The Streams and Rivers of Minnesota

The John K. Fesler Memorial Fund provided assistance in the publication of this volume, for which the University of Minnesota Press is grateful.

The contribution of the McKnight Foundation to the general program of the University of Minnesota Press, of which the publication of this book is a part, is gratefully acknowledged.

The Streams and Rivers of Minnesota

Thomas F. Waters

Photographs and maps by the author

University of Minnesota Press • Minneapolis

Published by the University of Minnesota Press
2037 University Avenue Southeast, Minneapolis, MN 55414
Printed in the United States of America on acid-free paper
Fifth printing, 1992

Library of Congress Catalog Card Number 77-81466
ISBN 0-8166-0960-8

To my father

Ray E. Waters

who introduced me
at a very early age
to the joys of a
free-running stream

Acknowledgments

It has been my great pleasure to visit the streams and rivers in the farthest corners of Minnesota. I have fished, paddled, hunted along, camped by, or researched to some degree the great majority of those named in this volume. Nevertheless, a book of this scope could not have been written without a great deal of assistance —both the written accounts of other researchers and the generosity of time by many friends and associates.

Lloyd L. Smith, Jr., my colleague in the University of Minnesota's Fisheries program, first introduced me to Minnesota's rivers and streams. And Alexander C. Hodson, then Head of the Department of Entomology, Fisheries, and Wildlife, initially encouraged me to write about them.

To L. Daniel Frenzel, University of Minnesota, and Calvin R. Fremling, Winona State University, I owe much for the impressive field experiences they made possible for me in spite of their own crowded schedules.

Many of my students in the university's fisheries program, while pursuing their own researches into the mysteries of stream and river ecosystems, have assisted me on their own time in many ways: guiding me into regions with which they were familiar, paddling the canoe, modeling for photographs, comparing ecological hypotheses and favorite trout flies; these are: David L. Hanson, Charles E. Petrosky,

G. David Heberling, Paul G. Heberling, James I. Stewart, Stanley L. Smith, Malcolm B. MacFarlane, Dennis K. Shiozawa, Paul C. Marsh, Austen S. Cargill, and Charles C. Krueger.

The literature I have consulted has been, for the most part, general texts and compilations; I make no claim to original historical or literary research. The Minnesota Historical Society's *Reference Guide to Minnesota History* proved an invaluable bibliographic aid. Most of the statistics on physical characteristics of the major rivers were obtained from the Hydrologic Investigations Atlas series which describes specific watersheds and was prepared by the U.S. Geological Survey and the Minnesota Department of Natural Resources. Among serials I found most helpful were the publications of the Minnesota Historical Society and the Minnesota Canoe Association, as well as *The Minnesota Volunteer*.

I have enjoyed unrestricted access to the extensive files of unpublished data and reports in the Department of Natural Resources, Division of Fish and Wildlife. Many friends and colleagues in several divisions of the department gave much time and effort in assisting me with the acquisition of these data and other information; the details of Minnesota's stream and river resources could not have been compiled without their help.

The watershed maps were prepared with the use of U.S. Geological Survey topographic maps and aerial photographs. I owe many thanks to John Miss, of Merle Morris Photographers, Minneapolis, for his special endeavors in the production of the black-and-white photographs.

I am notably fortunate—and so is the reader—to have had the entire manuscript reviewed by Herbert E. Wright, Jr., University of Minnesota, and John B. Moyle, now retired from the Minnesota Department of Natural Resources, and his wife, Evelyn W. Moyle. And I am particularly appreciative of the special efforts of Margaret S. Ewing in assisting with the preparation of the manuscript.

My subjective impressions of Minnesota's streams are based in large part upon a wealth of field experiences with a fishing and hunting companion of long standing, Leroy R. Genaw, with whom I have shared many wet tents and riverbank campfires.

Most of all, I am thankful for the encouragement and support of my family—wife Carol, Dan, Liz, and Ben—who helped in many ways and accompanied me on many river excursions.

I am grateful to all.

T. F. W.

Contents

THE CALL OF THE RIVER TRAIL*

There were great things seen, both grand and mean,
    in the land of the Northern Star,
And the river trails have their secret tales
    you hear on the gravel bar;
Here the Indian walked, and the Frenchman talked
    of an empire of trading posts,
But the beaver's through, and the white pine, too,
    to leave only the steamboat ghosts.

Now the riffle glides where the brook trout hides
    from the flash of a paddle stroke,
And the pool is deep where the Boy Scouts sleep
    in the dying campfire's smoke.

So tramp along to the rapids' song,
    through sun or misty vale;
We'll toast our toes where the campfire glows,
    tonight on the river trail!

I say there, chum, have you ever run
    that stretch where the rapids roar?
And then come out with a curse and a shout,
    and you're wet but you grin for more?
Have you felt the rush of a woodcock flush,
    from a streamside alder glade?
Have you cast a fly to the brown trout's lie,
    in the brooding spruce's shade?

Can you stand the damp of a soggy camp
    by a roiled and rising creek?
Do you love the spray of an autumn day,
    with the storm upon your cheek?

Then tramp along with your pack and song,
    where the rapids tell their tale;
We'll camp tonight 'neath a Northern Light,
    by a winding river trail!

*With apologies to Robert Service

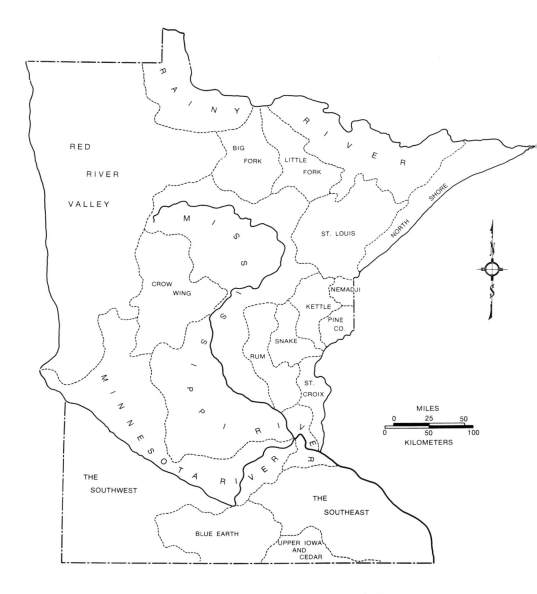

RED

RIVER

VALLEY

RAINY RIVER

BIG
FORK

LITTLE
FORK

MISSISSIPPI

CROW
WING

ST. LOUIS

NORTH SHORE

NEMADJI

KETTLE

PINE
CO.

SNAKE

RUM

ST.
CROIX

MINNESOTA RIVER

THE
SOUTHWEST

THE
SOUTHEAST

BLUE EARTH

UPPER IOWA
AND
CEDAR

MILES

0   25   50

0   50   100

KILOMETERS

The Major Watersheds of Minnesota

Introduction

The Magic of Flowing Waters

The Giants Range is the major highland feature of northeast Minnesota, dividing the region into its two principal watersheds. Ancient mountains composed of very old granite, still resistant to erosion, they tower 400 feet above surrounding glacial plains. Running in an east-west direction for fifty miles, the Giants Range is broken by the Embarrass River, which drains northern glacial lake beds through a magnificent forested gorge that was cut by meltwaters when the great ice sheets were retreating.

From the north slope, streams flow to the Canadian border and Hudson Bay. Streams on the south slope flow southwest around the North Shore highlands of Lake Superior and through Minnesota's international seaport of Duluth to the Great Lakes. But on a western spur of the Giants Range, in west-central St. Louis County, these two drainages meet the headwaters of yet a third, the largest in Minnesota and also in the United States, the immense watershed of the Mississippi River.

Here then is formed a rare three-way continental divide. Located on a slight elevation of land just north of Hibbing, it is identified by a marker. A rain shower falling on this spot splits into three parts —and these parts discharge after long journeys into three widely separated seas: icy Hudson Bay, the north Atlantic, and the warm waters of the Gulf of Mexico. Beginning at this three-way separation, Minnesota's streams and rivers flow through thousands of creek channels, rocky gorges, and broad river floodplains.

Because Minnesota lies astride the transition between eastern woodlands and the western prairies, from northern coniferous forests to the corn belt of mid-nation, and encompasses three continental drainages, the variety of streams is almost infinite. Our flowing waters creep through beaver meadows and wild rice flats with the quiet persistence of geologic time; they rush down mountainside and rocky gorge in a crescendo of sound and beauty; in flood they can awe and terrify. But in the spring they join bird song like that of the thrush, to create harmony along a favorite forest stream.

The rivers of Minnesota were the thoroughfares of Indians, guided the early explorers and trappers, military expeditions, and the settlement of immigrants, and determined the present location of most of our modern cities and towns. The shape of Minnesota is outlined largely by its border rivers—Red River of the North, Rainy, Pigeon, St. Louis, St. Croix, and Mississippi. On the remainder of the state's borders, Minnesota's waters (with few exceptions) only flow out to our neighbors.

Our rivers still serve as major navigation routes, still provide drinking water for our homes, water for industry, for cleaning, cooling, and electric power production. And, unfortunately, some are still used as sewers to carry away our wastes.

But Minnesota is rich with running water resources in many ways other than these practical uses. For those who would pause a moment at streamside—to listen in the shadow and solitude of a deep gorge, to breathe the downstream wind filtering through springtime creek bottoms coming to life—stream banks and river trails constitute a rich treasure.

Whether by snowshoe in winter or a hike in the spring, with canoe paddle, fly rod, or shotgun in the fall—to those who would listen, the river valley is a magic music box. To those who would observe, the pattern of color and movement paint a picture that is a masterwork resulting from millions of years of nature's efforts, yet dynamic and ephemeral. Minnesota is rich with stream and river resources that, beyond economic utility, make up our living environment, delight our senses, and, indeed, form and mold our culture.

So let's pause a while. Pick out a good sitting log at streamside; there is one every little way on almost any creek or river. Pull the canoe up on a sand bar, lay down the fly rod, prop the shotgun in the crotch of a bush, or stand the snowshoes in a snow-bank. What are these rich resources of our rivers? Basically, of course, they are the characteristics of moving water and of the valley milieu created by moving water that impinge upon our senses.

Threading through all is the stream itself, with the sound of its passage, whether a murmur, a roar, or the noiseless flow of flat water. But the sounds of streams and river bottoms are not confined to this music. The symphony of bird song, buzzing of insects, croaking of amphibians, the whistle and sigh of down-canyon winds in the treetops must all be counted among the auditory treasures of quiet-water stretches. And to the night-fishing angler listening intently for rising trout during a mayfly emergence, the baritone slurp of a giant brown trout is pure delight.

The songs of several woodland birds I recognized along favorite streams long before I ever saw them or learned their names. Still their voices come as old friends, expected, familiar, integral parts of the day afield. However, along stream banks the kingfisher probably comes closest to being a characteristic river denizen, racketing his way downstream from one perch to the next. I like the evening sounds best: from high in the deepening gloom drops the night-hawk's nasal voice, and in otherwise quiet openings along the river-bank the veery's downstairs-falling, rolling whistle adds its wild note to the end of the day. The brown trout fisherman listens at this time too for the night's first lonesome call of the whippoorwill, the traditional signal to take fly rod in hand and head for his secret pool.

Scientifically, a lot more has been made of lakes than of rivers. A monumental three-volume reference work on limnology (the science of inland waters) hardly acknowledges the existence of streams. But science is often cold and without music. For centuries men and women in anguish, joy, and love have poured their emotions into song and poetry about rivers — "Old Man River," "The Beautiful Ohio," "On the Banks of the Wabash," or "Red River Valley."

What about Kipling's:

> . . . do you know that racing stream
> With the raw, right-angled log-jam at the end;
>
> "The Feet of the Young Men"

and do you know Service's:

> Black canyons where the rapids rip and roar?
>
> "The Call of the Wild"

What visions, what scenes of past thrills these lines evoke! What fetters they unshackle!

Indeed folklore and songs of America are haunted by the images of her great rivers and the sounds of mountain and hill streams. The cowboy's trail wound beside the prairie river; the thrashing of paddle wheels stirred the wanderlust of every itch-footed riverbank boy; the whippoorwill's song still echoes over many a loved one's grave beside a rippling brook in a lonesome hill valley; and on the frontier a most loyal and trusted companion was a "man to ride the river." Even the whistle of an old steam-driven freight train was transformed to an evening hymn or an augury of adventure by its echoes in a high, timbered valley above a rushing stream. The Wabash Cannonball, legendary fast train of every proud Midwest community, pulls out each time "from the hills of Minnesota, where the rippling waters fall."

Names often tell us something about the location, color, flora, fauna, and history of streams. Which raises the question: What is a stream? Or a river? Why a creek or a brook? Obviously, a river is larger than a creek—but when does one become the other? Just as obviously, there is no good answer. A brook is smallest, perhaps a creek larger, a river largest—and all are streams. Science has its own solution: all are *running waters*; but that's not very romantic—it sounds like something coming out of a faucet.

My mother tried to correct my *crick* as being illiterate, just as she would try to keep me from saying *ain't*. But *creek* is almost exclusively American—there are kills, rills, runs, branches, forks, becks, burns, pots, and brooks, all over the English-speaking world, but nowhere except in America (and in Australia) are there creeks. Another exception occurs in Europe; there is a creek, but not on a hillside or in a mountain gorge—for it is a name for a small estuary or inlet on the seacoast. And it's pronounced *crick*. To this day, I stumble mentally over *creek*.

The names of rivers are good clues to geographic location and vegetational zones. Such names as Popple Creek, Pine River, and Cedar Creek immediately give away the region as somewhere in the northern Midwest, as Cottonwood Canyon and Dead Horse Creek do the Far West, Black River and Tamarack Creek the boggy spruce-fir forests, and Buffalo River the plains and prairies. Indian names for streams are common across the country, as are the names of explorers and kings.

Colors were frequently used to name streams and indicated something of the quality of water: Red or Yellow—muddy, clay, or turbid; Black—bog-colored swamp water; Green, Crystal, Clear—hard-water, clear, with deep green pools. The local fauna figured in stream names, too, particularly original fish species and those terrestrial animals that were most important to the early hunter and trapper. The number of Pike, Trout, Beaver, Deer, and Bear creeks is probably inestimable.

However, a few local river names are unique to their areas. Where else but in Michigan's upper peninsula is the Yellow Dog? Where else but among New York's fabled Catskill trout streams are the Beaverkill and the Neversink? Where but in Wisconsin, the Flambeau, or in Missouri, the Eleven Point?

Here in Minnesota, too, we have unique names: Devil Track, Blackhoof, Manitou, Zumbro, Blue Earth. These mean Minnesota and nowhere else. The names bring different mental pictures to different kinds of river devotees: singing voyageurs along watery border trails, settlers in the coulees of the southeast, or brigades of oxcarts fording a prairie stream. Trout fishermen have visions of fat brook trout from the brushy, cold creeks of the Arrowhead country, canoeists hear the swish of paddles in quiet water or the roar of boulder fields.

There are storied streams here in Minnesota that call forth old memories: steamboats on the Mississippi, St. Croix, Minnesota, and even the Red River of the North; river log drives on the St. Croix, Snake, Kettle, Rum, and Big Fork; the great settler migrations north and west. Some are newer: a big trout on a dry fly on the Straight River; canoes and kayaks in the Kettle rapids; or stream side alders thick with woodcock along Pine County creeks.

Take an old trout fisherman, blindfolded, to any one of his half-dozen favorite streams, and he will tell you which one it is—by the smell. It's a personal thing, not easily definable. Some combination, perhaps, of sweetfern and jack pine broiling on the uplands in the noon sun, or the springwater-washed odor of white cedar on a curving river terrace in a shaded gorge. Or it's a down-on-the-farm, old-home fragrance of a pasture creek after a summer shower. But it is unmistakable. A stream can have its unique, identifiable, never-to-be-forgotten smell. Sometimes it is more personal than environmental: an old wicker creel—with the accumulated memories (and odors) of a thousand trout—stuffed with bracken fern, white cedar boughs, or just reed canary grass, depending on the stream. The local smells of local materials are frequently unique.

Take a streamside campfire. There is a difference between the pungent, woodsy smoke of recently dropped red oak branches and the sweet fragrance of a fire made from pieces of a white pine stump, cut in the halcyon days of Minnesota logging and left to cure in the sun and rain for a hundred years.

The old fragrance of citronella, the universal bug dope of pre-World War II days, brings a nostalgia for dark brook trout and a can of worms in a cool cedar swamp. Fortunately nostalgia is stronger than the memory of those clouds of savage mosquitoes the citronella was intended to repel. But the fragrance remains evocative; citronella takes me back to younger, joyous days along some hidden creek.

Whatever the combination is, whatever the magic olfactory chemistry, a stream can have a unique fragrance. No wonder spawning salmon can find the way back to their nursery stream by its smell!

Many wild flowers are common along stream banks and in marshy woods, contributing to the seasonal change of color and fragrance along our rivers and creeks. One special advantage to the creek-bottom traveler, of course, is that springtime comes earlier here than in the uplands. South-facing slopes absorb a greater intensity of sunshine, steep gorges protect from chilling winds, and the relative warmth of waters in groundwater seeps tributary to a stream all add to an advance of the season. Probably the earliest bloom that the hiker will notice is the low, white flower of the blood-root, identified by its bright orange sap when the stem is broken; this is often the first sign that winter is on the way out, appearing before any green vegetation or even before the trout season opens! The marsh marigold, or cowslip, soon lines stream banks, oxbow marshes,

and small tributary springs, painting the lowlands with its bright yellow. And soon after, many more spring flowers appear in profusion—
pink spring beauties, yellow bellworts, pristine white trilliums, purple
and yellow violets, and trout lilies (delightful name!) with unique
purple-and-green mottled leaves.

Many late summer and fall flowers are low or small. But higher
plants, like the jewelweed or touch-me-not, line the water's edge with
gold, and Indian paintbrush strokes its brilliant red on gravel bars.
Fall colors are enhanced, too, by many fruits that mature at this time
—wild cherries and berries, grapes and plums, apples from a long-
abandoned riverside settler's orchard. The return home with a canoe
load of wild fruit can be enjoyed again and with interest—with wild
blackberry jam on a cold winter morning or chokecherry wine at the
fireside on a cold winter night!

However, not all is bird song and wild flowers
in the future of Minnesota's streams and rivers. Long before remem-
bered or written history, man was fascinated with wild rivers and
with his engineering ability to make flowing water serve his own purposes. We have never been modest in applying that engineering capacity. From the small boy damming and channeling the overflow of a
spring shower down a streetside gutter, to giant government agencies
and their immense projects, we are fascinated with the results that
can be wrought by our imagination and the application of materials
and machines to flowing water. We have dammed, channelized, and
dredged; we have extracted water for irrigation until streams dry up;
we have made artificial, polluted, and even buried streams for yet another highway. We continue to feel that the wild waters of our land
must be "tamed."

We are perverse, of course; we love the beauty of free-flowing
streams and also the work they can do; but we destroy them and lose
their music, and we complain that our outdoor living space does not
give us the satisfaction it should.

And we are not through yet, in Minnesota. Plans for immense
dams are on the drawing boards. Drainage of marshes supporting waterfowl continues. The U.S. Army Corps of Engineers, some time
ago, prepared plans for the connection of navigation between Lake
Superior and the Mississippi River—a project that was chilling in its
portent for the landscape of northeast Minnesota.

Nevertheless, we are learning slowly to live better as a plain member, as Aldo Leopold, author of *A Sand County Almanac*, put it, rather than as a conqueror of our natural community. New legislation and citizen activism now expose destructive development of our natural resources to closer scrutiny. Water pollution control, under strengthened legislation and powers of the Minnesota Pollution Control Agency, backed by strong public support, is reversing the trend of water pollution in a number of Minnesota rivers.

Paradoxically, one of the greatest threats to our streams in Minnesota appears in the form of those who would use them the most for recreational purposes. This threat is twofold. Simple crowding is one aspect—leading to too much competition for a single recreational use or to competition between uses. Severe as competition can be, it is nevertheless manageable. Use-specific management—that is, deliberately encouraging the type of use for which a river appears best suited—and management for diversity, can be employed to separate and diffuse crowded or conflicting uses, at least to a point.

The second half of the problem is more threatening—the increase of those types of recreational use that are, intrinsically, inappropriate or damaging to the stream environment. Several types of inappropriate use can be listed, but one is outstanding in Minnesota today, both in its degree of damage to streams and in its magnitude: the off-road, motorized recreational vehicle.

Where is the music of running water beneath the ice when our ears are filled with the whine of snowmobiles? How can the warbler song from springtime alders compete with the popping of trail bikes? Where is the delight from rising evening mists or the fragrance of a pine-knot campfire when the valley is blue with exhausts from all-terrain vehicles?

River bottoms, floodplains, and stream banks are fragile resources, quickly subjected to erosion when mistreated by machine-driven wheels and tracks. Beyond the physical damage is the obvious fact that no other use—hiking, canoeing, skiing, fishing or hunting, or just dozing on the stream bank—can compete with the overwhelming roar of engines.

I doubt that everyone loves a river. But somebody said that every river has someone to love it. Just threaten a river with a dam, with channelization, or a new industrial development, and a committee of irate citizens, rising with righteous anger, will come forward to protest the proposed despoliation of their favorite stream.

Probably every major river that appears as a central figure in a chapter in this volume will be considered by someone to have received short shrift. Someone will think that a tributary river within a chapter should have been the subject of a chapter by itself. Or (worst of all) someone's little but treasured stream is not mentioned at all.

I apologize for that, because some of my own favorites, being so small, are not noticed by anyone else either. In fact the very favorite from my first trout fishing days may even be gone—it was only a foot wide but at the time holding its own against encroaching cultivation. No doubt it now only amounts to a few moist rows of corn.

Well, enough for now. We'll leave the sitting log, slightly more polished, for the next river traveler who passes this way. Pick up the paddle or the fly rod. There is a rapid to be run around the next bend or a new rise at the head of the pool.

I hope for the next traveler that the trout lily will bloom in the spring, that the water will be clear, and that in the fall the woodcock will be back in the alder thickets. The sitting log may be a different one next year, for this one may go with the spring flood. Another, ready for more streamside polishing, will probably be somewhere near.

But I hope the music and the magic will be the same.

Chapter 1

The Nemadji Basin

Rivers in Red Clay

The traveler driving from southern Minnesota to Duluth or the vacationlands of the Arrowhead country may leave the busy interstate and instead take the Evergreen Memorial Highway — actually part of Minnesota 23 — a byway bordered by dark spruce, pines, and thick, glistening stands of birch. Just north of the village of Nickerson, the road drops sharply over the rim of a hill, and the forested roadside suddenly gives way to a clear view of a great depression in the land, stretching far ahead to shadowed distances and beyond to the hills of the northern horizon.

This is the basin of the Nemadji River, a broad, low plain that once was covered by great glacial lakes. The basin is a western extension of the glacier-carved trough that, to the east, now holds the world's largest expanse of fresh water, Lake Superior. The hill down which the northbound traveler speeds is the Nickerson moraine, which held back the waters of ancient Glacial Lake Nemadji and formed its southern shore.

The Nemadji basin — the part that lies in Minnesota — is a tiny watershed compared to those of our other great and larger rivers. The stream rises in Minnesota, but soon flows into Wisconsin, and it is not a river that everyone knows much about or has even heard of. Yet the Nemadji basin is different from any other watershed in Minnesota, and the tributary streams, as a group, are unique. This seems a profitable place to begin, for even within the basin the streams are diverse, giving us the opportunity to understand, at the very start, some basic principles of flowing waters that make our exploration of streams and rivers so fascinating.

Let us begin our exploration of Minnesota's rivers where the Nemadji tributaries begin, and follow them first to headwater trickles in their boggy hills. It is here in the peat meadows of northern Pine County, on top of the high glacial moraines, that the southern affluents of the Nemadji River have their origins.

Here the Net and Little Net rivers are small and sluggish; black with organic matter, warm and soft bottomed, they wind slowly to the north. But near the village of Holyoke, in Carlton County, these become two of the most enchanting little rivers in Minnesota. Rapidly they fall some 200 feet in elevation down the slopes of the old lake basin, bouncing over sandstone ledges, rushing through rocky riffles, and carving deep pockets with their cascades. Picking up cold spring water in this downward flight from the gloom of bog origins, the waters become clearer, cooler, and the concentration of mineral salts increases.

The Net and Little Net now become trout streams, primarily because the water is cooler, but also because rock and gravel substrates harbor more kinds of aquatic insects and other invertebrate animals that trout use for food. Also, the pools and rocky crevices formed by falling water provide essential cover for the fish. There are naturally reproducing brook trout in these reaches as well as stocked brown trout. In lower reaches migrating rainbows, or steelheads, ascend from Lake Superior, by way of the Nemadji River itself, leaving their progeny to spend their first two or three years in running water. The Net River's waterfalls and wild cascades enhance picnics, ball games on Sunday, or just a short stop for lunch at the delightful little park near Holyoke.

Farther downstream both the Net and Little Net take on a different character. Reaching lake-deposited red clay at the bottom of the basin, the streams have cut sharply into the ancient lake deposits to carve steep-sided gorges more than 100 feet deep. The Little Net River empties into the Net River about four miles downstream from the Holyoke park, and the Net, in another mile, enters the South Fork of the Nemadji River.

In all, the Net River flows about twenty miles from its origin in

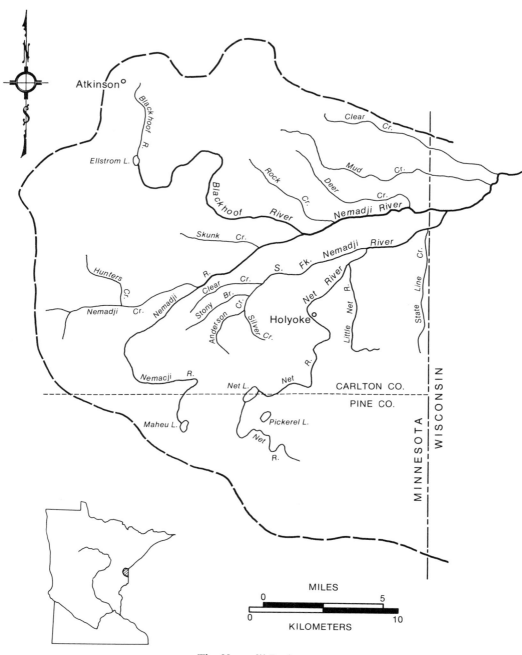

The Nemadji Basin

Pine County to its mouth in the South Fork, dropping about 500 feet in elevation. Half of this fall occurs in only about three or four miles of river, accounting for its wild, rushing character.

Farther to the west the main Nemadji River, or North Fork, begins on the same glacial moraine. It has its origin in Maheu Lake, small, shallow, and perched high on the moraine. As the Nemadji leaves the lake, it takes on the black, soft-water character of a peat meadow stream, typical of many headwater streams in the Nemadji basin and in many other areas of the northern Great Lakes region.

Bog streams collect rainwater and melted snow that saturate the spongy peat, filtering through mats of *Sphagnum* moss and swamps with black spruce and tamarack. These waters have almost none of the minerals, primarily calcium, that give to water the property we call "hardness." Instead they are deeply stained with brown, colloidal, organic matter derived from partially decomposed peat. These colloidal particles, much too small to be seen even with ordinary microscopes, give a yellow color to the water in a bottle and a black or deep reddish-brown cast when flowing in the stream. The red color is not, as sometimes thought, a result of iron. Such water is frequently called "bog water" described as tea- or coffee-colored.

The aquatic ecologist is much concerned with the property of water termed "alkalinity," for it is closely related to the productivity of aquatic life both in streams and lakes. Technically, all alkalinity means is that the water reacts with acid—and the technician in the field measures it by adding acid in carefully measured amounts to a known quantity of water until a chemical reaction is revealed by color change. The most common alkaline substances present in natural waters, including Minnesota's lakes and streams, are forms of calcium carbonate, so alkalinity is measured as parts per million (p.p.m.) of calcium carbonate. "Hardness" is another property of water, closely related to alkalinity, and although technically alkalinity and hardness are different, the two usually occur at about the same levels in natural waters, and the two terms are often used interchangeably.

But what is the relation between alkalinity and biological productivity? In lakes we know that higher alkalinities make more nutrients available for photosynthesis by aquatic plants, and a positive correlation between alkalinity and productivity has been observed in the lakes of Minnesota, generally ranging from low in the northeast Arrowhead country to high in western and southern lakes. In rivers, too, we note the same general correlation — from northeast to southwest — but the exact reasons for the relationship are not so clear in streams as in lakes.

At any rate, by the time an aquatic ecologist measures the alkalinity of stream waters, he or she has a pretty good idea of the type stream it is, and of what kinds and quantities of stream life may be present, including fish. The northeastern streams may have a low alkalinity in the range of only 15 to 25 p.p.m.; alkalinity of streams in central Minnesota is about 100 p.p.m. and in the south 200-300. Of course this measurement is not always a reliable index of productivity, but it is one factor in the field biologist's checklist of stream characteristics that tells a great deal. Alkalinity is not always the same for a given stream; in drought conditions more of a stream's water source is in springs and groundwater, and the alkalinity is high; in high water and floods more water comes from surface runoff, and the stream is "softer." Soft waters are usually colored with the brown colloids of bog water, like the Nemadji's tributaries; high alkalinity waters, such as from springs or well water, are almost always crystal clear.

The upper Nemadji flows from Maheu Lake north into Carlton County and wanders as a typical dark swamp stream for five or six miles. Here the alkalinity is only about 20 p.p.m., similar to the upper Net and Little Net rivers. But soon the Nemadji too begins to tumble down the basin slope, forming pools and rocky riffles, and then it carves a typical steep-sided gorge through the red clay deposits that characterize the Nemadji basin, and here the alkalinity increases to over 50 p.p.m.

In its narrow, deeply incised valley the Nemadji is lined by slumping, red clay banks on the outside of bends and bars of red clay, silt, and sand on the inside. The bars can be treacherous — the unwary foot of a fisherman or exploring canoeist will sink uncomfortably deep. The banks are never stable for very long; the clay slumps, and mature trees that line the top slide down and into the water, forming brush and log jams in the river. Flash floods tear these apart and further erode the red banks. These eroding banks are the chief source of the clay and silt that color and muddy the Nemadji. The muddy waters, in fact, are a problem of some importance where

Cutting its way through the thick red clay that was deposited on the bottom of glacial lakes, the Nemadji River leaves raw, steep banks that continue to erode. Slumping red clay carries with it the trees and brush from the channel edges.

they are discharged into Lake Superior, contaminating with silt water supplies drawn from the lake in that area. Eventually the silt and clay settle out in Lake Superior, becoming part of the bottom. Solutions to the clay-erosion problem are being sought by the Department of Agriculture's Resource Conservation and Development program; but any erosion control here will be immensely difficult.

In addition to a variety of small streams, the main Nemadji picks up Nemadji Creek (also called North Fork Creek) and the Blackhoof River. A half mile down from the mouth of the Blackhoof, Minnesota's Evergreen Memorial Highway spans the river as the major highway crossing the basin. Then, without road access, the Nemadji winds and wanders to the Minnesota-Wisconsin border, picking up the South Fork and its accumulated waters from the Net and Little Net.

Red, muddy, and warm, the Nemadji meanders the rest of its way toward Lake Superior, gathering in the waters of Wisconsin's Black River on the way. In all, the river flows from its source in Maheu Lake about sixty-five miles to its mouth in Lake Superior, dropping over 500 feet in elevation, and ends ignominiously beneath the steel and concrete of waterfront industrial development in the city of Superior, Wisconsin.

Two additional streams entering the Nemadji system from the southern edge are Anderson and Silver creeks— cold, clear, little trout streams. Their main water sources are not in the high peat lands but in springs among the steep, rocky sides of the ancient glacial lake basin. Consequently these are harder waters (60 p.p.m.) as well as cold and clear. The creeks contain wild brook trout. Although small—either can be jumped in many places—Silver and Anderson creeks contain riffles rich with aquatic insects and other trout-food organisms as well as pools that harbor the fish.

Anderson and Silver creeks join to form a larger stream that really constitutes part of the upper reaches of the South Fork of the Nemadji River. Quickly joining also are Stony Brook and Clear Creek, two other small streams that begin, not in the steep edges of the basin, but down in the flat glacial lake bed itself. They are both slower and muddier than Anderson and Silver creeks, but are cool and contain some trout. No doubt the initiated angler in search of hidden pools takes a share of secret brook trout from these less attractive waters as well as from Silver and Anderson creeks. The South Fork continues on northeast to collect the waters from the Net and Little Net and to flow on to Wisconsin.

The Blackhoof River is the largest and longest Minnesota tributary of the Nemadji. It is also the richest in running-water magic, for in the lower reaches it is characterized by broad riffles and deep, green pools. In contrast to the other major tributaries, the Blackhoof heads in the northwestern part of the watershed. From that area near the village of Atkinson, situated on a high glacial moraine, also flow the beginnings of Little Otter Creek, northeast toward the St. Louis River and Lake Superior, and the headwaters of the Moose River, which run via the Kettle and St. Croix to the Mississippi. From Atkinson the Blackhoof runs south about six miles as a small, sluggish creek, through pastures, meadows, and cultivated fields, including a short passage through Ellstrom Lake, actually an impoundment of the stream. Swinging east and north, the Blackhoof then enters the head of its valley, and its character changes strikingly.

Here it begins its descent through a typical Nemadji basin gorge, carving ever deeper an incised valley with forested hillsides. The waters cool, and the gradient increases to form rocky riffles, gravel bars, and deep pools. And for over ten miles it will be a shining trout stream.

The valley of the lower Blackhoof is a delight to the eye. In very early spring, when the steelhead season draws the angler to the stream, deciduous branches are still winter naked, and the waters may be swollen and muddy. In the heat of summer almost full foliage shades the cool stream banks at the gorge bottom, and like mother hens, dark spruces brood over deep river bends. But in fall there is a riot of color—silver waters mix with golden aspen and the ruby splotches of red maples, exaggerated even more by the still-dark spruces. And the silver steelhead returns again from Lake Superior in its autumn migration.

The Blackhoof's waters are harder and more alkaline than the Nemadji's headwaters (75 p.p.m.); its source is in the northwestern part of the watershed where ground waters occur in more alkaline glacial drift. Accordingly, productivity is higher in the Blackhoof; rocky riffles have invertebrate populations that include most of the trout's favored items of diet: immature stages of mayflies, stoneflies, and caddisflies. The alternation of pools and riffles is as nearly perfect as a trout stream manager could wish. The Blackhoof is not large enough to be canoed, at least not without more dragging of the canoe over riffles and downed trees than would be worthwhile. On the other hand, this feature ensures the trout angler the solitude that is an essential ingredient of the sport.

One major detraction from the beauty of the lower reaches of this stream is the siltation that occurs in the pools and interstices of the gravel riffles. This factor undoubtedly results in a low rate of production of stream-bottom food organisms, and thus it reduces trout production. Silt also probably decreases successful reproduction of brook and brown trout, whose eggs must incubate in an oxygen-rich aquatic environment through the winter; a coating of silt or clay will suffocate the eggs. Both brook and brown trout reproduce to some extent in the Blackhoof, spawning in the fall, but populations are low.

The steelhead, or migrating rainbow, spawns in the spring when waters are high and swift and the silt is kept constantly moving; consequently, the rainbow, aided by the shorter incubation period required for its eggs, may have the advantage in the Blackhoof. Evi-

Although the Blackhoof River drains part of the Nemadji watershed, it is considerably clearer than the Nemadji itself. The shining riffles and cool waters of the Blackhoof have both brook and brown trout, and also receive a steelhead run from Lake Superior, via the red, muddy waters of the Nemadji in Wisconsin.

dence of this probability is the apparent abundance of young rainbows compared to brooks and browns. After partaking of stream foods for two years or so, and competing with the young brook and brown trout during this time, the rainbow approaches a size almost attractive to the angler; then the rainbow flees downstream to Lake Superior. And so the Blackhoof's aquatic fish food, limited in the first place by excess silt and clay, is consumed by young steelheads that leave just before reaching a size attractive to fishermen. Naturally the steelhead fisherman is overjoyed at all this, taking the big silver fighters in early spring as they return from Lake Superior to spawn.

Perhaps the Department of Agriculture's erosion control research will solve the problem of the Blackhoof siltation. If so, it would benefit both the summer stream fisherman seeking brook and brown trout and the steelhead angler.

There are several other small streams in the basin that, because of their size or other ecological characteristics, play minor roles in the Nemadji watershed. These include Hunter's Creek, an upper tributary of Nemadji Creek, which used to be a trout stream; Skunk Creek, which flows into the main Nemadji between Nemadji Creek and the Blackhoof; and Deer and Rock (or Pleasant Valley) creeks, relatively hard-water streams (75-100 p.p.m.) flowing into the Nemadji from the northwest. Clear Creek and Mud Creek, in the northern part of the watershed, also head from the west and have very hard water (200 p.p.m.). These creeks flow east out of Minnesota, join in neighboring Wisconsin, and then empty into the Nemadji. (This is a different Clear Creek from the one in the south that forms part of the headwaters of the South Fork.) Farther downstream on the South Fork is State Line Creek, a small, cold, brushy, trout stream flowing northward to the river and parallel to the Minnesota-Wisconsin boundary.

The Nemadji basin is wild and unspoiled. It is sparsely populated, and nowhere are its streams polluted. Its total watershed area in Minnesota, only 270 square miles, is small relative to the other major river basins in the state, and this fact has probably been largely responsible for its present character. There are no major industries in the watershed, no cities or commercial concentrations, nor even any significant tourist business. The waters of its streams are singularly free of the contaminants commonly associated with concentrated industry.

The Nemadji's wild lands are covered with young, growing forests—aspen and birch, white spruce and balsam fir, scattered pines. The Nemadji State Forest is one of the largest in the state, but it does not include the Nemadji River. In fact, very little of the Nemadji watershed—only some of the northern Pine County peat lands—is included in the Nemadji State Forest. There is one state forest campground in the Nemadji watershed, Gavfert State Campground on Pickerel Lake, near the Net River above Net Lake.

Grouse and woodcock are fairly abundant, but hunting is light. The deep gorges, through which the streams flow, are magnificent in the autumn, yet tough going on the rugged hillsides for the upland bird hunter.

Canoeing is possible on only one stream—the main Nemadji. The reaches just above Minnesota Highway 23 can be canoed even at normal water levels if you are willing to drag over some of the short rapids that alternate with long, quiet pools. Here the gorge is deep, and the clay banks almost sheer. Generally forested, the valley sides vary from the greens of spruce and aspen to the red of slumping clay.

Fishing in the Nemadji basin streams is mostly for trout although some warm-water species and various minnows are present in most waters, and occasionally there are northern pike and crappies. Trout fishing falls into several categories: Wild brook trout are available in the small, brushy streams such as Silver, Anderson, Clear, and State Line creeks. Also, some brook trout and larger browns as well are available in the Net and Little Net rivers. The principal trout stream is the Blackhoof—large enough to wade, to fly fish, to explore long reaches of pools and riffles—over ten miles of trout water crossed by few roads. The lower four-mile stretch, from the last county road bridge to its mouth in the Nemadji, is wild, little accessible, and lightly fished. The stream banks are tough going but worth the effort. Finally, steelhead can be fished in the spring—mostly in the Blackhoof.

The development of the Nemadji country is similar to that of most forested lands in Minnesota. Settlement began in the mid-1800s, and the Nemadji was the scene of brawling, early log drives. But around the turn of the century the big pine was gone, and the logging era was quickly over. Today most of the watershed is forested, though with second growth, and only about 10 percent is used for agricultural purposes, largely pasture.

When the glaciers were melting back in the old Superior basin, some 10,000 to 12,000 years ago, huge glacial lakes of meltwater extended west over the Nemadji basin. At an elevation of about 450 feet above present Lake Superior, Glacial Lake Nemadji drained west to the Mississippi River and south. Later as ice in the Superior basin continued to melt, the much larger Glacial Lake Duluth also covered the Nemadji basin. During these times the red clay that is now typical of the basin was settling out as a thick, stiff lakebed deposit. The bright red color is characteristic of glacier-transported materials in the Superior lobe of ice that came from the northeast. The thickness of these clay deposits has been estimated at 200 to 500 feet, and present river gorges are cut into the clay more than 100 feet without reaching bedrock.

Formed beneath lake waters, the surface of the Nemadji plain is generally flat with little slope, and surface runoff during precipitation is slow. But because of the nature of the red clay, gorges formed by streams are steep-sided and narrow. Consequently storm flows produce flash floods, as evidenced on many stream banks by severe erosion, and valley development is called "flashy." Bridges and culverts are constructed oversize, with auxiliary culverts or spillways, to accommodate rapid increases in discharge.

The erosion of clay, as evidenced by the red turbid waters of the lower Nemadji River, is extensive. Silt dredged from the Superior, Wisconsin, harbor is equivalent to the removal of about ten tons per square mile from the Nemadji watershed, annually.

Soils in the western and northern parts of the watershed, however, contain less red clay and more coarse material, such as sand and stones, from the glacial moraines that form the northern border of the basin. Consequently the streams originating in the north and west, such as the Blackhoof, are less burdened with red clay, at least until farther downstream. They are also harder and more alkaline than streams heading up in southern, softer water sources.

Nemadji, from the Chippewa, means "left hand." As we approach the head of Lake Superior and the mouth of the St. Louis, the Nemadji is the first river on the left. There are none of the usual tourist attractions in this unspoiled river basin, no high waterfalls nor magnificent stands of virgin pine. The lack of cities and industry combines with wild, young forest, to form a valuable recreational resource.

The streams and rivers give the basin its particular character. From the high southern headwaters in their dark meadows, to the flashing riffles of the Blackhoof, from cold brook trout creeks to the sluggish red rivers in their deep gorges, the streams weave a treasured recreation potential.

Minnesotans in the future will appreciate even more the riches of this bit of running-water wilderness in the Nemadji basin.

Chapter 2

The St. Louis

River of Glaciers

The St. Louis River flows indolently past the twin ports of Duluth, Minnesota, and Superior, Wisconsin, through its wide, flat estuary—St. Louis Bay. The bay is lined with the harbor facilities, industrial wharves, and commercial dockyards of the largest inland navigation port in the United States. In its final reach the St. Louis flows beneath Interstate 535 bridge, which spans the river between Duluth and Superior, adding its waters to Lake Superior, the head of the Great Lakes-St. Lawrence River drainage.

But the St. Louis did not always flow docilely as it does now in St. Louis Bay, nor enter the Lake Superior basin at the location of its present mouth, nor did it always flow into Lake Superior. The history of the present St. Louis River channel is turbulent, shaped by the most important agents to mold the topography of our land and the flow of our rivers: the massive glaciers of the Pleistocene epoch, 10,000 to a million years ago. It is a fascinating chronicle of enormous quantitites of icy water eroding broad stream channels, of vast expanses of glacial lakes which drained away and formed again, of mile-thick lobes of ice that repeatedly advanced, retreated, and advanced again as climate changed over thousands of years, of diverse and changing river courses including the flow of the St. Louis.

The ice sheets that once covered almost all of Minnesota and the Great Lakes region ground the surface and smoothed much of the area intermittently for nearly a million years. However, the present topography, the river courses, lake formations, and most land forms remaining today are primarily the result of glacial activity during only the last few thousand years—when the glaciers were melting and the Pleistocene was coming to a close. It was the complex patterns of flowing meltwater, deposition of moraines, sedimentation on the bottoms of lakes of meltwater, and the temporary re-advance of glaciers that formed our present topography. In this period of glacial retreat, the ice edges receded—the glaciers themselves of course did not move backward—as ice melted. In fact, our largest glacial moraines formed when ice moved forward at the same rate as it melted back, so that the edge remained stationary, and giant mounds of rock, sand, and clay that the ice had been carrying were deposited as today's ranges of morainic hills.

The ice did not advance and melt along a uniform, continuous front. Instead, from the main centers farther north, several tongues of ice protruded, following preglacial lowlands—such as the Superior Lobe in the Lake Superior basin and the Des Moines Lobe which came south in the Red River Valley. Several lobes were involved in the development of the St. Louis River, advancing and retreating in different directions and at different times. These lobes rode over each other's previous paths and occasionally collided, in a complex pattern that left Minnesota its splendid topographic diversity. Two principal tongues of ice concern us with respect to the St. Louis River—the Superior Lobe that advanced southwest down the Lake Superior basin from the northeast and the St. Louis Sublobe (an offshoot of the Des Moines Lobe) from the west.

In an early period of melting, the meltwater from the western tip of the Superior Lobe flowed northwest up the developing St. Louis channel and formed a giant glacial lake north of present Floodwood—Lake Upham. Glacial Lake Upham drained west, to another great lake—Lake Aitkin—and from there south down the Mississippi when that stream was forming. But then the St. Louis Sublobe advanced from the west, covered up Lakes Aitkin and Upham and the western outlets, and forced the meltwaters from the Superior Lobe into other outlet channels. The first of these extended west from the site of present Cloquet to connect with the Kettle River, the St. Croix, and the Mississippi. As the Superior Lobe continued to melt back and downward into its basin, outlets formed successively at

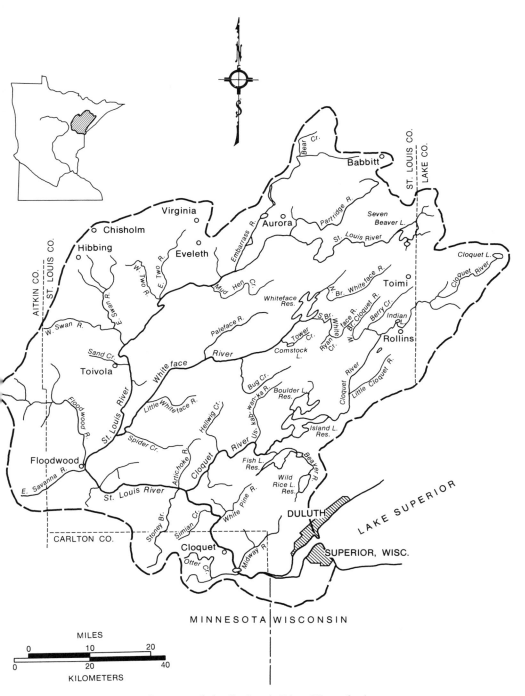

MILES

| 0 | 10 | 20 |

| 0 | 20 | 40 |

KILOMETERS

Streams of the St. Louis River Watershed

lower levels, also draining westward to the Kettle. The St. Louis Sub-lobe at this time began to retreat, too, adding its meltwaters to the same outlets and eventually causing Glacial Lake Upham to form again. In time, the western tip of the Superior Lobe melted sufficiently to form Glacial Lake Nemadji (over the present Nemadji Basin), which still drained west to the Kettle.

But with further melting of the Superior ice to even lower levels, a southern outlet was formed through an early St. Croix River channel to the Mississippi—up the present valley of Wisconsin's Bois Brule River, now a famous trout stream, and across to the headwaters of the St. Croix. Glacial Lake Nemadji disappeared, the western outlet to the Kettle was closed, and Glacial Lake Duluth, lower but larger, filled the Superior basin.

And then—significantly for our present concern—the St. Louis River, almost in its present form, drained Glacial Lake Upham, and enormous quantities of water began to course down the river channel to erode its lower gorge. As the glacial Great Lakes continued to find lower, more eastern outlets (eventually the St. Lawrence River), the level of water in the Superior basin also was lower, increasing the gradient of the St. Louis River and consequently also its erosive power. Now at the present level of Lake Superior, the St. Louis drops a total of 450 feet—from the strandlines of old lake Nemadji (near Carlton) to the river's mouth. The rocky lower valley of the St. Louis was carved as a result, a remarkable stretch of river we know today as the Dalles of the St. Louis. It is preserved for us in present Jay Cooke State Park, our heritage of the glaciers 10,000 years ago.

The lower gorge of the St. Louis was not always considered a place of beauty and enjoyment. In fact, it was at one time a formidable obstacle to early travel, overcome only for reasons of pride and profit.

For this was part of a major route of exploration and trade between the Great Lakes and Mississippi watersheds—an important route at that time. The early explorers toiled up a trail beside the St. Louis rapids—the Grand Portage (not to be confused with the Grand Portage to the northeast that connected Lake Superior with the border lakes country)—and then up the more placid waters above on the St. Louis. The voyageurs continued to about the present site of

Floodwood, and then turned west up the diminutive East Savanna River, a small stream that had eroded its shallow channel into the bed of old Glacial Lake Upham. The headwaters of the East Savanna River are separated only by a low continental divide from the head-waters of the more western Savanna River, which flowed west and, in turn, into Big Sandy Lake and the Mississippi River (Chapter 12). The divide between the East Savanna and the western Savanna River was low and swampy, but the track connecting the two streams, over the low divide, made a natural route of transportation. Its muddy, mosquito-ridden trail was considered by the voyageurs one of the more unpleasant routes. Now the portage and its significance are commemorated in Savanna Portage State Park, located at the western end of the trail.

The St. Louis River watershed is one of the largest in Minnesota, 3,584 square miles, lying mostly in St. Louis County with small portions in Lake, Carlton, Aitkin, and Itasca counties. Only sixty-three square miles are in Wisconsin, along the south side of the lower river, including part of the city of Superior. Essentially, the watershed is a high, flat plateau, bordered by higher glacial moraines and old mountains. The outlet of the watershed is the Dalles of the St. Louis, the lower river gorge leading to the head of Lake Superior.

The north-central area of the watershed is on the flat lake bed of Glacial Lake Upham, 650 feet above Lake Superior. Parts of the St. Louis and Whiteface rivers now flow across the dry lake bed. Bordering the north edge of the Lake Upham plain are the old mountains of the Giants Range, and along the south slope of these highlands are the more recent rocks of the Mesabi range, once the richest known source of high-grade iron ore in the world. The range cities, from Grand Rapids to Aurora, crouch in an irregular line along the base of the range, and the upper St. Louis River winds roughly along this northern border of the plain. Much of the area is covered with shallow, lake clay deposits and is poorly drained. Streams are of low gradient, slow, and often colored with bog water. Scattered farms are located in the area, but agriculture is not a major land use.

East of the lake bed is the Toimi drumlin field, regionally flat land with long, oval, low mounds of glacial debris that were molded by the glaciers moving slowly in a southwest direction. Consequently, streams and rivers in this area, including the Cloquet River and its tributaries, all flow southwest parallel to the drumlins.

Bordering the southeast edge of the watershed are the moraines that form part of the Lake Superior highlands, rising up above the North Shore to elevations well over 1,000 feet above the big lake. Rugged morainal country also dominates the southwest corner of the watershed, through which flow the lower St. Louis and some of the smaller, swift tributaries.

In this central, wild region of the St. Louis River basin run the three major rivers—St. Louis, Whiteface, and Cloquet—and their tributaries. These are largely forested lands, and although white pine once dominated the area in seemingly unlimited abundance, the principal tree species now are the result of second growth—aspen and birch, spruce, fir, and jack pine. Harvest and use of these species now constitute a major economic activity for the area, supplying the wood products industry of Cloquet.

Dams and impoundments are major features on the rivers of the St. Louis watershed. Five hydroelectric power plants are located on the lower St. Louis itself, from Cloquet downstream. Four of these are public utility plants operated by the Minnesota Power and Light Company, at Cloquet, Scanlon, Thomson, and Fond du Lac. The fifth is a private installation of the Northwest Paper Company at Cloquet. These plants provide power to the heavily populated Duluth area, as well as to industries at Cloquet.

The Thomson plant, considerably larger in capacity than all the others combined, utilizes water that is diverted from the main St. Louis by Thomson reservoir, the diverted water actually being run through an underground channel for about a mile. The diversion removes a considerable portion of the river's flow from the most rugged part of Jay Cooke State Park, reducing the potential scenic value of the gorge at low water levels. Although the waters impounded by these hydroelectric dams are of considerable area, the shorelines and water surfaces are not much used for recreational purposes, since there is little public access and pollution remains at objectionable levels from Cloquet downstream.

To regulate stream-flow for the operation of the hydroelectric plants, five large storage reservoirs were established in the Cloquet

River and Whiteface River watersheds between 1908 and 1923. The reservoirs receive additional water during times of heavy rainfall and river flow in the spring and early summer, and they release water during times of low river flow, primarily in winter. Consequently, the level of these man-made lakes fluctuates, the annual fluctuation ranging up to twenty-five feet. Furthermore, of interest to canoeists and campers downstream from the reservoirs are the occasional daily fluctuations in river levels as a result of the reservoir operations.

Four of the impoundments are in the Cloquet River drainage and include previously existing lakes. Island Lake, on the Cloquet River itself, is the largest and suffers the greatest water level fluctuation. Fish Lake and Wild Rice Lake, both impoundments of the smaller tributary Beaver River, lie to the south of the Cloquet River in rugged morainic terrain. Boulder Lake, north of the Cloquet River, is formed by a dam on tributary Otter Creek and impounds the waters of several streams; it is almost contiguous with Island Lake.

The Whiteface Reservoir, fed by the North Branch and the South Branch of the Whiteface River and several smaller streams as well, now marks the start of the main Whiteface. It is a man-made flowage and does not include existing lakes. Together, these five storage reservoirs have a total capacity of about one-third million acre-feet of water, Island Lake itself constituting about one-half of that.

Considerable cottage construction and development of shoreline have occurred on these artificial lakes. Although the water-level fluctuations create some problems, water surfaces are maintained at fairly stable levels during the summer vacation period. Considerable fishing is done in these lakes; the walleye and northern pike head the list of larger species, and some panfish are available as well.

The St. Louis River is generally considered to have its beginning in Seven Beaver Lake, one of the few large natural lakes in the watershed. However, several small tributaries enter the lake, and these may well be considered higher headwaters. These beginnings of the St. Louis are the uppermost headwaters of the St. Lawrence River system, flowing through the Great Lakes to the Atlantic Ocean, dropping 1,700 feet. The river was named by an early explorer after Louis IX, who was king of France at the time of the Crusades.

The St. Louis leaves Seven Beaver Lake as a moderately wide, slow stream and meanders slowly west in a tortuous, winding route through both narrows and wide-waters along the northern edge of the watershed. Its path roughly parallels the southern edge of the Mesabi range and the string of iron range cities from Babbitt west to Hibbing. The major tributaries along this west-flowing reach of 100 miles are, from the north, the Partridge River (thirty-two miles) emptying into the St. Louis near Aurora, and the Embarrass River (forty-two miles). The Embarrass originates near Babbitt and flows through a series of ice-block lakes in the Embarrass Narrows, a scenic glacial drainage channel cut through the Giants Range. Also from the north come the West and East Two Rivers, each about twenty miles long, emptying into the St. Louis at about the same point, southwest of Eveleth. The upper reaches of these northern tributaries are mostly wooded, with aspen and spruce, and the lower stretches are in swamp and some farmlands. From the south, the major tributary is Mud Hen Creek (seventeen miles), flowing through swamp and farm country.

From the mouths of the Two Rivers, the St. Louis turns abruptly south. Then it is joined by the East Swan and West Swan rivers, each about twenty miles in length, which originate in the lower outcrops of the Giants Range to the northwest near Hibbing. These are extremely dark, very soft waters. Farther south, the Whiteface empties into the St. Louis upstream from the town of Floodwood. And at Floodwood, the East Savanna River (the route of early travelers and voyageurs to the Mississippi drainage), and the Floodwood River (twenty-five miles) flowing from the northwest, are major tributaries. At this point, the St. Louis turns southeast toward Brookston, soon picks up the Cloquet River from the east, and then flows to the town of Cloquet, the lower gorge, and Duluth. Other, smaller streams along this reach include Sand Creek near Toivola, the Artichoke River and Stoney Brook near Brookston, and Simian Creek and White Pine River between Brookston and Cloquet.

The river, for all its wild remote character throughout the major upper portion, is a relatively quiet canoeing stream, with few difficult rapids or portages. It is included in the new river guide, *A Gathering of Waters*, prepared by Greg Breining and Linda Watson of the Minnesota Department of Natural Resources, Rivers Section. From the recommended starting access point, on the north side of the river just west of the U.S. 53 highway crossing, to the end of the route at Cloquet, is ninety miles. Recent development of the St. Louis canoe route includes construction of several additional campsites and accesses, described in a new pamphlet available from the Department of Natural Resources. Upstream from the U.S. 53 crossing it is about sixty miles to Seven Beaver Lake. This stretch is heavily forested, and most of it can be canoed, but there is poorer access and shallower, more unreliable water.

From its source the St. Louis flows a tortuous semicircular path of over 160 miles, dropping nearly 1,100 feet to its mouth in Lake Superior. Approximately half of this drop occurs in the lower river gorge downstream from Cloquet, a river distance of only ten miles. At its mouth the average discharge is over 2,000 cubic feet per second, but in the high waters of 1950 this discharge reached a maximum of nearly 38,000.

The St. Louis is a wild, splendid river, unspoiled throughout most of its length. In the headwater regions, it is heavily lined by coniferous forests. Little cabin or cottage development is visible along stream banks, and there is only one maintained campground. The only communities on the river, Floodwood, Brookston, and Cloquet, are in the lower section. Unfortunately the impounded, inaccessible, and polluted section of the lower river has generally given the river a poorer reputation than the quality of its upper reaches deserves.

The Cloquet River begins, appropriately enough, at Cloquet Lake—a remote body of water surrounded by the Superior National Forest in the eastern part of the St. Louis watershed. A primitive campsite with no facilities, but a magnificent view of the lake and wild shorelines, is accessible by a forest road. The stream running out of the lake is small, slow, meandering through black spruce bogs which are just as wild and remote as the lake. A small tributary stream flowing into Cloquet Lake from nearby Katherine Lake might also be considered the initial sector of the Cloquet, but the absolute beginning of a river is always difficult to determine. The river was named by explorer Joseph Nicollet for a French fur trader, although it was previously known as Rapid River.

The upper stretch of some thirty-five miles of stream down to Indian Lake is relatively inaccessible except by County Highway 2, which crosses about midway, and a few forest service roads. It is generally too small for canoe travel, except in high waters, from the county road to Indian Lake. It is characterized by many short boulder rapids, beaver dams, and black spruce bogs. The upper part of this section contains wild brook trout, originally stocked from the "fish car" on logging railroads. There are some cold-water tributaries, but because of their inaccessibility, the streams are lightly fished.

In this headwaters area, many small tributaries contribute to the main stream. For the most part, these are dark, slow streams, generally flowing southwest, as does the Cloquet, past the low drumlins oriented in that direction. Some of these small streams, such as Indian Creek and Pine Creek near Rollins, are trout waters, although slow and swampy.

A state forest campground located on Indian Lake, through which the Cloquet flows, provides access to the river. From here the Cloquet flows through remote country, with little access, to Island Lake, a distance of over thirty miles. But along this stretch is state forest Cedar Bay Campground, partly on nearby Bear Lake and also along the river, including canoe access. Farther downstream, the river is connected with several lakes that have some cottage development. The major tributaries above Island Lake are the West Branch of the Cloquet (sixteen miles), and the Little Cloquet (twelve miles).

Island Lake, largest of the five water-storage reservoirs in the St. Louis watershed, is the only one that directly impounds the Cloquet River. A canoe trip across the lake to the dam outlet is over six miles, the lake shores are heavily developed, high-speed motorboats are common, and the open reach of water is subject to high winds and waves. A canoe trip might more profitably include an overland transfer around the lake.

Below Island Lake the major tributaries are the Beaver River from the south, on which are two other water-storage reservoirs, Fish Lake and Wild Rice Lake, and the Us-kab-wan-ka (or Rush) River (fifteen miles) from the north. Several small trout streams, including Hellwig Creek, are tributary to the Cloquet in the vicinity of Independence.

From the Island Lake dam to its mouth in the St. Louis River near Brookston, the Cloquet flows more than twenty-five miles in a meandering but generally southwest direction. Its drainage area is nearly 800 square miles, over one-fifth of the St. Louis watershed. It is a broad stream, with moderate rapids and boulder fields in the upper portion, but with more rapids in the downstream sections near Independence. The last mile is a continuous rapids, the result of the steep drop in elevation into the St. Louis Valley.

The Cloquet provides an excellent experience for canoeists. The river can be generally characterized as having numerous rapids and short falls with long, deep pools. The rapids, especially in the high water of springtime, might better be left to the more expert. Canoeing on the Cloquet, including that stretch above Island Lake from Indian Lake downstream, is described in detail in *A Gathering of Waters*.

Fishing in the Cloquet River is primarily for northern pike, walleyes, smallmouth bass, and channel catfish, especially in the lower sections including the reservoir. Several small cold-water tributaries enter the main river and provide some trout fishing, already noted. Brown trout are stocked in some of these streams, and apparently some wander into the Cloquet River, where conditions may be suitable for their survival and growth to a large size in the main river. Local reports indicate some good brown trout fishing in the section where Hellwig Creek enters the main river.

From its sources in Cloquet and Katherine lakes, the Cloquet River flows about 100 miles to its mouth in the St. Louis, dropping about 300 feet. At its mouth the Cloquet contributes a mean annual discharge of about 500 cubic feet per second, approximately one-third of the flow of the St. Louis at that point.

Lying almost entirely in the Superior National Forest and the Cloquet Valley State Forest, the river is reasonably assured of stewardship in public ownership. Above Island Lake, ownership of land along its banks is largely federal, county, or state, and below the reservoir the stream margin is owned mainly by the Minnesota Power and Light Company. It is not spectacular country, but it is heavily forested and remote and has a wilderness quality. It should rank as one of Minnesota's finest recreational streams and deserves strong protection.

The main Whiteface River now has its real beginning at the outlet of Whiteface Reservoir. The name is a translation of an earlier Chippewa name. Drowned beneath the impounded waters of the reservoir is the junction of the two major branches, the main stem or North Branch and the South Branch. The waters of both upper branches are moderately soft and dark colored. The North Branch may afford some canoeing, being the larger of the two, although it is filled with boulders in low water, and the South Branch, a marginal trout stream, is too small for navigation.

Below the reservoir, the Whiteface is a moderately large river, with an average discharge of over 300 cubic feet per second. Flowing through the Cloquet Valley State Forest, the river is dark, deep, and heavily wooded. It will gain more attention as a wild, scenic route through unspoiled country.

Between the reservoir and the mouth above Floodwood, the main tributaries are Bug Creek, Paleface River, Jenkins Creek, the Little Whiteface, and Spider Creek, all generally too small for game fish management or canoeing. However, an even smaller stream, Tower Creek, is a brushy, cold, clear trout stream tributary to the Whiteface River, via Comstock Lake, not far below the reservoir. Wild brook trout provide fishing along most of its five-mile length above the lake.

The Whiteface, at its mouth in the St. Louis, is a soft-water, dark stream about a hundred feet wide or less. At this point it has drained about 600 square miles, or roughly one-sixth of the St. Louis watershed, in a distance of eighty miles including the North Branch above the reservoir. In this interval, from its marshy beginnings very near the headwaters of the St. Louis, it drops 430 feet. Its mean discharge at the mouth is about 400 cubic feet per second, approximately doubling the size of the St. Louis at this point and making it darker and softer water. It is a major member of the St. Louis family of rivers.

The streams of the St. Louis watershed as a whole range from low to medium in alkalinity and hardness—usually 25 to 50 p.p.m.—and are also moderately colored. Of the three major rivers, the upper St. Louis is both highest in alkalinity and lightest in color, and it changes noticeably in both respects where it is joined by the softer and darker waters of the Whiteface. Some of the smaller streams, originating in remoter swampy areas, are dark and low in alkalinity. The few trout streams, such as the White Pine River and Tower, Hay, Hellwig, and Chelberg creeks, have higher alkalinity concentrations (80 to 100 p.p.m.) and are virtually colorless, reflecting the spring-water sources that also produce the cooler water necessary for good trout habitat. These harder waters may also be expected to be more productive of bottom invertebrates and other aquatic life.

The larger streams of the St. Louis watershed played important roles in the lumbering industry during the last few decades of the nineteenth century. The upper St. Louis, the Embarrass, the Whiteface, and the Cloquet were all considered easy-driving streams, slow and of low gradient. The lower St. Louis, however, with its rocky gorge and the falls at Thomson presented an insurmountable obstacle to the transportation of logs to Lake Superior. Attempts to improve this section of river for driving logs met with failure. Consequently it was the town of Cloquet above the gorge, and not Duluth, that prospered first as a sawmill town, for it received the vast supply of pine that was floated down the upper rivers from almost the entire St. Louis watershed. In the late 1800s and early 1900s, up to 100 small dams were built on the St. Louis and its tributaries to facilitate the river transportation of logs. The remains of a few of these dams are still extant.

Nevertheless, Duluth was recognized as a potential sawmill town of great importance, since its lumber could be transported via the Great Lakes waterway to eastern markets that by this time had few sources of pine. But it was not until railroads were built into the northern pineries that Duluth received a large supply of logs. Then its sawmill activity soared. It was the last great western source of pine on the Great Lakes water route; and in the last decade of the century the number of sawmills in Duluth nearly doubled, and the cut of pine increased more than threefold while other mills down the Mississippi were declining. Such prosperity, however, was short-lived. The peak year was 1902, and the cut dropped after that. The pine, once thought to be virtually inexhaustible, was gone. The last river drive was made in 1925. The rugged lower St. Louis River had delayed lumbering prosperity in Duluth almost until the pine supply was depleted. Cloquet remains an important wood products industrial community, even though the trees today are not white pine and the upper rivers no longer carry the big log drives.

W̲ater pollution problems are minimal in the streams of the St. Louis watershed except in the lower section of the St. Louis from Cloquet downstream. Here the problems are severe. Wastes from the wood products industries in Cloquet contribute to the depletion of oxygen in the waters of this section of river, so that fish populations are seriously affected, even though reductions in waste effluents and improvements recently have been made. No drinking water supplies are withdrawn from the St. Louis River in this section; the water supply for heavily populated Duluth, for example, is from Lake Superior several miles northeast of the city.

On the Mesabi range, iron mining activity previously created turbid conditions in streams tributary to the St. Louis in that area. However, settling basins for the deposition of mining wastes have now been constructed by most mining companies, and processing water is largely recirculated. Today there remain virtually no turbidity problems in these streams as a result of mining.

The large region between the range cities and the heavily populated, industrialized Cloquet-Duluth area is lightly populated and free of stream pollution. This area constitutes the greatest proportion of the watershed, and the streams flowing through it, particularly the St. Louis, Whiteface, and Cloquet, remain clean and clear, valuable recreational resources.

Fishing in the St. Louis streams is only light to moderate, except in the few small trout streams and the large water-storage reservoirs. All of the larger streams—the St. Louis, Cloquet, and Whiteface—generally produce a fishery of walleye-northern pike, rather than bass-panfish. Smallmouth bass are common in the St. Louis River in the stretch between the town of Cloquet and the mouth of the Whiteface River upstream, and also are present in the Whiteface itself and the Cloquet below Island Lake reservoir. Certain reaches, particularly the St. Louis between Floodwood and Brookston, and the Cloquet River below Island Lake, are known for their channel catfish. However, the walleye and northern pike remain the principal game species in these rivers.

Fishing in the water storage reservoirs is an increasingly popular recreational activity, especially as resort and vacation home development increases. The principal species caught are the walleye and northern pike, among the large predators, and yellow perch and crappies, among the panfishes. There appears little success in management for largemouth bass, which are rarely found despite attempts to introduce and maintain this species by stocking.

The generally flat terrain of the St. Louis watershed, heavily covered with swampy glacial lake deposits which are poorly drained, and the underlying crystalline rock formations combine to produce a system of slow, warm, and sluggish streams. In the central part of the basin there are few sources of the cool groundwater necessary for springs and trout streams. With some exceptions the trout streams are small and relatively unproductive. The greatest concentration is in the more rugged morainal regions of the southwest part of the basin, between Duluth and Cloquet, and somewhat to the north. Several small streams, such as Miller, Keene, Kingsbury, and Sargent creeks, tumble down through Duluth itself. Others in this area include Hay Creek and Rocky Run, tributary to the Midway River which joins the St. Louis near Thomson.

South of the St. Louis, Otter Creek and Little Otter Creek are two of the better known, heavily fished trout streams in the area; much of Otter Creek flows through the University of Minnesota's Cloquet Forest Experiment Station at which research in forest management and forest-wildlife ecology is conducted.

Slightly farther north, but still associated with the southern moraines, are Squaw Creek, Joe Martin Brook, and Dutchess Slough. Here, too, is the lovely White Pine River, which winds through the rugged hills north and east of Cloquet, flowing under heavy forest cover, and tumbles through deep pools and riffles rich with invertebrate trout foods. In addition to resident brown and brook trout, the White Pine is reported to receive an annual run of large brown trout in late summer, presumably from the St. Louis River.

Aside from this southern group of trout streams that are the result of morainal topography, there are scattered small streams that either hold stocked trout for a time or, in some cases, have wild, naturally reproducing brook trout. These include Chelberg and Hellwig creeks, tributary to the lower Cloquet, and Humphrey and Ahlenin's creeks on the upper Cloquet. In the far northern tip of the watershed, Bear Creek, tributary to the Embarrass, is known locally for trout fishing. In the Whiteface drainage, two small, cold, brushy streams providing wild brook trout fishing are Tower and Ryan creeks. Ryan is a very short tributary of the South Branch of the Whiteface, which itself is a marginal trout stream.

Brook trout, although native to the Lake Superior tributaries, originally existed only in the estuaries following the last glaciation. They were not native to the North Shore streams above impassable barriers. The presence of brook trout in the small headwater areas of these streams today is the result of introduction. This is true also of all the streams of the St. Louis watershed, since the gorge and falls in the lower St. Louis presented insurmountable obstacles to the fish. Brook trout were introduced to the upper streams when they were

Much of the St. Louis drainage basin consists of a high plateau with little gradient for its streams; the region is notable for swamps, poorly drained glacial deposits, and slow streams. However, the rugged morainic area in the southern part of the watershed, near Cloquet, has produced a few trout streams, including the tumbling White Pine River, which contains wild populations of both brook and brown trout.

first planted in the Cloquet River in 1898. Rainbow and brown trout, of course, are not native to this part of the country, having been introduced from the western United States and Europe, respectively. Both species have long been raised in Minnesota hatcheries and stocked where appropriate in some of the St. Louis trout streams by the Department of Natural Resources.

The northern pike is the most abundant large game fish in the St. Louis watershed and is common in the rivers as well as the reservoirs. The northern, as well as the walleye, yellow perch, and smallmouth bass all appear to be native to the watershed.

A large part of the St. Louis drainage is in state or national forests, including much of the Cloquet and Whiteface rivers and part of the upper St. Louis; these areas are largely open for public use. Cloquet Valley State Forest, about twenty miles north of Duluth, includes about thirty-five miles of the Cloquet River, from Indian Lake to near Island Lake reservoir. There are two maintained campgrounds along the river in this stretch: Indian Lake Campground near Rollins, actually on Indian Lake through which the river flows, and Cedar Bay Campground, mostly on Bear Lake and partly along the river. About twenty miles of the Whiteface River, from the reservoir downstream, and Whiteface State Forest Campground, on the river about one mile below the outlet, also lie within the Cloquet Valley State Forest.

Small portions of other state forest lands lie within the watershed, such as Finland, Bear Island, Whiteface River, Savanna, and Fond du Lac state forests; the centers of activity of most of these areas, however, are outside the St. Louis watershed.

An important portion of the Superior National Forest is within the eastern part of the St. Louis watershed. The upper thirty miles of the St. Louis, the many upper branches and tributaries of the Whiteface, and the upper twenty-five miles of the Cloquet, all flow largely through federal lands. Cadotte Lake Campground, centrally located in this portion of the national forest not far from the North Branch of the Whiteface; St. Louis River campground, on the St. Louis a few miles southeast of Aurora; and the Whiteface Reservoir Campground, on a northern edge of the reservoir, are all operated by the U.S. Forest Service within the national forest.

Jay Cooke State Park is the only state park in the watershed, but it is one of the most scenic and one of the most historically significant of Minnesota's state parks, lying along the deep river gorge of the St. Louis River Dalles. Camp and picnic grounds, scenic overlooks, many miles of river trails, and a swinging suspension footbridge across one of the wilder sections of the river, are included.

Savanna Portage State Park, to the west, has a significant relationship to the St. Louis River. Actually the major portion is located in the Mississippi watershed although the east end of the portage trail is in the St. Louis watershed.

Of growing recreational interest in the St. Louis watershed is

The St. Louis-Savanna Rivers route provided the major link between the upper Great Lakes and the Mississippi River to early explorers and fur traders. The lower St. Louis River, however, was a mad torrent of white water and necessitated a long, arduous portage around the rocky gorge. Jay Cooke State Park now encloses this cascading stretch of river.

canoeing. Both the St. Louis itself (down to Cloquet) and the Cloquet River (which does not go through the town of Cloquet) are included in the state river guide, *A Gathering of Waters*. Both flow through wild country, with remote, long stretches having a wilderness quality. Although the established and designated canoe routes include only the lower parts of the two rivers, the more adventurous canoeist, with some additional difficulty expected with low water and obstacles, can also ply parts of the upper reaches as well as some of the larger tributaries. The Whiteface River, too, may provide good canoeing below the reservoir; however, like the Cloquet below Island Lake, fluctuations in water level immediately below the reservoir may require special precautions and careful timing.

An increase in recreational use of these streams, particularly for canoeing and camping, probably can be expected, especially in the Cloquet Valley State Forest. The unspoiled nature of these streams is an attractive lure. It will be a major recreational area close to the population centers of Duluth, surrounding communities, and the range cities. Good management of the resource to maintain the wilderness quality will be a challenge.

During the time of the great glaciers, more than ten thousand years ago, glacial ice which was thousands of feet thick —up to about two miles thick, in fact—pressed the land down with its immense weight. When it melted, the weight was removed, and the land responded with gradual uplift.

So it was at the western end of Lake Superior and over the lower St. Louis River Valley when the Superior lobe of ice first began to melt. The uplift in this region further increased the gradient of the river and assisted in the erosion of its deep gorge. The ice melted back to the northeast—up the lake—but this process took a long time and did not occur at a regular rate. By the time the ice was finally gone at the east end of the Lake Superior basin, uplift had already occurred at the southwest end, at the mouth of the St. Louis.

Then, with the relief from the glaciers' weight at the east end, uplift occurred there, and water consequently edged back to the western end of the basin, increasing its depth. It was like tilting a great bowl. The mouth of the St. Louis and part of its gorge thus became filled with Lake Superior water, resulting in a "drowned" river. St. Louis Bay was the result.

The St. Louis River, which had roared with glacial meltwaters, now lies aged, quiet, and drowned—but it constitutes one of the important international seaports of the world.

Chapter 3

The North Shore Streams

A Crown of Waterfalls

Most Minnesota North Shore streams rise on the Highland Moraine, a steep, rugged range of hills deposited by the glaciers on ancient rock, overlooking Lake Superior. The moraine parallels the big lake and forms the upper border of this narrow watershed. Here the streams seep slowly through upland bogs and marshes; then later, downslope, they course through a jumble of old lava flows and glacial boulders, traversing some of the most diverse landforms in the world. Finally, they plunge down the last few hundred feet in spectacular cascades and waterfalls that crest the northern border of Lake Superior.

There are many places on earth—some even called the "North Shore"—that have a special meaning to the people of a region. Perhaps none so much, though, as Minnesota's North Shore: no one need ask, "The north shore of what?" here. The words are capitalized, as are other proper place names, even when spoken!

This narrow strip of watershed bordering the northern coastline of the earth's largest lake is a very special place to Minnesotans. To be geographically correct, any complete discussion of the North Shore of Lake Superior should include that portion belonging to our northern neighbor, Canada—and that is beautiful country, too—but Minnesotans, provincially, do not usually do so. Minnesota's North

44

Shore extends—as does the subject of this chapter—from Duluth at the head of the lake, northeast along shores of spruce-clad hills, stony beaches, and sheer cliffs only to the mouth of the Pigeon River, the international border. The Pigeon has much greater significance than simply as a border—which we shall explore later; its character, and therefore its role in history, made it a very convenient line of demarcation.

The North Shore includes landforms unique in the north woods. Little in the way of dark, unbroken pine stands here—rather, there are the sweeping valleys of the high moraines covered with flaming maples in autumn; the soft, boggy muskeg that is inaccessible except to the wily canoe-borne duck hunter; the tumbling, rocky watercourses where the short streams find their way to the precipices of Lake Superior's rocky observation posts; the rugged, broken—sometimes sheer—gradients of solid rock that were scoured and scraped by the great glaciers, and, finally, the plunging, thundering waterfalls of the rivers that at last leap over the precipice.

Not all the waterfalls can be seen easily on an automobile trip up the North Shore highway, although there are enough almost beside the road—like those on the Gooseberry, Beaver, Cross, and Manitou—to satisfy most waterfall-watchers. Others—just as high and awesome—can be found by rugged hikes inland. For example, miles above the spectacular lower canyon of the Cascade are other falls that spurt from natural highland reservoirs to carom from one chasm wall to the next and delight the viewer with white water plumes against green spruce and blue sky. And far up the ever-deepening, every-darker slash of the Devil Track and Kadunce canyons are more waterfalls that block the river traveler and challenge steelhead fishermen to become rock-climbers just to get down into the river—and back out.

Many of the waterfalls are the focal points of state parks along U.S. 61, the North Shore drive, and are protected by park rules and trailside signs warning parents to keep small children in hand. The crowds thin out after Labor Day weekend. Later in the dead white of winter, hungry white-tailed deer leave their hoof slashes deep in the snow and ruffed grouse their smudged red trails on the surface after feeding on mountain ash fruits. But even then, a handful of waterfall-watchers appear at the state parks, the water now frozen into colonnades of ice as if the falls had suddenly been solidified in midair. And yet, although summer's throngs of tourists or winter's skiers may crowd around the waterfalls along the highway, the wild places farther up the slopes remain largely untrod.

The 1930 Shipstead-Nolan Act of Congress, prohibiting the construction of dams or other water-fluctuation structures in St. Louis, Lake, and Cook counties, supported by a Minnesota law of 1933, effectively protects the waterfalls, rapids, and beaches of North Shore streams.

The North Shore Watersheds

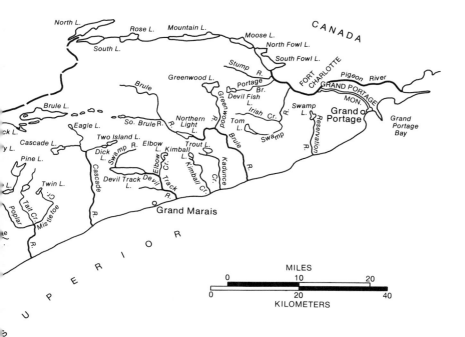

The entire Lake Superior region is thought to be underlaid by rocks over two billion years old, such as the well-known Ely greenstone. The trend of these rocks is generally east-west, somewhat parallel to present Lake Superior, a fact that has its expression today in the morphology of the great lake and also of its tributary streams. Then, about one billion years ago, violent volcanic activity occurred in the area and continued for some time; the old base rocks were folded downward, forming a trough or syncline that was the forerunner of the Lake Superior basin. The volcanic activity during this age—the Keweenawan period—also produced a great variety of lava flows in the basin and surrounding region.

After the period of volcanic activity, the Superior basin, then 2,000 feet deep and extending nearly 700 feet below sea level, undoubtedly filled with rock debris and other sediments owing to erosion on the bluffs and deposition in the trough. A major stream probably flowed down the center of the debris-filled basin.

Much later, during the Pleistocene epoch, when the glaciers ground their way down from the northeast, the Superior basin and its slopes were further modified. Glaciation continued intermittently

Although most waterfalls are in the lower sections of North Shore streams, other cascades and rapids occur farther inland. Here there are no crowds, but the falls are just as spectacular to the lone hiker or hunter. Ten miles from Lake Superior, the Cascade River starts its tumbling descent.

for at least a million years. Four distinct phases of ice advance and retreat have been identified in northern Minnesota for the period 20,000 to 11,000 years ago. Four times the Superior lobe pushed southwest through the basin and later melted back, each time scouring and pushing the accumulated rock debris out and, in melting back the last two times, forming huge glacial lakes of meltwater. The level of these was some 400 feet higher than present-day levels of Lake Superior. The fine sediments and clays deposited on the bottom of the glacial lakes are red because of the red rock that the glacier scraped from the Superior basin. These deposits were laid down in areas now easily recognized, such as in the Nemadji basin (Chapter 1) along the North Shore and even far up into stream valleys that must have predated the glacial lakes.

Today the North Shore watershed consists of a long narrow strip extending northeast-southwest along the lake, with many short tributaries flowing perpendicularly, or southeast to the lake. The streams have eroded through the surface deposits of glacial drift, and uplifted glacial lake sediments and even bedrock. The old lava flows that were laid down along the northern edge of the basin in the Keweenawan period were diverse in shape, thickness, fineness of grain, hardness, and chemical content. They now lie partially exposed at the edge of the basin sloping down or southeast to the lake. And it is down these slopes of base rock that present-day streams flow and in which they have eroded deep gorges to form the variety of stream environments we now enjoy in the valleys of the North Shore streams.

The rivers of the North Shore were never important as log-driving streams. They are generally narrow and short, draining small watersheds, and the rugged nature of these watercourses, especially in the torrential last rush to Lake Superior, made them unsuitable for carrying logs. The white pine, king of the great pineries of the St. Croix Valley and central Minnesota, grows in the rugged North Shore watershed, but it shares the forest with other trees considered less desirable at the time of original logging—red and jack pine, white spruce, and balsam fir in the uplands; black spruce and tamarack in the bogs and bottoms; and some great white cedar in swamps. Furthermore, the rocky slopes were not very productive of white pine, whose taproot penetrated much more easily the sand and loamy soils of the outwash plains and glacial till farther south.

A few small sawmills developed early at the mouths of some of the major streams, such as at Beaver Bay and Knife River, but the big mills that cut most of the timber from the North Shore were later built and operated in Duluth. The lumber milling industry in Duluth, starting in the 1860s, was seriously limited by the difficulty of transporting logs safely down the lower St. Louis River, and the city depended primarily on logs from the Nemadji River and the pine forests to the west, as well as a few rafts of North Shore logs floated down on Lake Superior.

But the railroads arrived about 1870 and soon spread north and east to transport timber from the Arrowhead country to Duluth. Many small, temporary railroads were built into the rugged country, in an attempt to reach within skidding distance of the timber. A vast rail network developed along the North Shore, and terminals were located at the mouths of the Knife, Gooseberry, Split Rock, and Beaver rivers, from which log rafts were floated to Duluth. Yards at the

Knife included docks that permitted direct loading of ships bound for eastern markets via the Great Lakes. Lumbering then boomed in Duluth, for the city, located right on the Great Lakes-St. Lawrence waterway that led to eastern markets, shipped great quantities of milled lumber via steamers and barges—not on lumber rafts like those used on the Mississippi, because Great Lakes storms would have torn them apart. About this time the pine was gone from eastern forests, and Duluth remained the last large lumber supplier for the east.

By the turn of the century, little remained of the original white pine along the North Shore. Duluth's lumber industry declined after its peak year of 1902, for the profitable stands of the northern Minnesota forests, like those in the east, were becoming exhausted. However, interest had developed in setting aside for conservation purposes some remnants of the original stands; General Christopher C. Andrews, former Civil War officer, then United States' Minister to Sweden and impressed with that country's forest conservation practices, urged the preservation of some of the forested public domain. The lumber industry reacted with both scorn and fear, threatening the northern communities with the loss of jobs and other calamities (some trumped up), a story of conflict with a familiar ring today. Andrews's plans went largely unheeded at the time, and the virgin timber was cut almost to exhaustion; nevertheless his ideas later stimulated the establishment of state and national forests, state parks, recreational areas, and historic sites, albeit on cutover lands. General Andrews went on to become Minnesota's first chief fire warden in 1895 and later, Forestry Commissioner. The first state forest reserve was established in 1900 and our many state forests followed; the Superior National Forest, embracing much of the North Shore, was established in 1909 as a result of General Andrews's efforts and today includes nearly three million acres.

Logging continues today as one of the major industries along the North Shore, but it now primarily harvests pulpwood to serve the paper products industry. With the advent of the truck and tractor in the 1920s, thousands of miles of small, private railroad tracks were torn up. The industry was then served by logging roads, penetrating the farthest corners of cutover country, and sought new pulpwood of many species far from the streams along the rugged shore. Fires that followed logging left much of the North Shore bare, rocky hills, but second-growth forests, now fully developed, have benefited the streams by stabilizing flow and cooling the waters.

Most of the North Shore streams are small to moderate in size, short, and steep. The usual main stem length is only about twenty miles, and the average gradient is 50 to 100 feet per mile. However, local gradients may be as high as 300 in rapids and waterfall sections. At the southwest and northeast ends of the watershed are the St. Louis and Pigeon rivers, respectively, both considerably larger than other North Shore rivers. Although there is some variation, the many streams in the middle section are cold, and trout are the principal game fishes; the St. Louis and Pigeon, on the other hand, are warm-water streams with game fish populations consisting primarily of walleyes and northern pike.

In their classic early work on the North Shore streams, Lloyd L. Smith and John B. Moyle list twenty-eight major streams and many smaller ones emptying directly into Lake Superior or tributary to the larger ones. Of these, about ten approach or exceed a watershed area of 100 square miles. These same ten have total lengths of approximately 100 miles, including their winding headwaters, but the main stem length is about twenty miles.

The hydrological character of the streams changes from Duluth northeast toward the Canadian border. Near Duluth the streams are flashy and poorly regulated; virtually no lakes exist in the headwaters, so that during times of snow-melt or heavy rain, floodwaters develop rapidly and run off quickly, and during drought, flows are extremely low. To the northeast, the streams have a more stable flow; lakes and marshes in the headwaters act as natural regulators, retarding high flows during storms and slowly releasing stored water during drought to maintain higher minimum flows. For example, the ratio of maximum discharge to watershed area for the Baptism River (with no lakes or marshes in the headwaters) is four times the ratio for the Pigeon River (with substantial headwater area in lakes). The fisherman or photographer will notice that the streams farther north maintain a higher flow in the drought of late summer than do the streams closer to Duluth, which are nearly dry.

The North Shore streams are all colored to some degree, and alkalinities are generally low, ranging only from about 15 to 50 p.p.m.

in most streams; those near the northernmost end of the watershed usually have the lowest alkalinities. The biological productivity of these streams is correspondingly low, although the reasons for this are not entirely clear. Production of bottom-living invertebrate animals that serve as fish foods is reduced, and consequently resident fish populations remain small, especially compared to the hard-water, clear streams of southeast Minnesota. The small catches and size of fish, however, do not detract from the quality of the angling experience, enhanced by the brilliance of wild brook trout and the scenic character of the streams themselves.

Starting near Duluth the first few streams have common traits that allow some grouping. These are among the smallest and shortest of the major North Shore streams. Yet they are important recreational resources, particularly because of their proximity to Duluth and Two Harbors, and they are heavily used. This group includes the Lester River (watershed fifty-eight square miles, main stem length fifteen miles), French River (thirty-one square miles, twelve miles long), Sucker River (thirty-seven square miles, fifteen miles long), Knife River (ninety-three square miles, nineteen miles long), and Stewart River (thirty-three square miles, length twenty miles). All these streams provide good brook trout habitat in the headwater reaches, but generally the waters are too warm and often silty in lower sections below the old beach lines of Glacial Lake Duluth. The lower reaches are rugged, with exposed igneous rocks and boulders, cascades, and rapids, although they lack high waterfalls. All receive runs of rainbow, or steelhead, from Lake Superior into their lowest reaches. Angling for trout is now open year-round in the lower reaches of all North Shore streams, and considerable winter fishing is done by the more hardy in the estuaries and off stream mouths. A Minnesota record-size rainbow was taken in the lower Knife River in January 1974, weighing an impressive seventeen pounds. Lester River, in this group, is the most metropolitan, flowing in its lower reaches along the edge of Duluth and Lester Park; the mouth of the Lester, including the section immediately beneath the U.S. 61 highway bridge, is the scene of boisterous smelt-dipping during the spring run from Lake Superior, usually around the first of May.

Next up the shore from this group of streams is the Gooseberry River, a spectacular stream in its lower reaches. Gooseberry Falls State Park, one of Minnesota's most popular, is located along the highway crossing. Here the river plunges more than 100 feet in a se-

Below U.S. Highway 61, the North Shore drive, the Gooseberry River plunges over the last of three spectacular waterfalls in its final descent to Lake Superior. The falls are in Gooseberry Falls State Park, one of the North Shore's largest and most popular parks.

ries of three waterfalls; the two major ones are located on either side of the highway, a third farther up. The park contains many features for the tourist, including camping near the lake away from the highway, many miles of trails along the river and falls, scenic lookouts, wildlife habitat, and rocky Lake Superior beaches. The Gooseberry's headwaters include many miles of brook trout fishing, but seeps into fractured bedrock consume much of the flow before it reaches the mouth. Consequently, the lower sections may become nearly dry in late summer while the upper headwaters and tributaries contain adequate flows to maintain trout populations. The Gooseberry, considerably larger than most of the streams in the first group, drains a watershed of ninety-seven square miles, and the main stem flows for about twenty miles, with a major East Branch and many headwater tributaries.

The Split Rock River, almost two streams in one, consists of the West and East branches, joining together only about three miles above the mouth of the main stem in the lake. Whereas the upper reaches of both branches provide brook trout angling, the West Branch (larger than the East) is generally considered better water; intensive management through stream habitat alteration by the Department of Natural Resources some years ago produced significant increases in wild brook trout populations. Below the junction of the two branches, the main stem courses through a wild section of cascades and rapids that terminates in a high falls about a mile above its mouth, and the stream drops in this reach a total of 400 feet. The lower mile is a wide, flat valley. The Split Rock drains forty square miles; the length of each branch to the mouth is about fifteen miles. A notable historic landmark is Split Rock Lighthouse, located on a cliff-top promontory up the shore a short way from the mouth of the river. It is now preserved as a state park.

The Beaver and Baptism rivers share some characteristics and yet differ significantly in others. Each possesses a fairly large watershed of about 135 square miles, with a main stem length of about twenty miles. Both streams, like those to the south, lack water storage in their headwaters, and consequently discharge fluctuates seasonally over wide ranges, leading to virtual drying up in late summer. Trout fishing in the Beaver and Baptism is probably best for browns, which tolerate warmer waters than do the brook trout. However, Big Thirtynine Creek, tributary to the Beaver, is known locally for its brook trout. The Beaver River system consists of two branches, the main East Branch and the smaller West Branch, joining the main stem about two miles above the mouth in Lake Superior. Below this confluence, the main stem flows through long pools and then drops 300 feet in a series of cascades and falls. The Baptism, on the other hand, is noted for the waterfalls with the highest sheer drop in Minnesota— seventy feet. Another falls of about fifty feet, Illgen Falls, is located farther upstream. The main stem, or West Branch, of the Baptism is joined near the town of Finland by the East Branch and Hockamin Creek; from the confluence down, a distance of about ten miles, the river is rocky and rugged, dropping over 700 feet in cascades, rapids, and the two high falls. Baptism River State Park includes the highest of the waterfalls and the lower gorge but no camping facilities. Finland State Forest campgrounds are located along the river farther upstream, in rocky rapids reaches below the town of Finland. Parts of the stretch down from Finland, very bouldery, are sometimes run by kayaks or covered canoes in high water, but this undertaking is for experts only and requires a number of portages, described in *White-water; Quietwater*, by Bob and Jody Palzer.

In the mid-1970s, a threat new to the North Shore watershed and its streams was raised, catapulting several North Shore streams into environmental controversy. For many years, Reserve Mining Company had disposed of waste taconite tailings from its Silver Bay processing plant by daily dumping 67,000 tons directly into Lake Superior. Through the years public concern developed over the possible degradation of Lake Superior and the safety of drinking water drawn from the lake. As safety and environmental evidence mounted against continued discharge into the lake, the case entered the courts, and in 1974 a cessation of the discharge was ordered. An on-land site for the tailings disposal would have to be found.

The first major controversy centered around Palisade Creek, a brook trout stream in its headwaters and the recipient of a significant steelhead run in its lower reaches. Palisade Creek originates in a spectacular valley in the rocky highlands above Silver Bay. The site was opposed by the Minnesota Department of Natural Resources, which considered the high valley a potential state park. The presiding judge of U.S. District Court, Miles W. Lord, after touring the Palisade Valley on foot, agreed with North Shore environmentalists and vetoed the plan. It appeared that the high valley of Palisade Creek had been saved.

But the next choice of Reserve Mining Company was a site in the Beaver River watershed. This site became the center of years of debate and so occupied the efforts and emotions of many Minnesotans and other Americans that its name was burned into the state's history and the nation's record of landmark environmental causes: Mile Post 7.

Mile Post 7 is the seven-mile point from Silver Bay on Reserve's railroad, but it is only three miles on the steep basin slope from Lake Superior. It lies, therefore, well within the North Shore watershed. The objections to Mile Post 7 were many, but in brief this proposal for a major new industrial activity in the North Shore corridor was judged by the state hearing officer to be "inconsistent with the main land uses which have developed over time for the corridor." The proposal called for gigantic dams holding back tailings; the main dam would be 180 feet high and over two and one-half miles long, perched 600 feet above the Lake Superior shore. It would be among the thirty largest dams in the world. As the hearing officer pointed out, the threat of catastrophe from failure of this dam would persist not only for the forty years of Reserve's proposed operation, but *in perpetuity*. The Mile Post 7 site would necessitate the diversion of Big Thirtynine and Little Thirtynine creeks, causing the loss of ten miles of trout waters. The site would remove eight square miles of watershed from the Beaver River drainage, a reduction of water source that would in all probability mean the loss of steelhead production in the lower reaches.

After a full year of intensive public hearings, including testimony from 160 witnesses, the State Hearing Officer in 1976 recommended against the Mile Post 7 and instead requested planning for a site *outside the North Shore watershed*. These recommendations were accepted by the Department of Natural Resources and the Pollution Control Agency. Reserve's permits were denied. The North Shore and Beaver River streams appeared, like Palisade Creek, to have been saved.

But Reserve appealed to the Lake County District Court, which substituted its own judgment on natural resource questions and overturned decisions based on years of study and testimony by resource experts. Permits were ordered for Mile Post 7. The battle for the North Shore continued with appeals by the state to the Minnesota Supreme Court. The state's charges against the District Court were serious: the court ignored the state's administrative hearing process and erred in a matter of law. Yet the high court, in a crushing defeat for the North Shore, simply reiterated the District Court decision and in April 1977 permits were again ordered for Mile Post 7. The integrity of the upland trout streams and the Beaver River is probably lost, and the threat of a taconite tailings catastrophe will hang over the lakeshore forever. It was not one of Minnesota's proudest moments.

The Manitou, Caribou, and Two Island rivers present a modest change from streams to the south in that they have some headwater storage in lakes and swamps, and stream water level fluctuations are not as great. The Manitou and its tributaries drain a watershed of 103 square miles, including many tributaries, eleven small lakes, and ten square miles of alder, tamarack, and cedar swamps; the main stem length is about eighteen miles. In the lower seven miles the Manitou flows through a deep, preglacial gorge, plunging over eight major waterfalls; the last falls drops almost directly into Lake Superior. Along the lower Manitou is an experiment in state parks, the George H.

Crosby-Manitou State Park, where only backpacking is permitted. No campsites are directly accessible by automobile or other motorized vehicles, but the trails wind along the lovely lower river gorge, including some of the high waterfalls. The Caribou River is a shorter stream (twelve miles) and drains a smaller watershed (twenty-three square miles); it, too, originates in swampy headwater areas. In its lower reach it drops over a series of rapids and waterfalls up to sixty feet in height. Caribou Falls State Wayside is located at the U.S. 61 highway crossing; it is a small park with trails and tables but no campgrounds. Two Island River is a small stream draining thirty square miles, about fifteen miles long, with a number of lakes and swamps in its headwaters. It is noted for its rapids and falls in the lowest one mile, including three tumbling falls, each dropping about eighty feet. The Manitou and Caribou, because of their copious spring water sources and relatively stable water flows are among the best trout streams along the North Shore.

The next group of streams—Cross, Temperance, Poplar, and Cascade rivers—exhibits a distinct change. The many lakes, ponds, and marshes in their headwaters result in more stable flows than in the streams to the south. The presence of the headwater lakes, many of them large, has another effect on the streams: the relatively high water temperatures in the upper reaches are more suited to warm-water fish species, such as northern pike and smallmouth bass, than to trout. Nevertheless, the middle reaches of these streams frequently yield excellent brown trout catches to skilled anglers, and some small, cold-water tributaries contain abundant brook trout. These four streams also provide wondrous river scenes—high falls, thundering cascades, veil-like rapids, and turbulent drops through gorges so narrow and deep they seem more like caves than river channels.

The Cross originates in a large group of lakes on the Lake-Cook county border, drains a watershed of ninety-one square miles with a main stem course of about twenty miles. In its lower six miles, it drops over five major waterfalls. A tumbling cascade presents a lacy white-water view to motorists at the North Shore drive crossing; unfortunately, these falls have lured the young and unwary to play among the cascades, resulting in some fatalities. Cross River State Wayside provides some trails to upstream riverbanks.

The Temperance River drains one of the largest North Shore watersheds, 180 square miles, and the river is also one of the longest, about twenty-five miles. It originates in a maze of many large lakes in the Boundary Waters Canoe Area. One of the Temperance River's headwater origins, Brule Lake, is unusual because it also serves as a headwater source for the Brule River. A single lake rarely serves as a headwater source for two separate river systems. In its lower reach of four miles, the Temperance descends rapidly in a narrow canyon so deep and dark that it is impossible to see some waterfalls in the gorge from the edge. The roar can be heard from far below where the canyon walls at some points are only three to four feet apart. Temperance River State Park is located on this lower reach, and it includes campgrounds, picnic sites, and riverside trails. A Superior National Forest campground is located along the Sawbill Trail, farther upstream on a sweeping stretch of wide, rocky rapids of the Temperance. The river is said to have been so named because it lacked a "bar" at the mouth. The Temperance is not the only North Shore stream so deprived, but many streams often have a bar. (And in some years, so does the Temperance!) The bar is a coarse gravel strand laid across the mouth of a stream. This results from autumn storms and turbulent wave action on Lake Superior, combined with usual low stream discharges of late summer and fall. Stream flow simply percolates through the gravel and rock during autumn and winter, and the bar is flushed away by floodwaters the following spring. The bars do not form every year, for in some years autumn rains keep the streams high, and the gravel does not accumulate. The configuration of the Temperance's channel at its mouth is such that a bar rarely forms, which is also true of some other larger North Shore rivers. When a bar forms at the mouth of a smaller stream, the effect on stream fisheries may be significant. For example, a bar might preclude the entrance of fall-running migratory species like the coho and pink salmon, and the occasional fall run of rainbows would be prevented as well. But since the rainbow's main spawning run is in the spring, after meltwater floods have washed out the bar, this species can, without difficulty, migrate upstream to reproduce. The major ecological effect in the long run may be to favor the rainbow over the Pacific salmon.

The Poplar River originates in a large network of lakes, ponds, and flat-water stretches of river, drains 150 square miles, and flows in its main stem for about twenty miles. Approximately three miles above its mouth, the Poplar plunges over a series of roaring falls, spanned at the upper brink by a small wooden-floored bridge, not recommended for the faint-hearted. Below this upper falls, the river

A bar forms at the mouth of Kadunce Creek. After the bar is complete, no fish may migrate either into the stream from Lake Superior or out to the lake from the stream; but spring freshets will flush the bar away, permitting the migrating rainbow, or steelhead, to ascend the rushing currents to spawn.

flows through a deep gorge, broken by numerous rapids and cascades. A small hydroelectric power dam with a ten-foot head, the only hydropower installation on the North Shore streams, formerly served a resort located on the lower reach. Near its mouth is Ray Berglund State Wayside, actually along the lower cascades of the Onion River, just south of the Poplar. A small but attractive primitive national forest campground is located on the Poplar upstream near the crossing of the Honeymoon Trail.

The Cascade River drains a watershed of 120 square miles with a main stem length of only about fifteen miles, but numerous tributaries, the headwaters of which lie in many lakes in north-central Cook County, enter the Cascade along its entire course. Ten miles above the mouth, the Cascade abruptly drops over bedrock ledges to begin its fall to Lake Superior. In the final three miles it falls a total of 900 feet; in the last quarter-mile, through a deep and twisting gorge, it falls 120 feet. It is this series of spectacular cascades for which the river is named. The lowest reach is in Cascade River State

Park, where the Cascade Trail extends up one side of the gorge, across a footbridge high overlooking Lake Superior, and back down the other side of the gorge. The park, one of the North Shore's largest, also includes many miles of Lake Superior shoreline. A small national forest campground is located on the river a few miles upstream from the state park.

The Devil Track River, in name as well as character, must rank as one of the most unusual rivers in America. Rising in a series of lakes and swamps, it flows first as Swamp River to Devil Track Lake, one of the North Shore's largest. Much of the Swamp River is cold, brook trout water. At the outlet of the lake the stream is called the Devil Track River, and from there it embarks on an incredible journey. The first reach includes some slow water and beaver ponds; but then the stream enters its lower gorge, a narrow winding gash cut deep into igneous rock. From the forested top, this lower gorge of the Devil Track is barely visible; there is essentially no valley. But from below on the stream, the hiker or fisherman is faced with sheer, towering walls of vertical rock, sometimes only a few feet apart at the top. Thus much of the river bed is inaccessible except by walking up from the mouth or climbing down from the rim of the gorge, the latter sometimes requiring mountain-climbing techniques. The rock is red rhyolite, a fine-grained lava flow that characteristically breaks in vertical planes. The riverbed consists almost entirely of broken flat pieces dropped from the canyon walls. The river is clear and fast as it swings from one wall to the other, the water flowing from a deep pool at the bottom of the cliff, to a shallow riffle, then to another pool on the other side. In the gorge reach, the river drops over several falls that effectively block upstream migration of rainbows; the lower falls, however, is more than a mile from Lake Superior, so there is a substantial reach for some of the best rainbow fishing along the North Shore, as well as for nurturing the young rainbows in their juvenile stream life. Fishing here in the high water of spring, when the rainbows run, can be dangerous, for the unwary angler can be trapped in the narrow canyon by a storm freshet; the walls cannot be climbed. Between Devil Track Lake and the lower falls excellent brown trout angling is available, and in the two main tributaries — Little Devil Track and Elbow Creek — there is also good fishing. Brook trout are present throughout the watershed, and the best populations are in the upper headwaters of Swamp River, the tributaries, and the reaches above the lower gorge. The Devil Track system drains seventy-five square miles, flowing a main stem length of eighteen miles. Its water level is one of the most stable among North Shore streams. No campgrounds are located on the river itself, although good access is provided by a national forest campground located on Devil Track Lake and by the Gunflint Trail, which crosses the Little Devil Track and the main river at the mouth of Elbow Creek. Devil Track Falls State Park is under development, probably as a remote backpacking area where the unique lower gorge with its waterfalls and sheer walls will be protected.

Two of the smaller North Shore streams are located just past the Devil Track. Although small, Kimball and Kadunce creeks are important for their scenic value and fishery resources. Each creek drains fifteen square miles and flows about seven miles to empty directly into Lake Superior. Both the Kimball and Kadunce provide high-quality brook trout fishing in the wilder reaches of the upper courses, which are replete with quiet beaver ponds and rushing riffles. Each also has a significant rainbow fishery in the lower reaches, below falls impassable to both angler and fish. The Kimball has a stretch of about a mile and one-half, and the Kadunce of about one-half mile, available to spring-run rainbows. Each flows through a steep-walled gorge in the lower reach; the gorge of the Kadunce is more spectacular, and its sheer red rhyolite cliffs are very similar to those of the Devil Track canyon. The Kodonce River (Kadunce Creek) State Wayside is located at the mouth, providing picnicking facilities, stream fishing access, and hiking trails.

The Brule River is the third largest of the North Shore streams (the St. Louis and Pigeon are larger), draining a total of 282 square miles and flowing about forty miles in its main stem. (The Brule is also sometimes known as the Arrowhead River, a later name given to it to distinguish it from Wisconsin's Bois Brule River, a noted trout and canoe stream on the south shore of Lake Superior; the recent tendency is to use the older name.) Originating in a maze of lakes, swamps, and a network of tributaries, the Brule has perhaps the most stable discharge among the North Shore streams. Its main tributary, known as the South Brule River, has its ultimate source in Brule Lake on the edge of the Boundary Waters Canoe Area. Brule Lake also serves as the headwater lake of the Temperance to the west, as previously described. Some of the Brule's upper tributaries, notably Greenwood River, Stony Creek, Timber Creek, and Pine Mountain Creek, provide excellent brook trout fishing. The slow sections of the main river and the lakes through which it flows are warm waters and support northern pike and walleyes as the principal game fish. In the lower reach, migrating rainbows ascend from Lake Superior in both spring and fall and provide perhaps the North Shore's best steelhead angling. The lower gorge, carved into red rhyolite, extends one and one-half miles from a series of high falls and includes many cascades and smaller falls, a total drop of about seventy feet. Near the upper brink of the high falls, more than half the river's flow plunges into a great pothole, sometimes termed the Devil's Kettle, and disappears. The water presumably emerges in the pool below the falls, but the exact location of its reentry into the river is not known. The high falls prevent farther upstream migration of lake-run rainbows, but the lower reach provides an extensive angling area. It is a big stream, compared to others along the North Shore, and the angler must adopt a different style of fishing in its heavy rapids and deeper pools. Some canoeing is possible on the Brule in upper reaches, but the river becomes more rugged with falls and rapids downstream and access is uncertain. Beyond is a progressively wilder stretch of rapids and falls leading to the lower gorge (see *Whitewater; Quietwater*, by Bob and Jody Palzer). Judge C. R. Magney State Park, one of the North Shore's largest, is located near the mouth and provides camping, picnicking, and many trails, some of which lead upriver to the high falls. Judge Magney, former mayor of Duluth and Minnesota Supreme Court Justice, was a champion of the North Shore's streams and waterfalls and promoted many of the state parks of the area. This one on the Brule was his favorite and appropriately memorializes his stewardship of these unique resources.

One major stream remains along the North Shore before we reach the Pigeon—Reservation River, a relatively small stream draining twenty square miles and flowing only about six miles from its source in Swamp Lake near the northeastern tip of Cook County. The Reservation River is distinctive among North Shore streams because there is no waterfalls near the Lake Superior mouth. Consequently, lake-run rainbows ascend and spawn in almost the entire length of the stream. It is the only North Shore stream in which native brook trout originally were found far upstream. Brook trout are still found throughout the entire stream, getting along satisfactorily with the juvenile rainbows. Most of the stream flows through the Grand Portage Indian Reservation (hence its name), and fishing the river requires a special license from reservation officials.

The Pigeon River is larger than any of the North Shore streams between the St. Louis and the Canadian border. It drains a total of 610 square miles, of which 235, or less than half, lie in the United States. In several ways it is the most outstanding of the North Shore streams. The isolated lower reach is particularly rugged with cascades and spectacular waterfalls. And for a century it served as the major route of canoe transportation into the beaver country of the North-west; later, largely because of that role, it was designated the United States-Canada boundary for its entire length.

In northern Cook County, North Lake and South Lake lie on the boundary, and between them is a slight rise of land dividing the watersheds of Hudson Bay and Lake Superior. The Pigeon's water-shed begins in South Lake and drains east into Lake Superior, a distance of sixty miles. From South Lake, the drainage is through many other lakes, a lake-and-portage distance of thirty miles. It emerges as a recognizable river from South Fowl Lake to flow some thirty more miles as the Pigeon River. From the continental divide between North and South lakes, it drops some 950 feet, for a mean gradient of sixteen feet per mile. From the rapids at the outlet of South Fowl Lake to Partridge Falls, a little less than ten miles, the river is mostly flat water and easily navigable, either upstream or down. Partridge Falls, a drop of fifty feet, is a forerunner of the torrential reach of cascades and falls in the lower twenty miles, where the Pigeon tumbles in intermittent cascades and waterfalls. Here the river is completely unnavigable, and portages are impossible. The descent terminates in Big Falls (Pigeon Falls), a thundering drop of nearly 100 feet, near the mouth. In this lower reach, the river falls a total of about 650 feet, a mean gradient of thirty-two feet per mile. Big Falls, Middle Falls, and Horn Rapids in the lower reach may be easily viewed from the Canadian side; The Cascades, a stretch of violent rapids and deep gorges a few miles below Partridge Falls, is accessible by hiking in from the Grand Portage Trail. The Pigeon is well regulated in its flow by its many headwater lakes. For the same reason it is a warm-water stream, with good walleye and northern pike fishing. Entering the Pigeon below South Fowl Lake are the major United States tributaries, Big and Little Stump rivers, Portage Brook and Swamp (or Kawashka) River, and the Swamp's main tributary, Irish Creek. Most of these waters are slow and warm, although Portage Brook is cold and supports brook trout.

There is no angling thrill, many say, that can match the pulsating leap of a big rainbow in fast water. It is a scene repeated many times on the North Shore streams each spring and fall, as the big silver, red-sided rainbows ascend the streams from Lake Superior on their spawning migrations. Rainbows spawn in the spring, ascending the rivers on the first flood of warm spring rains to dig their redds in gravel bottoms, lay their eggs, and start a new generation. The rainbow is not native to the Great Lakes but rather to western North America. The term steelhead originated with the Pacific streams and their migrating populations. Some anglers claim the term should not be applied to freshwater populations, but the fish are all rainbow trout. Like other members of the salmon family, the rainbow as a species is quite adaptable—genetically speaking—and the species includes populations adapted to a variety of conditions, including the salt water of the Pacific Ocean as well as Lake Superior's fresh water, a major physiological feat. It was first introduced into Minnesota's North Shore streams (Lester and Poplar) in 1901, although earlier plantings were made in the St. Louis River system in 1885, and the first Lake Superior introductions were made by Ontario in 1883. Today it ranks first among the game fishes sought along the North Shore.

When water levels permit, the rainbow sometimes makes an upstream run in the fall as well as in the spring. The question is often asked, why does this happen since spring is the actual time of spawning? As yet, there is no definitive answer. Perhaps, some say, this behavior is instinctive, inherited from the Pacific strains that ascended long rivers in which the migration had to start in the fall to reach the headwater spawning grounds by spring. At any rate, the fall run is considered by many to consist of fish that are brighter and stronger. Many are caught, and lost, in both fall and spring, and many are the thrills—and lovely trophies creeled—along the North Shore during the steelhead run.

But fish migrating upstream on most North Shore rivers cannot go very far, for the first major waterfalls are barriers to farther upstream travel, and spawning must be done below the barrier. Most streams receiving steelhead runs have less than a mile of river between the mouth and the first barrier.

Just as well. For upstream from the high falls and boiling cascades is the realm of the brook trout, which, without competition from the rainbow, brings delight to many angler-epicures. Herein lies an interesting paradox: although today the headwater reaches produce and nourish the colorful brook trout, this species was native to the North Shore streams only downstream from the barrier waterfalls; the brook trout arrived after the glacial lakes had receded downslope to lower levels. Then man introduced the rainbow to the lower reaches, where steelhead populations developed, and the brook trout to the headwater creeks and brooks, where they have the beaver ponds and small riffles to themselves.

There are other game fishes in the North Shore streams, of course, besides the brook trout and the steelhead. But, like these two, most are exotics—that is, species introduced from a different region and habitat that have become successfully adapted. The brown trout is one, although it is not as common as the brook or rainbow and not as important here as in southern Minnesota streams. The brown, tolerating waters slightly warmer than the brook trout, offers good angling in some North Shore stream reaches that otherwise would have little to offer.

The scourge of the Great Lakes is the sea lamprey, another exotic species from the Atlantic Ocean, a primitive, boneless, jawless fish that parasitizes our highly prized species. It arrived in the Great Lakes via the Welland Canal many years ago. It spawns in the North Shore streams, the larvae live a nonparasitic stream life for several years, and then the metamorphosing adults descend to the big lake where they seek a victim, often a lake trout or a steelhead. By 1950 the sea lamprey (it is not an eel) had nearly wiped out the native lake trout and other lake species, as well as the rainbow, in the lower Great Lakes. Then various control measures were developed by the U.S. Fish and Wildlife Service, first in the form of traps, weirs, and electrical shocking devices. Later, chemical control successfully brought the lamprey to low enough population levels to allow other species to prosper again.

Populations fluctuated, and species changed repeatedly over the next twenty years in a story too long to chronicle in detail here. The alewife (another exotic) was observed in Lake Superior in 1954, and it then proliferated. Several species of Pacific salmon were introduced, first by the state of Michigan—coho salmon in 1965, chinooks in 1967—to utilize the abundant alewife as forage.

Lake Michigan salmon populations prospered on a diet of alewife, and today the coho and chinook salmon in Lake Michigan are sought by hordes of anglers attempting to catch the big (twenty- and thirty-pound) salmon. Minnesota released coho into Lake Superior streams in 1969 and chinooks in the 1970s, but neither species added much to the stream fishery for steelhead; today cohos are no longer stocked, and the chinook will be managed primarily to be caught in the big lake. The steelhead remains the choice migratory species in the North Shore streams.

Two other fish species—both exotics—have now made the scene along the North Shore. One, the smelt—a native of the Atlantic Ocean—runs up all the tributary streams, big and small, in a spawning migration that is often the first augury of spring along the North Shore. The Great Lakes smelt populations originated in a 1912 stocking of an inland lake in Michigan; these escaped to the Great Lakes and reached western Lake Superior in large numbers in the 1960s. A small but delicious fish, smelt run in sometimes unbelievable numbers up small streams to deposit their adhesive eggs in rocky riffles, and it is in these small streams that hungry, winter-weary, but happy fishermen with dip nets harvest smelt by the tubful. Frozen in meal-size packages, such catches may supply a family nearly a year, until the next spring draws the smelt and fishermen together again. The run occurs from mid-April to as late as June, depending on unreliable spring weather.

The other newcomer is yet another species of Pacific salmon, the pink or humpback. This population is more an oddity than a significant addition to our fisheries because once it enters the stream for spawning, the pink salmon's body deteriorates rapidly. Pinks from the Pacific coast, of course, are favored food fish but are caught in the ocean, not in the streams. The pink's life history is unique among salmon in that it follows a strict two-year cycle; the run in Lake Superior occurs only in the fall of odd-numbered years, and the progeny come back as adults two years later to spawn. Like all Pacific salmon, the pinks die after spawning once. The introduction of the pink, unlike the coho and chinook, was not intentional. Young fish, reared for stocking by Canada in some Hudson Bay watershed streams, accidentally escaped into a Lake Superior stream in 1956. These spawned in 1957, and their progeny first showed up in Minnesota as two specimens caught in the Cross and Sucker rivers in 1959. Since then the population has been increasing, and the runs in 1973 and 1975 approached spectacular levels, even to the point of littering some streams with dead and decomposing bodies after spawning.

Smelt dippers await each spring for word from the North Shore: the run is on! The tasty little silvery fish is an introduction to fresh water from the salty ocean. The smelt has prospered in the Great Lakes, making a spawning run up tributary streams each spring. One of the most popular smelting streams is the Lester River, on the edge of Duluth, where crowds gather around campfires to await the nocturnal run.

Perhaps angling methods will be developed that will take pink salmon from Lake Superior before the spawning run and utilize them for sport and food. North Shore fishermen are resourceful enough to do that.

The wild region extending northwest from Lake Superior's North Shore was a vast area rich with timber, water, and wildlife. Before the Europeans' incursion into this country, its riches were largely unexploited, for the native American population was thinly distributed, and natural productivity more than balanced their consumption. When the European came, his immediate concerns were, first, to find a water route to the riches of the Orient—the mythical Northwest Passage—and, second, to exploit the riches of the Northwest itself, taking furs for the markets of Europe. The popularity of the beaver hat in Europe led to a concentrated effort by traders to harvest the beaver that inhabited the myriad watercourses of the Northwest.

There were two major avenues of approach to the beaver country of North America: Hudson Bay, the shortest and easiest, was discovered by Radisson and Groseilliers and was rapidly organized by the English as the Hudson's Bay Company; the St. Lawrence River-Great Lakes route was used by the French. At first, the English were content to maintain their trading posts near the shores of Hudson Bay; they depended on attracting the Indians to the posts to exchange peltries for trade goods. The French were more aggressive; they penetrated to the westernmost reaches of the Great Lakes—the North Shore—and beyond. Unfortunately for the French adventurers, there were difficulties: between Lake Superior and the northwest hinterland lay the steep and broken slopes of the North Shore, virtually impenetrable by any sort of watercraft. There were, however, two possible entrances to the back country. The earlier one used was the Kaministikwia River, emptying into Lake Superior at the present site of Thunder Bay (Fort William and Port Arthur) and, later, the Pigeon River was used. The Kaministikwia route, coursing north and west and back south to the Rainy drainage, was the longer and the more difficult because of the high Kakebeka Falls and the route's many swampy portages; the Pigeon route was shorter and navigable—except for the tumultuous, twenty-mile jumble of cascades and waterfalls in its lower course. Still, there was a way around. Fortunately, the course of geological events had left an indentation in the North Shore—Grand Portage Bay, the east side of which roughly paralleled the river's lower reach. From the bay, an overland route of nine miles by-passed the lower Pigeon and climbed gently up and through a natural pass in the high, rugged hills, from which the Pigeon could be rejoined on quieter waters. And from there, the Northwest lay open to exploration, and its furs to exploitation, by the trader in his bark canoe.

Certainly the native Indians knew and used the trail around the Pigeon cascades long before the Europeans. They probably showed them the route. At any rate there is evidence that by shortly after mid-17th century, the French had penetrated the country northwest of Lake Superior and along the North Shore. In the 1680s early settlements were established at Grand Portage Bay, and French explorers were known to have wintered on Rainy Lake. In 1688, Jacques de Noyon apparently was the first European to view Lake of the Woods. However sketchy these early records may be, it is definitely known that on August 6, 1731, Sieur de la Verendrye landed at Grand Portage Bay with a company of canoemen from Montreal, including three of his sons, a nephew, a priest, traders, and soldiers. Some of the party continued on via the nine-mile portage and the border lakes to Rainy Lake, and the next year La Verendrye followed, thus opening to written history the famous Grand Portage route of the French-Canadian voyageurs. The French, dreaming of empire, went on to build a host of trading posts to the north and west.

However, we shall not dwell here on the story of the voyageurs, a chronicle that belongs more appropriately to the chapter on the Rainy River and the border lakes. It will be sufficient to record that the Pigeon River and the Grand Portage trail served for a century more as the gateway to exploration, fur trapping, and trading in the Northwest and became symbols of the romantic and rigorous era of the voyageurs. It passed from French to English possession and, finally, after the Revolutionary War, to the United States. Today the post at Grand Portage has been reconstructed; the trail is marked, as is the site of Fort Charlotte at the northwestern terminus of the nine-mile portage. All are now incorporated in Grand Portage National Monument.

The Pigeon River was to play one further role in the history of North America and, more specifically, of Minnesota. Following the Revolutionary War, the 1783 Treaty of Paris between Canada and the newly independent United States set the international boundary from Lake of the Woods to Lake Superior along the customary line of "water communications." But this line varied with time, was in places disputed, and lay in remote country. It was still in contention after the War of 1812, when the Treaty of Ghent provided for further study of the boundary. Consequently, in the 1820s two teams of surveyors—one American, one British—were dispatched to the border lakes country to establish the true boundary. Three possible lines emerged: the St. Louis River, farthest south, advocated by the British; the Kaministikwia, farthest north, preferred by the Americans; and, in the middle, the Pigeon River. All three had served as routes of the voyageurs. Long delays ensued, and no firm decisions were made. Then, in 1842, the treaty worked out by Daniel Webster, Secretary of State for the United States, and English Lord Alexander Ashburton finally settled the boundary question with the choice of the Pigeon River. For the United States, Webster foresaw some of the great advantages of the land between the Pigeon and the St. Louis; Lord Ashburton saw little value in the wilderness region of the time. For Minnesota, Webster's efforts ultimately won the fur and timber resources of the Arrowhead region and the rich Mesabi iron range. Because of these efforts, we enjoy today the recreational wilderness of the Boundary Waters Canoe Area, the Superior National Forest, the national monument of the Grand Portage trail, and the waterfalls of the North Shore streams.

Modern voyageurs, with nylon backpacks and aluminum canoes, leave the Grand Portage stockade for the dark hole in the woods that is the entrance to the trail. But the path is the same old trail, its soil compacted through centuries of use by the moccasins of Indians and voyageurs. For nine miles it winds to the northwest, paralleling the Pigeon's lower course, avoiding the impassable twenty miles marked by Big Falls, Middle Falls, Horn Rapids, and The Cascades. The trail ends now in a tiny clearing in a spruce woods on the banks of the Pigeon, a primitive campsite constituting the remains of the once bustling base of Fort Charlotte. Below the campsite, the first small rapids can be heard. But upstream for two miles it is flat water to Partridge Falls, a spectacular series of cascades almost hidden by the lush forest. A portage trail here winds up along the American side. Then the Pigeon is flat water again, and there are no more falls.

Two miles up from Partridge Falls is a grassy meadow where the voyageurs of old made their first camp. More river miles, and then South Fowl Lake, North Fowl, Moose Lake, Lower and Upper Lily, then spectacular Mountain Lake. In succession, Watap, Rove, Rose, and little Rat Lake. Finally, South Lake, the ultimate source of the Pigeon River's waters on the border trail, and at a northwest corner of South Lake the Height of Land Portage. Here the voyageur made his last camp in the Great Lakes drainage. And here he became an *homme du nord* — man of the north — a title of honor among voyageurs.

Ahead of them lay the interior and northwest-flowing waters, the Rainy River drainage and the *pays d'en haut*—the upper country—a vast land of lakes and forests of the northwest wilderness, reaching to the wintering post of Fort Chipewyan at Lake Athabaska and beyond to the Pacific Ocean.

Chapter 4

Rainy River

The Border Trail

Three thousand miles, from the deep-water depot of Montreal on the St. Lawrence River to Fort Chipewyan on the far Northwest's Lake Athabaska—this was the Voyageur's Highway, life-line of the North American fur trade. It was an incredible route apart from its vast distances and forested wilderness. It included some 120 grueling portages, 200 rapids so violent they could not be run by canoe, 50 lakes large enough that wind and waves could suddenly bring grief and tragedy. But it was a magnificent route, too —this trail of the French-Canadian canoemen—with its dark virgin forests, blue lakes, and whitewater cascades.

Encamped on Height of Land Portage between North and South lakes, the voyageur looked ahead eagerly to the segment of trail that lay through the series of lakes and rivers to Fort St. Pierre, his next objective, at the outlet of Rainy Lake. For ahead—in contrast to the Pigeon River segment behind him—the canoes went with the current instead of against it, going down the rapids instead of toiling up through them. Although they would portage some rapids, they would run many, too, sometimes with tragic accident but more often with the thrill of adventure in white water that is still pursued by modern canoeists.

Many of the canoemen starting into North Lake and the northwest-flowing watershed of the Rainy River were retracing the track they had recently followed in the opposite direction. These were northmen, *hommes du nord*, the "winterers" who were experienced on this trail and had spent the winter in the north woods trading with Indians for furs. They had left their wintering posts in the spring, bound for Grand Portage to exchange furs for trade goods.

But for a few, the camp on Height of Land had meant a ceremony in which they became *hommes du nord*; thereafter each could wear a plume in his hat, a mark of the winterer. These few had started the year's journey from the civilization of Montreal, carrying trade goods from New France.

The French-Canadian canoemen most often were recruited from the lands along the north shore of the St. Lawrence River. Many of the people of this region came originally from Normandy, and some of the ancestors of the population were ocean-roaming Vikings — perhaps contributing to the canoeman's love of free-running waters. From Montreal and surrounding villages and countryside the fur companies contracted with young men experienced with canoe travel who desired the adventure of the Northwest. A contract was drawn up for each individual, spelling out wages and all details of working conditions on the trail, whether lake, river, or portage. Then, in the big "Montreal" canoes, each of which held a crew of twelve or fourteen and a cargo of about three tons, or sixty *pièces*, the brigades left about the first of May from Lachine, upstream from Montreal. They carried almost all the trappings of European civilization that would be useful or attractive to the northern Indian tribes — guns, powder, and musket balls; tools of all kinds; kettles, pots, and cutlery; beads and trinkets; kegs of liquor. The Montreal brigades were meant to travel on big waters — large rivers and lakes — not on the smaller streams of the north woods. However, their route did not simply follow the chain of the Great Lakes; that would have been much longer and more dangerous in the country of unfriendly tribes. Instead, they traveled up the Ottawa River (whose mouth in the St. Lawrence is near Montreal), up the Mattawa River, portaged into and canoed through Lake Nipissing, down the French River into Georgian Bay, over the top of Lake Huron via the North Channel and to Sault Ste. Marie and the rapids emitting from Lake Superior. Their route through Lake Superior, 450 miles along the north shore, was a journey made difficult by high winds, massive waves, great water distances, and storm-bound encampments along rugged shores. For the most part, the voyageurs hugged the shore for as much safety as possible. Frequently they encountered the open waters of a bay, and then a decision had to be made whether to make a traverse across the open water and save time (if the weather was favorable) or to creep along the shore around the bay (if it was not). And they were in mortal danger if a sudden squall came up to catch them on open water far from shore. Even the big Montreal canoes could not stand the pounding waves of storm-tossed Lake Superior, and many canoes, with their voyageurs, were lost off the mouths of wide bays or along shores of sheer cliffs.

The landing at Grand Portage Bay marked the end of the easternmost segment of their route—1,000 miles completed—and was the turnaround point for the Montreal canoes. After exchanging trade goods for furs, most voyageurs returned to the St. Lawrence. But here at Grand Portage some decided to continue on to the adventure of the Northwest—by way of the Grand Portage Trail and the Pigeon to Rainy Lake, or beyond—to become winterers of the north.

In June and July the community at Grand Portage was bustling. Here company agents negotiated and bartered; the value of goods and furs was assayed and tallied, and credit was given. The voyageur reveled, sang, and yarned around his campfire, boasting of the loads he had carried on previous trips. The Montreal canoemen used their larger canoes as shelters, temporary homes, while the Northmen lived in tents. The two groups had to be kept separate, for rivalry was keen and fighting frequently broke out.

All goods and furs were packaged into bales or *pièces* of standard weight—ninety pounds. A single voyageur routinely carried two such bales—sometimes more, for which he received bonus pay. Credible records have come down to us of loads up to five *pièces*, or 450 pounds. Boasts were made of eight *pièces*, but these were not always believed. It is clear that the voyageur was no weakling, although because of limited space in the canoe, only men five feet, eight inches tall—and smaller—were contracted for! Not surprisingly hernia was a common affliction, and occasionally the cause of death, for voyageurs along the trail.

The big Montreal canoe was not usually used beyond Grand Portage; rather the North canoe (*canot du nord*), smaller and more easily portaged, was used in the upper country. The North canoe employed a crew of eight to ten and carried a cargo of one and one-half

tons, or about twenty-five *pièces*, half that of the larger Montreal canoe.

Grand Portage was not the only rendezvous for the traders
along the 3,000-mile route. For, from Lake Athabaska, at a more
northern latitude and with both a later spring and an earlier winter,
the north brigades could not leave at spring thaw, canoe to Grand
Portage, and return to Fort Chipewyan before freeze-up. Consequently, Athabaska House was established as an intermediate rendezvous near La Verendrye's old Fort St. Pierre at the outlet of Rainy
Lake. Here the Athabaska men from Fort Chipewyan exchanged
their furs for the trade goods brought by a special group of canoemen from Grand Portage. And then the Athabaska voyageurs returned on the Rainy River to Lake of the Woods, and north from
there to their wintering posts at Lake Athabaska. But primarily that
segment from Grand Portage to Rainy Lake, with its chain of lakes
and forest trails, has come down to us in Minnesota as the Voyageur's Highway, eventually to be incorporated into present-day
Grand Portage National Monument, Boundary Waters Canoe Area,
and Voyageurs National Park.

North American Indians used the canoe trails
and portages of the Northwest, finding over the centuries new tracks
and shorter routes by different lakes. By the time the adventurous
French first discovered the route in the late 1600s, or were shown it
by the Indian, the trails were virtually in their present form. The
Grand Portage route's extant record began in 1731 when La Verendrye's company landed at Grand Portage Bay and passed over the old
trails and string of lakes to build Fort St. Pierre on Rainy Lake. Actually the French had earlier used the Kaministikwia River route, farther north, which joined the Grand Portage-Rainy route at Lac la
Croix. But the Pigeon River route, even with its initial grueling nine-
mile portage to bypass the waterfalls of the lower river, was better
as well as shorter. The French used the route for some thirty years,
competing with the English traders who operated from their Hudson
Bay posts. The Seven Years War, pitting the French and English in
conflict in North America as well as in Europe, concluded with the
1763 Treaty of Paris by which France conceded all its possessions in
New France to Great Britain. Although France was forced from the
historic trail and all its posts in the Northwest, the working force of

the fur trade—the French-Canadian voyageurs—was left virtually intact; the experienced, efficient, and knowledgeable voyageurs, without whom the fur trade could not have continued, were inherited by the British.

At first, many individual traders—English, Scottish, Yankee, Canadian—used the northwest routes and competed with Hudson's Bay Company and among themselves, often bitterly and sometimes violently. But soon they came to terms, at least with each other, and in the late 1770s loosely organized a business association that was destined to become the famed North West Company. This aggressive and adventurous organization plied the fur trade routes into the North American interior for nearly fifty years, leaving its name to history as the embodiment of the voyageur era. Its vast network of posts extended across the continent to the mouths of the Columbia and the Fraser on the Pacific shore. The North West Company ended its use of the Grand Portage route with the assertion of territorial rights by the newly independent United States. In 1803, fearful of duties attached by the Americans at Grand Portage, it retired from the Grand Portage post and established its business on the old Kaministikwia River route, with the Lake Superior depot at Fort William near the Kaministikwia's mouth. The North West Company continued to use the Kaministikwia route until 1821, when the company was incorporated by the Hudson's Bay Company; after that, the easier and cheaper route via Hudson Bay and the Hayes River was followed. John Jacob Astor's American Fur Company used the Grand Portage route and the working force of voyageurs until 1842, when the company failed. After that the fur trading enterprise in the Northwest gave way to other endeavors that were to bring civilization to the Rainy River country—logging, settlement, and agriculture. By 1860 the trade of the entire area, American and Canadian, was served primarily by faster, cheaper land transportation through St. Paul and up the Red River Valley.

But it was the fur trade that opened the northern wilderness to the Europeans. It was not the logger's ax followed by settlement of pioneers as in other parts of the state, nor missionary zeal, nor the thrill of discovery, nor even the search for the Northwest Passage to the Orient—it was the fur trade that provided the economic stimulus for the trader's enterprise, the daring of the voyageur, and the exploration of the Voyageur's Highway.

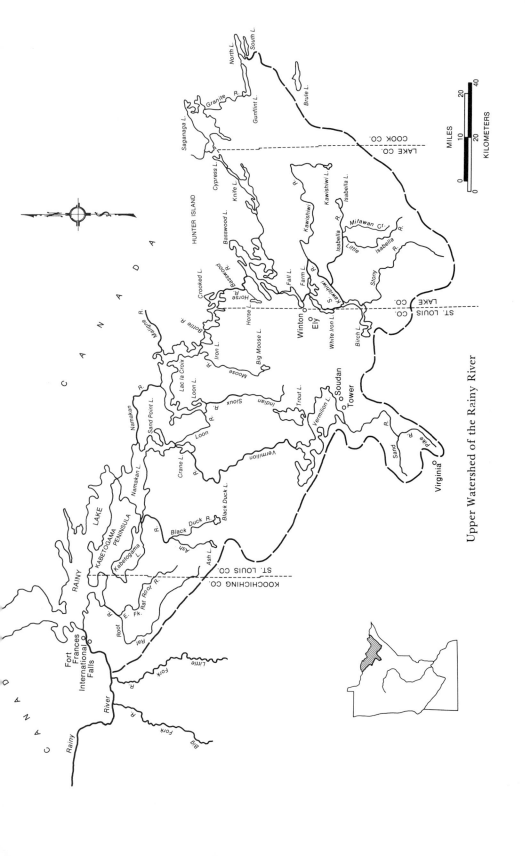

Upper Watershed of the Rainy River

The Rainy River watershed is readily divisible into two distinctly different areas. The upper, or eastern, part lies entirely on the Canadian Shield, a broad plain of eroded ancient rock covering much of central Canada and some of northern United States (mostly Minnesota). Whereas most of this bedrock is extremely hard, some weak spots were ground out by the moving glaciers. These produced many westward-trending excavations that now hold the lakes of the region and many of the streams that connect the lakes. This pattern is evident in the Quetico-Superior, the border lake country of Minnesota and Ontario. But nowhere in this upper watershed is there any stream named the Rainy River, although there are many that would qualify as the headwater of this stream. At the western edge of this region of lakes and forests, the Canadian Shield's waters collect in Rainy Lake and pour over the great waterfalls known first as Koochiching Falls. Here the Rainy River proper begins, a stream large enough that it once accommodated giant log drives and steamboats.

Below the falls is the other distinctive area of the watershed, where the Rainy flows as a broad stream over Glacial Lake Agassiz's flat bed, and the lakes, streams, and forests of the Shield are left behind. Across the old lake bed the Rainy flows fairly straight, with slight gradient, having carved very little valley. Here it picks up tributaries that drain the vast bog and swamplands on the poorly drained, flat glacial clay. There are few lakes in this lower watershed, except along the southern outer edges where higher moraines held back the waters of the ancient lake. Bedrock and moraines underlie the relatively thin veneer of lake clay so that the Rainy and some of its tributaries tumble over rock outcrops and through gravel riffles in some places. But for the most part, the Rainy is broad and unruffled. Finally, it empties into Lake of the Woods, itself a remnant of Glacial Lake Agassiz. At the Canadian outlet of Lake of the Woods, at Kenora, is a dam and hydropower facility, which regulates the level of the lake. Originally there were three natural outlets at the north end of the lake, all in falls; these were dammed, raising the lake level nine feet. From these dams, the waters of the Rainy watershed continue northwest down the Winnipeg River to Lake Winnipeg, and finally, by way of Canada's Nelson River, to Hudson Bay.

North Lake is not the only headwater for the Rainy River watershed, but it is usually considered the main one because of its historic and geographic significance. There are others in the United States and Canada that could just as well be considered the ultimate source of the Rainy. For the Canadian Shield is a vast area that is regionally flat, despite the rugged character of local topography. The two main watersheds, Lake Superior and Hudson Bay, are both like wide, flat saucers with low rims. This characteristic of the region produced a great maze of navigable waterways and permitted relatively easy access by the Indian and the traders' voyageur in birch bark canoes.

Nevertheless, we shall consider that the Rainy River starts its roughly 275-mile course at the voyageurs' camp on Height of Land. Ahead of them lay a route first wandering some 200 miles, through large, irregularly shaped lakes to Fort St. Pierre at the outlet of Rainy Lake; then it followed the Rainy itself for another 80 miles, and finally (for the Minnesota segment) it traversed Lake of the Woods to its northern outlets.

Many large lakes that now comprise the border chain are treasured by canoeists, campers, and fishermen as nearly pristine remnants of the North Woods: Gunflint, Saganaga, Basswood, Crooked, Lac la Croix, where the old Kaministikwia route rejoined the Grand Portage route, Namakan, and finally giant Rainy Lake. Few actual rivers exist along this waterway route, although the lakes are usually connected by rapids and waterfalls that tumble over the rock rims damming up the lakes. (These interconnecting rapids gave the voyageurs much trouble with occasional loss of goods and lives; today the pools below these rapids and falls are subject to investigation by underwater archaeological teams who have turned up many items, such as muskets and balls, kettles, tools, and trinkets lost in canoe accidents. Some of these finds have helped to more precisely identify the routes of the fur trade as well as to establish more accurately the customs and activities of the men and women of that era.)

There are, however, a few short rivers along the route. One is twelve-mile-long Granite River between Gunflint Lake and Saganaga Lake, a river of small interconnected lakes and shallow waters and, with sufficient water, some rough rapids. From Saganaga the main water flow is north into Canada, joining the voyageurs' old Kaministikwia route, then back to Lac la Croix by way of the Maligne River. This section in Canada flows around a large area known as Hunter Island; the voyageurs followed the south side of it, also a water route except for a short portage between Saganaga and Cypress lakes. At

Upper Basswood Falls, the start of Basswood River, was one of many impassable waterfalls and cataracts on the voyageurs' route that required a portage. Today, canoeists start mile-long Horse Portage at this point, circumventing many falls and rough rapids.

the outlet of Basswood Lake, the Basswood River starts its approximately eight-mile course in Upper Basswood Falls; Horse Portage circumvents not only these falls but also a long curving loop of the river with more falls and rapids. Farther downstream are Wheelbarrow Falls, more rapids, then, finally, Lower Basswood Falls where the river empties into Crooked Lake. At the west end of Crooked Lake, Curtain Falls drops over wide ledges. Then the route passes through more rapids and cascades into Iron Lake, but there is really no river. Between Iron Lake and Lac la Croix is the Bottle River, about one mile long. From Lac la Croix the main water route flows into Canada to Namakan Lake via the Namakan River, with many waterfalls and difficult rapids. The voyageurs, therefore, used alternate routes in this reach, sometimes making several portages and passing through other lakes south of the Namakan River, from the western arm of Lac la Croix to Loon Lake. This is the location of the present boundary. Between Loon Lake and Namakan is the Loon River and several more lakes and bays; this eighteen-mile-long river includes falls and cascades that require portages and also long stretches of shallow slow water with bullrushes and water lilies. It is the last river above Rainy Lake. The lower bay of Sand Point Lake, just above Namakan, receives the waters of Crane Lake and the Vermilion River, another

The great Koochiching Falls, on the Rainy River at International Falls, now is harnessed to power the industries on both sides of the international border. The falls had a significant effect on the Rainy River country — on the fur trade, lumbering, river navigation, and industrialization. Smoke from the plants on the United States' side, on the left, clouds an otherwise brilliant summer day.

early voyageur route that came up from Lake Superior via the St. Louis River and Vermilion Lake. Then between Namakan and Rainy lakes is Kettle Falls, with a modern dam to maintain water levels for the hydroelectric plant at International Falls. But there is no more river until the Rainy itself begins below the dam at what used to be Koochiching Falls.

Rainy Lake, Lac de la Pluie to the voyageurs and the last of the large border lakes, is thirty-five miles long from east to west and extends far north into Canada. With an area of over 150,000 acres in both Canada and United States, it is also the largest border lake. The southern shore is actually a vast, sweeping peninsula, extending twenty-five miles west to east with Kabetogama Lake to the south; this is 75,000-acre Kabetogama Peninsula, and most of its area is now incorporated into Voyageurs National Park. At the western outlet of Rainy Lake is Koochiching Falls, originally a cataract with a twenty-four-foot drop; this source of power had great impact on the history and development of the area. The falls is now harnessed by the dam at International Falls-Fort Frances, which serves the paper products industries of those two cities.

The Indian name for the river — Koochiching — referring to the mist and spray from Koochiching Falls, was applied to the entire stream: Rainy River. Below Rainy Lake the Rainy River proper begins, continuing to flow eighty miles to its mouth in Lake of the Woods. Here, the watershed includes part of the bed of Glacial Lake Agassiz; the river's gradient is low, with only a few minor rapids in its entire length. From the mouth of the Rainy, the traders' route was through Lake of the Woods to its northern outlet. Lake of the Woods, remnant of Glacial Lake Agassiz, spreads out over nearly 1,500 square miles (960,000 acres), about one-third of that in Minnesota and the United States. Minnesota's portion consists largely of a section of open, wide water, known as the Big Traverse to the voyageurs. Canada's portion, twice as large, is a maze of some 14,000 islands, with countless peninsulas and twisting waterways; the islands originally were covered with choice stands of pine timber, accounting for the lake's name.

In the 1783 Treaty of Paris, following the American Revolutionary War, the border between the United States and Canada was traced along the old voyageurs' route to the northwest corner of Lake of the Woods, and thence due west to the Mississippi, the source of which was not yet known! When Lake Itasca was eventually discovered, the border, of course, had to be modified. A later boundary commission, established after the War of 1812, decided on the 49th parallel from Lake of the Woods west to the Pacific Ocean. But this parallel did not intersect with the northwest corner of the lake, and, to close the gap, a line was dropped straight south from the corner to the 49th parallel. This resulted in the Northwest Angle, 150 square miles of Minnesota, left separated from the rest of the state by Canadian territory and the open waters of Lake of the Woods. This is the northernmost part of Minnesota and also of the contiguous forty-eight United States.

In the border lake country the major Minnesota tributaries are the Kawishiwi and Vermilion rivers, each draining a large watershed, each having its own characteristics and unique values. The Kawishiwi heads up in Kawishiwi Lake, in northeastern Lake County, and from there its course is westerly to near Ely and then north, flowing almost entirely through lakes or slow, lakelike stretches of river. A dozen miles east of Ely, the Kawishiwi divides into two separate streams, the more southern river known as the South Kawishiwi River. These rejoin later near Ely below White Iron Lake. This phenomenon of stream separation is common on the Canadian Shield, the re-

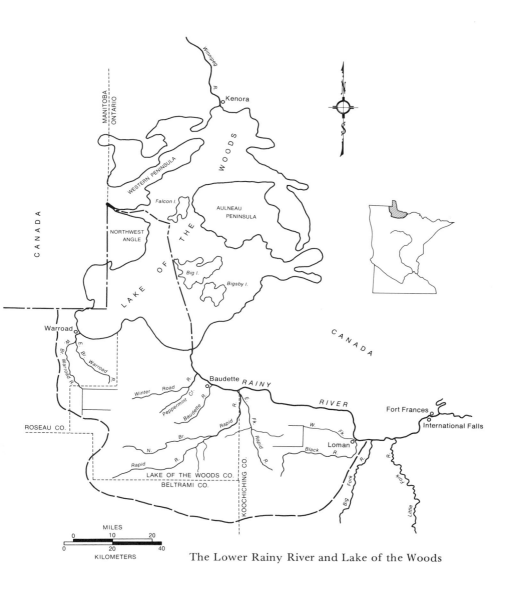

The Lower Rainy River and Lake of the Woods

sult of regionally flat but locally rugged terrain with few well-defined, eroded valleys. Another such major separation produced Canada's Hunter Island, nearly surrounded by navigable water, at least at high levels. Other separations such as the Loon River route to Namakan Lake, were used by the voyageurs at different times. And when the United States-Canadian boundary was in dispute, these separations were the cause of much of the contention, for the usual route of "water communication" had varied from time to time along the different separations. Geologist Dr. Ulysses Sherman Grant, an employee of the Minnesota Geological and Natural History Survey, complained in 1895 that Minnesota and the United States had lost considerable land and valuable resources because the final boundary followed the southernmost waterway separations in some cases. The nub of the problem facing those who tried to accurately interpret the 1783 treaty, as well as the geography of the region, was whether the boundary should follow the major route of water flow or the track the voyageurs used. In other words, should the emphasis, in the treaty phrase "water communication," be on the "water" or the "communication"! Both varied with time. Grant suspected that the survey teams were guided by old voyageurs who accompanied them; consequently it was the canoemen's portages that were usually followed, rather than the water routes.

Waters of the Kawishiwi flow north from White Iron Lake through another series of lakes and rapids between the lakes to empty into the border chain at Basswood Lake. In all, the Kawishiwi's waters flow a total of seventy miles (excluding the South Kawishiwi) in both lake and river, with a mean gradient of less than five feet per mile; the drop of 340 feet occurs mostly in occasional rapids and falls between lakes. The Kawishiwi's average discharge near Ely is about 1,000 cubic feet per second, its total drainage area 1,376 square miles.

The Vermilion River starts at a north bay of Vermilion Lake, dropping over a dam at the lake outlet, and runs north for forty miles to its mouth in Crane Lake, connecting with the border chain south of Namakan Lake. The Vermilion differs from the Kawishiwi in several ways. It has almost no lakes in its course, and although its mean gradient is only a little higher, six feet per mile, there are spectacular falls and rapids that require portages, including The Gorge with its sixty-foot-high vertical walls a mile above the river's mouth in Crane Lake. It also has a substantial slow-moving reach through wild rice beds. Although the Vermilion is not included in the state's canoe guide, a small individual map and guide has been prepared by the Department of Natural Resources, "Vermilion River Canoe Route"; and Sid Rommel, writing in the Minnesota Canoe Association's *Hut!*, presents an excellent description of the Vermilion as one of Minnesota's outstanding canoe streams. The Vermilion's mean discharge below Vermilion Dam is more than 300 cubic feet per second

—it is undoubtedly greater at its mouth; this stream drains a watershed of 1,030 square miles.

Other tributaries in the Shield area include the Horse, Moose, and Indian Sioux rivers between the Kawishiwi and the Vermilion, as well as the Ash and Rat Root rivers emptying farther west into Namakan and Rainy lakes, respectively.

Below International Falls, on the old Agassiz lake bed, the major Minnesota tributaries of the Rainy River are the Little Fork and Big Fork rivers (Chapter 5); then the Black River, at Loman; the Rapid River with its three large branches; the Baudette River, above Baudette; and the Winter Road River between Baudette and the mouth of the Rainy. The Warroad River empties into the southwest corner of Lake of the Woods, at Warroad. These streams are considerably different from those flowing on the Shield; for the greater portion of their courses, all flow slowly across the flat, swampy glacial lake bed, and most are ditched in their bog headwaters. Only the Rapid enters the Rainy with turbulence, tumbling over falls and rapids. The Warroad drains the northern portions of Beltrami Island State Forest, where Lake Agassiz's old beaches now stand out in timbered ridges. The state forest is an area of increasing recreational importance.

In all, the upper Rainy's drainage on the Canadian Shield, from Height of Land Portage on North Lake to lower Rainy Lake, is nearly 200 miles long and drops 438 feet for a mean gradient of 2.2 feet per mile; most of this course is in lakes rather than in recognizable rivers. Above International Falls, the watershed includes a total of 14,499 square miles, 4,489 in Minnesota and 10,010 in Canada. In the lower Lake Agassiz area, the Rainy River flows eight miles from International Falls to its mouth in Lake of the Woods; the total drop is only about ten feet, and the gradient is therefore very low. This lower watershed is composed of 13,805 square miles; the Minnesota portion is 7,285 including that of the Big Fork, Little Fork, and the Minnesota share of Lake of the Woods, whereas Canada's part totals 6,520 square miles.

The discharge of all streams in the Rainy River watershed is remarkably stable, with neither extreme flood nor drought, the result of the excellent retaining capacity of the many lakes of the Canadian Shield and the bogs and swamps of the glacial lake bed in the lower course. The Rainy's mean discharge at International Falls is about

10,000 cubic feet per second and downstream, at its mouth in Lake of the Woods, about 18,000. The alkalinity of all waters in this region is low, ranging from about 10 to 50 p.p.m., reflecting the igneous rock and bog sources of the water. All waters are colored to some degree, ranging from small swamp streams which are extremely dark to some lake outlets which are almost crystal clear.

The short, rugged rivers of the upper Rainy River watershed did not play a large role in the timber harvest of the border lake country. A few sawmills, notably those at Tower, Virginia, and Winton, used logs from some river drives. These mills also produced lumber from timber floated or rafted on lakes, but most logs from the larger areas were hauled out by small logging railroads. The period of intense harvest of the virgin pine stands began in 1893 and lasted until 1930, when the depression and other factors brought operations to a halt.

In the lower watershed the Rainy River played a most important role as a driving stream. It carried pine logs from the Big Fork, Little Fork, Black, and Rapid river pineries in great numbers to mills at Baudette and Spooner (a small sawmill town now merged into Baudette) and many Canadian mills.

The arrival of railroads in 1907 at International Falls, permitting the transport of lumber and other forest products to distant markets, spurred the development of the milling industry in that area. In 1910 the paper mill of the Minnesota and Ontario Power Company (later Minnesota and Ontario Paper Company, or Mando) was built and, the next year, the large sawmill of the International Lumber Company, a branch of Mando. The latter ran for twenty-seven years, operating a total of 186 logging camps. The peak year was 1917, when twenty-seven camps were in operation at one time. This was the last of the big sawmills in Minnesota, and it closed in 1937 when readily available timber was exhausted.

Logging came first to the Rainy River country on the Canadian side, however, as did settlement, agriculture, railroads, and industry. In the late 1870s, the Canadian Pacific Railway reached out from Rat Portage (later Kenora) on the Winnipeg River outlet of Lake of the Woods, and sawmills sprang up to provide lumber for the industries and settlements stimulated by the railroad. These mills used pine from the American side, much of it obtained illegally, for there was little white or red pine north of the border along the Rainy. By 1890 many Canadian mills were in operation on the Rainy and Lake of the Woods, cutting pine plundered from across the border. But around 1900 new laws and strict enforcement, combined with increased settlement and the arrival of American railroads, ended the trespassing, although not until nearly a billion board feet had been removed from the Little Fork, Big Fork, and Rapid river country.

In 1857 Canadian surveyor Simon J. Dawson was sent to explore the feasibility of an improved road to generally follow the old voyageurs' Kaministikwia track between Lake Superior and the Red River settlements. Although the route was laid out and later some work was actually done on it, it was not until 1870 that the Dawson Trail became a reality in this region. In that year Colonel Garnet Wolseley made his historic military expedition from Port Arthur to Fort Garry on the Red River to quell a rebellion of Red River settlers. Wolseley built fortifications and storehouses, dammed streams for improved waterways, cleared obstructions from the portages, and constructed bridges and corduroy roads as he passed. The value of the road was more than evident to the Canadians, and later it was further improved. The portages were supplied with carts, vans, and lodging houses. And then steam tugs appeared on Rainy River and some of the large border lakes, including Rainy and Lake of the Woods.

Thus the steamboat period began on the Rainy River and lasted thirty years. Construction of locks was begun around Koochiching Falls at Fort Frances for the steamboats' passage, although it was never completed. Still, the steamer was the principal form of heavy transportation from 1870 until after the turn of the century, when the railroad replaced it. Steamboats carried settlers west and supplied communities with goods all the way from the upper end of Rainy Lake to Rat Portage. They helped maneuver big log rafts on the river —even on the Rainy's Little Fork and Big Fork tributaries—and they carried lumber from the mills.

The building of the dam at Koochiching Falls, now providing power to the industries of International Falls and Fort Frances, was begun in 1905 and took five years. It was to have great impact on development of the Rainy River country. In 1965 Mando was purchased by the Boise Cascade Corporation, which now operates the mills and paper-products industry at International Falls.

Today's production of the paper industry is impressive; so was the waste that once left the plants to drift downstream in the Rainy. Here wood fibers from the paper pulp process settled out in huge quantities to coat the bottom of the river in great sludge mats sometimes several feet thick. The sludge consumes oxygen from the bottom waters and produces hydrogen sulfide, a powerful poisonous gas, killing walleye eggs and fry and invertebrate organisms that live on the bottom. It was a sad fate for waters that had flowed through the blue lakes of the canoe country and the rapids of the Voyageur's Highway. Today modern techniques of waste retrieval and new, more stringent laws have brought about a slow improvement. Significant research on the wood fiber mats' hydrogen sulfide effects, carried out in the fisheries laboratories of the University of Minnesota, has assisted in finding solutions to alleviate this particular pollution problem.

The walleye is undisputed king of the sport fish of the Rainy River region, in both the upper canoe country and the large lakes and river in the lower area. Pools below the rapids between lakes were favorite places for the voyageurs and the modern canoeist as well to catch walleyes, particularly since the necessary portage at a waterfalls or rapids was also chosen for a night's camp. Archaeological teams searching for voyageur artifacts have also recovered much fishing tackle, from small lures to outboard motors!

Virtually all lakes in the upper region contain sizable walleye populations, and northern pike are also common. Yellow perch are frequently encountered but are often held in disdain by anglers — unfortunately so, because the perch, a close though smaller relative of the walleye, makes a tasty dish. Smallmouth bass, newcomers to many of the northern lakes, but native to Lake of the Woods, are also considered to be undesirable by many anglers and a serious competitor to the walleye. But the smallmouth is also delicious and a much more vigorous fighter on a line than the walleye. Many small, deep lakes in the upper watershed have been reclaimed and restocked with stream trout, both brook trout and rainbows, providing fishing for some large trout. They are not self-sustaining populations, however, since trout do not spawn in lakes, and their populations depend on periodic replenishment from hatchery stock.

Trout streams are few in the upper watershed. The flowing waters interconnecting lakes are lake surface waters and are generally

The dark waters of the Little Isabella River flow north between colonnades of tall jack pines to join the Rainy River drainage and eventually Hudson Bay. In its upper reaches it is one of the north's most popular brook trout streams.

too warm for trout; other flowing waters are small, swamp streams, cold enough for brook trout but brushy and difficult to reach. There are no major trout streams; two of the most popular small ones are the Little Isabella River and nearby Mitawan Creek, which empty into the South Kawishiwi.

Many lakes in the canoe area are deep, rocky, and clear, offering good habitat for lake trout, which were indigenous to many border lakes as well as to Lake Superior. Carved from hard igneous rock by the glaciers, these lakes are cold and well-oxygenated, conditions necessary for lake trout. The Minnesota border lakes constitute the only substantial group of lake trout lakes, exclusive of Alaska, in the United States, although Canada has an equally important group in Quetico Provincial Park across the boundary.

In the Rainy River, the walleye is still the principal sport species. The river and Lake of the Woods also have significant populations of lake sturgeon, which used to be taken in great numbers and huge sizes. They are still fished for but under strict regulation.

Lake of the Woods is Minnesota's most productive walleye fishery. Here, the catch rate of walleyes is twice the average for the rest of the state, even though fishing pressure is high. Other game species, notably yellow perch, northern pike, and saugers, are abundant but fished for infrequently. The muskie angler takes some trophy-winning specimens from little-known haunts in Lake of the Woods.

Commercial fishing is permitted and is highly productive in Rainy Lake, Rainy River, and Lake of the Woods. Again, the walleye is the principal species, in economic importance. At one time the Lake of the Woods commercial fishery accounted for one-fifth of the country's commercial walleye production. The commercial fishery also takes other species, such as tullibees, burbot, and suckers. These are not taken much by sport fishermen and generally are not used for human consumption; but they supply pet food and fur farm markets. The burbot, a freshwater cod, was once processed for the vitamin content of its oil.

Considerable conflict has continued over the years in Lake of the Woods between commercial fishermen and sport anglers competing for the walleye. Although arguments on both sides have valid points, it appears that the walleye population may indeed be over-exploited. Commercial fishermen have been encouraged by state fishery biologists to take nongame species instead, and sport anglers have been urged to reduce their take as well. Species such as the sauger and yellow perch, highly prized elsewhere, could be taken in greater numbers.

Spread over that part of the Rainy River watershed on the Canadian Shield are a thousand sparkling lakes. Many are huge, with great wind-swept distances. Many more are narrow, but long and straight, oriented east-west as the glaciers gouged their jagged troughs. The canoeist plying these waters is apt to conclude that this is not a land mass sprinkled with lakes but rather a vast expanse of water laced by a network of narrow islands. Indeed, the presence of countless small islands and rocky points adds immeasurably to the variety of scene and availability of access and campsites. It is fortunate that so many of the lakes are interconnected by water routes and short streams or by relatively easy portages—a consequence of the flat topography of the Shield.

This is the border lake country, largely roadless, in much the same condition as when the voyageurs paddled through; it is the only extensive wilderness area of its kind in the United States. The special recreational value of the border lake country was recognized two centuries ago. The earliest explorers, as occupied as they were with the deadly serious business of profits and survival, still noted in their diaries the striking beauty of the wild environment in which they found themselves—the sweeping lakes, brooding forests and rocky eminences, the roaring cataracts.

After the fur trade declined, the next major economic activity to have an impact in this region was logging. Particularly south of the border, the white and red pine stands were outstanding. But even while intensive logging was just beginning, there was a recognition of the important recreational potential and an interest in protecting the virgin timberlands for their aesthetic value. General Christopher C. Andrews, Minnesota's first Chief Fire Warden and Forestry Commissioner, along with his supporters, began campaigns for protection programs in the state's remaining virgin areas. In 1902 a half-million acres of forest land in Cook and Lake counties was withdrawn from homesteading and settlement. With a later addition of more than another half-million acres, the Superior National Forest was established by proclamation by President Theodore Roosevelt in 1909. In that same year, Canada set aside the Quetico Forest Reserve north of the border, later to become Quetico Provincial Park. Additions were made to the Superior National Forest in subsequent years until it reached its present size of three million acres; the forest now includes numerous campgrounds and recreational areas, vast areas open to public hunting, a myriad of waterways open to fishing, and a wide variety of resources available for other recreational activities.

After World War I there was a sharp increase in recreational use of the forest, and then concerted efforts began to be made for protection of certain areas, largely because they provided unique opportunities for canoeing. But in the 1920s ambitious proposals of intensive development were raised, including creation of a network of roads to carry America's new and popular vehicle, the automobile. Also proposed was a series of hydropower dams that would have drastically altered the streams and water levels of many of the large lakes in the border country. The public was aroused to one of the nation's first environmental struggles, and the result was the creation in 1926 of a designated primitive area in the national forest. In 1930 Congress passed the Shipstead-Nolan Act, prohibiting alteration of existing water levels and logging along natural shorelines of lakes and streams. And in 1938 the Superior Roadless Primitive Area was established, setting aside about one million acres of the Superior National Forest, with management objectives very similar to those for the present Boundary Waters Canoe Area.

After World War II recreational use increased sharply again, this time including private aircraft and fly-in resorts, which stirred additional concern for the region's wilderness value. Consequently, President Harry S Truman issued an executive order in 1949, effective 1951, prohibiting recreational use of aircraft into the area.

The present name for this region, Boundary Waters Canoe Area, was established in 1958, and in 1964 the BWCA was incorporated as one of the initial units of the National Wilderness Preservation System. Since then conservationists and resource managers have been in conflict many times with private landowners already legally established in the wilderness area. Recent challenges by developers have been met and fought, in Congress and in the courts. Dams, pollution, mining, motorized recreational use, and logging have been the critical subjects of conflict. At one time in the industrial development period of the 1920s, a hydropower scheme proposed dams for Lac la Croix, Basswood, Crooked, and Iron lakes, as well as at other locations; the

Shipstead-Nolan Act, along with similar legislation in Canada, effectively brought a halt to these plans and all future similar proposals in the BWCA.

Commercial logging is the present major point of contention being fought between lumber interests and environmentalists; at issue are several remaining large tracts of virgin timber. Totaling more than a half-million acres, the virgin forest in the BWCA is the largest remaining in the eastern United States. A Federal District Court ruled that logging virgin timber in the BWCA was illegal under the Wilderness Act; then the ruling was reversed by the 8th Circuit Court of Appeals. Central to the present difficulties is language in the original 1964 act that established the National Wilderness Preservation System. The act included the BWCA as an initial unit, but added special language for the BWCA that kept the door open for logging and use of motorized vehicles. These contradictory purposes have been responsible for intense controversy and a management dilemma for the Forest Service, which has principal administrative responsibility. A recent bill in Congress would prohibit logging and mining, phase out the use of motorized vehicles, and change the name to the Boundary Waters Wilderness Area. Many citizens' groups are intensely active in this important, though probably not last, struggle to protect the priceless border lake country.

The BWCA includes over one million acres, in the northern parts of St. Louis, Lake, and Cook counties. Eighteen percent of the area, or 175,000 acres, is water. It was principally created out of the Superior National Forest although it also includes parts or all of several state forests—Lake Jeanette, Burntside, Insula Lake, and Lake Isabella.

Other state forests in the Rainy watershed include Bear Island, near Babbitt; large Kabetogama State Forest, some of which has been incorporated into Voyageurs National Park; Koochiching, Smokey Bear, and Pine Island state forests, most in the Little Fork-Big Fork drainages; Beltrami Island State Forest, which includes the headwaters of the Rapid, Winter Road, and Warroad rivers; and Northwest Angle State Forest, on that isolated, northernmost corner of Minnesota in Lake of the Woods.

Additional state parks include Bear Head Lake and Tower-Soudan in St. Louis County, the former offering wilderness recreation and the latter a historic park including the famed underground

Soudan iron mine. On the shores of Lake of the Woods is Zippel Bay State Park, composed of an outstanding three-mile-long sand beach, wooded beach slopes, and primitive camping areas.

For decades, the idea of a national park in northern Minnesota had periodically been brought out for discussion and debated. In 1891, at the very start of logging operations in the border country, long before the establishment of the BWCA or even the beginnings of the Superior National Forest, the Minnesota State Legislature petitioned the United States government for a national park along the border. Active efforts began again much later, in the 1960s; the Park Service made its initial recommendations in 1964, and in 1975 Voyageurs National Park was officially established.

The park includes about 100,000 acres of land and 60,000 acres of water, including major portions of Rainy, Kabetogama, and Namakan lakes. The main body of the park is Kabetogama Peninsula, a land mass of 75,000 acres, lying between Rainy Lake on the north and Kabetogama Lake to the south. No roads will be built on the peninsula; it will be available only by boat. Indeed, recreational activity in the park will center on boating and canoeing. Historically, the great significance of the park is its relation to the Voyageur's Highway, which the northern border of the park follows. There are few streams or rivers in the park, although the waters of the Vermilion, Ash, and Rat Root rivers empty into the park's big lakes.

Lying at the western end of the Shield segment of the Rainy watershed, complementing the Grand Portage National Monument, Superior National Forest, and the Boundary Waters Canoe Area, Voyageurs National Park assumes a prominent position in preserving a segment of the unique land-and-forest border country. It will help to keep fresh in the nation's consciousness our heritage from the French-Canadian canoemen who plied the lakes and rapids of our northern border.

Chapter 5

Big Fork-Little Fork

Wild Waters North

The Big Fork and Little Fork rivers flow north to our border with Canada in superb wildness. Notable for their free-flowing aspect, they include long pools, waterfalls, and swift rapids—and some great remote stretches.

Settlement and industry came early to the streams because they empty into the Rainy River, part of the canoe trails of early explorers. Fur traders from Lake Superior and New France routinely passed their mouths. And later, because their watersheds had some choice tracts of native white pine and other valued timber, they served as important log-driving rivers, discharging their loads to the Rainy and the lumber mills on Lake of the Woods. Both were navigable by larger craft, including steamboats, in their lowermost reaches. But early industry and commerce long ago left these waters in quiet isolation, flowing through forests recovering the former beauty of regal pine and spired spruce.

They pass through a wide variety of environments—from the morainic hill country of north-central Minnesota with its lakes and marshes rich with waterfowl and wild rice, from the north slopes of the Giants Range, down by way of rapids and falls to the flat bed of Glacial Lake Agassiz covered with wild swamps of white cedar, black spruce and tamarack, arctic plants, and vast peat lands. They form

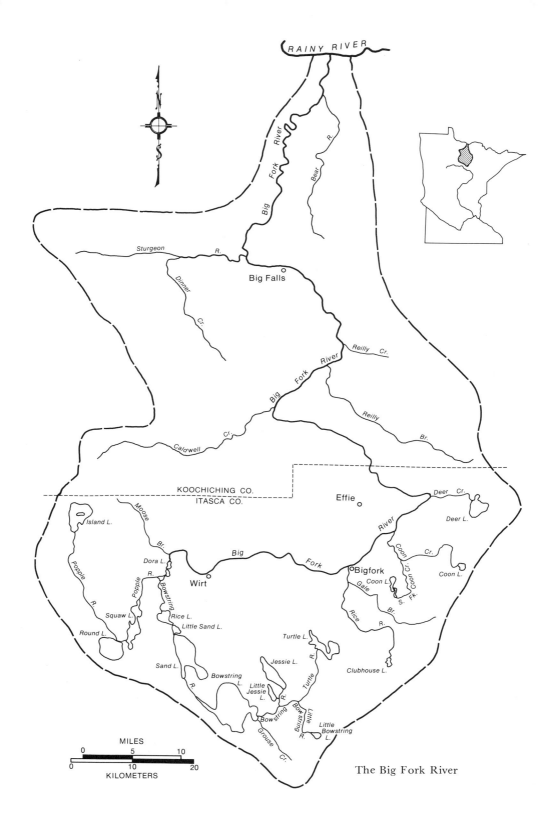

RAINY RIVER

Big Fork River

Bear R.

Sturgeon R.

Dinner Cr.

Big Falls

Reilly Cr.

Big Fork River

Reilly Br.

Caldwell Cr.

KOOCHICHING CO.
ITASCA CO.

Effie

Deer Cr.

Deer L.

Island L.

Moose Br.

Big Fork River

Coon Cr.

Coon Cr.

Popple R.

Dora L.

Bowstring R.

Popple R.

Wirt

Bigfork

Coon L.

Coon L.

Gate Br.

S. Fk. Coon Cr.

Squaw L.

Rice L.

Little Sand L.

Rice R.

Round L.

Turtle L.

Sand L.

Bowstring L.

Jessie L.

Clubhouse L.

Bowstring R.

Little Jessie L.

Turtle R.

Bowstring R.

Little Bowstring R.

Little Bowstring L.

Grouse Cr.

MILES
0   5   10
0   10   20
KILOMETERS

The Big Fork River

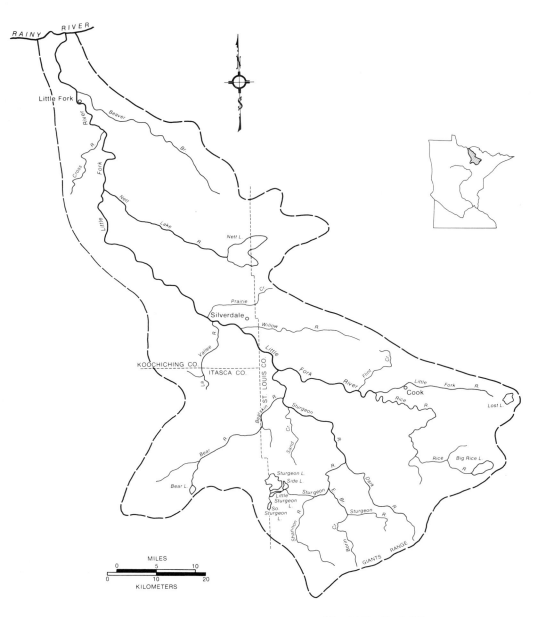

The Little Fork River

part of the north-flowing Hudson Bay drainage, their waters joining those of the Rainy River to flow into Lake of the Woods and eventually the icy salt waters of the north Atlantic.

Today the watersheds of the Big Fork and Little Fork include some of our finest recreational resources, certain to become more appreciated as wilderness values are rediscovered. The watersheds comprise much of several state forests, parts of both the Chippewa and Superior National forests, two superb state parks, important historic and archaeological sites, areas for excellent wild stream angling, immense acreages open to hunting and, on the rivers themselves, several canoeing routes with unsurpassed wilderness qualities.

Lake Agassiz, the vast inland sea that spread over middle North America 10,000 years ago, stretched east at its greatest extent from western plains to the rocky Canadian Shield of the north, across what is now northern Minnesota and the Rainy River country, including the lower watersheds of the present Big Fork and Little Fork rivers. On the bottom of the great lake, glacial clay sediments were deposited as a relatively thin, gray counterpane over earlier glacial drift. Poorly drained, much of the land in the lower watersheds is now also covered with several feet of peat in bogs and muskeg swamps.

Ice Age man hunted prehistoric mammals along the lake's beaches and followed the melting ice north, building ceremonial and burial mounds in the Rainy River country that we recognize and identify today. Only a few thousand years later, when the European explorers first used these northern water routes, the area was peopled by the Sioux, or Dakota—who soon were forced to retreat before the pressure of the warring Chippewa, driving westward with the help of arms obtained from the French. The fur traders followed, exploiting that ubiquitous mammal of northern creeks and ponds, the beaver.

Logging began in the watersheds in the latter half of the 1800s, but most occurred in the early 1900s; islands of glacial drift that had protruded above the surface of Lake Agassiz were now covered with large stands of white pine, the preferred timber of the loggers. Both streams carried great river drives, vast seas of logs that, entering the Rainy, almost choked the larger river. Steamboats that plied the Rainy River also entered the Big Fork and Little Fork. Homesteaders built cabins and attempted to make the peaty land produce, but failed. It was the railroad, here too, that finally introduced civilization, extended trade, accelerated communication, and brought the pioneer period to a close in the early years of the twentieth century.

Today economic activity in the watersheds of the Big Fork and Little Fork is principally logging of second-growth timber, mostly aspen and pine for pulpwood; there is some raising of livestock and some wild ricing. However, by far the greatest resource of the Big Fork-Little Fork country is the immense recreational opportunity afforded by a million acres of wild lands and several hundred miles of wilderness rivers.

The origin of the rivers' names is simple; the streams are the big and little forks of the Rainy River—even though they are not greatly different in size, with respect to discharge or watershed area.

The Chippewa name for the Big Fork meant "bow string," and that name persists in the upper reaches. Bowstring River heads up in Jessie Lake and several of its tributaries in other lakes located in a morainic region of big lakes and wooded hills. These lie in that portion of the Chippewa National Forest just north of the continental divide separating the Mississippi and Hudson Bay drainages. From Jessie Lake the Bowstring winds through a succession of lakes and sloughs, meandering through extensive wild rice beds, a favorite area of many local people for ricing. Although wild rice flourishes in the many lakes and the river as well, the quality of the rice differs, depending on whether it is from river or lake. The rice heads from the river are made up of grains that tend to be short and ripen early; this is called "bird rice." The rice heads from the lake beds contain grains that are long and ripen somewhat later. This rice is preferred, especially for gourmet markets, although the flavors of the two are usually conceded to be identical.

The Bowstring River flows from Jessie through Bowstring Lake, Sand Lake, and Rice Lake to Dora Lake; Dora is really three small lakes closely connected. The Bowstring's major tributary, Popple River, enters at Dora Lake. The Popple also flows through several lakes before joining the Bowstring.

Below Dora Lake, then, the river is the Big Fork; the canoe route described in *A Gathering of Waters* begins at a landing on Dora Lake. The river's course is at first an eastward meandering, roughly paralleling the northern edge of the moraines. In this reach the river begins to drop into the flat terrain of old Lake Agassiz. This upper reach of the Big Fork flows through a diverse area, and many persons may prefer the recreational qualities of this stretch. It includes lakes and slow-moving river, with beds of wild rice, dense stands of sugar maples, brilliantly colored in autumn, on the morainic ridges, and modest rapids as the Big Fork drops to the old lake bed. Sport angling in this reach includes some of Minnesota's best muskie fishing.

East of the town of Effie the Big Fork takes a sharp turn north across the plains of the glacial lake to its confluence with the Rainy. Here the river flows in a deeper channel, worn through the glacial clay, and meanders less. Most of it is flat water, but water currents increase downstream. In this reach are two notable waterfalls, as well as rapids that may challenge the canoeist. North of Effie, in an area of exposed granite below high banks, is Little American Falls, a short but abrupt drop that must be portaged. Below the falls is a convenient campsite, accessible only by canoe, beside a deep pool where a camper may obtain a supper of northern pike or walleye. Stretches with rapids some miles above the falls (Muldoon Rapids) and a few miles below (Powell Rapids) are frequently rough.

At the town of Big Falls the river drops again over granite outcrops in a raging, broken torrent of wild, white water. The only hydroelectric installation in either river is located here, utilizing some of this fall; the mandatory portage is through town. A most pleasant municipal park with campgrounds is located beside some of the wilder rapids.

The Sturgeon River, a major tributary, enters from the west a few miles below Big Falls, where a state forest campground is located. The Sturgeon flows from a region of old "islands" in the glacial lake, mounds and ridges that protruded above water and had valuable stands of white pine; the largest of these, Pine Island, is a central feature of Pine Island State Forest, through which the Sturgeon flows.

From Big Falls down, the river is slower and more meandering, winding through the lower reach of swamp and peat land. It is a long reach of generally flat water interspersed with modest rapids, and it finally empties into the Rainy a few miles east of the village of Loman. Minnesota Highway 11 crosses the river just above its mouth, and good access is available. At the mouth is the Grand Mound historical site, where the largest prehistoric burial mound in the upper Midwest is located.

The Big Fork drains a watershed of 2,063 square miles, about one-third of it in the morainic region of lakes and ridges in northern Itasca County; the lower two-thirds are in the flatter terrain of the

Little American Falls, on the Big Fork River. A "study stream" in the National Wild and Scenic Rivers System, the Big Fork is one of Minnesota's best candidates for inclusion in the national rivers protection program. The Big Fork, in the Rainy River and Hudson Bay drainage, is both wild and scenic, a canoe stream of the highest quality. Here a member of a canoeing and camping party fishes for northern pike in the plunge-pool below the falls.

bed of Glacial Lake Agassiz in Koochiching County. From Jessie Lake to the outlet of Dora Lake, the Bowstring is about thirty miles long, including both lake and river reaches. From Dora Lake down, the Big Fork flows a total of 170 miles to its mouth, dropping 250 feet in elevation for a mean gradient of 1.5 feet per mile; the area of highest gradient is a twenty-mile stretch including Little American Falls and the rapids reaches above. Another major drop is in the cataract at Big Falls. The mean discharge at the mouth of the Big Fork is close to 950 cubic feet per second; the maximum was near 20,000 in 1950. The Big Fork's waters are generally clear, especially in the upper reaches, and alkalinities are moderate, about 75 p.p.m.

Backed against the northern slope of the Giants Range, the Little Fork's tributaries begin in many small, dark, brushy streams. These originate in lakes and swamps on the highlands of the ancient mountain and the morainic hills on the north side of the

Range. The Little Fork itself begins in a flat, swampy region around Lost Lake, south of Lake Vermilion, and flows northwest. From the junction of these dark tributaries and swampy brooks near the village of Cook, the Little Fork begins a wild journey toward its mouth in the Rainy, through some of the most remote river reaches in Minnesota and over many sparkling falls and rapids. About fifteen miles downstream from Cook, the Little Fork plunges in a cascade over Hananen's Falls, a total drop of more than twenty feet. Through another twenty miles the river drops over numerous other falls and rapids as the stream descends to the more level terrain of the bed of Glacial Lake Agassiz. From the bridge of Minnesota Highway 65 near Silverdale (Silverdale Bridge), the river flows for forty miles without a road crossing and with hardly a glimpse of civilization; here it is mostly flat water, though there are some widely interspersed rapids. In this area the stream passes through a portion of the Nett Lake Indian Reservation. Flowing across the lake bed sediments, the Little Fork has cut a channel with steep sides of slumping gray clay; access to the water's edge may be slippery and difficult, and getting out may be impossible except at rocky edges or road crossings. Below the reservation are more wild rapids alternating with long pools until Highway 65 crosses the river for the second time. Downstream toward the village of Little Fork, access is better, but rapids continue virtually into the village. Below Little Fork, however, the river is wide and flat, now tame, the wilderness left behind in the upstream reaches.

The first major tributary of the Little Fork is the Rice River (or South Branch of the Little Fork), entering just downstream from Cook, having originated in Big Rice Lake in moraines north of the Giants Range. The Little Fork's largest tributary, the Sturgeon River, enters in the rapids-and-falls reach a few miles below Hananen's Falls, having originated in many small tributaries of its own on the slopes of the Giants Range. (The Little Fork and Big Fork each have a major tributary river named the Sturgeon.) The Sturgeon itself is a moderately large stream and can be canoed for thirty wild miles. It offers the canoeist a choice of several reaches of varying character and length, including some fine white water and some "embarrasses," log jams caused by vertical clay slumping along the banks. La Vallee (Valley) River enters just down from Silverdale Bridge, a cold, dark-water stream that offers tough fishing but an occasional trophy brown trout. Below the lower Highway 65 bridge crossing, Nett Lake

Hananen's Falls on the Little Fork. Here the stream tumbles its way northward to the Rainy River and the Hudson Bay drainage. The Little Fork includes some of the most remote river reaches in Minnesota.

River enters from the east, coming from the Nett Lake Indian Reservation and its origin, large Nett Lake. The original Chippewa name for the Little Fork meant "river of two choices for canoe routes"—that is, the present Little Fork or Nett Lake River—and its English-sounding word was shortened to "net," or, as it is now, Nett Lake River.

The Little Fork drains a watershed of 1,849 square miles, almost all of it on the bed of Lake Agassiz except for the area of small upper headwaters in the moraines north of the Giants Range. Almost all of the southeastern upper watershed is included in the Superior National Forest in St. Louis County; the northwestern or lower half, roughly, lies in Koochiching County in Koochiching State Forest, and a small portion of the western headwater tributaries of the Sturgeon drains the northeastern corner of Itasca County. From its ultimate source in the Lost Lake swamp, south of Vermilion Lake, the Little Fork flows a total of 150 miles to its mouth in the Rainy River about twelve miles west of International Falls. From Cook, however, the recommended start of the canoe route in *A Gathering of Waters*, the river flows 110 miles to Little Fork, a wild reach of stream. From

Lost Lake to the mouth, the total drop is 300 feet, for an overall mean gradient of only two feet per mile; between Cook and Little Fork, however, the drop is about 200 feet, including Hananen's Falls and many other falls and rapids. The Little Fork's mean discharge is about 1,000 cubic feet per second, although it has reached a maximum of about 25,000. Like other north-flowing streams, the Little Fork sometimes has ice-jam floods in the lower reaches because the upper, or southern, headwaters melt first in the early spring. These floods are not violent, however, and the river has not suffered severe damage. Low flows are sustained well through the summer because of ample storage and slow discharge from the spongy peat and muskeg of the lower watershed area. Compared with the Big Fork, water in the Little Fork is generally darker, a bit muddier, softer, with alkalinities of about 40 to 50 p.p.m., and much lower in its small headwater streams. Despite the names of the two streams, their sizes are virtually the same. However, the Little Fork surpasses the Big Fork in beauty, with its wilder character, longer remote reaches, and abundance of tumbling falls and rapids.

The fisheries of the Big Fork and Little Fork rivers are little known—at least to science. Like most of our northern warm-water streams, however, the principal sport species are the walleye and the northern pike; river campers and canoeists should normally have little difficulty in obtaining at least a mess for supper. The rock bass, primarily a river species, is also common. Local rumor has it that immense sturgeon still roam the long pools of these rivers and that both streams also offer some of the finest river muskie fishing in the state. These monsters of the pike family may strike a flashing canoe paddle!

Many small trout streams, mostly in the Little Fork drainage, contain small populations of naturally reproducing brook trout, some supplemented by hatchery stocking. These include tributaries of the Sturgeon, Rice, Dark, and Bear rivers in the upper Little Fork area near Cook: Dean, Leander, and Sand creeks, Stony Brook, and Venning, Forsman, Johnson, and Spring creeks. In the Big Fork drainage, there are Shine Brook, near Effie, and Trout Creek, near Big Falls.

A large proportion of the two watersheds lies in state and national forests, including vast acreages of public land available for recreational use. The Big Fork's headwater reaches lie in the lake and ridge country of George Washington State Forest, the Big Fork State Forest, and the northern part of the Chippewa National Forest; the lower watershed lies mainly in Pine Island State Forest. The Little Fork's watershed includes part of the Superior National Forest and much of Koochiching State Forest, with smaller areas in Sturgeon River, Kabetogama, and Smokey Bear State forests. Both watersheds contain numerous state and national forest campgrounds, as well as some provided by the Boise Cascade Company, on both rivers and lakes in the headwaters morainic regions. The Lake Agassiz Peatlands Natural Area, athwart the two watersheds in Koochiching State Forest, has been set aside to preserve for scientific study the unique muskeg and peat land now occupying the glacial lake bed. Scenic State Park, a superb park with virgin pine and wild lakes, is located on Coon and Sandwick lakes in Itasca County, headwaters of one of the Big Fork's tributaries, the South Fork of Coon Creek. McCarthy Beach State Park, noted for its white sand beaches, is on Sturgeon and Side lakes on the St. Louis-Itasca county border, headwater lakes of the Sturgeon River in the Little Fork watershed.

The Big Fork and Little Fork rivers are outstanding for canoe travel. Both are mapped in the state's *A Gathering of Waters*; in addition, the Big Fork is the subject of detailed canoe guides available commercially in the town of Bigfork as the "Bigfork River Canoe Trail."

Both streams traverse the north woods in unspoiled beauty, but the Little Fork provides the wilder waters. The streams with their wild riverbanks and clean waters are excellent examples of natural resources that may become less wild as they are discovered and more heavily used. The Big Fork was designated in 1970 as a study stream in the National Wild and Scenic Rivers System. In the meantime, both streams should be given the maximum protection possible; they are two of the better candidates for rapid inclusion in Minnesota's Wild, Scenic, and Recreational Rivers System.

Chapter 6

The Red River Valley

Legacy of Glacial Lake Agassiz

When the last of the glaciers retreated through northwestern Minnesota and North Dakota, the meltwaters began to form a vast freshwater lake. It was destined to become, in known geologic time, the most extensive body of fresh water ever to have existed on the North American continent: Glacial Lake Agassiz, named for Louis Agassiz, Swiss-American geologist.

As the glaciers melted in the region of modern-day Browns Valley on the Minnesota-South Dakota border, water was trapped north of the moraine near present Lake Traverse. Northern outlets were blocked by glacial ice, while the southern margin of ice warmed and melted.

Lake Agassiz, over the period of its existence, covered 200,000 square miles of North America; as the ice melted northward enlarging the lake, lowered lake levels in the south reduced its area there. The greatest extent at any one time probably was about 80,000 square miles—22,000 in the United States, 17,000 in Minnesota. Lake Agassiz covered all of northwestern Minnesota and parts of present North Dakota, Saskatchewan, and much of Manitoba and Ontario as well. It was much larger even than the combined areas of all the present Great Lakes. North to south, it was over 700 miles long; its maximum depth, at the northern ice border, was 700 feet.

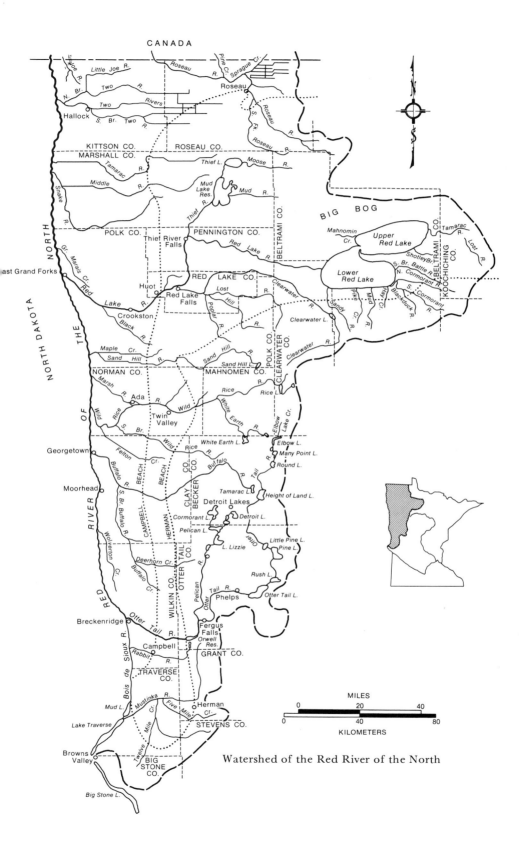

Watershed of the Red River of the North

Lake Agassiz lay for over fifty centuries in the center of the continent following the Pleistocene. Huge prehistoric mammals roamed its cool shores and were hunted by stone-age man. It ceased to exist as a glacial lake less than 6,000 years before the birth of Christ.

The lake surface was not always at one level. Rather, as outlets were worn down to lower and lower levels, or lower outlets in Canada were uncovered by the retreating ice, the lake successively occupied lower planes. At times the ice in the north advanced again temporarily, and the lake returned to previous, higher levels. Each water plane is evidenced by strandlines such as beaches formed by centuries of wave action and ridges of water-washed sand and gravel that can be traced and located today. Early roads and railways often followed these ridges.

More than fifty separate strandlines have been identified. Many of course are not in Minnesota, but are in Canada because the dwindling lake, in its last stages, drained to the north. Five major beaches exist in Minnesota and, of these, two concern us primarily as evidence of the major geologic changes that affected northwestern Minnesota and created the present Red River Valley. The Herman Beach, named after the village of Herman in Grant County, was at the outer, uppermost shore; it was the edge of Lake Agassiz in an early stage. The beach runs from the northeastern end of the Lake Traverse-Mud Lake channel, loops slightly south, runs far north, and then extends east below Red Lakes and into the present Rainy River drainage in St. Louis County. This was Lake Agassiz at its greatest extent in Minnesota, 12,000 years ago. Water poured from its southern outlet through the Lake Traverse and Browns Valley gorge and flowed southeast as the great Glacial River Warren. But the lake remained at the level of the Herman Beach for only 500 years.

The huge torrents eroded the outlet, and lake levels dropped, leaving several lower strandlines. Eventually the outlet was worn down until the lake stood at the level of the Campbell Beach, named after the town of Campbell in Wilkin County. Here the water plane remained much longer, perhaps for a total of 2,000 years, although it was interrupted periodically by retreat and advance of the northern ice. Consequently the Campbell Beach is the most massive and the most visible of the Lake Agassiz beaches in Minnesota. It, too, starts near the northeastern tip of the Lake Traverse channel, runs almost straight north, west of the Red Lakes, then east to the Lake of the Woods area, and eventually into Canada. The Campbell stage was the last at which water drained south as the Glacial River Warren. As eastern and northern outlets were uncovered by melting ice, lake levels fell from the Campbell strandline. Water no longer flowed down the Warren channel; River Warren was "beheaded." This occurred about 9,300 years ago, after the giant lake had existed for about 3,500 years; in another 500 years the lake left Minnesota; and in yet another 1,500 years (7,500 years ago) Lake Agassiz disappeared, and the Red River and Rainy River watersheds now empty into Hudson Bay.

While Lake Agassiz existed, melting glaciers poured collected debris, silt, sand, and gray clay into the lake, and these settled to the bottom. The flat lake bed was formed of sediments hundreds of feet thick. Today the prairie drains gradually north with a slope of about one foot per mile.

Some relatively shallow depressions in the lake bed remain undrained: Upper and Lower Red Lakes, Rainy Lake, Lake of the Woods, and Manitoba's Lakes Winnipegosis, Manitoba, and Winnipeg, many potholes, and some great marshes. Otherwise, the broad flat plains have no natural lakes. Instead, many streams, the subject of our concern in this chapter, now dissect the glacial clay and silts, and slowly discharge runoff waters from the flat plains.

The Red River Valley, unlike some other major watersheds in Minnesota, was not shaped by the streams that drain and erode its surface. Its modern topography is entirely the product of Lake Agassiz. That topography, in turn, has shaped its streams and rivers. It is an error, for example, to consider it the "valley" of the Red River of the North, for it was not the present river that eroded the valley. The Red has no sharply defined valley, only a shallow channel; the river merely collects the drainage of an extinct lake bed and remains a meandering stream that is small relative to its vast watershed.

The ultimate source of the Red River of the North, as we recognize it from its geologic history, is in Lake Traverse and, immediately to the north, Mud Lake. The two form a twenty-four-mile-long channel that was the southern outlet of Lake Agassiz and was eroded by the exiting meltwaters. Its drainage then was southerly. But when Lake Agassiz began to discharge northward, Glacial River Warren ceased to flow. The Little Minnesota River, a tributary coming into

Browns Valley from the west, deposited an alluvial fan in the valley and effectively dammed the southerly drainage of Lake Traverse. Consequently, it now drains north and is the head of the Red River of the North watershed.

Into the lower, or northeast, end of Lake Traverse flows the Mustinka River, emptying just above the U.S. Army Corps of Engineers dam that now controls the Lake Traverse level. Below the dam Mud Lake begins, and at the end of this lake, from another Army Corps dam, flows the beginning of the Bois de Sioux River. This stream, really the headwater of the Red River, flows north some thirty miles to the mouth of the Otter Tail where the city of Breckenridge is located. The Red River of the North is considered to begin here. The Bois de Sioux is hardly a river now; it consists of the barest trickle in low water and flows mainly through straight, deep ditches that serve only to carry overflow from Lake Traverse and Mud Lake in high water. The Otter Tail, usually the larger river and much more consistent in its flow, was understandably thought to be the main upper reach of the Red River system by early explorers. Hydrologically it is; from the standpoint of geologic history, of course, it is merely another tributary.

The Red River of the North commences its long, tortuous path from the junction of the Bois de Sioux and Otter Tail at Breckenridge north through the center of the old Lake Agassiz bed, 400 river miles to the Canadian border, about 200 more to its mouth in Lake Winnipeg.

Why it should be called the "Red" is virtually lost to history. If the color had any significance, it surely must have been tangential to the nature of the water in the river. The Chippewa had a name for it in its lower reaches that suggested a flaming sunset on its flat waters; the French then called it Riviere Rouge, and the English and Americans translated that name.

But the river's waters are anything but red. Almost any other stream in Minnesota is redder than the Red River of the North. Turbid with the gray clay that settled to the bottom of Lake Agassiz, the river reflects the same gray—grayish-brown in low water when the clay is mixed with the brown of humic soils.

For its entire distance in the United States, the Red serves as the border between Minnesota and North Dakota, flowing across flat plains that were originally tall-grass prairie. It flows through no forested areas. It touches only the woodlands of its own riverbank and floodplain and those of its tributaries. Originally these river-bottom woods were the only source of timber to Indian and early settler—cottonwood, elm, willow, green ash, box elder. And today the course of the Red River can usually be detected several miles away across flat fields by a phalanx of distant trees.

Tributaries flow in from both sides, but their watersheds are different—from Minnesota, streams flow from the edge of the glacial lake plain bordered by eastern woodlands; from North Dakota, tributaries flow from what were originally western short-grass prairies of glacial drift plains. The Red is usually muddy, is badly polluted in some stretches and looks it; its steep, barren clay banks are not inviting. It is not utilized much for fishing, canoeing, boating, or other recreational purposes. There are few public parks along its banks.

In its Minnesota-North Dakota course of 400 miles, the river drops 210 feet in elevation, an average gradient of little more than half a foot per river mile; it is thus very flat water. There are no rapids of consequence, although about eighty miles downstream from Georgetown a shallow stretch known as Goose River Rapids (named for a North Dakota tributary) caused problems for steamboats in low water. The alkalinity of the Red is high, usually over 200 p.p.m. and close to 400 in the low water of summer. There is no evidence of bog color, but the river is to some degree always turbid. The average discharge near the Canadian border is about 2,700 cubic feet per second, but it has reached nearly 100,000 in maximum flood. In Minnesota the Red drains 16,400 square miles, more than that in North Dakota, and a little in South Dakota—a total of 38,200 in the United States. The Herman strandline, the outermost limit of Lake Agassiz, encompasses about 17,000 square miles in Minnesota; this area includes part of the Rainy and Lake of the Woods drainages but not all the drainage of the Red. The Campbell line encompasses 7,500 square miles in Minnesota, almost all within the drainage of the present Red River.

Streams tributary to the Red from the Minnesota side share many characteristics. Among those in the upper (southern) part of the watershed are several originating in the pine-hardwood regions of high moraines that bordered Lake Agassiz. Their headwater streams are clear and rocky, often connecting chains of lakes; some flow through wild rice marshes as well as swift riffles.

In the lower sections they become typical turbid plains streams of slow, meandering waters. These streams include the Mustinka, Otter Tail, Buffalo, Wild Rice, and Sand Hill rivers.

In the lower (northern) part of the watershed the headwaters of all major tributaries originate on the Lake Agassiz bed between the Campbell and Herman beaches. Their origins are in aspen parklands, conifer forests, and bogs of north-central Minnesota, rather than in the morainic region. These were timbered uplands, and although they were not prairies originally, they are still part of the old lake bed and regionally flat. They include the big Upper and Lower Red Lakes and the vast Big Bog north and west of the lakes. Streams include Red Lake, Snake, Middle, Tamarac, Two Rivers, and Roseau rivers.

Below the moraines and bogs, rivers have eroded the beach ridges of the glacial lake, most noticeably at the massive Campbell Beach. Here, in the middle of seemingly flat plains, it is surprising to come upon deep gorges and rocky rapids. Some of the outstanding scenic river environments in Minnesota occur where prairie streams have cut into the Campbell Beach. A number of state parks have been established at these sites—Buffalo River State Park (on the Buffalo River, Clay County), Old Crossing Treaty State Wayside (Red Lake River, Red Lake County), and Old Mill State Park (on Middle River, Marshall County), as well as many county and municipal parks and state waysides.

Below the beaches, all streams take on the character of the slow, turbid plains stream. In the lowest reaches many of these have been severely ditched, even some of the larger ones such as the Mustinka, Sand Hill, Middle, and Tamarac, and extensive ditching is proposed by the Corps of Engineers for the lower Roseau. Many smaller tributaries to the Red originate on the lake bed and are plains streams for their entire courses. Most of these have been converted to straight ditches.

Alkalinities of the Red's tributaries are variable, although most are high. Only in the headwaters of the northern tributaries is alkalinity lower, and then only as low as 100 p.p.m. Most tributaries range from 150 to 300—north to south—with an occasional reach as high as 400. Alkalinity is highest at low water levels, because a greater proportion of water source is then in the groundwaters of highly calcareous glacial lake sediments.

Two Red River tributaries stand out as significant rivers in their

Cyr Creek, a tributary of the Red Lake River, erodes a gully through the gravel of the Campbell Beach, which is the most prominent existing strandline of Glacial Lake Agassiz.

own right, with respect to their size and length as well as their importance as recreational, water power, and scenic resources: the Otter Tail and Red Lake rivers.

The Otter Tail rises in the high, rugged region of lakes and woods in Otter Tail and Clearwater counties, a land of white pine, shining birch, and sky-blue waters. There is little hint here of the muddy plains stream the Otter Tail becomes in lower reaches.

Its origin is in Big Rock Lake in southern Clearwater County. Then, in a brief reach just before it enters Elbow Lake as Elbow Lake Creek (or Solid Bottom Creek) on the Clearwater-Becker county line, it is a cold, dark, alder-shaded little trout stream with fat brook trout. In its outlet from Elbow Lake the lake-warmed waters contain trout no longer. From here down to the Lake Agassiz plain it is nevertheless one of Minnesota's most beautiful streams — clear and clean, gravel-bottomed, rich with aquatic invertebrates and fish, repeatedly passing from lake to wild rice marsh and back to stream.

An outstanding canoe stream in the hilly, glaciated region of west-central Minnesota, the Otter Tail River is famous for its clear waters. In its upper reaches, the river flows through many lakes. Where it drops down through glacial lake beaches, it provides hydroelectric power for much of western Minnesota. Then the Otter Tail becomes a slow, turbid prairie river flowing across flat Red River Valley. Here a group of girls from a local camp starts out below Round Lake in Becker County on a trip of several days through the Tamarac National Wildlife Refuge.

The Otter Tail flows through scores of lakes in this upper reach —so many, in fact, that it might well be classed as a waterway of connected lakes and marshes rather than a river. Elbow, Many Point, Round, Height of Land, Pine, Rush, and Otter Tail lakes are some of the larger ones. Of the total course from the mouth of Elbow Lake Creek to Friburg Dam near Fergus Falls, a distance of 125 miles, 50 miles are in lakes and 75 in flowing stream.

Five hydroelectric dams have been developed to harness the potential power of reaches with high gradient and deep gorges where the river falls over the slopes of Lake Agassiz's shores. These now supply electricity for the Otter Tail Power Company. The first is Friburg Dam, forming Red River Lake northeast of Fergus Falls. Downstream, a diversion dam impounds the river for about two miles and virtually dries up a twelve-mile-long loop of river around the east side of Fergus Falls; a canal diverts the impounded water into Hoot Lake, then into Wright Lake, and from there through a generating station and back to the river channel. This so-called Hoot Lake station has the highest head of the five, seventy feet, and produces the greatest amount of electricity. In the city is the small Central Dam, and on the west side, Pisgah Dam. Dayton Hollow Dam, southwest of Fergus Falls, also is a relatively high dam impounding Dayton Lake; the company maintains a recreation site on the lake; it is open to the public and includes a picnic area and boat-launching ramp.

Immediately below Dayton Hollow, the Corps of Engineers' Orwell Dam impounds the large Orwell Reservoir; generating no hydropower, the Orwell Dam was built for flood control and for augmentation during low flow in the Red River. A waterfowl refuge and state wildlife management area have been developed on the reservoir and adjacent lands.

Below the high-gradient reach of dams and reservoirs, the Otter Tail flows out upon the glacial lake bottom and then west to meet the Bois de Sioux at Breckenridge. It becomes a plains stream — slow, meandering and shifting, sand-bottomed, and muddy. Rough fish, particularly carp, are abundant here. In the plains stretch, like many other streams to the north, the Otter Tail has practically no valley — only a deep, steep-sided channel cut into flat glacial lake clay.

At Breckenridge the Otter Tail and Bois de Sioux join to form the official beginning of the Red River of the North. Here it commences its long journey toward Hudson Bay and the waters of northern oceans.

In its upper course the Otter Tail flows through an area containing some of the finest recreational resources of the region — the lake country of northwestern Minnesota. There are many opportunities for fishing walleyes, northerns, black bass, and panfish in the many lakes through which it flows. And the Otter Tail as a canoeing stream is remarkable for its clear water and variety of habitat. A canoe journey is not simply a river trip — the canoeist must also be prepared to paddle through wild rice marshes and large lakes. Many small dams are located at lake outlets to control water levels, and these may require portages. In the upper reaches the river flows through Tamarac National Wildlife Refuge, a large area including thousands of acres, much of it open to public hunting for waterfowl, grouse, deer, and other game. Hubbel Pond Wildlife Management Area, near Tamarac, as well as the Orwell area, provides state public hunting grounds. A short way below Otter Tail Lake is the old Phelps Mill, preserved now in an Otter Tail County park, with picnic area, museum, and old country store. There are few developed public campgrounds along the river, though Little Elbow Lake State Park and Maplewood State Park are in the watershed as are many private resort campgrounds.

Flowing through the lake country with many lakes, ponds, and marshes in its watershed, the Otter Tail may be the best naturally regulated waterway in the state. Water levels and discharge are remarkably constant throughout its course, and flooding is rare.

The major tributary of the Otter Tail is the Pelican River, originating essentially in Detroit Lake, Becker County, and flowing successively through many other lakes in its upper watershed. Its entire course is through the morainic hill and lake region, emptying into the Otter Tail at Fergus Falls. From Detroit Lake it flows through Lake Sallie, Lake Melissa, Pelican Lake, Lake Lizzie, and Prairie Lake, near the town of Pelican Rapids. All are popular fishing lakes, and walleyes, northern pike, and panfish are the usual quarry. Wild rice flourishes in the marshy areas between lakes.

From Pelican Rapids down, the stream flows through no more major lakes. Canoeing and boating are possible in the upper lake reaches but are pursued primarily as a means of travel between lakes. A number of dams are present, maintaining lake levels and requiring portages by the canoeist; the lower river reaches are usually too narrow and shallow for canoeing.

From Detroit Lake the Pelican flows sixty miles to its mouth in the Otter Tail. It has a relatively high gradient, 3.5 feet per mile, although much of its course is through lakes. It drains 518 square miles, and the average discharge at Fergus Falls is about 70 cubic feet per second. There is little fishing in the river except in pools below dams; the species present are essentially the same as those in the contiguous lakes. The Pelican is somewhat unusual because the carp has not thus far been able to establish itself in abundance in the watershed.

The Otter Tail flows 200 miles: 125 through the lake country, 35 in the dam and reservoir stretch through Fergus Falls to Orwell Dam, and 40 miles from this lowermost dam to the river's junction with the Bois de Sioux on the Red River plains. It drops a total of 540 feet, a mean gradient of 2.7 feet per mile; the greatest fall is in the dam and reservoir section. It drains 1,922 square miles, including the Pelican's watershed; its annual mean discharge is nearly 300 cubic feet per second at Breckenridge, and the maximum is only about 2,000.

With its many lakes, clear waters, rich wild rice marshes, and abundant water power, the Otter Tail must be classed as one of Minnesota's choicer flowing water resources.

The Red Lake River flows across the bed of Glacial Lake Agassiz throughout its course. It starts as the outlet of Minnesota's huge Red Lakes—remnants of the glacial lake—and through its full length courses over lake plains and beaches.

Whereas the Red Lakes are nominally its headwaters, other streams tributary to the Upper Red Lake constitute sources farther up in its watershed. These are the brown-stained waters of Tamarac River and Shotley Brook, entering Upper Red Lake from black spruce and tamarack bogs. Southern tributaries of Lower Red Lake and the upper reaches of the Clearwater originate in the morainic region south of the big lakes.

At the outlet of Lower Red Lake the Corps of Engineers has constructed a dam to control water level. Nearby a small recreation area consisting of picnic tables and parking is provided for public use. Lower Red Lake and a small part of the Upper Lake are in the reservation of the Red Lake Band of Chippewa Indians and are closed to fishing by others. The walleye is the most important species in the Indians' commercial fishery in the lakes. On almost any day a few sport anglers in pursuit of walleyes may be found along the bank of the river below the dam. Freshwater drum, or sheepshead, are also common in this stretch of the river, but this species is generally held in disdain by fishermen. The stretch below Red Lakes has been channelized for many miles.

West of Red Lakes the river flows through part of the Big Bog, an immense, flat, poorly drained area of peat lands and wooded islands remaining from Glacial Lake Agassiz. About sixty miles from Red Lakes, at the town of Thief River Falls, the river makes a sharp bend to the south. Here it picks up its first major tributary, Thief River, which comes from the north after supplying water for the state's Thief Lake Wildlife Management Area and, below that, Agassiz National Wildlife Refuge surrounding large Mud Lake Reservoir.

Between Thief River Falls and Red Lake Falls, twenty-five river miles to the south, is the most scenic reach of the river. In the lower fifteen miles of this section, below St. Hilaire, the stream has cut a deep gorge in the gravel and sands of Campbell Beach. Here the river has exposed steep bluffs and gravel deposits, with boulders and rubble in the stream's rapids. To one traveling in an east or west direction here, the river may be a surprise because the channel is an abrupt, deep, and rugged gash in what seems an otherwise flat plain.

At Red Lake Falls, attractive Sportsmen's Park lies in the triangle of land between Red Lake River and its largest tributary, the Clearwater River, at their confluence. Both streams have a high gradient at this point, flowing between high clay bluffs and over rugged boulder bottoms.

Unlike the Red Lake River the Clearwater originates in a morainic region to the south of Red Lakes, actually very near the headwaters of the Mississippi. Where it is small in its headwater reaches, the Clearwater is cold and tumbling and a popular trout stream. After flowing through Clearwater Lake, it quickly drops down to the glacial lake bed and becomes a plains stream like the Red Lake River. Flowing northwest the Clearwater constitutes the border of the Red Lake Indian Reservation for many miles and then swings west toward Red Lake Falls and its mouth in the Red Lake River. The Clearwater is sometimes as large as its receiving stream, the Red Lake River, depending on recent patterns of precipitation. Approximately the lower fifty miles of the Clearwater has been dredged and channelized for flood control; thus this major section of the stream flows almost straight, or in wide smooth curves, in an uninteresting course.

Between Red Lake Falls and Crookston, near the village of Huot, is located Old Crossing Treaty State Wayside on the Red Lake River. This park commemorates the treaty of land cession with the Chippewa in 1863 by which the United States received 5 million acres in the Red River Valley. Camping, picnicking, canoeing, and fishing are available at the park. An Army Corps dam and reservoir are proposed as a flood-control program in this stretch, intended for the protection of Crookston at flood times. The reservoir would cover over 2,000 acres at normal pool level, including woodlands important to wildlife, part of a major canoe route, and the Old Crossing Treaty Park.

Before reaching Crookston the river flows down and out of the Campbell Beach region and enters the low plains. From Crookston west, the river meanders across the plains as a slow stream, turbid

Minnesota stretches from the pine and spruce forests of the North Woods to the plains of midnation. Along the turbulent Basswood River (*above*), our border with Canada, tramped the voyageurs of the fur-trading era; but under a prairie dawn the frozen Redwood River (*below*) winds gently across the southwest plains, accentuating the great diversity of Minnesota's streams and rivers.

The Straight River (*above*) is perhaps Minnesota's most widely recognized trout stream. Its clear waters, flowing over gravel bars and silt beds rich with invertebrate trout foods, yield trophy brown trout to the skilled angler.

The mighty Mississippi River, rising in the wilds of northern Minnesota, serves the civilization of the Twin Cities and provides a commercial highway to the central United States. Approaching downtown Minneapolis (*upper right*) the Mississippi steams in the intense cold of midwinter. Farther downriver Lock and Dam No. 4, near Kellogg, is a component of the Upper Mississippi navigation system (*lower right*).

North Branch Creek, in the Root River watershed, rushes from its headwater cave. Surface waters from agricultural uplands percolate through the crevices of underlying limestone, creating caverns and underground streams. The North Branch is one of the most productive trout streams in the southeast. Several other creeks in the region originate in caves.

Below the hovering bluffs of Gribben Creek valley, also part of the southeast Root River system, an angler reaches with rod and fly for a rising trout. In the background are the crumbling remains of an old mill, a reminder of the early settlement of the driftless area with its productive floodplains and clear streams.

The headwaters of Kadunce Creek begin in a quiet, upland pool (*left*), high on glacial moraines that border the northern Lake Superior watershed; downstream it becomes a cascading torrent flowing through narrow, rock-lined canyons. But in winter (*below*) the mouth of the Kadunce is hidden beneath a bar of gravel, which is covered by deep snow marked only by fox tracks. Here the river flows through the gravel into the lake.

Sheer cliffs of red rhyolite, an ancient lava rock, border the narrow canyon of the Brule River in Judge C. R. Magney State Park on the North Shore. The Brule is one of the best steelhead streams along the Lake Superior shore, offering good angling upstream from its mouth to the high waterfalls in these deep canyons, beyond which the migrating trout cannot ascend.

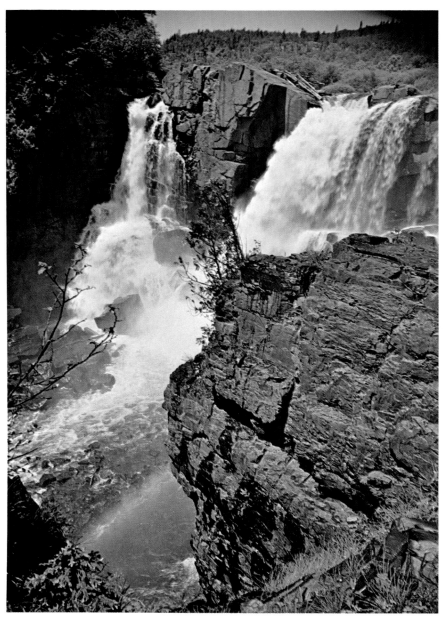

The waters of Big Falls on the Pigeon River thunder down a hundred-foot drop. Rugged cascades and sheer waterfalls in the lower twenty miles of the river forced explorers and fur traders to take the Grand Portage trail that led to quieter waters on the upper Pigeon and the Voyageur's Highway of lakes and streams to the northwest interior.

with the gray clay of Lake Agassiz deposits, and empties into the Red River of the North at East Grand Forks.

The Red Lake River canoe route is described and mapped in the state's new guide, *A Gathering of Waters*. This varied route of 165 miles includes wild bog country, the rapids and pools of the Campbell Beach stretch, and the plains of the Red River Valley. From the outlet dam on Lower Red Lake the river flows 60 miles to Thief River Falls, 25 miles through gorge and rapids from Thief to Red Lake Falls, and 80 miles from Red Lake Falls to the mouth at East Grand Forks. In its total course it drops 345 feet, an average gradient of slightly over two feet per mile; in the steepest section between St. Hilaire and Red Lake Falls, however, the gradient is eight feet per mile. The Red Lake River drains a total of 5,988 square miles; of this the Thief River drains 959 and the Clearwater 1,370; the Red Lakes alone comprise 450 square miles of water surface within the watershed. The mean discharge at Crookston is 1,000 cubic feet per second, the Thief River contributing a little more than 100 at its mouth and the Clearwater nearly 300. Flood flows at Crookston have reached about 30,000 cubic feet per second.

For the record, the hydrology of the other tributaries is as follows:

The Mustinka, 68 miles long, drops 160 feet from its lake sources in Otter Tail County, an average gradient of 2.5 feet per mile. It drains a total of 909 square miles and has a mean annual discharge of over 50 cubic feet per second, emptying into Lake Traverse. Tributaries Twelve Mile and Five Mile creeks drain the southern part of the Mustinka's watershed. The Rabbit River, also originating in morainic lakes very near the source of the Mustinka, drops quickly to the low plain and empties into the Bois de Sioux at the end of a course of twenty-five miles. It drains 282 square miles and has a mean discharge at Campbell of 36 cubic feet per second. Contiguous areas draining directly to the Bois de Sioux from the Minnesota side include an additional 796 square miles.

The Otter Tail joins the Bois de Sioux at Breckenridge, as described above, forming the Red River in Wilkin County.

The Buffalo River, from its origin in Tamarac Lake in Becker County, flows a total of 88 miles and drops 635 feet, a gradient of seven feet per mile. It drains 1,189 square miles, including 522 drained by its main tributary, the South Branch. The Buffalo's mean discharge is about 150 cubic feet per second. Contiguous areas on both sides of its mouth, drained primarily by Wolverton Creek to the south, include another 500 square miles of watershed draining directly into the Red. Some romanticists maintain that early Vikings ventured up the Buffalo in a journey of discovery from Hudson Bay.

The Wild Rice River originates in high Clearwater County lakes near the Mississippi headwaters. It flows for 200 miles and drops nearly 700 feet for a gradient of 3.5 feet per mile, although the gradient in the glacial beach area from Faith to Twin Valley is 5.5. It drains a total of 1,681 square miles. The South Branch and White Earth River, its main tributaries, drain a large portion of the southern part of the watershed including part of the White Earth Indian Reservation. Near the town of Ada two diversions into the upper Marsh River, one natural and one constructed, divert high waters from the Wild Rice during flooding. Mean discharge of the Wild Rice is more than 200 cubic feet per second. A reservoir on the Wild Rice near Twin Valley, Norman County, has been proposed by the Army Corps of Engineers to control flooding in the Ada area. The reservoir itself would flood a gorge where the river has eroded the glacial lake beaches; it would inundate 530 acres in the conservation pool and 1,600 acres in maximum flood, covering up 7 miles of river in the conservation pool and an additional 6.4 miles in the flood pool.

The Marsh River does not originate in the morainic lake region, but rather in the lower beaches. During floods it receives water diverted from the Wild Rice. The Marsh is 46 miles long and drops only 100 feet, a gradient of 2.2 feet per mile. Its watershed is also small, 300 square miles, and its average flow is about 90 cubic feet per second.

The next stream to the north is the Sand Hill River, whose watershed extends far east to the upland lake region where the stream originates in eastern Polk County. It is 100 miles long and drops 480 feet, a gradient of 4.8 feet per mile. The Sand Hill drains 484 square miles and has a mean discharge of 60 cubic feet per second. Areas contiguous to the Wild Rice, Marsh, and Sand Hill rivers draining directly into the Red comprise 131 square miles. Below (north) of the Sand Hill watershed is that of the Red Lake River at East Grand Forks.

North of the Red Lake River is the watershed of the Snake River and its tributary the Middle. The Snake watershed contains 1,224 square miles, of which the Middle River drains 324. The Snake is fifty miles long, but the Middle is sixty-seven miles long to its mouth in the Snake. Both streams start on an upland above the Campbell Beach but within the glacial lake bed. Gradients are low in both streams except in lake beach sections, and discharges are also low; frequently there is no flow. North of the Snake is the Tamarac River, fifty miles long and draining 333 square miles, with low flow and gradient. Contiguous areas, drained by ditches and small intermittent channelized streams, comprise 266 square miles of watershed emptying directly to the Red.

The Two Rivers, consisting of a main stem and the North and South branches, empty into the Red near Hallock in Kittson County, the most northwestern county in the state. The North and South branches each are about sixty miles long, although the South Branch is by far the larger stream, and the middle or main stem is about eighty miles long. Together the three branches drain 1,112 square miles, but the headwaters of all three are completely ditched and interconnected so that the drainage of the separate branches cannot be precisely measured. These headwater ditches are in higher marshes behind lake beach ridges, and gradients are quite high, ten feet per mile; in the lower plains reaches, gradients are much lower. Discharge of the Two Rivers is more than 100 cubic feet per second, but it often falls to nearly zero. Lake Bronson State Park is located on a small impoundment of the South Branch. In the extreme northwest corner of the county, and state, the Joe River drains 120 square miles, flowing into Canada.

East of the Two Rivers watershed is that of the Roseau River, lying mostly in the United States and partly in Canada. The river flows about ninety miles in both Canada and the United States, emptying into the Red about fifteen miles north of the Canadian border. Much of the watershed is timbered, the southern part in Beltrami Island State Forest and the northwestern part in the large Roseau River Wildlife Management Area. Most of the watershed is flat, marshy, and subject to flood; Roseau Lake, a shallow body of water that once covered more than 2,000 acres and moderated flooding, has now being drained, and the predictable result is aggravation of flooding conditions. The watershed includes 1,150 square miles in the United States; another 440 square miles in Canada drain into the U.S. via the Roseau's tributaries. Gradients in the southern tributaries are as high as seventeen feet per mile. The Roseau's mean discharge at the Canadian border is about 300 cubic feet per second. The Army Corps of Engineers has proposed an extensive straightening and channelizing of about 45 miles of the river from Roseau downstream, including those reaches flowing through the wildlife management area.

If we can believe the narrative carved in an "ancient" stone found in 1898 near Kensington, southwestern Douglas County, as well as the authenticity of other certain artifacts found in the Red River Valley watersheds, Europeans first paddled and waded up the valley headwaters in the mid-fourteenth century. Thirty Norwegians and Goths, the runic message reads, on a search for other Norsemen lost from their western settlement on Greenland, entered Hudson Bay and, finding the mouth of the Nelson River, embarked instead on discovery. Up the Nelson, across huge Lake Winnipeg, up the Red. Then up the Buffalo, and they became lost in the maze of lakes in the upper valley highlands. On Cormorant Lake in the Pelican River watershed, ten of the thirty were massacred, apparently by aboriginals. The survivors eventually made their way down the Pomme de Terre, the legend goes, to the Minnesota, thence to the Mississippi. The trail ends there, but a controversy continued around the Kensington rune stone.

Eminent Minnesota historian Theodore C. Blegen, albeit sympathetic to the romance of Scandinavian history in Minnesota, has, along with noted archaeologists, runologists, and other historians, labeled the stone a modern forgery. Its historical importance appears to be merely "a monument to Scandinavian humor on the American frontier." It is pleasant, nevertheless, to imagine a Viking penetration of mid-America, specifically the Red River region, a century and a half before Columbus.

But it was no legend that, 300 years later, the French made a daring sweep of exploration into the Great Lakes country via the St. Lawrence River. Radisson and Groseilliers learned, from western Sioux at their Mille Lacs capital, of the Red River country and the Hudson Bay route to the interior. They sailed back to Europe to raise support and fit out an expedition, but their own country spurned them. The two French adventurers turned to the English, who, already knowing of Hudson Bay, listened carefully to their accounts of water routes and great sources of furs in the northern Red River country. Charles II and the English staked them to two ships and another trip, under the supervision of Prince Rupert and a company of merchants; only one ship, with Groseilliers, returned, but it brought an unprecedented load of peltries. The English then were so impressed that the Prince and his associates were given one of the most comprehensive commercial grants ever to be issued and implemented: the fur-trading rights and the territory that included all lands draining into Hudson Bay, 1.5 million square miles. Thus in 1670 "Prince Rupert's Land," including the Red River Valley, came under the British flag—and venerable Hudson's Bay Company, destined to dominate the British-American Northwest, was formed.

Although the English thus claimed it, they knew little of the Red River Valley. And while they proceeded to exploit the fur resources around the shores of Hudson Bay, the French continued their penetration through and beyond the Great Lakes. It fell to Sieur de la Verendrye and his sons to explore. They found and used the Grand Portage route from Lake Superior to Lake of the Woods and the Winnipeg River; they named Lake Winnipeg, Pembina, Turtle Mountains, and Grand Forks (at the mouth of the Red Lake River); they traveled the plains of western Dakota, saw the Badlands and the Black Hills. Deservedly, the La Verendryes are known as the "Discoverers of the Northwest." And in 1734 the second son, Pierre, formally claimed the Red River Valley for France.

At the conclusion of the bitter Seven Years War in 1763, the British won the lands of New France. The British were quick to rush west from Montreal to take over the fur empire, and in the winter of 1783-84, the Montrealers formed the North West Company. One of this group, Connecticut Yankee Peter Pond, explored widely to the west and into the northwest—and drew maps. It was Pond's map that was used by American and English commissioners to establish the boundary between British Dominions and the United States Territories. The Red River was thereby finally and formally divided.

The American settlement of the Red River Valley frontier is a complex chapter in the growth of Minnesota, and the United States as well. It was not a simple encroachment of explorer-trader-settler from civilization to the frontier. Rather, it was the result of a pincer movement by two strong competing forces: England's imperial Hudson's Bay Company and the young, ambitious United States of America, moving from two different directions.

The Company brought employees and colonists to the Red River Settlement, or Assiniboia, at the confluence of the Red and Assiniboine rivers, in two steps. First, wealthy Scot nobleman Lord Selkirk applied for and received in 1811 a huge grant, part of Prince Rupert's Land, for a colony to receive the displaced and oppressed peasants of large Scot and Irish estates. Second, in 1821, the Hudson's Bay Company merged with the North West Company and then sent displaced servants and their families to the colony. They expected the new community to yield food and a continued source of labor for their far-flung fur empire. Just south of the border, on the west side of the Red, developed Pembina, a rough settlement primarily of the *métis*, half-breeds who were the offspring of earlier French and English explorers and trappers in Indian lands.

Initially, points of contention and competition across the border were fur-trading rights—for buffalo robes and muskrat pelts from the plains, and beaver, mink, and otter from the forests.

The competition developed into a contest for the profits to be gained from the trading routes, and in this the Americans won. Eventually, for the Americans, the greater prize was the opening of the vast agricultural lands in the glacial lake bed, some of the richest soil on earth. Before the 1850s the English trade routes were almost the only feasible routes—ocean steamer to Hudson Bay and the main depot York Factory; then an arduous paddle-and-portage trip up the Hayes River and lake chains, through giant Lake Winnipeg; and finally up the Red to the Red River Settlements at the mouth of the Assiniboine. Earlier the English had enjoyed a similar advantage over the North West Company, who had used the longer St. Lawrence-Great Lakes route.

In the 1850s, however, railroads stretched from the east coast of the United States to the Mississippi, steamboats ascended to St. Paul, and the Red River oxcarts groaned their way to Pembina. Using the English route it took at least a month for the ocean trip and two more for the passage from York Factory to the Settlements; in contrast, the Americans brought provisions from New York to St. Paul in five to seven days, and by oxcart to Pembina in about three weeks. Soon Hudson's Bay Company accepted, though reluctantly, provisioning by the Minnesota route.

The rosy future of American Red River transportation, however, was soon to be dimmed by a succession of catastrophes. First, the Panic of 1857 slowed investment and the creative development that needed capital; then the Civil War burst upon the country, and Minnesota lost many young men needed to push the frontier forward; finally, the Sioux Uprising in the summer of 1862 was a crushing blow, leaving much of western Minnesota desolate with burned way stations and deserted farmsteads. It was not until final retaliations against the Indians were carried out some years later and the end of the Civil War that profitable Red River traffic began again. Thus far, the Red River itself had not played a part in the development of this trade. However, in the interim, some creative minds and ambitious spirits had been at work.

In 1859 Anson Northup ran his small steamer up the Mississippi over the Sauk rapids to the Crow Wing River, then dismantled it and dragged the pieces through winter wilderness west to the Red. In the spring, he steamed north downriver to the Assiniboine Settlements, and a new era was opened in Red River Valley transportation. The Hudson's Bay Company was quick to utilize this new development, and a business arrangement for transporting company goods was made. From 1860 to 1862 the route was: steamboat from Minneapolis to St. Cloud and the Sauk rapids; covered wagon up the Sauk River Valley and across to a base the Hudson's Bay Company acquired at the mouth of the Buffalo, later Georgetown; steamer again down the Red across the international border to the Red River Settlements. Northup refurbished the *Anson Northup* and named it the *Pioneer*, and soon a new steamer, the *International*, was added. The dependence of Hudson's Bay Company and the Red River Settlements upon the United States was increased, and trade flourished despite bad times and the Civil War. And then it came to a complete halt in the bloodbath of August 1862. The desolation on land was compounded by the virtual loss of river transportation because of low water in several successive years; the *International* was stranded for at least one season at Goose Rapids, eighty miles down from Georgetown.

Yet, in 1862, Minnesota's first railroad, the St. Paul and Pacific, completed ten miles of track between St. Paul and St. Anthony. In 1863 Alexander Ramsey concluded a treaty with the Chippewa for a vast land cession in the Valley; Old Crossing Treaty State Historical Park near Huot on the Red Lake River now memorializes the treaty-signing. In the next year, the St. Paul and Pacific was laying track out toward the Red River Valley. And James J. Hill, his young eyes on this primordium of empire, became shipping agent for valley free-traders.

After 1865 and the end of the Civil War, settlement and trade began again in the broad prairies. With their triumph in transportation some Americans, including Alexander Ramsey, focused their ambition on the annexation of all of Rupert's Land. They argued that the Hudson's Bay Company empire, separated from eastern Canada by the rugged country north of Lake Superior, was linked to the destiny of Minnesota, not England, by reason of transportation via the Red River Valley.

Railroads played an ever larger role. In 1866 the St. Paul and Pacific linked St. Paul and St. Cloud, and the steamer segment of the route on the Mississippi was abandoned; then the same line was extended to Breckenridge and the Red River in 1871.

In the early 1870s, James J. Hill further challenged the Hudson's Bay Company. He built the *Selkirk*, steamed it into Fort Garry in 1871, and roused the Company to competitive action. Eventually Hill and the Hudson's Bay Company formed a coalition; the Red River Transportation Company—manager, Norman Kittson—added three more steamers and twenty barges. For most of the rest of the decade, this coalition carried on a brisk and profitable trade; they also brought more immigrants, scores to northwest Minnesota and—at last, by the American route—thousands to the Red River Settlements and Winnipeg. A rival steamship line developed and introduced the steamers *Manitoba* and *Minnesota*.

Steamers on the Red were unreliable but still maintained an important segment of the Red River route. The efforts of Ramsey and his associates who coveted Rupert's Land came to an unsuccessful close when the Canadian government purchased the Hudson's Bay empire from the company in 1869. A large part of Rupert's Land became Manitoba; the Red River Settlements, Winnipeg.

The history of transportation in new lands often includes the replacement of steamboats by railroads. On the Red River, stern-wheelers of the mid-1870s literally caused their own demise—by carrying rails and ties to Manitoba. It was the *Selkirk* that delivered the coup de grace to its own future, when, in October 1878, it delivered to Winnipeg, from a flatboat it was pushing, a locomotive under full steam. And in December tracks from Winnipeg and the

St. Paul and Pacific were joined at the international boundary. Red River steamboating would soon come to an end.

Development of the Red River Valley turned away from reliance upon the winding, turbid waters and toward the productivity of the rich prairie that one day would be known as the Breadbasket of the World. Wheat, the great bonanza farms, and waves of immigrant settlers were to have their day on the Red River prairies, but the river itself was to play no further important role in development.

Fishing on the many lakes in the eastern valley highlands is among the best in the world, for this part of Minnesota is included in the state's renowned lake and resort region. On the other hand, with few exceptions the streams and rivers contribute little to sport fishing, except below lake-control dams where migrating fish often concentrate in tailwater pools. There are a few trout streams in the highland region, mostly quite small, such as Lost River (Red Lake River drainage) and Elbow Lake Creek (Otter Tail), both in Clearwater County, and the larger upper reaches of the Clearwater River in Clearwater and Beltrami counties. Other small trout streams are Felton Creek (Wild Rice watershed), in Clay County, and Lawndale Creek (Buffalo watershed), in Wilkin County, where they cut through Campbell Beach in relatively steep ravines.

In lower reaches of most Red River Valley tributaries, the sport fishes utilized are almost entirely walleye, northern pike, and channel catfish. In some streams glacial lake beach reaches provide the best fishing, that is, where higher gradients have permitted the development of productive riffles interspersed with good pools; the stretch of the Buffalo in Buffalo River State Park and the Wild Rice near Twin Valley are examples. The Red Lake River is an excellent walleye stream for much of its length from Red Lakes to Crookston; the stretch immediately below Red Lakes is not easily reached and has been heavily channelized, but between Thief River Falls and Red Lake Falls the stream is a splendid wild river with good fishing opportunities. Catfish are important in the middle reaches of several streams such as the Red Lake River between Red Lake Falls and Crookston. The Roseau is unique in Minnesota because it has an unusually large northern pike population. The pools in the Roseau River Wildlife Management Area are used for spawning by many northern pike, and up to 100,000 fingerlings and larger pike are removed from these pools each year for stocking elsewhere in the state. The Roseau in the vicinity of the wildlife management area is heavily utilized by fishermen; about as many anglers as hunters use this area each year.

Rough fish populations are usually larger than those of sport species, however, in almost all streams; redhorses, suckers, and drum are the most abundant species. Although carp are common in the watershed, this is not the predominant species (which it frequently is in other Minnesota streams). In the upland sections of the major streams, such as the Otter Tail, Red Lake River, and Wild Rice, carp are rarely present; they are sometimes abundant in the lower plains stretches, including those of the Red.

Wildlife populations in Minnesota's Red River Valley were once immense. Outstanding were waterfowl in the prairie potholes and beach ridge marshes, and prairie chicken in grasslands. The extent of both of these habitats is now severely reduced from original conditions. Drainage, cultivation, and the high agricultural yields of rich Red River Valley soils have led to exploitation of almost every corner of tillable or reclaimable land. However, many small areas have been acquired in state and federal wetland protection programs; these include the waterfowl production areas of the U.S. Fish and Wildlife Service and Minnesota's wildlife management areas. There are also the larger Roseau River Wildlife Management Area, Thief Lake Wildlife Management Area on the Thief and Moose rivers, Twin Lakes Wildlife Management Area on the upper Two Rivers, Hubbel Pond and Orwell Wildlife Management Areas on the Otter Tail (all state-administered), and Agassiz National Wildlife Refuge on the Thief River, and Tamarac National Wildlife Refuge on the Otter Tail. A large part of each of these is open to public hunting.

Already beset by serious pollution problems, the Red River of the North may have additional, more serious ones in store for it—from the huge Garrison Diversion project under construction in North Dakota by the U.S. Bureau of Reclamation. The project's objective is to divert water for irrigation from the upper Missouri River through hundreds of thousands of acres of North Dakota farmland; the water then will be returned to the Red, carrying with it chemicals and salts leached from cultivated fields as well as pesticides, fertilizers, and other wastes. The number of acres to be benefited by irrigation (250,000) is only slightly more than the number to be destroyed by construction of the project (230,000). Minnesota has objected that the project violates state pollution control standards, as has Canada. The pollution of Canadian waters would violate international treaty. Yet ditching by the Bureau of Reclamation continues, in a storm of protest and controversy. In addition to polluting the Red, the project will damage a number of national wildlife refuges, destroy innumerable acres of wetland where losses are estimated at 350,000 waterfowl annually, extend the distribution of rough fish species into rivers and lake systems in which they do not now exist, and degrade several of North Dakota's canoe streams; the project has destroyed many small farms already with its canal-digging. The irrigated soils, already high in soluble salts, may be quickly destroyed by additional concentrations, with the evaporation of irrigation waters. And the transfer of great quantities of water from the Mississippi-Missouri watershed to the Hudson Bay drainages could have unpredictable and calamitous effects on both watersheds.

Several Minnesota congressmen, acutely aware of damage to the Red River of the North, as well as to other resources, have opposed the project and urged the delay of funding and construction until further review of the project can be carried out. In response, President Carter withdrew the Garrison Diversion project, among many other questionable projects, from his proposed 1977-78 budget so that it could be subjected to critical review. The project is undoubtedly one of the nation's outstanding examples of unprofitable water schemes causing great losses of our nation's natural resources.

The bane of the Red River Valley is flooding, a problem that may be aggravated by the addition of waters from the Garrison Diversion. The reasons are two: first, the river flows north, backing up when the upstream sections are running full with springtime snowmelt and the downstream reaches are still locked in winter's ice; second, the main stream channel is so small, and the valley is so flat, that when water overflows the channel, it spreads widely. It has been said that the Red is the only river that runs amok while standing still. Man's activities, particularly in ditching the headwaters, have aggravated the flooding problem. Almost a century of draining upland stream headwaters and prairie marshes, which previously held back excess water, and the later channelizing of the lower main tribu-

Warning signs seem superfluous as Minnesota Highway 220, near Oslo, disappears beneath the spreading waters of the flooding Red River of the North, and a row of utility poles disappears into the mist of continuing rain. The flat valley is covered almost annually.

The flat glacial lake bed of the Red River Valley is the most intensively ditched and drained area in the world. Here what was once a small, meandering prairie stream is now a roadside ditch, devoid of pools for fish and of streamside wildlife cover. It now carries water only during spring runoff and after heavy rains.

taries have caused the spring meltwater to hurry downstream, swelling the tide even higher. No area on earth has been so intensively drained for agriculture as the Red River Valley.

And now the cry is heard for high dams on the tributaries to hold back waters sluicing down from upstream ditches. Dams are now proposed for the Wild Rice and Red Lake rivers. Unfortunately the only high dam sites are where these streams have cut gorges into the beach ridges, the most scenic river reaches.

As long as rain falls and snow melts, there will be floods on the Red River of the North. There is essentially no floodplain on the Red —except the vast, flat, old lake bed itself. And when the spring water spreads, it is not merely the Red River in flood; rather, it is Glacial Lake Agassiz, come back to haunt the flat plains.

Chapter 7

The St. Croix

Wild River to a Nation

The National Wild and Scenic Rivers Act, a landmark of American natural resource legislation, became law of the land in 1968, establishing the National Wild and Scenic Rivers System. Its purpose is to implement a declared policy of the United States to preserve in free-flowing condition those streams having "outstandingly remarkable scenic, recreational, geologic, fish and wildlife, historic, cultural, or other similar values," for the benefit of both present and future generations.

Initially about 675 streams or specified reaches were considered for inclusion. The battle for passage was long and intense; at the end only eight rather noncontroversial rivers remained in the bill, designated as "instant" components of the system. The St. Croix River was one of the eight, and the portion designated includes the upper section from Taylors Falls upstream including its major tributary in Wisconsin, the Namekagon.

The drafters of the final form of the act were farsighted. In addition to the eight instant components, twenty-seven additional rivers were designated as "study" streams, the "5(a)" classification, for potential addition after determination of their eligibility and approval by Congress. These twenty-seven received protection similar to the instant eight for a minimum of five years. Reports of these studies,

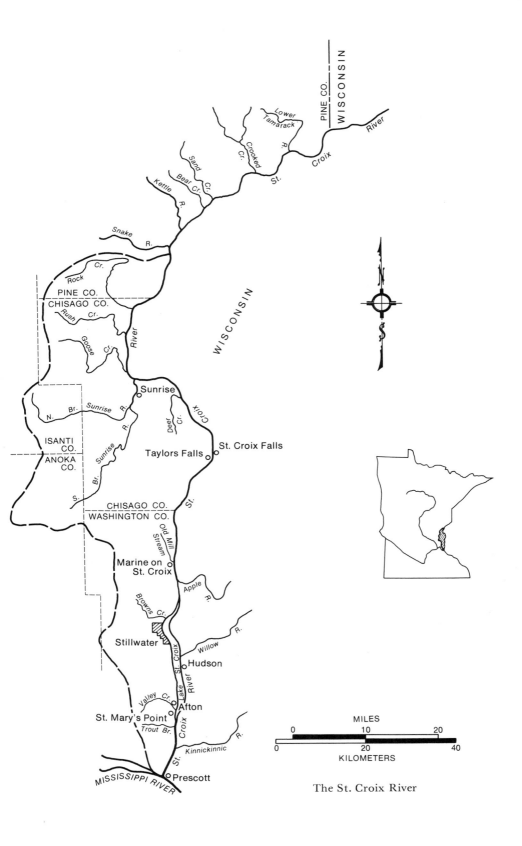

The St. Croix River

to be conducted by the Departments of the Interior and Agriculture, are due by 1978.

The Lower St. Croix, from Taylors Falls to its confluence with the Mississippi, was one of these twenty-seven; in 1972 this unit was added to the national system by Congress, the first federally protected addition to the original system. The addition of the Lower St. Croix received strong local support.

The system was divided into three categories: Wild, Scenic, and Recreational, in decreasing order of "wildness." This classification allows maximum protection to the pristine streams which are vestiges of primitive America, and it also provides at least minimal protection to others that do not qualify as pristine but still have outstanding qualities. The Upper St. Croix is designated Scenic down to the impoundment above St. Croix Falls, Wisconsin, which is classified as Recreational. The uppermost ten miles of the Lower St. Croix is designated Scenic and the lower reach, including Lake St. Croix, Recreational.

The Act also provides a means by which state-designated and administered rivers may be added by order of the Secretary of the Interior—for example, the Allagash in Maine and Ohio's Little Miami and Little Beaver were subsequently added by this means. Furthermore it provides encouragement and assistance to the states to develop their own wild river systems of stream protection; about half the states, including Minnesota, have now done so. The Act directs the Secretaries of the Interior and of Agriculture to make further studies and investigations for the determination of additional rivers to the system, the "5(d)" classification.

Progress has been slow. At this writing, the system contains about twenty streams. Roughly fifty remain for administrative or congressional approval or await funding for the necessary studies.

On September 10-12, 1970, the first National Symposium on Wild, Scenic, and Recreational Waterways was held in St. Paul and was attended by some 250 federal and state officials, scientists, writers, natural resource managers, and representatives from citizens' groups, industry, and government from all parts of the United States and from Canada as well. For three days discussions were held on the progress, problems, and programs of national and state river systems. On September 10 Secretary of the Interior Walter J. Hickel, addressing the symposium, announced the addition of forty-seven rivers in twenty-four states to the 5(d) classification for study and potential inclusion in the national system. Although they do not have the degree of protection of either the instant or study streams, their potential inclusion in the national system must be taken into account if any other water resource project is considered by a federal agency. Minnesota's Big Fork River was included on this list as was Iowa's Wapsipinicon whose headwaters are in Minnesota. In 1975 an amendment to the Wild and Scenic Rivers Act added Minnesota's Kettle River and the upper Mississippi from Anoka to Lake Itasca to the study 5(a) category.

The history of the use and development of the St. Croix River, to its inclusion in the National Wild and Scenic Rivers System, is a paradox. For the St. Croix, a great natural highway for transporting the fantastic timber riches of its valley, was the first site in Minnesota to undergo industrial development, namely, at the great lumbering centers of Stillwater, Hudson, and Marine-on-St. Croix. Although the lumber industry flourished on the river, it was the combination of the Mississippi-Minnesota rivers and St. Anthony Falls which grew into the great industrial and metropolitan development of the Twin Cities of St. Paul and Minneapolis. And when the timber was gone from the St. Croix Valley, when the sawmills were quiet, the last lumber raft had gone downstream, and the remaining few steamboat packets were converted to pleasure excursion craft, the St. Croix was silent once again. It returned to conditions of clean water, the lushness of second-growth timber, and new populations of wildlife. In the late 1920s Northern States Power Company, through its subsidiary the United Power and Land Company, acquired virtually all lands along the river upstream from Taylors Falls for about seventy miles for the purpose of future hydroelectric development. Since that time the company has retained ownership, allowed public recreational use, and leased certain lands for the development of St. Croix State Park, Chengwatana State Forest, and St. Croix State Forest. During the extensive public hearings held in preparation for the wild and scenic rivers legislation, the company declared it had no plans for damming the St. Croix and lent its full support to the proposed act.

Because of these conditions the noncontroversial St. Croix was one of the eight proposed instant streams, and its inclusion in the National Wild and Scenic Rivers System was assured.

In early 1968 before passage of the Wild and Scenic Rivers Act, a cooperative task force composed of representatives of the U.S. Department of the Interior, the states of Minnesota and Wisconsin, and

Northern States Power Company embarked on the development of a plan for management of the St. Croix-Namekagon waterway in the national system. The plan included the donation of 25,000 acres of Northern States Power Company land to federal and state governments.

Presently evolved plans for management of both the Lower and Upper St. Croix, including the Namekagon (the entire system now termed the St. Croix National Scenic Riverway) are the responsibility of the states of Minnesota and Wisconsin and the National Park Service. On the Minnesota side in the upper segment much land is already in public ownership or is expected to be donated by Northern States Power Company. Plans for this section include a maximum-preservation zone near the river's edge in which only "passive" activities—such as hiking, canoeing, fishing, snowshoeing, primitive camping—will be permitted. The major thrust of the plan is toward nonmechanized recreation.

Management plans for the Lower St. Croix will permit a wider range of use, especially for the lowest forty-two miles classed as Recreational. The addition of the Lower St. Croix unit was strongly supported locally, but approval of sufficient federal funds for management of the federally supported segment was difficult to obtain despite Congressional approval. In Minnesota's new Critical Areas Act, Governor Wendell Anderson in 1974 declared the Lower St. Croix the first "critical area" because of its outstanding scenic and natural value, and future development inconsistent with the national system's objectives was prohibited until federal protection was provided.

The St. Croix is perhaps the outstanding recreational river resource of the upper Midwest. Certainly in the border regions of Minnesota and Wisconsin it is a stream resource that will continue to serve present and future generations with a rich variety of outdoor experiences.

Principal recreational activities will probably remain canoeing and boating, fishing, and hunting, at least in some combination with camping, or just a day's outing. The river provides several distinctly different boating experiences, mainly in three areas.

The first of these, actually not in Minnesota at all, is the uppermost section of nineteen river miles from the dam near Gordon, Wisconsin, to the mouth of the Namekagon. Above the Gordon Dam, marshy sections of river and Upper St. Croix Lake extend the uppermost headwaters another twenty miles. But it is the stream below Gordon Dam (that part of the designated waterway included in the National Wild and Scenic Rivers System) that is of primary concern to the river traveler. Here the river is an intimate stream—quiet, shady stretches are interspersed with rocky riffles and modest rapids. Canoeing in this stretch is best in the higher water of spring, for many rapids would be too shallow in the low water of late summer.

The second section of river receives the major tributary, the 100-mile-long Namekagon River, an outstanding canoe stream and excellent brown trout water in its upper reaches. At their confluence the Namekagon is considerably larger than the St. Croix. This section of the St. Croix, seventy-nine miles from the Namekagon downriver to Taylors Falls, is noticeably larger and wider than the upper section. In fact frequent upstream winds may plague the paddler who will find it tough going just to make headway downstream against the wind. However, the sweeping valley with densely wooded hillsides provides superb wild scenery in this section. The oustanding feature for the canoeist is the Kettle River Rapids—not in the Kettle, but above and below the mouth of the Kettle in the St. Croix. The difficulty of these rapids depends on water levels, and at higher levels they are worthy of an expert river-runner's skill. Minnesota's St. Croix State Park is adjacent to these rapids; there are landings above and below the rapids. Below St. Croix State Park the St. Croix is flat water down to the Northern States Power Company's sixty-foot-high hydroelectric dam at Taylors Falls (St. Croix Falls, on the Wisconsin side).

The third section, fifty-two miles from Taylors Falls to the St. Croix's mouth in the Mississippi, begins with some of the most outstanding river scenery in the Midwest—the Dalles of the St. Croix. Here glacial meltwaters from the north cut deep vertical channels through ancient lava flows, leaving towering palisades and large rock masses jutting from the forest edges overhead. This scenic area is encompassed by Interstate Park, a state park of both Minnesota and Wisconsin, which lies on both sides of the river. Many potholes or "kettles," caused by the erosive action of rotating hard stones and sand grains in bedrock crevices are in evidence in the park, and some are as large as sixty feet deep. From Interstate Park downstream the St. Croix is a wide stretch of flat water, with many islands, that finally opens out into Lake St. Croix at Stillwater. This is the Lower St. Croix waterway of the national system; it is used heavily by motorized vessels as well as by sailboats. Marinas, small boat harbors, and boat clubs service large numbers of watercraft, which must share the lower wide waters with commercial barge traffic. The last twenty-five miles of the St. Croix is managed by the Corps of Engineers as a navigable stream, and a nine-foot channel is maintained up to Stillwater.

Recreational facilities along both sides of the St. Croix are many and varied, and there should be no problem in finding just the right level of wilderness (or lack of it) that is desired. Canoe access points are numerous and are clearly indicated in canoeing and recreational guidebooks; canoe rentals and shuttle services are ample, particularly at the state parks. The St. Croix is also included in the state's guide, *A Gathering of Waters*. In addition to the St. Croix and Chengwatana State Forests, public land and access are available at the several state parks, sites established by Northern States Power Company, old logging landings, and historic sites. The St. Croix has an abundance of islands—some 250 in all—under the administrative jurisdiction of the National Park Service, available for exploring, for lunch stops, and some for camping; these islands increase the sense of solitude for the canoeist on the river, especially where the channel itself is broad and straight. St. Croix State Park, Minnesota's largest with 30,920 acres, provides several canoe accesses, canoe rentals, many trails, camping and picnic areas, and access to the lower Sand, Bear, and Crooked creeks, which include some small tributary trout streams. At the downstream side of the park the Kettle River enters the St. Croix, and trails along the Kettle provide some of the most scenic hiking in the park. A short distance downstream from the park the Snake River enters; there is good access here on both sides (sites of the old Pine City Ferry).

Near the old village of Sunrise the Sunrise River, a major tributary, enters the St. Croix. Good access at the mouth of the Sunrise is available at the site of the old Sunrise Ferry and the planned St. Croix Wild River State Park. Headwater branches of the Sunrise originate in and flow through Carlos Avery Wildlife Management Area, a game refuge and public hunting ground of nearly 23,000 acres. The area is managed primarily for waterfowl, but grouse, woodcock, deer,

The Dalles of the St. Croix, eroded through ancient lava flows by glacial melt-waters, provide some of the Midwest's most scenic river environment, with vertical cliffs and towering rock overhangs. This formation, in the rough outline of a Maltese cross, is popularly but incorrectly credited as the source of the river's name. Rather, the St. Croix appears to have been named for an early fur trader, one Sainte-Croix, who plied rivers of the area to trade with the Indians.

squirrel, rabbit, and pheasant are hunted in the wetlands and stream-side woodlots of the upper Sunrise tributaries. Carlos Avery serves enormous numbers of persons, from the Twin Cities area particularly, not only for hunting but also for nonhunting uses of the area's wildlife by school and teacher-training groups, by scouting groups, by students and scientists studying ecology, and by bird watchers and photographers in the scenic impoundments created for waterfowl in the Sunrise River.

Interstate Park near Taylors Falls, marking the lower boundary of the Upper St. Croix National Waterway, also provides good canoe access and canoe rental for the lower segment, excursion boat trips through the Dalles, and camping, picnicking, and hiking areas along the precipitous river banks. Downstream a bit, little William O'Brien State Park offers wooded riverbank recreational activities; it is intensively used, its large campgrounds meeting recreational needs of many people near the Twin Cities. The St. Croix Island Scenic Reserve, administered by the National Park Service, provides island refuges and camping in the river reach just below O'Brien Park. The Boomsite Wayside Park at the head of Lake St. Croix marks the site of intense logging activity in the late 1800s, centered on the Stillwater mills and the great river lake. Lake St. Croix, like many other Minnesota lakes that were created in river valleys cut by glacial meltwaters, was formed when a delta partially dammed the river, and the water was impounded—the Mississippi with its great load of silt and sediment dropped an alluvial bar, or delta, at the St. Croix's mouth. On Lake St. Croix is historic Afton with its many marinas and luxurious motorcraft; scenic Afton State Park, in an area known for its excellent birding opportunities, is being developed. Canoe campsites are plentiful on many sandbars in the Afton area.

Maintaining the diversity of recreational resources on the St. Croix is essential to its proper management. The inclusion of the river in the National Wild and Scenic Rivers System will no doubt attract persons from all over the nation, if not the world, to view and experience the wonders of the sweeping St. Croix Valley. It lies within a day's drive for over 10 million people. It will attract persons seeking different experiences—guiding a plunging canoe through the upper rapids, fishing the quiet waters of the middle section, camping on one of the many islands, roaring over the surface

Sweeping out of the confines of its upper river valley, the St. Croix spreads out into Lake St. Croix, a "river-lake" impounded by the alluvial dam formed at its mouth in the Mississippi. Here, a few miles above Stillwater, the St. Croix Boom Company began operations in 1856. The boom consisted of floating timbers tied end-to-end and extending between the riverbanks. The huge spring drives of logs were stopped for sorting and combining into rafts. In the half-century of its operation, the St. Croix Boom passed 10 billion board-feet of lumber in logs. Rafts were sent downriver to the mills in Stillwater, Winona, and St. Louis. The area is now set aside as the Boomsite Wayside Park, providing unusual riverside hiking and recreational boating and camping.

of the lower segment in a high-powered launch, or just looking at the great wooded valley from some perimeter vantage point.

There are many popular explanations for the origin of the name St. Croix. An early map (1688) locates a Fort St. Croix along the upper river. Another source indicates it was named for the cross on a French voyageur's grave near the river mouth. There are others. Most likely it is named for a French trader, one Sainte-Croix, who dealt with the Indians along the St. Croix and Mississippi. Nicolas Perrot, an early French explorer, first called the river by this name—"Rivière de Sainte-Croix"—in 1689; both Du Luth and Le Sueur support this explanation. Most certainly the popular version, that the name originated from a crosslike rock formation on a cliff in the Dalles, is erroneous—despite the story that tourists now receive at Interstate Park.

The length of the St. Croix, from Gordon Dam in Wisconsin to its mouth in the Mississippi, is 150 miles; for the lower 125 miles it serves as the boundary between Minnesota and Wisconsin. Over the total length it falls 325 feet. The average gradient is a little over two feet per mile; thus it is a relatively flat-water stream, but interspersed rapids in the upper segment and the high gradients in the Kettle River Rapids provide some rough stretches. The total drainage area is 7,650 square miles, 3,500 square miles in Minnesota including the drainages of the Snake and Kettle rivers (Chapter 8) and the Pine County creeks (Chapter 9). The Sunrise River drains an area of about 100 square miles, and other smaller streams drain their own watersheds directly into the river. The mean discharge of the St. Croix at its mouth is about 5,000 cubic feet per second.

The St. Croix's waters are clean and relatively unpolluted. At the confluence with the Mississippi, for example, the difference, as seen in aerial photographs, between the clean St. Croix and the muddy Mississippi is striking indeed. The St. Croix's waters are slightly colored, reflecting the bog sources of northern waters, but without much turbidity or muddiness, especially in the upper reaches. Its alkalinity is relatively low, ranging from only 25 to 50 p.p.m. in its headwaters in Wisconsin to a maximum of about 100 p.p.m. in the downstream segment in low water; it is not likely that overpopulation of algae and other aquatic vegetation will occur in these soft, infertile waters.

As elsewhere in the upper Great Lakes region, striking hydrographic features wrought by the glacial epoch provided early explorers with easy routes of water travel. This was particularly true with the St. Croix. When Glacial Lake Duluth poured meltwaters down its outlet channel, the raging stream carved the valleys of two modern rivers: Wisconsin's Bois Brule, one of the nation's most famous trout streams, and the St. Croix. When the ice disappeared and Lake Duluth's level dropped so that it no longer discharged down the old channel, the middle portion of this channel was left high and (almost) dry—an area that serves as the headwater sources of both the Bois Brule, flowing north to Lake Superior, and the St. Croix, flowing south to the Mississippi. The route, long known to the Indians, connected the upper Great Lakes with the lower Mississippi River, a water road of some historic significance. Sieur du Luth, in 1680, was the first of the French explorers to ascend the Brule from Lake Superior, to make a two-mile portage to the upper St. Croix, and to paddle down through the wild splendors of the St. Croix Valley.

Trade with the Indians for beaver pelts soon stimulated much French activity along the Brule-St. Croix route, and it became one of the major arteries of fur transport between the Mississippi region and the Great Lakes and New France. For nearly a century the fur trade was the biggest commercial industry in North America. Le Sueur, La Verendrye, their voyageurs, and other early French explorers and traders used this route extensively. Later the English gained supremacy in the region's fur trade. Among these were Jonathan Carver in his search for the Northwest Passage and many traders of the North West Company, whose reconstructed wintering post may be visited today along the Snake River. The United States, even after its successful War of 1812, did not immediately penetrate the St. Croix; the British continued in what was technically an illicit trade with the Indians along the river until the establishment of powerful Fort Snelling brought a strong U.S. rule to the region. In 1832, immediately after finding and naming Lake Itasca as the origin of the Mississippi, Henry Rowe Schoolcraft, with a military contingent trailing behind, ascended the St. Croix's broad waters and upper rapids, making the first intensive U.S. exploration of the entire valley as well as of the Brule to Lake Superior.

The explorations, the canoe paddling and military expeditions, the beaver trapping and fur trading left no permanent mark of their passing. While their era was drawing to a close, the primal silence returned to the great valley, and the clear waters and pine-timbered hillsides remained as they were before the first French bark canoe probed the upper rapids. But five years after Schoolcraft's epic explorations an event took place at Fort Snelling that was to have, as a direct and intended consequence, the greatest impact the valley was ever to endure, and one that changed it forever.

In July 1837 a thousand Chippewa assembled on the fort's grounds from all parts of their land to the north. Governor Henry Dodge of Wisconsin Territory was the chief negotiator for the United States. At stake was an area of the richest white pine land on the continent, the so-called St. Croix Delta.

The treaty-making went according to the usual plan introduced by white men of the day: the Indians received a pittance for fabulous riches, and much of what they were to receive was retained to pay off the usual "traders' debts." In the same year the Sioux also became the object of the treaty-makers, and their chiefs were taken to Washington for their turn. The Sioux ceded lands to the south of the Chippewa's.

For Minnesota these treaties opened up the triangle of land between the Mississippi and the St. Croix, from the confluence of these two streams as the point of the triangle, north to a line from the mouth of the Crow Wing in the Mississippi east to the St. Croix. They opened the St. Croix Delta, fabulously rich with virgin white pine, to the ax and saw of the lumberman.

The exploitation of the St. Croix Valley pine was slow to start but increased rapidly. When the treaties of 1837 were ratified the next year, a few lumbermen and settlers rushed upriver to cut the logs and build sawmills. Officially they were squatters, for the United States Government did not begin to sell the Delta lands until a decade later.

This was a minor hindrance, however. Franklin Steele steamed upriver in 1838 to build a sawmill at the rapids just above the Dalles. Although this St. Croix Falls mill did not actually begin operations until 1842, in 1839 a primitive sawmill at Marine started producing the first commercial lumber in the St. Croix Valley and in the region that was to become the state of Minnesota as well. This early development was soon to be far overshadowed by the great milling and rafting industry built on Lake St. Croix in Stillwater, which, "with pine to the back of it, water power at its feet, and two thousand miles of navigable waterway ahead of it," was to become a giant among sawmill towns. Many of the lumbermen who built Stillwater came from Maine and Michigan when the pine ran out in the east; the town took its name from Stillwater, Maine.

The first mill began operating in Stillwater in 1844. And when Delta lands were officially for sale by the government in 1848, the lumbering business mushroomed. Land sales flourished and reached their peak in the mid-1850s. The peavey, a combination of spike and clasp which was a valued instrument on the river drives, was first made by Joseph Peavey, Stillwater blacksmith, in 1858. Stillwater became the roaring, booming lumbering town that it was to remain for fifty years. Millions of big white pines crashed to the ground in the upper valleys, ran the spring drives, and were cut in Stillwater.

In 1856 the St. Croix Boom Company was conveniently located about two miles north of Stillwater, at the head of Lake St. Croix. Here the river was divided by several narrow islands, facilitating the sorting of logs. The boom itself—a line of timbers stretched from bank to bank—caught the running logs from upriver just as the quieter waters of the lake were encountered by the river drives. The logs were sorted by log marks designating ownership and placed into boom pockets by mark—of which there were some two thousand different kinds. As many as 600 men were required at one time to handle the work on the St. Croix Boom.

For fifty years the Stillwater boom was an institution considered essential in the pioneer culture of the region. It handled many millions of logs, some of the best in the world. It sent rafts of logs to the Stillwater mills and the Winona mills. Logs were transported farther downriver too, joining those from St. Anthony to construct the dwellings and commercial buildings of the mid-nation, primarily through the great mills at St. Louis. The largest lumber raft ever to go down the Mississippi system left Stillwater in 1901; over a quarter of a mile long, it contained 9 million board feet of lumber.

In the half-century of St. Croix logging, 133 sawmills operated on the St. Croix; the lumber from logs passing through the boom and downriver amounted to 10 billion board feet. Including logs transported by railroad as well as those passed through the boom, the total from the St. Croix of both Minnesota and Wisconsin was nearly 15 billion board feet.

James Goodhue, pioneer editor, referring to the St. Croix Delta pinelands, wrote in 1852: "Centuries will hardly exhaust the pineries above us." But like other great stands of virgin timber that were once thought to be inexhaustible, the Delta pine, too, was exhausted — in little more than fifty years.

By the end of the 1800s the great days of logging on the St. Croix were over. The year 1890 was the peak on the St. Croix — 3.5 million logs, a half-billion board feet, passed through the boom in that year. The decline came rapidly after that. W. F. Gray, boom master, who sent the first log through the St. Croix Boom in 1856, also passed the last one — in 1914.

While lumbering dominated the valley in the last half of the 1800s as an economic enterprise, agriculture was introduced, too, and in this period local crop production served the settlers and lumberjacks as well. The first private gristmill in Minnesota was Lemuel Bolles's built in 1845 on a small tributary now known as Valley Creek near the present town of Afton. Bolles ground corn and wheat at his primitive facility and served as the region's first postmaster. Remnants of Bolles's sluiceways that carried water to his mill wheels are extant along parts of Valley Creek. Wheat production was, at first, the principal agricultural activity in the valley. But as the pine was removed and agricultural enterprise increased, greater activity was directed toward dairying and the more diversified agriculture that exists today.

As on other major Minnesota rivers, the steamboat played an important role in exploitation and settlement on the St. Croix. Franklin Steele ascended the river with the first steamboat in the valley, the *Palmyra*, and began to establish his mill at St. Croix Falls in the spring of 1838. And in the fall of 1838 the men from Marine, Illinois, on the *Ariel* selected the site of Marine-on-St. Croix and of the St. Croix River's first operating sawmill.

For fifty years the steamboat played a significant part in the St. Croix lumbering enterprise — hauling supplies and mail upriver, guiding rafts downstream — and it disappeared from the lumber business only when the pine ran out. But it was in the settlement of the valley by farmers that the steamboat made the greatest lasting contribution. For three decades beginning in the mid-1800s, steamboats brought the oppressed and anxious of Europe up from the downriver railheads on the Mississippi. Most of the immigrants who came up the St. Croix were Swedish, and they favored the fertile lake country of northern Washington and Chisago counties served by the St. Croix's steamers at Taylors Falls, the head of navigation. They worked in the lumber industry for wages to start, but their eventual goal was to settle and farm. The Homestead Act of 1862 lured many Swedish immigrants to the valley, mostly in the 1870s.

The years 1860-90 saw the greatest steamboat traffic. Regular packet runs served Taylors Falls from Stillwater—and Stillwater from Prescott and the Mississippi River lines. The St. Croix Boom was frequently an obstacle to navigation; the Boom Company was held financially responsible for navigation losses resulting from blockage of the river channel and often paid heavy damages. The lumber business, however, was more important to the valley's economy than the packet lines, and the boom stayed.

The first railroad operated in the valley in 1870, and thereafter, as on other Minnesota rivers, the importance of the steamboats declined. The regular packet lines disappeared, and the only traffic on the river was the steamboat continuing to pilot lumber rafts downstream or those that entered the new business of river excursions. And it was in this period of concern over the decline of river navigation that the idea of a ship canal between Lake Superior and the St. Croix was first seriously discussed and promoted by politician Ignatius Donnelly; it was to utilize the old explorers' route via the Brule and upper St. Croix. More recently staff of the Corps of Engineers prepared plans for a modern navigation waterway over the same route including channelization and lock-and-dam construction on both rivers. The feasibility of the plan was quickly and prudently rejected by the Corps itself.

By 1890 the railroads served most of the trade needs of the valley's people. By 1914 the last of the lumber rafts passed downstream, and a few excursion boats remain today.

The quiet waters did not last long, however, for modern commercial navigation was to come, and remain, in the lower river. Even while the last of the steamboats plied Lake St. Croix, the Army Corps of Engineers began to work to facilitate navigation. A three-foot channel was authorized up to Taylors Falls in 1878; dredging was completed by 1900, and one wing-dam was constructed in the vicinity of St. Mary's Point by 1910. It now lies buried under a sand bar. But the present nine-foot channel up to Stillwater made a greater impact on the lower river. The nine-foot channel was established in 1938 with the completion of Lock and Dam No. 3 on the Mississippi near Red Wing, backing water into the St. Croix at the same level as the Mississippi's Pool 3 and raising the original level of Lake St. Croix about six feet. Presently continual dredging maintains the nine-foot depth and results in the accumulation of spoil in the valley. Barge traffic up the St. Croix is considerable: about 120 barge trains per year, or an average of one every two days in the shipping season that runs generally from mid-April to mid-December. Most of the barge traffic carries coal to the industries along Lake St. Croix.

With all its other riverine treasures, the St. Croix also holds the distinction of being one of the finest sports fishing areas in the Midwest. Among streams that characteristically provide river fishing for walleyes, northern pike, and muskies, the St. Croix also offers outstanding angling for smallmouth bass, a species held in great esteem for its hard-fighting, aerobatic behavior. The smallmouth is found in lakes as well as streams in Minnesota, but essentially it is a river fish. Preferring moderate to large streams with fast currents and rocky bottoms, it takes advantage of the current in its fight for life on the angler's line and frequently takes to the air in high-flying leaps. It is a matter of some debate whether the rainbow trout or the smallmouth provides the more noble battle to the angler; a final decision, of course, will never be agreed upon. Meantime, in the riffles and currents of the St. Croix, over the boulder-strewn bottoms, and in the air above the surface, the smallmouth will continue to delight river fishermen.

The smallmouth is taken primarily in the upper stream reaches above Taylors Falls. However, as with other streams of similar habitat in Minnesota, other species, usually redhorses and suckers, are predominant among river populations. In the upper segment above Taylors Falls, the smallmouth, walleye, lake sturgeon, and channel catfish, as well as redhorses, are characteristic of fast-water reaches in boulder rapids and swift pools. However, in the reservoir above the St. Croix Falls dam, habitat is more lakelike, and fish species occur accordingly: here largemouth bass, crappies, yellow perch, bullheads, and the carp—all species of slower water—are more common. It is characteristic among many Minnesota rivers that in slower reaches the carp is the predominant species; in swifter reaches the redhorses usually are by far the most abundant.

In the lower river, essentially Lake St. Croix, fish populations and sports fishing are more like that in many inland lakes. Over sixty species of fish have been observed in this section of river, but of these, five species constitute the major sport fish: walleye, sauger, crappies (white and black), and white bass. The crappies and white bass vie for honors as the most abundant of these five. Other sport species in Lake St. Croix are the northern pike, smallmouth and largemouth bass, bluegills, lake sturgeon, channel catfish, and flathead catfish. Flathead cats and northern pike are rare, but those present are usually large. The lake sturgeon is also relatively uncommon, but a significant early autumn fishery has developed recently; there is a forty-inch minimum legal size, so all specimens creeled are large. The carp is the most abundant rough fish in Lake St. Croix, although the sheepshead, or drum, and redhorses are also common. The gizzard shad, also considered a rough fish, is represented abundantly by young individuals in the summer; this species is at the northern limit of its range, and it does not survive well in the northern winters here. However, tremendously successful reproduction by the few adults that do survive (probably in the warm, power-plant discharge waters), provides a large source of food for the walleye, sauger, and white bass. A popular fishing site, particularly in winter, is the warm waters of the Northern States Power Company power-plant discharge canal. Most sought in Lake St. Croix by sports fishermen are walleyes and sauger, although the greatest proportion of total catch is the white bass in summer and crappies in the winter. About one-fifth of the yearly catch is taken in the winter by ice fishing.

Several game species exist only below the St. Croix Falls dam (sixty-foot head), apparently having been unable to ascend the original falls there; these are white bass, sauger, and flathead catfish. Similarly, rough species such as bigmouth buffalo, sheepshead, and gizzard shad are not found above the dam or else there are so few that they are inconspicuous.

Several small trout streams originate along the steep banks on the Minnesota side, chiefly Old Mill Stream which flows through Marine-on-St. Croix, Brown's Creek in the gorge just north of Stillwater, and a few other small, spring-fed brooks. Better-known trout waters also enter the St. Croix from the Wisconsin side—the Apple, Willow, and Kinnickinnic.

Commercial fishing is permitted in the lower reaches of the St. Croix where the average annual yield of about 400,000 pounds is dominated by the carp. Also permitted in the commercial harvest are other rough species such as sheepshead, catfish, quillback, and various other species of suckers.

With designation and management in the National Wild and Scenic Rivers System, fame of the great valley's natural splendors has spread widely. Other designated "wildernesses" in the United States have consequently become increasingly popular, and unfortunately overuse has brought deterioration of the very natural sources of beauty and solitude that designation meant to preserve. But with deliberate, planned management for diversity, it should be possible to avoid overcrowded conditions in the St. Croix Valley. As long as all forms of river activity are given support—canoeing and boating, sport fishing, hunting, birding, photography— and there is diversity in user-density, the riverway will be a sustained store of treasures.

Many groups and individuals worked hard for the protection of the St. Croix and the inclusion of both the upper and lower segments in the national rivers system. Among Minnesotans, former Senator Walter Mondale and Congressmen Donald Fraser, Joseph Karth, Albert Quie, and John Blatnik, and, more locally, Jim Harrison, Executive Director of the Minnesota-Wisconsin Boundary Area Commission, and Don Vogtman of the U.S. Fish and Wildlife Service, have been at the forefront of the effort in their initiation and support of legislation.

Most citizens now believe the objective was worth the fight: to save the natural values of the stream Senator Mondale called "one of the truly majestic rivers of the world."

Chapter 8

The Snake and Kettle

White Pine and White Water

Down from the high divides in east-central Minnesota separating the Mississippi drainage from Lake Superior's, two of Minnesota's wildest streams come alternately brawling and gliding toward their mouths in the St. Croix. Brown with the organic stain of bog and swamp, and nearly stagnant in a few large pools in late summer, they rush crashing and frothing through white-water stretches in the springtime. In the final reaches they hurry down rapids as if they knew there would be no more.

Through the fabled St. Croix Delta, the Snake and Kettle carried large quantities of pine logs in great river drives. Today they provide in wildlife, stream currents, and new forests some of the state's outstanding recreational resources.

The Snake and Kettle country has a history of ruthless Indian war—Indian against Indian—and a half-century of logging that left the watersheds stripped and nearly worthless. Immigrants came to settle and cultivate the stubborn, stump-filled soil, only to meet bitter failure in the Great Depression of the 1930s. The anonymity of these lands in tax-forfeit status lasted for three decades; as late as 1960 tax-forfeited tracts in this region could be bought for less than in the original federal land sales.

During the 1960s, however, new eyes were turned to the for-

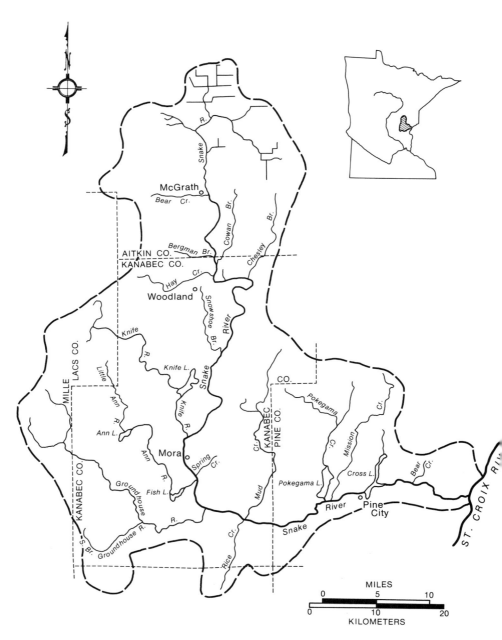

The Snake River

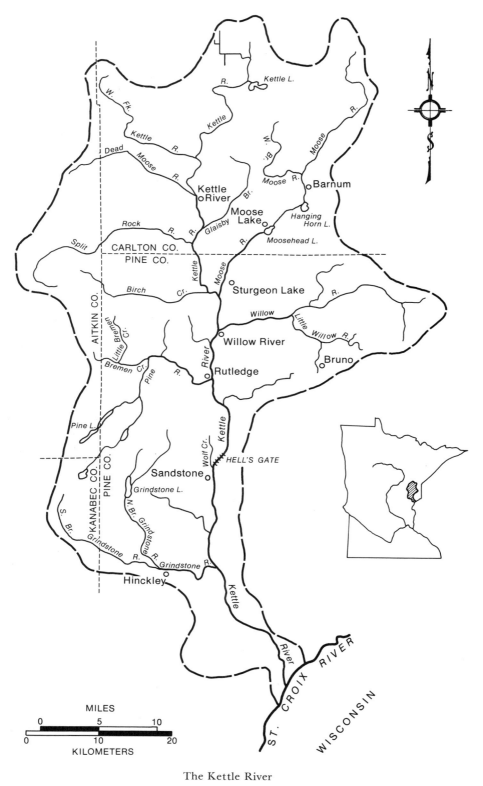

The Kettle River

gotten lands in Pine, Kanabac, Aitkin, and Carlton counties. Despite continued minor logging and some great forest fires over a seventy-five-year period, these woodlands that once were laid waste now had acquired a new coat of second-growth vegetation—maple, basswood, aspen, birch, and oak, and a sprinkling of pines, newly planted. Lakes and streams were abundant in the new woodlands, and deer, bear, and upland game flourished. The region now is one of the major areas of the state for fishing, hunting, canoeing the wild rapids, or just plain river-hiking.

The region known as the St. Croix Delta—a roughly triangular area between the Mississippi and St. Croix—contained in its northern part in 1837 the richest stands of virgin white pine in the whole area that was to become Minnesota. It was looked upon by ambitious lumbermen with envious eyes. In that year the first large Minnesota land cession (it was not yet Minnesota Territory) was made by the Chippewa and the Sioux to the white man with his saw and ax.

Fifty years of intensive logging in the St. Croix Delta, providing millions of logs to the St. Croix and Mississippi mills, began in the watersheds of the Snake and Kettle. And the logs that continued to pour from these two streams into the St. Croix constituted a large proportion of the Delta production. At times, the rivers' volume of flow was too low to carry the logs. So temporary dams were built on the main streams and in the tributaries as well to provide a spring flood that would carry the big pine. Logging rose to a peak in the 1880s, then slowed, and by the end of the century the white pine was gone. The loggers moved north to new stands, leaving remains of their old dams and massive white pine stumps, which can be found today almost everywhere along riverbanks.

The Chippewa, living along the St. Croix River near the mouth of the Snake, had a name for their traditional enemies, the Dakota, who lived up along the tributary stream: *Kinebik*, or "Snake in the Grass." Consequently, the French, who came upon the Minnesota scene as the Chippewa-Dakota conflict moved southwest across the region, applied their own name for "snake" to the Dakota: "nadouesse," or in the plural form, "nadouesioux." The

In the latter half of the 1800s, lumbering in the upper Great Lakes states meant white pine. Forests of the St. Croix Delta contained some of the finest and largest white pine in the country, with base diameters up to six feet. Only scattered trees remain in the Delta, towering over the streams, such as the Snake River in the Lower Falls area, that once carried the giant logs.

English-speaking settlers in characteristic fashion shortened this to the last syllable — and the Dakota were commonly known as the Sioux from then on.

Eventually, in a series of bitter battles, the Chippewa successfully drove the Sioux out of the river valleys and finally out of the northern Minnesota woodlands altogether. But the name of the Snake River remains, and it is located in the county with the Chippewa-derived name for the same word, Kanabec.

The Snake River is formed from the junction of several small branches located in southern Aitkin County. These small, sluggish, bog-colored streams originate in large alder, willow, and black spruce swamps. The branches come together near the tiny village of Pliny, and from here the Snake proper flows to McGrath and south.

This upper section of river down to a bridge on a township road east of Woodland, a distance of a little over twelve miles, has undoubtedly some of the wilder and more scenic river environment in Minnesota. A major access below McGrath is the excellent Aitkin County Snake River Campground—but from there down are wild rapids and plunging torrents through high, granite-walled gorges that both delight and torment the river traveler. These are the Upper and Lower Falls of the Snake, accessible only by canoe or a good hike. The Minnesota Canoe Association utilizes them to test the mettle of their wild-water enthusiasts in the high water of springtime. In the usual low water of summer, the rapids become a boulder-strewn water course with only trickles wandering through, and canoe travel becomes virtually impossible. The average stream gradient in this section is a respectable twelve feet per mile; in the falls areas the drop is thirty feet in one mile between walls of granite.

Below the township road east of Woodland, the river enters the new Snake River State Forest for ten or twelve miles and, in all, flows twenty-eight miles to Mora. This is a stretch of long pools and rapids, and it, too, is tough going in low water; but at medium to high levels it is an enjoyable though fast trip. Remains of the old Bean Logging Company dam are found about four miles from the upper end of this section, holding back a large pool. But the overall gradient of the section is still good, at about five feet per mile.

From Mora to Pine City, a distance of thirty miles, is a stretch of mostly long, quiet pools; only a few minor rapids are found here, and the reach would be classed for novice canoeing. There are several access points between Mora and Pine City for shorter trips. The mean gradient for this section is only two-thirds of a foot per mile, a very flat stretch.

Below Pine City and toward the mouth, however, the nature of the Snake changes again. After flowing through Cross Lake and over a new dam that maintains the lake level, almost continuous rapids occur for twelve miles to the mouth in the St. Croix, except for one long, deep pool near the mouth of Bear Creek. The river narrows gradually toward its mouth, the banks become higher and the current swifter. There are no road crossings in this section, but considerable cabin development and private accesses are here; a public landing is available near the mouth in the St. Croix. Gradient in this stretch is again high, with a mean of ten feet per mile.

The upper half of the river—down to near Mora—is wild and heavily forested with second growth but includes a few majestic remnants of old white pine; from Mora to Pine City the watershed is mostly put to agricultural use, pasture and forage production predominating; the lower section is wooded with second growth of hardwoods and some pine.

Numerous recreational areas and historic sites are to be found along the Snake. Foremost, perhaps, is the Aitkin County Snake River Campground located on the riverbanks just before the river leaves Aitkin County to enter Kanabec; it is off the main track, quiet, and surrounded by many protected acres of county park in natural condition. The Snake River State Forest, through which a good portion of the river flows near Warman and Woodland, is largely undeveloped; it provides much public land, available mostly by canoe, for use in primitive camping, fishing, and hunting. The canoe route is described in *A Gathering of Waters*. The Rum River State Forest and the Mille Lacs Wildlife Management Area include the headwaters of some of the western tributaries, and the lower few miles of the Snake flow through the Chengwatana State Forest.

West of Pine City is the North West Company Fur Post on a winding ridge overlooking the Snake. Recently rediscovered and reconstructed by the Minnesota Historical Society, it is a carefully restored replica of the trading post built by voyageurs in 1804 as an outpost of the British company.

Considerable fishing is done in the Snake and the principal lakes of its watershed. Best known is smallmouth bass fishing in the river itself. Although among the larger game fishes both the walleye and northern pike outnumber the smallmouth, the smallmouth, prized for its fighting ability, deservedly has the greater reputation. The principal areas for the smallmouth are the pools and rapids of the swifter uppermost and lowest sections. The smallmouth in the Snake is often most available in isolated reaches known only to the dedicated angler specializing in technique and equipment and willing to undertake difficult access. However, the rapids area below Cross Lake at Pine City provides readily available smallmouth fishing and is the site of annual smallmouth outings by the St. Paul Fly Tiers and Fishermen's Club. Campgrounds among high riverbank woods are available at this site, too. The walleye and northern pike, taken more frequently than the smallmouth, are usually found in quieter pools. The channel catfish is also a favored and sought-after species, especially below Cross Lake in the one large pool midway in that section.

Fish populations found in the river, as distinct from those sought and taken by anglers include some rough fishes dominated mostly by several redhorse species of the sucker family, followed in abundance by carp and sheepshead. Panfish such as the bluegill, crappies, and yellow perch are common in places. Once common but a relative oddity now, the lake sturgeon still is found in the Snake, principally in areas of strong current like the uppermost and lowest sections. There was a time when the sturgeon was taken by the wagonload, individual fish weighing up to hundred pounds.

The Snake has many tributary streams, and some are large. In the forested headwater sections several small woodland streams enter as tumbling, rocky creeks; these include Hay and Spring creeks, and Bergman, Chesley, Cowan, and Snowshoe brooks. Just north of Mora the Knife River enters after leaving Knife Lake, a major area of recreational and cottage development; a dam at the outlet of Knife Lake maintains the lake level, although several breaches of this dam occurred after the severe floods in the summer of 1972. South of Mora the Ann River enters the Snake after flowing through Ann Lake and Fish Lake, also important cottage and fishing areas.

A little farther downstream the Groundhouse River empties into the Snake. The Groundhouse originates with several tributaries that extend upstream west into the Rum River State Forest and the Mille Lacs Wildlife Management Area as do the headwaters of the Ann and Knife rivers. The Groundhouse is a moderately large river and was an important route for log transportation in the Snake River country.

Above Pine City, Pokegama Creek flows from the north into Pokegama Lake which then drains directly into the Snake. Pokegama Lake and Cross Lake, through which the Snake flows at Pine City, constitute the major recreational home development areas near Pine City. Below Pine City there are no major tributaries; the only significant one is the small Bear Creek from the north which enters the Snake near the beginning of the one big pool in this section.

Some tributaries and their associated lakes, particularly Ann River and Fish Lake, and Knife River and Knife Lake, also contain important fisheries including the walleye, northern pike, largemouth bass, and panfishes. A few of the smaller tributaries, such as Chesley Brook northeast of Woodland and Spring Creek just south of Mora, were once classified as trout streams, although they are marginal at best.

In all, the Snake drains 1,020 square miles. For a length of 100 miles, it drops a total of 500 feet from its origin in several headwater ditches in Solana State Forest which is about 1,300 feet above sea level to 800 feet at its mouth in the St. Croix. The overall mean gradient is thus five feet per mile, one of the highest in central Minnesota, but it has a range of up to thirty feet per mile in the falls area of the upper section. The mean discharge is about 600 cubic feet per second; the maximum, occurring in the summer floods of 1972, may have been nearly 20,000. The Snake and its tributaries have alkalinities of low to moderate levels, ranging from about 40-50 p.p.m. in the upper section to near 100 p.p.m. at the mouth; the wide range is primarily the result of igneous bedrock in the upper sections and the more calcareous sedimentary rock in the downstream part of the watershed. Color of the water is associated with the alkalinity: brown bog color in the upper sections and tributaries and clearer water in the lower reach, particularly during the lower water levels of late summer and winter.

No set of statistics, however, can convey the rush of white water, the color of lichen-covered granite boulders, or the green sweep of the forested valley of the Snake River.

Occasionally on the bedrock bottom of a stream a tiny pebble or a few grains of sand collect in a small crevice and, if the river currents are just right, start spinning around in place. Soon a depression is formed, now circular, as the result of the abrasive action of the spinning pebble. Eventually a larger rock falls into the depression and serves as the grinding tool, and the forming "pothole" grows larger. Such round holes or "kettles" are common along rivers, particularly where soft sedimentary rocks such as sandstones form the bedrock river bottom. Often these can be found well above the present river surface, indicating a previously higher level of the stream. Such is the case along the St. Croix and Kettle rivers, particularly along the Kettle River gorge and in the lower rapids. The numerous kettles are responsible for the river's name.

The Kettle River includes extremely diverse stretches along its course, and therein lie its beauty and value. Geology, topography, stream-bank vegetation, canoeing conditions, fishery resources, bottom type, gradient, and current velocity all vary widely. It is this great diversity that makes the Kettle one of Minnesota's outstanding recreational rivers.

The Kettle begins in a number of small tributaries that flow sluggishly from an alder-swamp and willow-marsh area known as the Corona Bog in west-central Carlton County, actually near Kettle Lake. These small streams are mostly ditched, warm, and dark-stained. But a mile or so south of County Road 4, the small tributaries combine to form the Kettle proper, and from here for a distance of about twenty miles it is one of the most productive smallmouth streams in the state. Rocky and swift, with excellent gravel bars, this stretch of the Kettle is ideal for the wading bass fisherman who loves fast water, although the slippery boulder bottom makes footwork difficult. Average gradient is about ten feet per mile in this section of rapids. The bottom types are also ideal for smallmouth spawning and for production of preferred invertebrate food organisms. Although the state-designated canoe route starts in this section near the village of Kettle River, the sector is difficult to canoe except in high water, and so the wading smallmouth fisherman will not be bothered too much by canoes. In this stretch, several tributaries enter from the west—West Fork of the Kettle, Dead Moose River, Split Rock River, and Birch Creek; flowing swiftly through rocky, deeply incised ravines, some of them also have unique scenic value.

Where the Moose River enters the Kettle from the east, the character of the stream changes abruptly. The Moose River also offers an interesting canoe trip, starting at Barnum (at least in moderately high waters) and going through two lakes—Hanging Horn and Moosehead—to empty into the Kettle near the town of Sturgeon Lake. It is sometimes called the Moose Horn River above Moosehead Lake; the headwaters near Atkinson are designated trout waters. The Moose is virtually the same size as the Kettle at the confluence of the two streams, and after their junction the Kettle is noticeably larger. It is also much slower, with a sand and silt bottom instead of rubble and boulders and with a gradient of only about three feet per mile. For canoeing it is a flat-water stretch of about fifteen miles; the only rapids is short and steep, and is just above the Interstate Highway 35 crossing. For the angler it is walleye and northern pike water. Two major tributaries enter in this reach: the Willow River from the east, entering near the village of Willow River, and Pine River from the west, emptying into the Kettle at Rutledge. Both these streams can be canoed for a distance at high water stage, especially the Pine.

Just north of Sandstone at the site of the abandoned village of Banning is perhaps the outstanding reach of scenic river in Minnesota. This is the Kettle River gorge, including Hell's Gate, a wild two-mile stretch of racing water, chutes, cascades, and rapids with a gradient of forty feet in one mile. At very low water, the river makes an impressive but quiet gash in the ground; at high water, it is noisy and awesome. The remains of Banning, a sandstone-quarrying town named after St. Paul banker and railroad contractor William L. Banning, are still to be seen on the riverbanks—standing sandstone walls, artifacts, and debris from the quarrying. There is little fishing in this stretch because of its wild character, but it is the ultimate in white-water canoeing, and the Minnesota Canoe Association holds annual spring and fall expeditions through the gorge. It is, of course, for experts only; unfortunately a number of inexperienced canoeists and others have lost their lives here. But the gorge is unquestionably the outstanding feature of interest and beauty in the Kettle River, and it is protected now by the recent establishment of Banning State Park. Wolf Creek with its lovely hidden waterfalls enters on the west side, near the lower end of the gorge.

In Sandstone is Robinson Park, below the gorge and just upstream from the Minnesota 123 bridge, where easy access is available. From here down to Big Eddy landing in St. Croix State Park is a twenty-mile section that varies greatly. Most of it is flat water, but this alternates with some rapids. Average gradient over this reach is only one to two feet per mile, despite the presence of short rapids. The Grindstone River enters this section from the west, coming from Grindstone Lake. The North Branch of the Grindstone in its upper reaches is a marginal trout stream and, in the lower reaches, a small-mouth stream.

Downstream from the Big Eddy is the lower rapids, a stretch of five miles to the St. Croix with plenty of white water and an average gradient of thirteen feet per mile. The last two miles is an especially steep, fast run in high water, but it can hardly be canoed in low water. The Kettle is also described in the state's guide, *A Gathering of*

Plunging through Hell's Gate rapids on the Kettle River, kayakers fight for control of their light craft in the whirling waters. Wearing wetsuits against the cold of springtime water and helmets and face-guards against the blows of subsurface boulders, most of them upset in the worst of the rapids. Placid for most of its length upriver, the Kettle drops precipitously into its gorge in the Hinckley Sandstone formation, brawling through stair-step rapids and swirling slides. This reach is now included in Banning State Park. The Kettle is the first component designated in Minnesota's Wild, Scenic, and Recreational Rivers System.

Waters and provides details of the run through the Banning rapids and Hell's Gate. This entire lower stretch of rapids is primarily smallmouth water, whereas walleyes and northern pike would be more likely in the flat-water stretches including the Big Eddy itself. The banks are high, and a climb along the rim in St. Croix State Park rewards the hiker with magnificent river scenes.

Developed recreational facilities are minimal along the Kettle River; most of the area remains wild. But campgrounds are available at the large Willow River Campground in General C. C. Andrews

State Forest near Willow River on an impoundment of the Willow; at Banning State Park along the Kettle gorge; and in St. Croix State Park. The large Moose Lake Recreation Area, recently developed, borders the west side of Moosehead Lake. Considerable hiking and roaming space is available along the river; streamside state park land extends for nine miles in Banning and seven miles in St. Croix park. Canoe access is ample, with small areas available for parking at road crossings and village parks.

In 1973 the Minnesota legislature passed the state Wild and Scenic Rivers Act, and in 1975 the Kettle was the first stream to be designated as a component of this Minnesota system. Differing from the national program, the state program does not include the right of eminent domain (condemnation of property) and cannot prevent the construction of federally authorized dams (as the national program can). The Minnesota system does, however, provide much-needed protection of river resources—for the public and riparian owners as well—without creating a public park in which there is a high density of users. The Kettle was also added to the national system in a study category in congressional bills in 1971 and 1975, but action has not been taken on these proposals.

The Kettle and its tributaries drain 1,060 square miles of watershed. The Kettle itself flows some eighty miles from a 1,320-foot elevation in the ditches above Kettle Lake to 820 feet at its mouth in the St. Croix, for a total drop of 500 feet and an average gradient of 6.3 feet per mile. Although this gradient is only moderate, the average, of course, does not begin to describe the excitement of the Banning gorge or the lower rapids, or the swift-water smallmouth fishing in the upper reaches. Mean discharge at the mouth is about 750 cubic feet per second, but the record high was probably similar to that of the Snake after torrential summer rains in 1972.

The Kettle's water is very soft, only 20-30 p.p.m. alkalinity in the upper reaches, although some tributary waters have an alkalinity of about 50. All waters are deeply brown-stained, reflecting the bog sources of headwaters and tributaries.

It is true that logging in the latter half of the last century left the Snake and Kettle watersheds desolate. Virtually all of the magnificent white pine was taken out, and extant stumps are impressive by any standard. But the succession of second growth during these last seventy-five years brought unforeseen riches in wild-life habitat that now gives the region a priceless character. Vegetation in its varying successional stages provides the optimum environment for woodland species such as the ruffed grouse and white-tailed deer.

The virgin white pine forests, with high crowns that blocked out the sky and shade that left the forest floor needle-covered and cool but with only a sparse growth of green plants, must have been majestic. But as wildlife habitat, except for pinecone-eating red squirrels, the pinelands were virtually a desert.

With the removal of the pine and the second growth of aspen and birch, dogwood, holly, wild grapes, and ground plants like wintergreen and blueberries, grouse and deer populations increased greatly. Such an abundance of foods for wildlife had not been known before in the Snake and Kettle watersheds, and wildlife prospered.

We like to think of the ruffed grouse as a northern species and therefore adapted to life in the pine woods and spruce and balsam swamps. We thought, for a long time, that grouse needed the conifers for winter cover. But as a result of research done by University of Minnesota wildlife biologist Gordon W. Gullion, at the Cloquet Forest Experiment Station, we now know that such is not the case. Actually the presence of conifers only increases predation by owls and goshawks, providing cover to the predator more than to the prey. What the grouse really need to come through the winter in good condition is deep, fluffy snow and a nearby supply of good food. The supply of snow, of course, is out of man's control (at least for the present), but the food supply that really counts for grouse is the large bud of the mature male aspen tree, which can be provided in abundance with proper forest management. The male buds are so large, and so nutritious, and sometimes so abundant on the mature trees, that the bird may require only about fifteen minutes to take in enough calories to last the coldest day of a Minnesota winter. That kind of food supply was never available when big white pine covered the St. Croix Delta. But fortunately for the grouse and grouse lovers —whether they tote shotgun, camera, or paintbrush—aspen is now one of the principal tree species in the region.

The Snake and Kettle country in the fall is a magic land. From the fiery red maple in September, through October's glory that ends with gray November skies, grouse is king here. The thunder of wings on the aspen-covered slopes is relatively new to the valleys and has replaced the rush of autumn winds in the high pine tops and the ring of the logger's ax as well. But today it is music to match the roar of river rapids.

Chapter 9

The Pine County Creeks

Of Trout Streams and Timberdoodles

The St. Croix River, after first touching Minnesota, rushes westward in a great sweeping curve and then flows south, forming the border with Wisconsin. From north of this rough westerly curve, a number of small streams drain a part of Minnesota's Pine County, flowing south to join the St. Croix. Separated from all other watersheds of the state, these little creeks — more than forty in all — compose a small watershed of their own. And although the drainage area is relatively small — 510 square miles — the Pine County creeks impart a unique natural character to this corner of Minnesota.

The explanation for the isolation of this drainage pocket is found in the subsurface topography. From near Hinckley toward the northeast, a zone of lava bedrock long ago became elevated as a result of earth movements; on top of this elevation, moraines formed as the melting glaciers halted along the zone, leaving a low ridge from which streams now flow both north and south. The northern streams enter the Kettle River watershed to the north and west, and the Nemadji watershed to the northeast, but those flowing south drain across southeast Pine County to the St. Croix.

Most of these rise in broad marshes and swamps on the tops of the moraines. These waters are deeply brown-stained and very low in alkalinity, as low as 25 p.p.m. In periods of high water they become

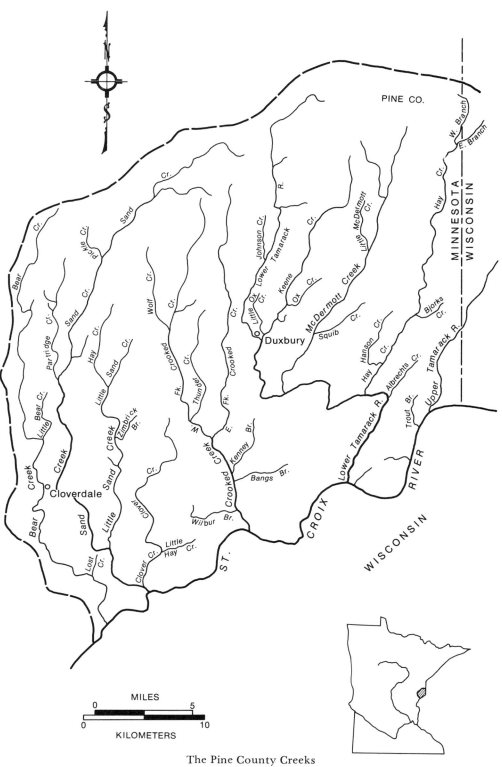

The Pine County Creeks

almost black, like the swampy peat from which they flow. Gradients become relatively high as the streams tumble down the moraine over rocky riffles and gravel bars; they flow more slowly again in the last few miles over sandy outwash plains that formed below the moraine.

Many of the streams are exceedingly small, yet they are named, and most, of course, empty into receiving streams that are successively slightly larger. Thus the basin drains into the St. Croix via four primary streams: Lower Tamarack River and Crooked, Sand, and Bear creeks. A few other smaller creeks flow directly into the St. Croix, and one additional larger stream, the Upper Tamarack (or Spruce) River, flows into the St. Croix very near the state border, having originated and coursed mostly in Wisconsin.

This watershed was included in the St. Croix Delta, richly timbered with native white pine. Its frozen valleys echoed with the crack of the lumberjack's ax and the roar of the great pine dropping into the snow. Its logs went out to the St. Croix and the Stillwater mills; thus even these small streams had spring log drives. Auxiliary driving dams were required to move the giant logs — temporary dams built to hold back the spring freshets until sufficient water was available, which was then released with a rush. Some remains of these logging dams are extant on the Sand and the Lower Tamarack, but not much remains of the pine. The few notable stands, such as those in St. Croix State Park and some individual trees along upper stream reaches, little resemble the deep woods of shadow and huge trunks that was the milieu of the lumberjack. In some places, though, fields of great stumps give an idea of what it was once like along these creeks.

Today the great pines have been replaced by the aspen or poplar, now highly utilized for paper pulp and other wood products. The soils of the Pine County creeks do not support great agricultural production, and although there is considerable pasturing of livestock, there is little crop cultivation. Aspens, however, grow well, and the countryside is now one of aspen ridges and brushy pastures. At first glance, the traveler might consider this landscape uninteresting. But the aspen is valued for more than its wood products; it provides richly for wildlife, primarily deer and grouse which were not abundant in the big pine woods.

Along hidden creek bends and swamps are many private recre-

Alder thickets along the banks of Sand Creek provide excellent coverts for the American woodcock. This bird finds high-quality habitat and an abundance of its favorite food, the earthworm, in the moist streambanks along creeks and rivers.

ational sites—deer-hunting cabins, summer homes, and cottages; there are some commercial campgrounds and recreation areas here as well. But extensive public lands are also available for outdoor recreation in this watershed. Most of the southern part along the St. Croix is included in St. Croix State Park, Minnesota's largest park, with 30,920 acres. Bear, Sand, and Crooked creeks all flow through the state park to the river. Northeast of the park and also along the river is the St. Croix State Forest, through which the Lower Tamarack flows to its mouth. And in the northern part of the watershed near the headwaters of the Lower Tamarack and some of its tributaries are the southern portions of the Nemadji State Forest. All along the St. Croix are lands of the St. Croix Scenic Waterway, a component of the National Wild and Scenic Rivers System. Much of the state forest land is open for public use, including fishing and hunting; St. Croix State Park, like all state parks, is open for many types of recreation, including fishing but not hunting.

There are few state wildlife management areas for public hunting in the watershed. Opportunities exist, however, for their development along some presently inaccessible stream reaches where land is still in tax-forfeit status. Wildlife management areas that could be established along some of these streams for upland game and deer hunting would be superb.

Large areas of the watershed are wet—extensive swamps, bogs, and wet meadows occur here in addition to the plethora of little streams, mostly in the upper reaches atop low moraines. As the streams tumble down the moraines, conditions in several creeks become suitable for trout, and the brook trout has been successfully introduced. Today this species reproduces naturally and is maintaining itself in several small streams. These wild populations are mostly in the Sand and Crooked creek systems; wild brook trout occur in Clover (or Hay) and Little Hay creeks, tributary to the Sand in St. Croix State Park, and, in the Crooked Creek drainage, Wilbur Brook and Bangs Brook. Browns and rainbows are stocked in other streams that are a bit warmer than the brook trout creeks but are able to hold trout for a short period in the early part of the season. The best of these are an upstream section of Sand Creek and the lower reaches of Crooked Creek up to and including part of the West Fork. Although other streams hold promise for additional trout management if streambank cover continues to increase and waters cool, a major problem persists—the beaver.

The relationship between beaver and trout has long been hotly debated. Around streambank campfires and in deer-hunting shacks the debates are often spirited. The question is always the same—Resolved: That the beaver ponds are good/bad for trout streams.

Some anglers from the cold north woods maintain that their little forest creeks will not produce good-sized brook trout except where beaver ponds occur. Here more space and deeper water are available to larger trout. But others argue that a beaver pond inundates food-producing riffles, slows the current and allows silt to deposit, and—worst of all—permits the water to warm up so that temperatures in the pond and stream below are then too high for trout.

Who's right? Are beaver ponds good for trout streams—or bad? The answer, of course, is not satisfactory to either side, for it is equivocal. What is the stream like in the first place? If it is a very small, very cold woodland stream, clear and silt-free, with pools and cover hardly adequate to shelter a tiny brook trout, then a beaver pond may provide the space and food lacking in the stream. Because the stream is initially very cold, the warming that occurs as a consequence of the larger surface area of the pond will not exceed temperatures suitable for trout. In fact some small forest streams are so cold (40 to 50°F) that fish growth is limited simply by low temperatures, and some warming (to about 50 or 60°F) results in better fish growth even given the same food supply. But if, on the other hand, the stream waters are already near the thermal limit for trout (60 to 70°F) and if they frequently carry a silt load, a beaver pond—or any other impoundment for that matter—may very well warm the water above a temperature tolerable to trout, as well as cause silt to deposit, filling the pond and suffocating trout foods that normally are produced in stream-bottom riffles.

Unfortunately most Pine County creeks are in the latter category. Most are too warm to support trout, and those that can, may be near the upper thermal limit in summer. If a series of beaver ponds is added, even these few streams would no longer be suitable for trout. Of course just one or two small beaver impoundments probably would not make much difference. But severe restrictions on beaver trapping over many years, no doubt because the animal was trapped nearly to extinction in the early days, have permitted populations of this aquatic mammal to increase tremendously. Some Pine County creeks, otherwise suitable for trout, have scores of beaver dams and ponds!

To some extent, beaver control is now practiced on the best of these trout waters, and dams and beavers are removed to improve trout habitat. But intensive management will be required to keep the few trout streams free of impoundments, for the beaver is a persistent animal and will soon return in the night to rebuild.

There is another secretive denizen along the Pine County creeks and alder lowlands, an important wildlife resource of this small watershed. Elusive quarry of hunters afield in October days with shotgun and dog, this is the timberdoodle, or American woodcock.

The woodcock really belongs to a shorebird family, fleeting dwellers of grassy pools and brackish marshes. But long ago this member deserted the family along reedy shorelines and evolved to an upland inhabitant. Seldom noticed until the fall hunting season, the woodcock spends the warm months of the year in the woodlands of northeast North America, including eastern Minnesota, raising its young and storing food reserves for its fall migration south.

The timberdoodle's ecology has been the subject of intensive studies at the University of Minnesota by William H. Marshall and his students for some thirty years. Though the details of the woodcock's life history remain elusive, the basic outline has been unraveled by Professor Marshall along the creeks and swamps of northeastern Minnesota.

In the winter, though, the woodcock spends the waiting months in the warm moist swamps of the south Atlantic and Gulf coasts, largely in the broad wetlands of eastern Louisiana, and returns for breeding in April when Minnesota snow is barely off the ground. Unlike the spectacular migrations of waterfowl, the woodcock's comings and goings are rarely observed.

Why does it seek southeast Pine County? Woodcock are not restricted to this area, of course. They may be found in Minnesota's southeastern valleys and north along the Mississippi and St. Croix to the rocky stream courses of the North Shore and beyond. But the Pine County creeks offer particularly suitable habitat to the woodcock.

Its prime habitat is a young forest in an early successional stage, with light tree cover and openings interspersed. Its food includes small insects and other invertebrates of the soil and forest duff, but it prefers succulent earthworms and probes in the ground for them with a specially adapted prehensile bill. It is not very active on the ground, moving slowly in wet places looking for worms. Consequently, the woodcock does not like thick undergrowth of either dense brush or grass. The moist bottoms of small creeks, particularly under the relatively open willow and alder thickets, provide the best woodcock habitat—a combination of thin ground cover and rich, wet soils with earthworms. And the Pine County creeks, flowing through second-growth forests of aspen and birch, alder and willow brush, and lightly pastured woods provide this combination of habitat features.

The woodcock season opens in early September in Minnesota, and it closes in early November, a two-month span that can include a sweep from summer's heat to frost, cold, and sometimes snow. October is the prime month, with blue skies and autumn woods, and the sound of rocky riffles.

However, despite an abundant supply, the woodcock is not hunted very intensively in Minnesota. Of about 300,000 small-game hunters in the state, perhaps only about 1,000 search specifically for the timberdoodle; of probably 1.5 million birds shot annually in the United States, only about five to ten thousand are taken in Minnesota. Hunting pressure is low undoubtedly because this bird is not big or showy and certainly yields little food for the table compared with the traditional Minnesota game birds like pheasants, ducks, and grouse. However, each year a few more hunters discover woodcock hunting as high-quality sport. Picking along a trail of golden aspens and alder thickets on a Pine County creek bottom, especially with a well-trained pointing dog, this hunt becomes the quintessence of upland bird shooting.

Try the fringes of the big alder swamps and the shallow bosky valleys of the headwaters; farther south, the flat creek bottoms where the Sand, Little Sand, West Fork of the Crooked, and Lower Tamarack come down the morainic slopes; search out the small tributaries and the open areas where pastures are bordered by alder-lined creeks and where aspen and bracken lightly cover the slopes up from the streambed.

In mid-October woodcock become more active in their daily foraging, and their crepuscular flights to feeding areas become longer. For a few days, woodcock, dogs, and hunters approach a frenetic peak of activity—the birds seem to be everywhere.

Then one night the moist swamps and bottoms freeze, and earthworms burrow deep. Now the instincts of the timberdoodle are stirred to southern hills and the warm swamps of Louisiana, and a ragged wave of birds, in small flocks of two or three, drift out of the pastures and alder thickets along the Pine County creeks.

For a few days more, they will linger in brushy valleys of southeastern Minnesota, and then, as northern storms push down through the state, they will move on, to follow the wide Mississippi River floodplain toward the warm Gulf.

Chapter 10

The Rum

River of Good Spirits

Mille Lacs Lake, Minnesota's second largest, and famous for its walleye and northern pike fishing, is the headwater of the Rum River. But before the French "discovered" Mille Lacs, this inland sea was the veritable center of another culture—it was the "Spirit Lake" and focus of the Sioux world. The French were the first explorers to visit the Indian capital—Du Luth in 1679, Father Hennepin (as a prisoner of the Sioux) in 1680—but the area was finally occupied by another Indian nation. Bitter war between the Chippewa and Sioux through most of northern Minnesota finally resulted in a fierce, three-day battle in 1745 at Kathio, the community of Sioux villages at the headwater of the Rum River. The Sioux were harshly displaced, and the Chippewa were permanent residents thereafter.

Indian war along the Rum River continued for nearly another century. In 1839, after members of both tribes had left their camps at Fort Snelling, where the commander had been struggling for reconciliation between the two groups, Sioux warriors sought revenge for the murder of one of their hunters. They followed their old enemies from the fort and overtook them by ambush along the Rum. Seventy Chippewa, mostly women and children, were killed on their way to Mille Lacs. It was not the last Indian blood to be spilled along the ill-defined Sioux-Chippewa border.

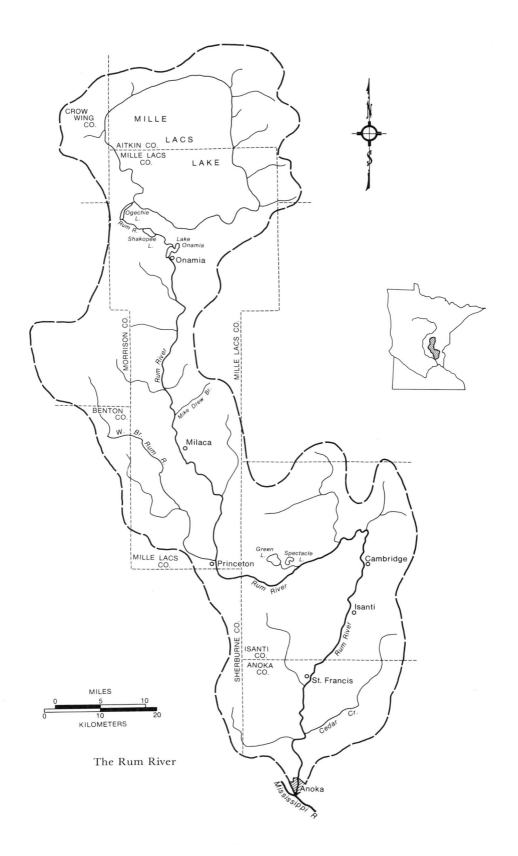

CROW
WING
CO.

MILLE

LACS

AITKIN CO.

MILLE LACS
CO.

LAKE

MILLE LACS LAKE

*Ogechie
L.*

Rum R.

*Shakopee
L.*

*Lake
Onamia*

○ Onamia

MORRISON CO.

Rum River

MILLE LACS CO.

BENTON
CO.

Mike Drew Br.

W. Br. Rum R.

○ Milaca

MILLE LACS
CO.

*Green
L.*

*Spectacle
L.*

○ Princeton

Rum River

Cambridge ○

Isanti ○

SHERBURNE CO.

ISANTI
CO.

ANOKA
CO.

Rum River

○ St. Francis

Cedar Cr.

MILES

0   5   10

0   10   20

KILOMETERS

The Rum River

Anoka

Mississippi R.

The name of the river running out of the Sioux's "Spirit Lake" apparently is the result of a mistranslation by whites: "Spirit" to "Rum."

Mille Lacs Kathio State Park, which now encloses the old Indian village, includes some of the richest archaeological sites in Minnesota. Excavations continue; artifacts dating to 2,000 B.C. have been recovered. Until the 1700s, Indians harvested wild rice in the lakes through which the Rum flows after leaving Mille Lacs; modern Indians still do. A historical interpretive center has been prepared in the park by the Department of Natural Resources; the Mille Lacs Indian Museum at Vineland, operated by the Minnesota Historical Society, depicts the lives of the Sioux and Chippewa, as well as the battle, along the Rum River headwaters. Father Hennepin State Park, near Isle on the south shore, commemorates the French missionary's travels to the big lake.

Today Mille Lacs Lake bustles with another activity, especially in the early weeks of the walleye season, and the Rum itself echoes with the splash of canoe paddles.

Most of us do not think of Mille Lacs Lake as a reservoir, an impoundment. Yet the big lake is just that—and the giant dam is natural, formed by the most important agency to shape the present surface of Minnesota, the glaciation of prehistory. The dam, of course, is the Mille Lacs terminal moraine that curves around the west and south sides of the lake basin and holds back waters flowing south. Wooded hills and lakes mark this morainic area, much of it included in the state park, the Rum River State Forest, and the Mille Lacs Wildlife Management Area.

Farther south, landforms consist largely of sandy outwash plains deposited by flowing glacial meltwater when moraines formed. Here in the sandy plains, lakes and hills are less common.

The big lake constitutes the headwater source of the Rum River which cuts through the Mille Lacs moraine to the south. But to be more precise, farther sources of the Rum lie among the several small streams that flow out of low swamplands into Mille Lacs Lake on the north and east sides. Discounting these, however, the Rum clearly begins as it spills out of the lake (at least in years of normal to high waters) to start its south-flowing course to the Mississippi. But the

Rum is interrupted in its course by three other lakes—Ogechie Lake, Shakopee Lake, and Lake Onamia—in close succession. At the outlet of Ogechie Lake a state-operated dam controls water levels, including that of Mille Lacs; this is the site of old Sioux Indian grounds and is now near the center of recreational activity in Mille Lacs Kathio State Park.

From Mille Lacs, 1,250 feet above sea level, the Rum flows 140 miles to its confluence with the Mississippi in Anoka, dropping about 145 feet. Nearly half the drop occurs in a thirty-mile stretch of river between Onamia and Milaca. The Rum's watershed contains 1,552 square miles, 200 of which are in Mille Lacs Lake. In its course the Rum receives many small tributaries; the only substantial ones are the muddy West Branch, which enters the main stem at Princeton, and Cedar Creek in the lower section. Downstream from Princeton the river diverges temporarily from its southerly course and flows northeast to Cambridge; then it continues south toward Anoka. The alkalinity of the Rum's water is only moderately high at its head (about 75 p.p.m.), but most of the small tributaries, and the West Branch as well, have waters of greater hardness (120 to 130 p.p.m.) so that when the Rum reaches Anoka, its alkalinity is about 100 p.p.m. This is indicative of fairly productive water.

Upstream from Milaca, the Rum is usually clear so that canoeing or wading is a real visual pleasure. Below Princeton, however, the water is much less clear, perhaps due to the West Branch's turbidity, and the river is usually muddier through the rest of its course.

Woodlands along the Rum are predominantly hardwood—oak, elm, ash, maple, willow—with only an occasional pine to remind the river traveler of the pine stands of earlier years. Although the spruce and pine of northern streams are not found here now, the Rum has plenty of wild woods.

Stream flows in the Rum River are not normally subject to frequent or drastic fluctuations, particularly in the upper reaches, because Mille Lacs Lake acts as a natural regulator of flow. Consequently the Rum is notable as a reliable stream for recreational purposes. The annual mean discharge at the mouth is about 600 cubic feet per second, and the minimum flow, even in late summer, rarely is less than 200. The discharge from Mille Lacs Lake typically constitutes about half the total discharge of the Rum in its lower reaches. The record flow, occurring in the spring of 1965, was more than 10,000 cubic feet per second. Some flooding occurs after heavy summer rains, particularly in the reach between Princeton and Cambridge where the valley is shallow, and it results in snags and log jams in this stretch. Flood control projects, including a ditch between Mille Lacs Lake and Onamia to reduce high water levels in the lake and a diversion channel below Princeton, have been proposed; although these projects might possibly alleviate some flooding, they would diminish the natural values of the river, and plans for them have been dropped.

In the mid-1800s the fur trade in Minnesota began to give way to the state's second great industry—logging and lumbering. Sharing honors for great timber resources with its Great Lakes neighbors, Wisconsin and Michigan, Minnesota had an advantage because its many rivers were conveniently located so that logs could be floated out easily from its vast pineries. Furthermore, Minnesota could more easily supply logs to markets on the lower Mississippi, especially the mills at St. Louis, Missouri. The Rum was a significant driving stream; in fact, its location made it perhaps the most important logging stream to the developing Twin Cities.

The Rum bisected the great pine lands of the St. Croix Delta, which, as already noted, contributed great numbers of logs to downstream mills via the St. Croix, Snake, and Kettle rivers. But although it shared the job of carrying the big logs out of the Delta, the Rum was especially important because it emptied into the Mississippi *above the Falls of St. Anthony.* Flowing south through Mille Lacs, Isanti and Anoka counties, it was a perfect transportation route for logs from the Delta to the mills of Minneapolis (then St. Anthony) and other developing markets. The water power of the falls, the rich pineries only forty miles to the north, and the river highway constituted a powerful combination that very early attracted the attention of lumbermen.

As early as 1822 the U.S. government cut pine on the Rum, operated a small sawmill on government reservation lands on the west side of St. Anthony Falls, and cut lumber for the construction of Fort Snelling. The Delta's timber lands were ceded by the Chippewa in 1837, the Rum was first cruised by lumbermen in 1847, and in 1848 commercial sawmills began operation at the falls, cutting Rum River white pine.

During the 1850s land sales were brisk in the Rum River water-

shed, and for two decades the logs rolled down the Rum and Mississippi. Estimated to last almost indefinitely (albeit in early years when
equipment was primitive), the Rum River pine was soon gone. As
early as the 1870s loggers began leaving the Delta, and by the end of
the century the lumberjacks trying to harvest the last of the pine bat-
tled farmers who impatiently awaited the lumbermen's departure.
Together with the Mississippi on the west and the St. Croix on the
east, the Rum, Kettle, and Snake rivers carried away the riches of the
Delta in less than a half century.

Canoeists making the full run on the Rum from
Mille Lacs to Anoka will note three distinct reaches of the stream.

The uppermost, from Onamia to Princeton (excepting the three
lakes at the head), is small, rocky, and clear. It runs almost straight
south from Mille Lacs in this reach, a distance of about sixty-five
river miles. This stretch is not wild—it is crossed by many roads, including U.S. 169. The riverside is not heavily wooded, and much of
the area is in pasture or open field. The course is low and rocky in
late summer of many years, and in high water the river flows under
some small county road bridges making canoe passage impossible.
But it is an intimate, narrow stream here, with rocks to dodge and
clear water and riverbank bushes close at hand. The fishing is good,
and if you do not mind jumping out once in a while to free a stuck
canoe, this stretch can be a lot of fun.

From Princeton to Cambridge, the second stretch, the Rum is
quite different. Here it has already received many tributaries, including the West Branch, and it is noticeably larger. In this stretch the
river flows east instead of south—in fact, it flows back north a little
—and the relationship between its direction of flow and the topography undoubtedly is responsible for the stream's different character.
Here it is slower, larger, deeper, muddier, and much more meandering. Its banks are heavily wooded, and marshy ground often makes
streamside travel on foot difficult. The valley is shallow and the riverbanks are flooded more easily. Four bridges cross this reach, but the
meandering stream has a wild quality despite nearby roads, for the
dense woods muffle the occasional car engine.

The woods, marshy banks, and possible flooding are most significant to the canoeist. Fallen trees and snags are common in this
section, some completely blocking canoe passage. Care should be

The Rum offers many miles of relaxed canoeing close to the Twin Cities. The middle reach, from Princeton to Cambridge, is wild, wooded, and isolated from civilization by the dense stands of hardwoods that line the banks. Streamside trees, however, continue to topple into the river, sometimes creating major obstacles to the canoeist.

taken in approaching these obstacles; the water is often deep, and it is difficult to walk on the banks. Another consequence, however, is that this is the wildest and most remote area of the river. For a distance of thirty-two river miles no whine of traffic is heard; rather, there are sounds of water, wind, and wildlife.

The third and last section of the Rum is from Cambridge to Anoka, thirty-five miles. The river here stretches to the south and runs almost straight again to Anoka and the Mississippi. The valley is deeper, and although woods persist on the high riverbanks, fallen trees and snags are rare. This lower section becomes more civilized, with dwellings and some manicured lawns. It is not as isolated as the previous reach, but the river is broader and the vistas longer. There is room for some fast paddling—or lazy floating. There are even some ropes dangling from overhanging trees, where you can stop for a swing over the river and a drop into the water.

The Rum is a stream for beginning and intermediate canoeists. There are few rapids, but an old dam under the St. Francis bridge may have to be portaged, as well as the municipal dam at Milaca. In low water some shallow riffles will be encountered below St. Francis. The "embarrasses" on the Princeton-to-Cambridge run are the only obstacle. A full week can be spent on the whole length of the stream, but the Rum is close enough to the Twin Cities to provide a canoe trip for just an afternoon. Many access points are available with good parking (and canoe camping at some). In addition to starting points in Mille Lacs Kathio State Park and Onamia, there are wayside parks at Milaca, Princeton, Cambridge, Isanti, and St. Francis, as well as the Anoka County Park at the fairgrounds in Anoka. This is the last landing above the Anoka dam. Parking, canoe rental, and shuttle-service are available at the Anoka site.

The Rum is one of the state's designated canoe trips in *A Gathering of Waters*. The entire river from Mille Lacs Lake to the Mississippi is included. A handy pocket guide entitled "A Boating Guide to the Rum River," also prepared by the Department of Natural Resources, encompasses only the stretch from Princeton to Anoka. The Rum is currently proposed for inclusion in Minnesota's Wild, Scenic, and Recreational Rivers System.

The Rum is well known for smallmouth bass fishing. Paradoxically the smallmouth is not the most abundant game fish in the Rum, even in its favorite spots. But such is the reputation of this species as a hard-fighting fish, especially in swift water, that the smallmouth fishery, like that in the Snake River, has an enthusiastic following. These fish need a moderate-size river—no little creek will do—cool water temperatures (just a little too warm for trout), and clean water flowing over a gravel or rocky bottom. The last provides the foods that smallmouths like: larger aquatic insects, crayfish, minnows, and other small forage fish.

The principal reaches for smallmouth in the Rum are the lower stretch below Cambridge and, in years with good water supply, the upper stretch above Milaca. The latter, when sufficient water is present, is probably the most attractive to anglers—it is small enough to be waded easily, waters are clear and cool, and there are plenty of boulders behind which a fancy fly cast can be laid.

There is also fishing for walleyes and northern pike, often more common in the Rum than the smallmouth, especially in the stretch between Princeton and Cambridge; both are cosmopolitan and not as particular in their choice of habitat as the smallmouth. Large-

Among several good smallmouth bass streams in Minnesota, the upper Rum provides clear water and rocky riffles for the wading fisherman. This one's lure is about to drop into the shaded pool under overhanging trees on the opposite bank, a choice spot for smallmouth.

mouth bass-panfish angling in the impoundment above the Milaca dam is notable, and the lower two miles of Mike Drew Brook, a few miles north of Milaca, as well as several other small tributaries, were once considered good trout waters. Many species characteristic of the lower Mississippi, including channel catfish, white bass, and lake sturgeon, apparently were unable to ascend St. Anthony Falls and thus did not occur in the Rum. However, the Minneapolis Upper Harbor project, completed in 1968, included a lock through the existing St. Anthony Falls dam and has probably permitted the upstream extension in range for these species, including immigration into the Rum.

Although most species of small game occurring in central Minnesota are also found in the Rum River watershed, no single area is particularly noted for hunting. An exception may be the wooded section between Princeton and Cambridge where gray squirrels are plentiful. The Mille Lacs Wildlife Management Area, containing some outstanding grouse and woodcock habitat, lies mostly in the Snake River watershed to the east, but it is closely associated with the upper Rum. Also along the Princeton-to-Cambridge run is the 400-acre Spectacle Lake Wildlife Management Area, which straddles Green Lake Brook, a tributary of the Rum flowing south out of Green Lake. The Spectacle Lake area is managed mostly for waterfowl, although most game species are present—plus wild land beauty and plenty of room for roaming.

Another tributary entering the Rum from the east in the lower part of the watershed is famous as a name in scientific history. Cedar Creek flows through the Cedar Creek Natural History Area, 5,400 acres of protected wild land established as a living museum for study and research by the University of Minnesota and the Minnesota Academy of Science. It is used extensively by students and faculty of the university. The late Raymond L. Lindeman conducted his now classic research on ecosystem dynamics here in Cedar Bog Lake during the 1930s; his work is familiar to ecologists throughout the world.

The shrill cries of Indian warriors are gone now, and so is the rumble of the big log drives. The Rum is not a wild river any longer, but it has acquired through woodland growth new wilderness value. It is close to densely populated centers and good access, and therefore meets many recreational needs. It can serve families and youth groups, and can lead the beginning river traveler to wilder, more distant waterways.

Its values are worth preserving.

Chapter 11

The Crow Wing

Oxcart to Canoe

They say you could hear them coming for miles, long before the string of dust plumes became visible. Made entirely of wood and rawhide, the utilitarian Red River oxcart was for a quarter century the mainstay of trade between the head of Mississippi River navigation at St. Paul and the frontier settlements on the northern Red River. It was a flourishing trade—to be replaced only by the steamboat and the railroad. An oxcart train consisted of as many as eighty or ninety carts divided into brigades of ten carts each; they groaned along at two miles per hour, twenty miles a day.

The all-wood construction and lack of lubrication caused them to squeal—so loudly and distinctively that the sound itself became identified in history with the oxcart era on the western plains. Heard faintly from afar, the shriek was a signal of impending arrival. When the brigades arrived, all other village activities ceased: livestock were frightened, children exhilarated; dogs barked; and church services were postponed because the sermon could no longer be heard.

It was inevitable that the Crow Wing River, with its unique central location, its course from the northwest frontier to the navigable Mississippi, would have at its mouth one of the important way stations and river crossings of the Red River oxcart trails.

From the standpoint of terrain, the easiest route between St. Paul and the Red River was farther south across the flat western prai-

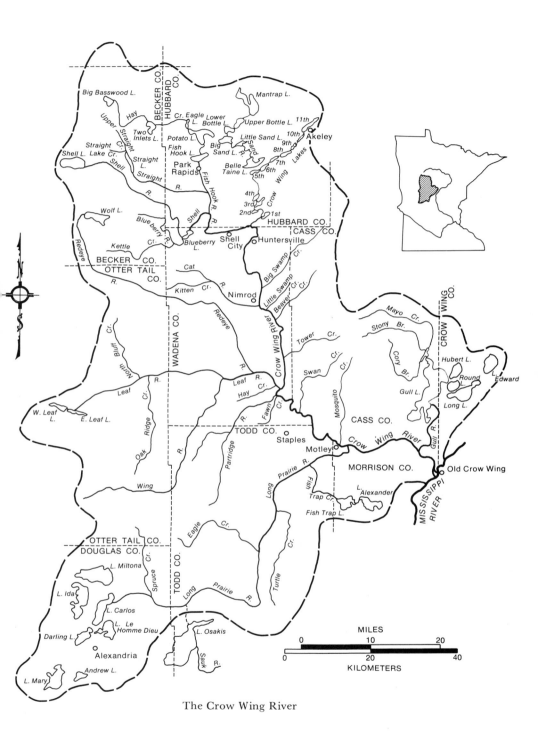

The Crow Wing River

ries. Two plains routes were first established. One, the West Plains Trail, followed the Minnesota River to near its head, crossed the Bois de Sioux north of Lake Traverse, and continued north down the Red River Valley on the west side of the river. The East Plains Trail was more direct: north along the Mississippi to Sauk Rapids, then west to the Red River Valley, and north again over the plains on the east side of the river. The oxcarts carried buffalo robes, other furs, and produce from the northern plains to St. Paul, and they brought general supplies and staples to the settlements.

However, cart trains following the Plains Trails were fully exposed on the prairie land of the Sioux, who were frequently hostile to the intruding brigades. Consequently the Woods Trail was developed to reduce the threat of Indian attack, especially after the 1862 Sioux Uprising along the Minnesota River. This route, in addition to passing through country of the more friendly Chippewa, was shorter. It ran up the Mississippi, crossed the Mississippi north of the mouth of the Crow Wing, followed the Crow Wing to the site of present Motley, and then turned west to the Red River Valley. It joined the East Plains Trail at the crossing of the Wild Rice River, far to the north.

The mouth of the Crow Wing was an important crossroads during several eras of Minnesota history. Early French traders camped and bartered with the Indians at the confluence of the two rivers in the latter half of the 1700s. The area was also the scene of some decisive conflicts between the Sioux and Chippewa. Later, in the early 1800s, English and then American fur-trading posts were established on the east side of the Mississippi across from the mouth of the Crow Wing, and the village of Old Crow Wing came into existence. Allan Morrison and William Aitken, after whom two Minnesota counties are named, operated a trading post and store, respectively, in Old Crow Wing during this period. The village also became the Chippewa capital of Minnesota.

But the decline of fur trading, brought on by overexploitation of fur-bearing animals and continued feuding between the two Indian nations, reduced activity in the settlement. Then in 1844 the first of the oxcart trains on the Woods Trail came through Old Crow Wing, trade became brisk, and the village grew as an outfitting center for the cart trains. The establishment of Fort Ripley in 1848, a few miles south of the Crow Wing on the Mississippi, also stimulated growth of the village.

Old Crow Wing played an important role in the logging of north-central Minnesota, for it lay at the junction of the two important driving rivers. The Chippewa land cession of 1837 stimulated the earliest logging activity. Although this treaty included only those lands on the east side of the Mississippi, and only as far north as the Crow Wing's mouth, some illegal cutting of logs began along both rivers. After the treaties of 1847 and 1855, upstream regions were legally opened to logging, and Old Crow Wing prospered again.

The first river drive from Crow Wing to St. Anthony was in 1848; then river drives came down the Crow Wing and the Mississippi to join at Old Crow Wing, and the village served as staging area and outfitting center for the upriver camps. Logs were driven to the small mill at Old Crow Wing itself and to the larger mills at Little Falls, St. Cloud, and St. Anthony Falls. Logging continued until the end of the nineteenth century, when the pine ran out.

The oxcarts passed into history with the advent of the steamboat and railroad in the Red River Valley. For a while the possibility of a railroad crossing near the confluence of rivers encouraged local hopes of further growth for Old Crow Wing, but in 1871 the Northern Pacific chose instead to cross the Mississippi at Brainerd, and the village withered away.

Today the sites of Indian war, trading posts, river ferry, village establishments, homes, warehouses, and missions are preserved in Crow Wing State Park on the Mississippi across from the Crow Wing's mouth. There are abundant opportunities for canoeing on the river, fishing and boating, picnicking, hiking, and searching out the past in one of Minnesota's most colorful historic centers.

The mouth of the Crow Wing in the Mississippi is divided into two parts. Between these is an island about one-half mile long, which resembles, prehistoric Indians thought, the wing of a raven. Their name for the river, Raven's Wing, was in due time translated, taking some liberty with ornithological nomenclature, to Crow Wing.

The Crow Wing River begins in several series of impressive lakes formed by the melting of rows of buried ice blocks after glaciation: the Crow Wing Lakes, numbered from First to Eleventh. The first, or uppermost headwater lake, is the Eleventh Crow Wing Lake (and the eleventh is the First), a possibly confusing situation. Furthermore, the Crow Wing's first significant tributary, the Shell River, would have been a much better choice as the headwater stem, because its discharge is nearly three times that of the Crow Wing at their confluence.

At any rate, the Crow Wing River starts in the Eleventh Crow Wing Lake in southern Hubbard County and flows for nearly twenty miles through the lake chains. The lower portion of the lake series, between the Fifth and First lakes, is navigable. The lakes, in aggregate surface area, comprise about 5,000 acres.

The Crow Wing River above the mouth of the Shell, the eleven Crow Wing Lakes, and the nearly fifty other lakes in the northern part of the watershed, all lie in what is locally known as Mantrap Valley, named for one of the largest of the lakes, Mantrap. The Crow Wing Lakes are all noted for good fishing; the upper ones (Eleventh through Seventh) are best for largemouth bass and panfish, and the lower ones (Sixth through First) are deeper and are classed as northern pike-walleye lakes. The Fifth is unusual because it has produced a few very large brown trout, probably originating in its tributary Hell Camp Creek, a trout stream. The Tenth is the only one with developed public access, although roads crossing the Crow Wing River between lakes provide fair access for canoes. The river in this lake section produces abundant wild rice, probably more important than the fisheries to local residents.

An interesting and somewhat mystifying phenomenon occurs in the Mantrap Valley; a group of lakes in the area has no visible outlet. The Sand River, which connects Mantrap, Upper and Lower Bottle, Big Sand, Little Sand, and Belle Taine lakes, is large enough for canoeing (up to 200 feet wide). The river flows from lake to lake and finally is tributary to Belle Taine Lake, but there is no surface flow out of Belle Taine. Because soils in the area are quite porous, Belle Taine's outlet may be underground and is thought to connect with the sources of Hell Camp Creek, which rises in several large springs and empties into Fifth Crow Wing Lake.

After leaving the First Crow Wing Lake, the Crow Wing River receives its first large tributary, the Shell River, near the Wadena County line. The Shell and its tributaries, the Fish Hook River (and its main tributary, the Straight River) and Blueberry River, drain another extensive lake area in southwestern Hubbard and eastern Becker counties.

The Shell originates in Shell Lake and flows forty miles to its

The Crow Wing, a superb recreational river for all canoeists, regardless of ability, carries its travelers through a mixture of tall pine and hardwoods.

confluence with the Crow Wing. The upper reaches, just below its source, flow through Smoky Hills State Forest. Although the Shell is a small stream in its headwaters, in the lower fifteen miles it is noticeably larger and can be canoed after it joins the Blueberry River in Blueberry Lake. An established canoe trail includes the lower section of the Shell, from Blueberry Lake to its mouth in the Crow Wing. The principal sport fish in this reach of the Shell is the northern pike.

The quantity of freshwater clams in the Shell is impressive; they are clearly visible in great numbers on the bottom and undoubtedly were the source of the river's name. Shell City, on the Shell River, is now a canoe access and campsite in Huntersville State Forest; before the days of plastic buttons, the town boasted a flourishing button factory utilizing the abundant clam shells.

The Fish Hook River, the major tributary of the Shell, flows from Fish Hook Lake ten miles through Park Rapids and down to its mouth in the Shell. A dam in the city impounds the Fish Hook River in two-mile-long Fish Hook Lake. The Fish Hook offers little sport fishing because the river population is dominated by suckers, although walleyes and northern pike provide some angling. A few brown trout are taken, probably having originated in the tributary Straight River.

From the mouth of the Shell the Crow Wing flows almost directly south through the entire length of Wadena County. In this stretch the Crow Wing collects many small tributaries from each side and two moderately large tributaries from the west—the Red Eye and Leaf rivers which drain lakes located in high morainic regions in the western part of the watershed. In southern Wadena County, Partridge Rivers enters; the Battle of Partridge River took place at its mouth in the winter of 1782-1783. A wintering post of the French and Chippewa was attacked by Sioux, who were successfully beaten off, marking one of the earliest conflicts between whites and the Sioux. The area is now developed as the Old Wadena Historic Site, with extensive picnic grounds and hiking trails.

Leaving the southeastern corner of Wadena County, the Crow Wing is part of the borders of Cass, Todd, and Wadena counties. Below this reach, near Motley, the Crow Wing receives its longest tributary, Long Prairie River, from the southwest. The Long Prairie originates in an area of many lakes near Alexandria in northeast Douglas County; in this area of headwater lakes is Lake Carlos State Park (on Lake Carlos), an area of hardwood timber and bogs. The park has a swimming beach, picnic and campgrounds, and trails. Some miles below Lake Carlos, a diversion ditch has been constructed to connect the Long Prairie with Lake Osakis to the south. This is the headwater lake of the Sauk River, thus connecting the two watersheds during high water. The Long Prairie flows for nearly 100 miles from its lake sources. River fish populations are dominated by redhorses and suckers, whereas the principal sport species is the northern pike, and some walleyes are present, too. Only in the Long Prairie and its headwater lakes have carp been observed in the Crow Wing watershed; they may have entered by way of the diversion ditch from Lake Osakis.

Below Motley, the Crow Wing flows as the border between Cass and Morrison counties to its mouth in the Mississippi at Crow Wing State Park. In this lowermost reach are the only two dams on the river, one at Pillager (forming Lake Placid) and the other near Sylvan (forming Sylvan Lake); each dam has a head of twenty-two feet; both are used to generate hydroelectric power. The Crow Wing also receives the Gull River from the north in this reach; the Gull originates in Gull Lake, a unit of the Mississippi headwaters reservoir system, and flows through a Corps of Engineers' dam at the lake outlet.

The Corps maintains a recreation area at the dam, including picnic and campgrounds and canoe access above and below the dam. The Gull flows fifteen miles to its mouth in Sylvan Lake, the lower impoundment on the Crow Wing; the river contains walleyes, northern pike, and panfish.

The central part of the Crow Wing watershed, through which the main river flows, is a plain of flat to undulating topography nearly surrounded by glacial moraines where many lakes occur. At the end of glaciation the Crow Wing drainage was blocked on the east by the melting ice, and Glacial Lake Wadena with waters up to 130 feet deep covered the plain. The northern part of the watershed is glacial outwash, composed of sandy, porous soils. The result of these topographic and soil characteristics is that the river flows relatively straight with moderate current but without rapids or major falls. The upper part of the valley in Wadena County is heavily forested with jack pine on sandy ridges and streambanks, providing excellent scenic character to the Crow Wing.

Both the Shell and Crow Wing flow through Huntersville State Forest, a flat, jack pine forest on the sandy outwash plain. Several campgrounds are located in the state forest on the streams, including the extensive, developed Huntersville State Forest Campground on the Crow Wing. Parts of Paul Bunyan, Badoura, Foot Hills, Lyons, Smoky Hills, Two Inlets, and Pillsbury state forests, Lake Carlos State Park, and parts of Itasca State Park also lie in the Crow Wing watershed but include no recreational developments on the river. Crow Wing State Forest, to the east in Crow Wing County, is not in the Crow Wing watershed. Crow Wing State Park, the subject of earlier sections of this chapter, is associated with the history of the Crow Wing River but does not lie in the Crow Wing watershed.

Including the headwater chain of eleven Crow Wing Lakes, the river flows over 100 miles to its mouth in the Mississippi. It drains 3,764 square miles, including 1,000 in the Long Prairie watershed. The drop through the eighty-five-mile stretch from the First Crow Wing Lake to the mouth is 215 feet, an average gradient of about 2.5 feet per mile. The mean discharge at the mouth of the Crow Wing is about 1,000 cubic feet per second; of this, the Shell contributes an average of 250, Leaf River about 150, Long Prairie River 200, and Gull River 100. The Crow Wing is remarkably stable in flow, seasonally and also from year to year, because of its sandy soils and the natural regulation of flow by many lakes in the margins of its watershed. Flooding is rare, as is extremely low water. Its usual spring flood discharge is less than 10,000 cubic feet per second, although under the extreme conditions of spring 1965 it exceeded 18,000. Water in the Crow Wing and its main tributaries is extremely clear, has little color, and is not turbid, the result of good groundwater sources, sandy soils, and lack of floods. Alkalinities are moderately high, ranging from 100 p.p.m. in the northern lakes and tributaries to 200 in lower reaches.

Fishing is excellent throughout most of the Crow Wing River and can be easily combined with most other river-based recreational activities. The northern pike is by far the principal sport fish, but rock bass and walleyes are also important elements of the sport fishery. Predominant in the river populations, however, are redhorses and suckers. Although habitat for smallmouth bass appears at first glance to be ideal, this species has not been successful; it occurs in moderate numbers only in the very lowest reaches of the Crow Wing. Species, such as channel catfish and freshwater drum, that originally were not found in the Mississippi above St. Anthony Falls are also absent from the Crow Wing. Except in the Long Prairie River, the carp does not occur abundantly in the Crow Wing watershed; it has recently invaded a number of the Long Prairie headwater lakes and probably will become more common. The species characteristic of lakes—largemouth bass, bluegills, crappies, yellow perch— are mainly limited to the lower reach with its impoundments. The Crow Wing ranks near the top among Minnesota rivers in its sport fisheries. Snapping turtles are also common in the Crow Wing, and "turtling" provides some sport and income for local residents.

The Crow Wing watershed includes the stream in Minnesota probably most widely recognized for trout fishing—the Straight River. Below Straight Lake in eastern Becker County, the Straight flows for fourteen miles. There is excellent brown trout reproduction here; in addition, rainbows are stocked, but these populations do not maintain themselves. The Straight is best known for its large, trophy brown trout, which may be more than twenty inches long. However, the brown is an exceptionally wary species and is taken only by the most skilled and persistent anglers. In late spring, during the nighttime emergence of large mayflies, the big browns are most susceptible, the abundance of mayflies on the water surface often driving the fish into a feeding frenzy. But the fishing is still difficult; pool and streambank must be learned so well that in almost total darkness an angler can cast to the sound of a rising fish and avoid branches and snags on the back cast.

Other trout streams in the watershed are Straight Lake Creek, tributary to Upper Straight Creek above the lake; Hell Camp Creek, tributary to the Fifth Crow Wing Lake; upper Cat River, tributary to the Crow Wing near Nimrod; and Hay and Fawn creeks, tributary to the Crow Wing near Staples. Several small, marginal trout streams occur in the eastern moraines of the watershed. And two small streams with significant good natural reproduction of brook trout are Cory and Stony brooks, tributary to the upper Gull Lake watershed.

The Crow Wing, with its large headwater tributary, the Shell, constitutes one of the major stream systems in Minnesota managed primarily for recreation. Its stable water levels and clarity impart a sparkling quality to the river, an outstanding canoe stream. Only beginning skills are required, yet it remains uncrowded and wild in its visual aspect along most of its length. It is currently proposed as a component of the Minnesota Wild, Scenic, and Recreational Rivers System.

A number of county campgrounds and other accesses have been established at convenient intervals along both the Shell and Crow Wing; most of these are primitive campgrounds where at least the basic needs of the casual canoe camper are met. These are located at the Shell River outlet from Blueberry Lake in northwestern Wadena County, at the old Shell City campsite downstream on the Shell, and at numerous other sites downstream on the Crow Wing. Such sites as Anderson's Crossing, Little White Dog (Little Round Hill), and Bullard's Bluff add historical interest to the route. In addition to county campgrounds, there are others such as the Huntersville Township Campground, Huntersville State Forest Campground, and Knob Hill (which is maintained by personnel of the Wadena Air Base). More than a dozen camp and access sites are located on the two streams. A canoe trip could continue to Motley for landing at a highway wayside or all the way to the mouth in the Mississippi at Crow Wing State Park.

For the canoeist, the Crow Wing can be divided roughly into four major distinctive reaches according to the river's character. The upper twenty miles, from First Crow Wing Lake down to Anderson's Crossing campsite, is relatively flat water with a gradient of less than one foot per mile, sandy bottom, and wide, deep water. This upper reach has a remote quality. Then between Anderson's Crossing and Knob Hill campsite is a rapids reach of some fifteen miles, including virtually all of the Crow Wing's rapids; this reach is shallower and narrower with boulder and rock bottom; average gradient for the entire stretch is about five feet per mile. Below the rapids stretch for thirty-odd miles the river is wider and deeper again, with sandy bottom and lower gradients, down to the town of Motley and the mouth of the Long Prairie River. Even in these wider waters below the rapids reach, the Crow Wing continues to flow past towering hardwoods and pine. Below the Long Prairie the river becomes obviously larger, and soon the effect of the hydroelectric impoundments becomes noticeable. This fourth reach is the dam and impoundment section, more lakelike than river, and extending twenty miles to the mouth; in this reach, crossing the two large hydroelectric reservoirs and portaging around the dams are necessary. There is considerable motorized boat traffic in this area.

Throughout its course, the stream and its densely wooded banks are visually superb. The bottom of the river, whether sand, gravel, or rock, is almost always clearly in sight, and fish are visible everywhere. In many places the river seems choked with rooted aquatic vegetation, but channels can always be found through it, and free flow continues even among the plant beds. For the most part the river is flat water, although strong currents make an easy float; the rapids are modest, and in the driest years the canoeist may merely have to drag over some rocks or, at worst, wade ashore. The Crow Wing canoe route is described and mapped in the state's *A Gathering of Waters*.

The commerce of the northwest no longer utilizes the rivers or the old trails; the high timber on the Crow Wing's banks does not now shelter the frontier trading post; nor will the clear waters ever again thunder with river drives of giant pine logs.

Now the squeal of oxcarts has been replaced by the gentle splash of canoe paddles. But along the river in Crow Wing State Park you can still walk in the ruts worn deeply by the slow carts bound for the markets of St. Paul or the grassy wilderness of the Red River plains.

Chapter 12

The Mississippi

I. The North Woods

The Mississippi River rises in the bogs and spruce swamps of a northern Minnesota wilderness, tumbles down through the state, and then downstream flows sedately through the country's heartland to the warm Gulf of Mexico. The history of the river's influence on the United States is virtually the record of the midnation itself. The river flows from the isolation of northern wild rice beds to the clatter of metropolitan industry. And below St. Anthony Falls, a cataract once wild but now tamed, the river is one of the world's notable commercial waterways, along which fuel, food, and building materials are transported through America's midlands.

The river's recorded history spans only three centuries. But in this period its valley was the source of wild and cultured produce, and the river was the highway to western exploration, a route of early navigation that meandered up the middle of the country and ended in the center of the rich northland that was to become Minnesota. The tragic conflict of two human races, the exultation of discovery, the intrigue of continents at war all took place in the spectacular natural beauty of an immense and verdant river valley.

Conventionally, and for several good reasons, the Mississippi is divided into the Upper and Lower rivers, the dividing point at the mouth of the Ohio River at Cairo, Illinois. The Lower Mississippi is

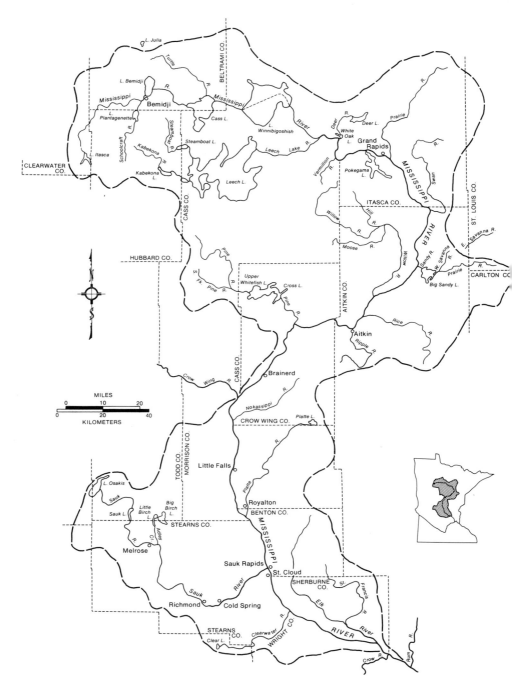

Mississippi River — Lake Itasca to the Crow River

deep, broad, more winding, slower, and muddier than the Upper; there are few obstacles, such as dams or swift rapids, to navigation; it flows through a land of cottonfields and cane, of fertile alluvial deposits, no glacier having penetrated this far south. But the Upper Mississippi country is different; it is a land recently shaped by the glaciers from the north, a land of prairie and forest; the river is smaller, swifter, shallower, and clearer—with so many rapids that twenty-nine locks and dams are required to permit modern navigation from St. Louis to Minneapolis, more than a third of them in Minnesota.

That portion of the river flowing either within or along the border of Minnesota—the portion with which we are concerned here—is only part of the Upper river. But even this relatively small portion, 660 miles, can itself be divided into upper and lower sections—namely, above and below the Twin Cities. Two significant natural events were responsible for this division. The first was the erosion of the valley of the lower Mississippi River by the Glacial River Warren with its huge load of glacial meltwaters. The second was the formation of St. Anthony Falls in the Mississippi, now about eight miles up the Mississippi from the mouth of the Minnesota.

The River Warren, the glacial river that some ten to twelve thousand years ago drained Glacial Lake Agassiz and carved the immense Minnesota Valley, also eroded the Mississippi Valley downstream from the confluence of the two. As a result a wide, deep channel and high bluffs characterize the Mississippi below the junction; in this lower reach it is more like the Minnesota's channel than the upper Mississippi's. Further, flow from the glacial St. Croix River, draining Glacial Lake Duluth, intensified erosion. After the glaciers melted back into Canada, and the glacial lakes found other outlets, the lower Mississippi Valley was partially filled with sediments to 200 feet deep, so that today it is a huge valley with a wide floodplain. In contrast, the upper Mississippi River within Minnesota is a small river in a shallow valley with modestly sloping sides, and it tumbles down from northern forests in many swift rapids.

St. Anthony Falls also significantly affected the character of the upper river. It was an obstacle to the upstream dispersal of river fishes as well as to the movement of the vessels of early travelers. The falls determined the location of Minneapolis, and the use to which man put the river was different above and below the falls. Even the characteristics of aquatic life above and below the falls are different. The contrast between the sections is so marked that the entire river above the Twin Cities is sometimes referred to as the Mississippi headwaters.

So, if you speak of the Upper Mississippi in Minnesota, define your term: It could be understood as either the stretch above Cairo or as the shorter "headwaters" above St. Anthony Falls!

Statistics are often boring; but concerning the Mississippi they are at least impressive. In terms of volume of flow, or discharge, it is the largest river in North America, the seventh largest in the world. (The flow of the Amazon dwarfs even that of the Mississippi—it is fourteen times as great; the Nile is considered the longest.) Draining all or parts of thirty-one states and two Canadian provinces, the Mississippi basin is one and a quarter million square miles in size (larger than the Nile's). The river drains the *Sphagnum* bogs of the North Woods and draws off the high mountain snows of the Rockies to the west (via the Missouri River) and the spring rains of the Appalachians to the east (via the Ohio River). From Lake Itasca the mighty river flows 2,350 miles to the Gulf of Mexico—660 of these within or along Minnesota.

The history of the Mississippi began many hundreds of millions of years ago. Several times warm tropical seas covered the base rocks of much of Minnesota, and the sediment at the bottom of those ancient oceans formed the stratified rock, such as sandstone and limestone, that now constitutes the great bluffs along the lower river.

But only about a million years ago the series of events having the greatest effect upon Minnesota's present landscape began to unfold across the region. This was the beginning of the Pleistocene epoch—when gigantic layers of ice as much as two miles thick ground across the land, melted back, and pressed forward again—scraping and leveling, mixing and molding, melting and depositing mounds, plains, and great ranges of morainic hills.

The Mississippi's course below St. Paul was essentially established before the last glaciation, although copious meltwaters carved it and shaped it locally. But the upper river, above St. Anthony Falls, is entirely the result of the most recent glaciation. Its course, its topography, the shape and thickness of deposits over and through which the Mississippi and its tributaries flow—all were determined by the moving and melting ice.

Ten thousand years ago the last glacial stage was ending. Primitive man had dispersed across the habitable parts of North America—perhaps coming from Asia—and pressed northward behind the retreating glaciers. South of the melting ice ranges, he followed the winding trickles of the early Mississippi and hunted the woolly mammoth, the mastodon, musk ox, and giant bison, gathered wild fruits and vegetables, and took shelter in caves under the river's bluffs. He first made weapons from chipped rock, later hammered out utensils and tools from copper, learned primitive agriculture, and began to make pottery. At about the time of Christ the woodland Indian culture was almost as white explorers first found it in Minnesota. Throughout the upper Mississippi watershed, the Dakota, or Sioux, lived amid the forests, streams, and lakes of northern Minnesota.

To the east, however, the Chippewa and their relatives, ancient enemies of the Sioux, threatened. Later, with guns and techniques acquired from the French, the Chippewa's aggressions were more effective, and the border between the two groups, always vague and in contention, moved sporadically but conclusively southwest across the upper Mississippi watershed toward the prairies. The conflict was not to end until the Sioux rose up in frustration to battle the white intruders along the Minnesota River in 1862 and thereafter were banned from the new state.

The French were the first Europeans to leave their mark upon the upper Mississippi. Arriving in the midst of the Indian conflict, they attempted to serve as peacemakers. They had, of course, discovered the rich supply of beaver, and they depended, after all, upon the Indians for the initial harvest of these aquatic mammals. Their peace-keeping efforts were sometimes successful, but only temporarily.

The French had a more lasting effect in another way, however, for the northern wilderness was opened by their quest for furs and was exploited in turn by the English and the Americans. Searching for a route to the Pacific and the riches of the Orient, Du Luth entered the upper Mississippi country from Lake Superior in 1679. Father Hennepin came from downriver the next year and was taken captive by the Sioux and kept at their Mille Lacs Lake capital. He visited the great falls on the Mississippi and named it after his patron saint, St. Anthony of Padua; Father Hennepin was later released from his captors by Du Luth.

Then, along the wind-swept marshes of the Gulf of Mexico at the big river's mouth, La Salle in 1682 claimed the vast, uncharted watershed of the Mississippi for King Louis XIV, naming it Louisiana. And the French proceeded with exploration from both north and south.

In 1763 following defeat in the Seven Years War, the French gave up their territory east of the Mississippi, and then the British took their turn. Jonathan Carver, also in quest of a northern inland passage to the Pacific, journeyed on the upper Mississippi and upstream on the Minnesota (Chapter 18).

Then came the Revolutionary War and independence for the United States. The British were slowly forced out—to Canada. When in 1803 Napoleon sold the Louisiana Territory to the Americans, all lands west of the Mississippi were included in the expanding new nation, and virtually all of the Mississippi country was then part of the United States. Shortly thereafter, President Jefferson ordered intensified exploration of the western American wilderness.

It has long been true that those who paddle up strange rivers become obsessed with the search for the source. So it was with the Americans surveying new possessions—especially because their territory now contained, at some unknown place in the northern wilderness, the source of the mighty Mississippi!

As early as 1700 Du Charleville, a relative of New Orleans founder Bienville, ascended the Mississippi and proceeded a short distance beyond St. Anthony Falls in search of the river's source. With tongue in cheek, the Sioux told him that the river extended up again as far as it flowed down to its mouth. Disappointed, Du Charleville returned, convinced that the Mississippi originated near the Arctic Ocean.

Lieutenant Zebulon Pike, under orders to acquire lands for military posts and to seek the Mississippi's source, sailed by keelboat from St. Louis in 1805, bound for the upper river. At the mouths of both the Minnesota and St. Croix rivers, he successfully negotiated with the Sioux for lands to build military posts—certainly one of the most important diplomatic achievements of the day. Eventually, on the parcel of land at the mouth of the Minnesota, historic Fort Snelling was built, and the city of Minneapolis was developed on the west side of St. Anthony Falls. Looking for the river's source farther upstream, Pike was caught by the northern winter, but he built a fort near Little Falls and, after the river froze, continued on by foot and sleigh. He arrived at Leech Lake via Leech Lake River, and the Indians informed him that the big lake was the source. Not satisfied, Pike traveled overland to Cass Lake (then known as Red Cedar Lake), which he proclaimed the source.

Italian adventurer Count Giacomo Beltrami was the next to try. Romantic, an exile and freebooter who defied contemporary custom, he arrived at Fort Snelling in 1823 on the steamboat *Virginia*, apparently already planning to search for the Mississippi's origins. From Fort Snelling, Beltrami accompanied an exploratory expedition up the Minnesota and down the Red River of the North. Beltrami left the group at Pembina and headed southeast by canoe and foot to find the source of the Mississippi. His search ended at a small lake north of present Bemidji, which he named Lake Julia, and he proclaimed it the source. Wrong again—but he was close. While returning to civilization with a Chippewa guide, the Indian told him of Lac la Biche (Elk Lake, later named Itasca!), west of Lake Bemidji; he reported that a tributary stream of the Mississippi originated there. Beltrami named it the *western* source, without having visited it, but named Lake Julia the northern and true source. Unknown to him, the outlet waters of Lake Julia flowed north only to the Red River.

In 1820, a few years before the Italian count's overland hike, Lewis Cass, Governor of Michigan Territory which then included Minnesota, led an expedition from Detroit through the upper Great Lakes and overland to Red Cedar Lake. The lake was renamed Cassina in the Governor's honor (later changed to Cass), but he went no farther. However, a young geologist in the party, Henry Rowe Schoolcraft, was unconvinced that this was the true source. Thus later, when Schoolcraft obtained governmental sanction to lead an expedition into the upper Mississippi country (once more, to attempt to reconcile the battling Chippewa and Sioux), the final search for the great river's origin began.

From Lake Bemidji, Schoolcraft's route took him, not by way of the actual Mississippi, but south through Lake Plantagenette and then up the smaller river that now bears his name, and overland to the Mississippi headwater lake. The party, with a Chippewa guide, arrived at Lac la Biche on July 13, 1832. The name was changed on the spot to Lake Itasca by dropping the first and last syllables of the Latin *veritas caput*. Lake Itasca, the true head, was found. The great search was over at last. Schoolcraft's expedition attained the previous explorers' principal objective, and the discovery phase of exploration on the Mississippi closed.

The Mississippi River below its origin in Lake Itasca winds down through a northern wilderness of spruce swamp and wild rice.

One more explorer, however, was drawn to the stream's upper course—not by adventure but by the desire to measure and record the river's resources and physical characteristics. In 1836 Joseph N. Nicollet, a Frenchman, ascended the Mississippi to Lake Itasca and spent three days surveying, measuring the lake's latitude, longitude, and elevation, and preparing maps of the area as well as records of his observations. Nicollet's trained, inquiring, and analytical mind provided the first reliable technical observations of the morphometry of the river's source; these were the first of many records of the northwestern wilderness he was to prepare.

When the French explorers, priests, and fur traders first probed the western Great Lakes and upper Mississippi region during the latter half of the 1600s, they found a strange, rugged country, where many narrow streams and innumerable lakes made travel difficult. But the French quickly adopted the Indian's means of relatively easy travel through the watery maze: the birch-bark canoe.

Unlike the heavy dugouts of the lower river's Indians, the bark canoe of the northern tribes was light enough to carry over portages, yet generally tough enough to withstand the pummeling of small, fast streams. Best of all, the materials for construction and repair were always handy—birch trees for bark, white cedar for ribs, spruce resin, and black spruce roots ("wattape") for binding.

With the canoe the French followed the Indians and the beaver, and trappers reached the tiniest streams and brought out furs of many kinds, mostly beaver, from the farthest corners of the forests. Jolliet and Marquette, in their first downriver probe, followed by La Salle, Hennepin, Le Sueur, Carver, as well as others later seeking the source upriver, employed the highly portable, readily constructed birch-bark canoe.

In the late 1700s and early 1800s traders of the North West Company removed great quantities of furs from the upper Great Lakes and Mississippi country (Chapter 4). In this exploitation of riches, the *canot du nord*—North canoe—was the usual means of travel on the streams and lakes of the Mississippi headwaters, and it was unsurpassed as a common carrier for two centuries.

The upper Mississippi country was not settled in the usual sense. The northern wilderness was tamed not by the immigrant settler with oxen and plow but by the logger with ax and saw.

The first large area of pineland acquired from the Indians was the St. Croix Delta in 1837; lying between the St. Croix and Mississippi rivers, it was the richest timberland in the land of Minnesota. Logging followed soon after. Ten years later another large section of pineland west of the Delta, on the west side of the Mississippi River, was ceded.

Logging along the uppermost Mississippi headwaters, however, began later, after 1855 when the Mississippi Band of Chippewa ceded a large area in north-central Minnesota including watersheds of the river and its tributaries from the mouth of the Crow Wing up. This cession opened vast new timberlands, triple the area of the Delta. True, they were not as rich as the Delta with its white pine five or six feet in diameter; but still, with white pine three or four feet in diameter and plenty of red, or Norway, pine, it was extremely valuable land.

The Panic of 1857 and then the Civil War at first retarded development of the upper river pinelands. But after the war, logging and the lumber industry grew at a rapid pace.

The timber cruiser, rugged individualist and lone traveler, was the first into a prospective area. Measuring the potential board feet of trees still standing, the cruiser provided the basic data on which lumber company decisions were made—the basis of fortunes risked and won. The cruiser was also concerned about the availability of close driving streams, for the value of standing timber was inversely proportional to the distance from a river capable of transporting logs.

Then the tote road was built from town, or other source of supply, to the location where the logging camp would be built; the tote road served not to haul logs, but as the route of supply and maintenance for the camp. From the camp where the lumberjacks were housed and fed during the winter cutting season, went the crews six days a week. Choppers felled the big pines, using their skill with muscle and ax. Later, in the mid-1870s, the crosscut saw came into use, and sawyers felled a tree and then cut it into convenient lengths, usually sixteen feet, as it lay on the ground. Oxen and horses were used to skid single logs out of the woods to the logging road, and here, on the road that was hard and slick with a bed of ice up to eighteen or twenty inches thick, big sleigh loads were piled high. Sometimes more than 100 tons of logs were piled on a single sleigh pulled by a team of two horses. The sleigh loads were hauled to the river landing and unloaded on the bank. There the logs were scaled, to estimate the yield in board feet, and then a distinctive log mark, like a cattle brand, was placed on them with a stamp hammer.

During the winter the piles of logs grew larger at these river landings or rollways. But when the snow melted in the warm days of spring, and the river swelled with meltwater, the logs were let go and the drive was on.

Many lumberjacks left the security of the lumber camps for the white-water adventure of the river drive. It was often a cold, wet job —and hunger was common, too, for the logs would sometimes outrun the floating cookshack. River driving was a dangerous job—a single misstep and a riverman was ground beneath the crush of oncoming great logs. Many anonymous graves lined the route of the log drives.

The crews attending the spring drive, ingloriously known as river pigs, were divided functionally into three groups. The *driving crew* was in the vanguard, keeping the logs moving and out of side channels and shoals. Following, in the main aggregation, was the *jam crew*; these were the elite of the river pigs, keeping the channels clear and jams from forming—if they did form, this crew risked their skill and their necks to find the key, offending log and break the jam. At the tail of the drive was the *rear crew*, searching out and freeing stray logs, moving from one side of the river to the other in their bateaux—sharp-prowed boats about thirty feet long—prodding and pulling stray logs out of flood-inundated swamps back into the main current.

On the smaller streams that fed into the Mississippi and its larger tributaries, auxiliary logging dams were built. These dams held back the springtime meltwaters until a large head accumulated; then it was released and a man-made flood would pour downstream, carrying the logs on the rushing tide to a bigger river. Many of these small dams were constructed in the upper Mississippi country, even in the uppermost headwaters where dams built just below the outlet of Lake Itasca raised the level of the lake itself to carry the logs that had been cut and landed on the lake. Parts of many of these old dams still remain on the smaller streams in the upper river country.

On the Mississippi, logs were first driven directly to the mill, which was powered by the river current and cut lumber for local use. Later, the floating logs were caught and held in large booms—strings of logs tied from one riverbank to the other—sorted by log mark, indicating ownership, into boom pockets and then tied together into huge rafts. These rafts were first floated and later pushed or pulled by steamboats down to the mills.

In the mid-1850s the first rafts were floated downriver on the Mississippi from the St. Croix mills to southern markets. These rafts of sawn lumber were made up of many *cribs*, each crib a 16-foot-wide, 32-foot-long pack of lumber. Cribs were joined into longitudinal *strings*, up to 500 feet long. A raft was made up of eight to ten strings, side by side. The whole raft, then, was about two acres!

It was soon discovered that log rafts, as well as lumber rafts, could profitably be floated to mills far downriver that also needed raw materials. These rafts were made up of strings, too, and were about the same size as the lumber rafts.

To guide the rafts around bends and to keep them off shoals and riverbanks, oars or sweeps were employed at the bow and at the stern. An oar, a forty-five-foot-long plank, was operated by one man. As the raft was to navigate a bend, the bow sweeps swung the bow end in one direction, and the stern sweeps made the raft follow around.

A particular problem in rafting on the Mississippi was the unreliable condition of Lake Pepin. In slow currents—or worse, with upstream winds—it was a long, tedious job of cordelling (hauling with lines) down the lake. The same difficulty occurred in Lake St. Croix on the St. Croix River above its mouth in the Mississippi. As early as the 1840s steamboats were employed to assist the rafts through these two lakes—by towing with a line astern. Later it was found to be more efficient to *push* rather than pull the rafts, predating the barge "tows" of modern time. Oars were used at the bow for steering, but later the steamboat was used at the rear as a movable rudder, shifting its position relative to the raft, to steer the raft. To assist in the steering of these "towed" rafts, small steamboats were sometimes used at the bow of the raft, to move the bow sideways.

Although the first commercial sawmills in Minnesota were at Stillwater on the St. Croix, giant mills were built not long after at St. Anthony and Minneapolis and were powered by St. Anthony Falls. And Minneapolis mills, in 1890, led the world in lumber production. Winona, on the Mississippi in southern Minnesota, was also the site of important lumber mills in this period, cutting logs from both the St. Croix and Mississippi.

Minneapolis and Winona were the principal sawmill towns on the Mississippi River, but other mills farther upstream also produced much lumber from headwater pinelands in the 1870s and 1880s. Mills at Anoka, St. Cloud, Little Falls, Brainerd, Aitkin, Grand Rapids, and Bemidji were developed in turn to cut the big pine as logging moved north up the Mississippi. Some especially rich white pine lands lay in Itasca and Cass counties, and much of this land, now in second-growth timber, is incorporated in the Chippewa National Forest. Logs from these lands were eventually driven down the upper Mississippi.

Many rafts, made up at Reads Landing at the lower end of Lake Pepin on the Mississippi, were towed all the way to St. Louis. That city was built largely of Minnesota white pine, as were the off-river cities of Omaha, Kansas City, Des Moines, and Topeka.

The sleigh-haul road, or "winter road," extended back from the riverbank or lakeshore at best only ten miles; large areas of standing timber were left unharvested, or at least not recovered. Some other way to bring out the logs was needed, and the logging railroad was the answer. After 1900 private logging railroads assisted in moving the logs out of the woods.

Not that the river drive was gone — far from it. The logging railroads simply brought the logs from the cutting grounds to the river landings where the river drive down to the mills began. Until the supply of big timber was exhausted, the major rivers — the Mississippi and its principal tributaries — continued to serve as the main arteries of log transportation. But the railroads penetrated remote corners of the north woods, bringing out to river rollways logs that were too far removed from the stream for horses to transport them. Before main-line railroads could replace the river drives, the big pine was gone.

The peak of lumber production in Minnesota occurred in 1905, and the Minneapolis mills declined rapidly after that. The Duluth mills took over leadership, sending lumber east through the Great Lakes. The last great log drive on the Mississippi was in 1919.

The logging industry along the upper Mississippi country was slow to start, gained momentum during the time the great pinelands were thought to be inexhaustible, created a boom that made fortunes, and died quickly. It left in its wake legends and a vast, treeless region further desolated by fires. A few scattered virgin pine, such as the stands in Itasca State Park and some in national forests, are extant; also, old individuals remain along the riverbanks.

Even after Henry Schoolcraft found his way to Lake Itasca in 1832, and Joseph Nicollet mapped the area more precisely in 1836, the question of who should receive credit for the discovery of the true source of the Mississippi remained in contention. Some claimed an earlier visit to Lac la Biche, and others claimed that a different lake was the real source. Some later geographers even contended that the Missouri is the major upper river and that, from a strictly geographic standpoint, it is the Upper Mississippi that is a tributary of the Missouri. (With some reason: the Missouri is 1,500 miles longer than the Upper Mississippi!)

It is true that Lake Itasca itself has several small tributaries and that these in turn flow out of somewhat higher lakes. Nevertheless, it is generally conceded that the Itasca basin is the essential reservoir of collected waters that form the head of the great river.

The outlet stream, little more than ten feet wide, flows past a lateral series of stepping-stone boulders and the famous post into which are carved statistics of the river's total fall in elevation and length (now in error since the Army Corps of Engineers shortened the river about 200 miles!) and leaves Lake Itasca with a discharge of barely one cubic foot per second but with an undisputed riverine character.

Surrounding the headwater lake and enclosing many other lakes and streams is Itasca State Park, Minnesota's second largest with 29,400 acres. In addition to memorializing the great river's headwaters, this park includes some of the oldest virgin stands of red and white pine. The University of Minnesota's Lake Itasca Forestry and Biological Station and the Itasca Wilderness Sanctuary of 2,000 acres dedicated to scientific study are also within the park.

Flowing north from the lake in southeastern Clearwater County, the river immediately enters an area of swamp and forest, with the remoteness and beauty of the wild north. Across the northwest corner of Hubbard County and southern Beltrami County, the river meanders—sometimes markedly—making a roughly quarter-circle path clockwise toward Bemidji, a distance of eighty miles, and finally entering Lake Bemidji. This is an area of spruce and fir, wild rice marsh, and pine-topped ridges. The river can be canoed for virtually the entire distance, although a start a few miles below Lake Itasca at a road crossing would probably be more convenient. Almost this entire reach is now enclosed in a segment of the Mississippi Headwaters State Forest. Most is quiet water, but some rapids, beaver dams, and confusing marshes are encountered. Several access points and campgrounds are available in this section, including places with intriguing names like Wannigan, Coffee Pot, Bear Den, Pine Point, and Iron Bridge landings. Bear Den is one of the more picturesque, as well as convenient for a midway stop. An excellent canoe guide for this sector is "Our Headwaters Canoe Trail," by Rivers R. Elliott; the state's river guide, *A Gathering of Waters*, maps the entire canoe and boating route from Lake Itasca down to the Twin Cities. Only one low dam (Vekins Dam, an old logging structure) and no large lakes mar the wild aspect of the upper section. And few tributaries enter—the only major one is Schoolcraft River, which rises in central Hubbard County and flows north through several lakes before entering the Mississippi just south of Bemidji. The uppermost reaches of Schoolcraft River are trout waters, as are Sucker Brook and La Salle Creek in and north of Itasca State Park.

Lake Bemidji State Park, with its virgin pine and timbered lake-

shore, graces the north end of Lake Bemidji. Leaving the lake, the
Mississippi swings to the east out of Beltrami County and then southeast across Cass County and into Itasca County toward Grand Rapids,
a distance of about 125 miles. This section, still forested and northern in aspect, nevertheless has lost the wild character of the previous
shorter reach. Here it is a river-lake stretch; after Lake Bemidji, it
passes through Cass Lake and giant Lake Winnibigoshish as well as
several smaller lakes. The river's power has been harnessed, for Army
Corps headwater dams have been constructed on the river at the outlet of Winni and in Grand Rapids (the latter impounding Pokegama
Lake tributary to the river), as well as on Leech Lake River at Leech
Lake's outlet. A hydropower dam has also been installed on the Lake
Bemidji-to-Cass Lake channel; in much of this reach the river flows
through beds of wild rice. The Blandin Paper Mill dam at Grand Rapids creates the Blandin Reservoir, downstream from the Corps dam;
it is about three miles long.

Lake Winnibigoshish, well known as one of Minnesota's most
productive walleye lakes, occupies fifteen miles of the river's route.
And about twenty-five miles below Winni is White Oak Lake, site of
the proposed and controversial Days High Landing dam across the
river. The principal purposes of the dam, its proponents argue, are to
enhance wild rice and wildlife production. The benefits to wild rice
and wildlife have been questioned, and there is little doubt that the
dam would impede river travel and create a more artificial landscape.

Also in contrast with the headwaters reach, this section of the
river receives a number of major tributaries. These include Turtle
River, which empties into Cass Lake from the north and which was
thought by Beltrami to flow from Lake Julia as the headwaters of
the Mississippi; Leech Lake River, a twenty-five-mile-long stream
emanating from Leech Lake, on which is the important Mud-Goose
Wildlife Management Area; Deer River, entering from the north
through the White Oak Lake project; and Vermillion River from the
south entering the Mississippi through Schoolcraft State Park, one of
the most attractive and uncrowded state parks on the river where the
primitive natural beauty of the riverbanks has been retained. Two important streams enter Leech Lake at its western, or upstream, side.
One is Steamboat River, the more northern, which flows through
Steamboat Lake and then into Leech through Steamboat Bay, one of
the larger sections of Leech Lake; in its upstream reach, Steamboat
River receives Bungoshine and Pockedee creeks, both small brook

trout streams. South of Steamboat River, however, is probably the best-known and most productive brook trout stream in the state — Kabekona River. Flowing for about fifteen miles, it empties into Kabekona Lake and Kabekona Bay of Leech and has some smaller brook trout creeks as tributaries.

At Grand Rapids the Mississippi crosses the western end of the Mesabi iron range. And then in its flow about 125 miles to Aitkin, southwesterly across most of Aitkin County, the character of the Mississippi changes markedly. Current velocity is much lower, and the stream meanders more. Grand Rapids was the head of navigation in the days of steamboat travel on the upper river. The watershed is wooded, with hardwoods here in contrast to the conifers of the north, and in places the river flows through open marsh areas. About halfway down this stretch, Big Sandy Lake, lying just to the east, discharges Sandy River into the Mississippi through another of the Army Corps of Engineers headwater reservoir dams. This lake was on the major route of exploration and fur trading from the Great Lakes, for the Savanna rivers through Big Sandy provided a link between the Great Lakes and the Mississippi (Chapter 2). Savanna Portage State Park, including the old portage trail, commemorates the historic passage; the park is surrounded and complemented by Savanna State Forest.

Downstream from Big Sandy Lake the river swings southwest and flows over the lake bed of old Glacial Lake Aitkin which, as noted earlier, once received the "upstream-flowing" waters of the St. Louis. The river is slower and deeper in this flat, marshy country with many wild rice paddies. Banks and bottom are clay-lined. One result of this topography was flooding in the vicinity of the town; this is now mitigated by the Aitkin Diversion Channel, a wide, six-mile-long ditch that cuts off a large meandering loop, bypassing Aitkin in time of flood.

Besides Sandy River, the outlet from Big Sandy Lake, there are four major tributaries in this reach: Prairie and Swan rivers, both with moderate current and some swift rapids, enter from woodlands northeast of Grand Rapids; the Willow and Rice rivers enter in the vicinity of Aitkin from the northwest and east, respectively — both drain the swampy, flat glacial lake bed. Along the upper Willow, in Hill River State Forest, is the large Moose-Willow Wildlife Management Area, including important breeding habitat for waterfowl and much wild rice; the area covers twenty-five square miles on the headwaters of the Willow, Moose, and Hill rivers. Rice River flows through the Rice Lake National Wildlife Refuge, east of Aitkin.

From Aitkin to the mouth of the Crow Wing River the Mississippi flows southwest roughly along the north edge of the Cuyuna iron range and west across Crow Wing County for a distance of sixty miles. Although here it still flows across the bed of Glacial Lake Aitkin into central Crow Wing County, the river is less meandering and has cut a deeper valley. Flowing almost westerly then, the Mississippi leaves the flat lake bed and enters one of the most delightful areas of its northern watershed, the pine ridges, sand hills, and clear-water lakes of the Crow Wing State Forest north of Brainerd. The river is shallow and swifter here, with sand, gravel, and rocky bottoms. The major tributary is the Pine River, a clear, gravel-bottom stream that originates in the lake-and-hill country of Foot Hills State Forest in western Cass County, flows through the Whitefish chain of lakes, the Army Corps of Engineers' dam at the outlet of Cross Lake, and down through jack pine hills and wild swampy forest to its mouth in the Mississippi. The Pine itself is an excellent, little-publicized canoe stream of great beauty, especially in the lower section of fifteen miles below the lakes. Good access is available at the Cross Lake dam, and there is a landing at the crossing of Crow Wing County Road 11, a mile above its mouth. The clarity of the water is outstanding. Below the mouth of the Pine, a dam in Brainerd spans the river—the Northwest Paper Company dam which impounds Rice Lake reservoir, affecting the river for about twelve miles.

The major reach of river from the mouth of the Crow Wing to the Twin Cities courses through the heartland of the state. It is little known and little used, moving from hardwood timber wilderness to broad treeless prairie to metropolitan industry. The river in most of this reach flows across the broad outwash plains between Little Falls and the Twin Cities, through oak savannah, originally a tall grass prairie with scattered bur oaks. The river runs fairly straight, with relatively little meandering, for 135 miles to St. Anthony Falls. It flows south from Morrison County, then forms parts of the borders of six counties—Stearns, Benton, Wright, Sherburne, Hennepin, and Anoka.

In this reach several of the largest tributaries enter; first the Crow Wing River from the west, the largest tributary above the Twin Cities (Chapter 11). Opposite the mouth of the Crow Wing is Crow Wing State Park, an area rich with history of Indian, explorer, and fur trader, and a major junction and crossing of the Red River oxcart trails. Downstream a few miles the Nokassippi enters from the east, a much smaller stream whose mouth is just across the main river from the site of pioneer Fort Ripley, built in 1849 as the northernmost military post on the Mississippi to help restrain the warring Chippewa. The Platte River enters the Mississippi from the east in northern Benton County near Royalton, after flowing about forty-eight miles from its source in Platte Lake in southern Crow Wing County.

In this stretch are located the major main-stem dams on the Mississippi in Minnesota: the Minnesota Power and Light Company dam at Little Falls, the Blanchard Dam near Royalton, which impounds six-mile-long Zebulon Pike Lake, the St. Regis Paper Company dam at Sartell, the old Whitney hydroelectric dam at St. Cloud (forerunner of Northern States Power Company but no longer operating), and the large inoperative Coon Rapids hydroelectric dam just above the Twin Cities.

The Sauk River, another major tributary in this reach, flows from Lake Osakis in the western Minnesota hill country of Douglas and Todd counties, and courses nearly 100 miles east and south. It passes through many natural lakes, the maze of Cedar Island Lake in southern Stearns County, and a hydroelectric dam at Cold Spring, dropping a total of 340 feet. It enters the Mississippi at Sauk Rapids, named for the turbulent rapids in the Mississippi at the confluence. The mean discharge of the Sauk at its mouth is approximately 250 cubic feet per second, about one-twentieth of the Mississippi's flow at that point.

Some lower portions of the Sauk, from Sauk Lake downstream (Stearns County), offer good canoeing when water levels are suitable. Some interesting river-lake canoeing is possible in the maze of lakes near Richmond, and moderate white-water runs can be made, at higher water levels, in the lowest few miles from Rockville to the mouth in the Mississippi. When the water is sufficiently high, the entire run from Sauk Lake to the mouth—nearly 100 miles—can be made by canoe. The dams at Melrose and the hydroelectric plant at Cold Spring, and perhaps smaller ones as well, must be portaged. The nearby state campground at Birch Lakes State Forest is particularly attractive, the lakes on the Todd and Stearns county line are extremely clear and reminiscent in many ways of more northern regions. Little Sauk, Duel, and Round Prairie creeks in the same area are tumbling, small brook trout streams.

Downstream on the Mississippi the Clearwater River enters from the west, heading in the northeast corner of Meeker County, flowing through Clearwater Lake near Annandale and into the Mississippi at the town of Clearwater. A number of small tributaries to the Clearwater River are trout streams; one of the more notable is Fairhaven Creek, which has a naturally reproducing brook trout population.

Elk River empties into the Mississippi at the town of Elk River; after flowing about fifty miles from its origin in northern Benton County and dropping 200 feet, the Elk enters the Mississippi through Orono Lake, a municipal hydropower reservoir of Elk River. Its mean discharge, similar to the Sauk, is about 250 cubic feet per second. The middle and lower reaches of the Elk, flowing through deciduous woodlands with waters of excellent clarity, should offer fine canoeing. A major tributary of the Elk is the St. Francis River, flowing through Sand Dunes State Forest and the Sherburne National Wildlife Refuge; the St. Francis offers some canoeing at higher water levels, including opportunities for wildlife observation.

At Dayton on the Hennepin-Wright county line, the Crow River enters the Mississippi. The Crow, draining one of central Minnesota's principal watersheds, is composed basically of two branches, the North and South forks. Of these two, the North Fork is perhaps the most important for recreational purposes. Originating in Grove Lake in eastern Pope County, the North Fork flows as a very small stream to Lake Koronis, from which the main North Fork is generally considered to start. For some miles below Lake Koronis, the stream has been ditched and straightened, but from the crossing of Minnesota Highway 22 (start of the canoe route in *A Gathering of Waters*) the North Fork is clear and free-flowing, alternating between scenic rapids and pleasant pools. It has neither north-woods character nor plunging white water, but the North Fork is not monotonous. The stream environment is a mixture of woodland, prairie, and farmland; the river is moderately challenging to the canoeist and altogether attractive. Except in the high water of spring, it is clear and fresh, with unspoiled wooded or pastured stream banks, a valuable part of the state's flowing-water recreational resources. It is featured in a canoeing guide map prepared by the Minnesota Department of Natural Resources, "A Boating Guide to the North Fork, Crow River," describing about forty miles from Forest City to Albright. Roughly the same reach of river has now been designated a unit in the Minnesota Wild, Scenic, and Recreational Rivers System, forty miles from Lake Koronis to the Meeker-Wright county line near Kingston.

Under the lacy greenery of early spring, entrants in a paddle-splashing canoe race on the South Fork of the Crow River near Lester Prairie compete for prizes and prestige.

For about fifty miles the North Fork maintains its character of gentle wilderness. Eventually, though, in central Wright County, its load of agricultural sediment increases and, in a ditched and channelized stream bed, it becomes a dull, muddy stream. The South Fork, a larger, slower, muddier stream, joins the North Fork near Delano; even the South Fork, though, has its attractions—one of which is the annual Lions-supported canoe race, a competitive event that draws both local and distant canoeists in a wild, paddle-flashing run down its spring-swollen course. Then from the Rockford dam downstream, the Crow main stem is a large river, dammed again at Hanover and again at historic Berning's Mill, where lumber was recently sawed with direct mechanical power. The Crow empties into the Mississippi at Dayton, where a convenient wayside park provides a good landing. The Middle Fork, the major tributary of the North Fork, flows through a number of small lakes near New London. Numerous bays and islands in the lakes contribute to a total of over sixty miles of shoreline for leisurely canoeing, exploring, picnicking, and camping; the Middle Fork empties into the North Fork near the village of Manannah.

In all, the North Fork flows 175 miles, the Middle 30 miles, and the South Fork 100 miles, and the main stem, from Delano to the Mississippi, flows another 25 miles. The entire Crow River watershed drains 2,756 square miles — of this the North Fork drains about 1,270, including the Middle Fork with 280, and the South Fork drains 1,250. The mean discharge of the main stem at Rockford is about 600 cubic feet per second, with a recorded maximum of more than 20,000. The gradient of the most scenic stretch of the North Fork — approximately from Forest City to Albright — is about 2.5 feet per mile.

At Anoka, the Rum River enters from the north after passing over the old hydropower dam, with an average discharge of 600 cubic feet per second (Chapter 10).

Except for the reach in the Twin Cities metropolitan area, this stretch of the Mississippi is the most industrialized; the river is used for hydropower and for cooling both fuel-burning and nuclear-fired power plants; water is extracted for industrial and domestic water supplies. There are numerous riverside municipal parks and waysides, and one state park along the main river in this reach. On the riverbank at Little Falls, the boyhood home of the late Charles A. Lindbergh is preserved in the delightful wooded Lindbergh State Park; Lindy himself was there to help dedicate the park's interpretive center on September 30, 1973.

Chapter 13

The Mississippi

II. GREAT River

Contrary to some understandable misconceptions, the name "Mississippi" is not of southern but rather of Minnesota origin. The Chippewa name was Mee-zee-see-pee, or Messipi; others called it Mese-sebe, or Missicipy, or Meschasipi, or other variations. In the end, "Mississippi" prevailed. It means "Big River," or "Father of Waters"—the Great River, the Mighty Mississippi—rising in the northern wilds of Minnesota!

But nowhere in the state of Minnesota has the Mississippi River had a more significant effect than in the metropolitan area of Minneapolis-St. Paul. The Mississippi and St. Anthony Falls in particular are responsible for the location and even the existence of the cities. The routes of exploration and early commerce; the head of steamboat navigation and later of commercial barge traffic; transportation of extensive timber resources from the north and prairie-grown grains from the west to markets in the south—all phenomena of the Mississippi River. Today, from the mouth of the Rum River at Anoka, past the mouth of the Minnesota at Fort Snelling, to the mouth of the St. Croix near Hastings, the Mississippi's course travels a diverse path, rich in history, culture, geology, and biology. Although marred by pollution from inadequate sewage treatment in a downstream reach, it is breathtakingly beautiful in the gorge created by the upstream retreat of St. Anthony Falls.

216

The city of Minneapolis plan for development of the riverfront area emphasizes the "river character" of the downtown area and its relation to both historic and contemporary values of the river. Nicollet Island would be restored as a historic village; upstream would be the industrial area, limited to those businesses that require the proximity of water; in the central reach, residential and shopping areas, restaurants, historic buildings, and plaza would be renovated and constructed; the lower, or gorge, section would be further developed for recreation, with improved pedestrian access. Clearly there are inspired plans for a corridor where city dwellers can live, play, and work in harmony with the great stream. "Think River!" is the planners' rallying cry.

There is much more than just the water and the riverbanks of the Mississippi, however, in this watershed that supplies the Twin Cities. A number of tributaries, though small, have come under increased scrutiny (and protection) because they are a valuable part of the environment of city and suburban dwellers. Minnehaha Creek, winding in from Lake Minnetonka and the southwest part of the city, was one of the first of these small streams to receive attention; Minnehaha Park, the winding, flowered parkway, and the veiled falls of Longfellow's legend found their way into the hearts of the Twin Cities. When the park was threatened by the intrusion of a major intracity highway, the howl of protest was loud and persistent—and effective. A number of other small streams, although not graced with a striking feature like Minnehaha Falls, nevertheless are recognized as resources that contribute to the beauty of the metropolitan environment: Shingle Creek in northern Minneapolis suburbs, Rice Creek in the northern St. Paul area, Bassett Creek in west Minneapolis and the downtown area (where it is now buried but would be exposed under the city's plan), Nine Mile Creek in southern Minneapolis (tributary to the Minnesota), Battle Creek in St. Paul. All have municipal parks, nature study areas, scientific reserves, picnic grounds, or recreational areas and playgrounds of some kind. Most have inspired the establishment of associations by nearby residents or other citizens concerned for the future and natural character of the creeks as they contribute to the city dwellers' quality of life. In addition there are at least fifteen municipal parks and recreation areas along or directly related to the Mississippi River in the cities. All citizens of Minneapolis and St. Paul are fortunate indeed to have these stream and river resources, as well as concerned people to look after them.

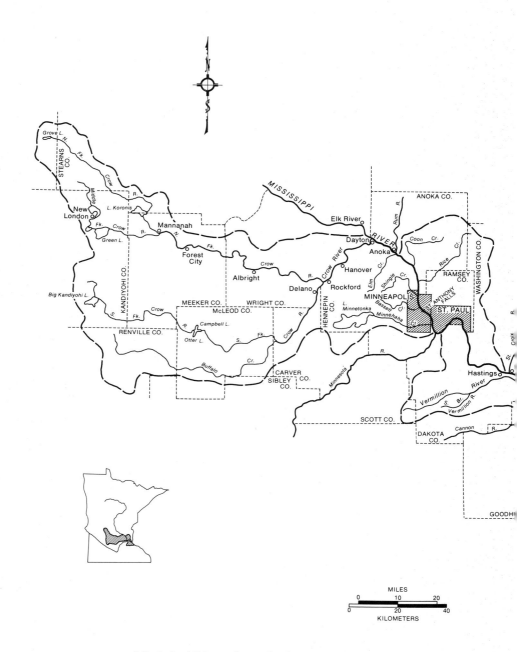

Mississippi River — from the Crow River to Iowa

The Mississippi below the Twin Cities is far different from the upper reach. It is many times wider, in a much deeper valley with a floodplain up to five miles wide; the river is nearly as wide north of the border with Iowa as it is at New Orleans (though shallower, of course). At Winona the discharge is almost four times what it is as it enters Minneapolis.

Leaving the metropolitan area the river forms the boundary between Dakota and Washington counties, and from there south forms the border between Wisconsin and the Minnesota counties of Goodhue, Wabasha, Winona, and Houston.

The entire reach from St. Anthony Falls to the Iowa border is about 135 miles long, almost all of it characterized by a broad, deep channel carved by the meltwaters from Glacial Lakes Agassiz and Duluth flowing to the Mississippi via the Minnesota and St. Croix valleys, respectively. The original lower Mississippi Valley was carved to a depth of 600 to 800 feet by these relatively clear glacial waters; but after the glacial lakes found lower, more northern outlets as melting ice retreated, the more turbid waters of modern streams, particularly the Minnesota, partially filled the deep valley with sediment. In places

these postglacial deposits are 200 feet thick, creating the broad flood-plain we see today.

Lake Pepin is the outstanding feature along this reach, located between Red Wing and Lake City in Goodhue and Wabasha counties. One to two miles wide and twenty-two miles long, this river-lake is an impoundment formed by the sandy delta of the Chippewa River from the Wisconsin side — the Chippewa enters at the downstream end of the lake. During the days of rafting logs and lumber on the Mississippi, Lake Pepin was often a major obstacle; its location in the long, deep gorge made it subject to violent storms and exceedingly turbulent surface waters that broke up rafts, and in upriver breezes rafts sometimes were becalmed. Even before steamboats were used to tow rafts down the entire course of the river, steamers plied the lakes to move the rafts through the lake. About halfway down Lake Pepin, on top of one of the highest hills, is Frontenac State Park, commemorating one of the very earliest French forts. The view down Lake Pepin and its broad deep gorge is magnificent. Lake Pepin is noted, too, as the place where water skiing was invented.

Farther down the river, north of Winona, is John A. Latsch State Wayside, extending two miles along the river; this timbered river-bank provided fuel for the old steamboats and includes a number of outstanding limestone bluff and rock formations, towering about 450 feet above the river.

Sand washing down the Chippewa from central Wisconsin has created a maze of islands and backwaters downstream. The intricacy of island and channel and the total area of water surface on the flood-plain were increased greatly when the Army Corps of Engineers built the nine-foot navigation channel with its locks and dams, because the intervening pools caused higher water levels. Now the constant supply of sand also forces the Corps to continually dredge to maintain nine-foot depths.

On these diverse floodplains, from the south end of Lake Pepin downstream, has been established one of the most notable wildlife and recreation areas on the North American continent — the Upper Mississippi River Wildlife and Fish Refuge. The refuge includes the entire floodplain (up to five miles wide), nearly 200,000 acres of marsh, timbered islands, backwater sloughs, sandy beaches, oxbow lakes, towering green hills and limestone bluffs, wooded, watery channels, and great sweep of river. It includes 33,000 acres in Minnesota, 88,000 in Wisconsin, 51,000 in Iowa, and 23,000 in Illinois,

Lake Pepin, a "river-lake," was impounded by the Chippewa River delta which was deposited in the Mississippi. The Chippewa drains much of central Wisconsin. With its frequent upstream winds, Lake Pepin was a major obstacle to log and lumber rafts of the late 1800s, but today it is a favorite for the walleye angler.

covering river bottoms from Wabasha, Minnesota, to near Rock Island, Illinois, a river distance of 300 miles. It is an immense public natural resource.

The Upper Mississippi River Wildlife and Fish Refuge was established by Congress in 1924 to protect the wildlife, fisheries, and flora of this extensive river-bottom area. The lands are publicly owned, the refuge administered by the U.S. Fish and Wildlife Service.

The name "refuge" may be misleading. Except for several designated areas of special significance to migrating waterfowl, it is not closed in the usual sense. Fourteen sanctuaries are scattered along its length, comprising some 41,000 acres in all, in which hunting is prohibited during the waterfowl seasons. Except at these times in the closed areas, the entire refuge is open to fishing, hunting, camping, and boating by the public, subject only to usual state fish and game laws.

As may be expected, the area offers some of the finest water-

The swamps and backwaters in the Upper Mississippi River Wildlife and Fish Refuge near Winona provide a river-bottom wilderness unique in America. There is an abundance of waterfowl, shorebirds, and marshland mammals, and many sport fishes. The refuge includes 200,000 acres of land and water open to public recreation. This reach of river is proposed for inclusion in the National Wild and Scenic Rivers System, but is threatened by dredging which maintains a navigation channel.

fowl hunting in the country, for it is heavily used by migrating birds of many kinds. Game mammals such as white-tailed deer, squirrels, and rabbits are common, as are aquatic fur-bearers such as muskrats, beaver, and otter. In addition to being productive of game species, the refuge is a favorite resting area for thousands of whistling swans, and hundreds of bald eagles from the central continental populations find their principal wintering ground here. The river bottoms abound in great blue herons, white common egrets, rails, and bitterns.

Although the refuge is used extensively for fishing, the angler desiring isolation has no trouble finding it. In fact the greenhorn boater, exploring the backwaters, may get lost temporarily. Walleye and northern pike fishing may be the most common, but bass and channel catfish are also popular, and yellow perch, sunfishes, and white bass are common in their favorite spots. No part of the refuge is closed to fishing or camping, except the designated sanctuaries during waterfowl migrations.

Refuge headquarters is located in Winona; also, district offices are in Trempealeau, La Crosse, Prairie du Chien, and Cassville, Wisconsin, in Lansing, Iowa, and Savanna, Illinois; further information about the river and refuge may be obtained at any of these offices.

Pleasure boating always should be undertaken with normal precautions, but some special attention must be paid to certain features in this area. The waterways are tremendously complex, and the nature of open passages and shoals changes with water levels and currents; excellent navigation charts are available from the Army Corps of Engineers and should be used. Operators of motor-powered craft should be aware of the location of old backwater closing dams, which were constructed of limestone rocks and often lie just under the water surface; similarly, many submerged rock wing dams angling out from the banks create a serious hazard to fast-running watercraft; these hazards are identified on navigation charts. Commercial barge traffic in this section of the river is heavy during the navigation season; a moving tow of big barges is not easily diverted from its course, and small craft should always give it wide berth. Locking is available to pleasure boats and can be done easily and safely with a minimal knowledge of procedures and normal safety rules. Several small craft may be locked together, but locking with a barge tow is not permitted.

Unfortunately, the unique area of backwaters and secondary channels remains threatened by the continued dumping of dredge-spoil in the river floodplain—mud and sand dug from the river bottom by the Corps to maintain the nine-foot navigation channel. Such dumping fills up backwaters and blocks off side channels, continually converting fish and wildlife habitat and other resources to barren piles of sand that each year cover more island vegetation and fill fish lakes and waterfowl marshes.

Only recently has there been broadly based citizen interest in the dredge-spoil problem, but this concern is growing rapidly as people realize that, should the present dredge-spoil disposal system employed by the Corps continue, the resources of this unique river valley will eventually and certainly be destroyed. Scientists and resource managers are concerned and are seeking to document more precisely the ecological effects of spoil disposal, as well as to search for alternative means of disposal; some local and state agencies have issued legal challenges to the Corps concerning their spoil-disposal operations. Various plans for other uses of the material and modification of the dredge-spoil disposal methods have been proffered, but one basic premise must be accepted if the river's rich bottomland resources are to remain—that dredge-spoil must eventually be removed from the floodplain entirely.

Such a program will be costly, although the technology exists to make it feasible, and dredges other than that used on the river today are available to do the job. Traditionally the navigation system on the river has been built and maintained at public expense, with no costs to navigation interests for either construction or operational expenses; however, it has been increasingly urged that user fees—paid by the shipping companies, shippers, buyers, and indeed all who profit from the low-cost transportation route—be imposed, not only for the costs of lock and dam structures, dredging, and harbor facilities, but for costs of environmental maintenance as well, including the removal of dredge-spoil from the floodplain. It is obvious that there are limits on the extent to which the valley can be used as a dump for dredge-spoil without eliminating resources of wildlife, recreation, and natural beauty.

The river bottoms in this lower reach constitute a wild land of cattails, rushes, and other marsh plants, beds of arrowhead, water lilies, and lotus bright with white and yellow blooms, as well as blue water and sky, and the rich green of wooded hills. It is a Tom Sawyer land of lazy summer days, a world isolated from noisy highways and busy cities; when you are on the river, they seem not to exist. The traveler is left with the islands, hills, and majestic river.

A major tributary of this lowest stretch of the Mississippi on the southern edge of the Twin Cities is the Vermillion River, rising in eastern Scott County and flowing across all of Dakota County to its mouth near Hastings, a distance of some thirty-five miles. The Gores Wildlife Management Area is located on the pool above Lock and Dam No. 3 on the Mississippi at the mouth of the Vermillion; it includes many small lakes and ponds, sloughs and backwaters, providing extensive wildlife habitat and waterfowl production areas open to public use, including fishing, hunting, and trapping. Besides Vermillion, other important tributaries in this stretch are the Cannon, Zumbro, Whitewater, and Root rivers, all draining the area of deeply dissected lands in the southeastern drift-less region (Chapter 14).

The flow of the Mississippi increases significant-ly as it courses through the state, acquiring the waters of its major tributaries. From its beginning trickles at Lake Itasca, it increases to mean discharges of about 100 cubic feet per second at Bemidji, 1,000 at Grand Rapids, 3,500 at Aitkin, over 7,000 entering the Twin Cit-ies, 10,000 at St. Paul after receiving the Minnesota River (but a flow of 171,000 was recorded at St. Paul in 1965!), and 15,000 below the mouth of the St. Croix. Doubling its discharge again in its course to the Iowa border, collecting many waters from Wisconsin as well as from Minnesota, it reaches the Iowa border with an average flow of 30,000 cubic feet per second, still only 1.5 percent of its flow at the Gulf.

The gradient varies widely. From Lake Itasca to Bemidji it is an average of 1.5 feet per mile, low but reflecting some rapids in its first course; across the lake-studded path to Grand Rapids it is only about 0.5 foot per mile; across the flat bed of Glacial Lake Aitkin, from Grand Rapids to the mouth of the Crow Wing, it is likewise low, about 0.7 foot per mile. But from the Crow Wing to St. Anthony Falls in Minneapolis, the gradient is higher, over 2.5 feet per mile, and it is here that a number of hydropower dams were installed— Little Falls, Blanchard, Sartell, St. Cloud, and Coon Rapids. The riv-er now drops fifty feet over St. Anthony Falls alone. But from the Twin Cities down, the gradient is again very low—less than 0.5 foot per mile in its course to Iowa. In Minnesota the river drops 833 feet, or 57 percent of the total drop over the entire river. The average gra-dient is 1.26 feet per mile in Minnesota; over the entire length of riv-er to its mouth, the gradient is just half that, or 0.62 foot per mile.

The alkalinity of the Mississippi ranges from about 100 to 150 p.p.m., indicating moderately high fertility, about the same as most streams in central Minnesota that have surface drainage across glacial drift as the main source of water. Alkalinity gradually increases from the river's source to the Iowa border. Some tributary streams in the north that drain swamps and coniferous forests are of typical bog color and somewhat softer or lower in alkalinity, around 50 p.p.m.; but these have little effect on the main stream. A few others, trout streams with springwater sources, are clear and have alkalinities well over 200 p.p.m.; this is true of most tributaries in the southeast, as well as some northern trout streams with springwater sources. The Mississippi generally has little color throughout its length. However, it is turbid, with mud and clay in the Lake Aitkin lake bed area and, in the lower reaches, brown with eroded silt from ditched and drained western prairies. Farther downstream, however, in the sprawling Upper Mississippi River Wildlife and Fish Refuge, river waters are relatively clear again. The Mississippi flows directly through parts of seven state forests and the Chippewa National Forest, and major tributaries flow through more than twenty additional state forests.

The Mississippi, at the Iowa border, has drained part or all of seventy-one Minnesota counties (of eighty-seven), as well as parts of Iowa, South Dakota, and Wisconsin—65,000 square miles in all, 45,000 in Minnesota, over half the total area of the entire state.

By the time Glacial Lake Agassiz began to drain its icy waters via the Glacial River Warren, the stage was set for the formation of one of the most significant river features on the continent—St. Anthony Falls on the Mississippi River. The placement of ancient ocean-bottom rock strata, the cutting of preglacial river valleys, the filling of valleys with deposits from the melting of old glaciers—all combined in proper chronological order and required only the immense energy of the water of Glacial River Warren to start the falls.

St. Anthony Falls determined the location of the head of navigation—from the steamboat days to modern barge towing. It was responsible for initial development of a lumber industry later to become the world's leader (1890); for the greatest flour-milling enterprise in the country (1880s); for the first hydroelectric station in the United States (1882); for the first permanent bridge to span the Mississippi River (1854); as well as the location of the Twin Cities of Minneapolis and St. Paul.

More than 10,000 years ago Glacial River Warren poured out of the western prairies, draining vast Lake Agassiz. In the area that was to become the metropolitan Twin Cities, the giant stream thundered along the surface of a hard bedrock layer, now called the Platteville limestone. Under the limestone was the thicker layer of St. Peter sandstone, a much softer rock that would easily have been eroded by the river had it not been protected by the hard layer on top. But at the point where the present-day Robert Street bridge spans the Mississippi in St. Paul, the glacial stream shot over a waterfall into a river valley that had earlier been cut into the bedrock and filled with older glacial drift. These older materials were rapidly washed out, and the falls, called by modern geologists the River Warren Falls, dropped 175 feet into the old preglacial valley. The soft sandstone then began to erode under the limestone caprock at the plunge-pool, and the caprock broke off in chunks. Rapidly, then, the waterfall moved upstream—the soft sandstone eroding and the caprock limestone breaking off to lay in great slabs on the riverbed below the falls. This is a history common to many waterfalls.

For perhaps 2,000 years, the River Warren Falls retreated upstream, moving up about eight miles to the mouth of the smaller Mississippi, the location of present-day Fort Snelling. For two miles more the River Warren Falls retreated upstream into what is now the lower Minnesota River Valley. Then it met the end of the limestone caprock at another buried river valley, and the falls was extinguished.

However, the retreat of the River Warren Falls past the Mississippi left the latter's mouth perched high above the gorge. Thus St. Anthony Falls was formed on the Mississippi, the river plunging some 180 feet over the limestone caprock edge. Then these falls in turn began to retreat upstream. Soon passing the mouth of Minnehaha Creek, on the west side of the Mississippi, the upstream-moving St. Anthony Falls left the mouth of this small tributary perched. Minnehaha Falls, thus formed, retreated upstream approximately 1,000 feet more until it reached its present location in Minnehaha Park.

Since its formation 10,000 years ago, St. Anthony Falls has retreated eight miles upstream on the Mississippi from the location of Fort Snelling to the falls' present location, an average rate of perhaps four feet per year, alternately eroding the soft St. Peter sandstone and causing the hard Platteville limestone to break off, leaving behind a deep scenic gorge through the center of the present metropolitan area. Tree-shaded winding streets lined with walks, park benches, and small parking areas now parallel the wooded blufftops on both sides of the gorge, marking two of the cities' most attractive parkways.

When Father Louis Hennepin visited the falls in 1680, it was not at its present location. Rather, it was about a mile downstream,

The Mississippi River gorge, separating St. Paul and Minneapolis in the heart of the metropolitan area, was formed by the migration of St. Anthony Falls from the mouth of the Mississippi in the Glacial River Warren (at the present location of Fort Snelling) upstream eight miles to the falls' present site. The falls' retreat took about ten thousand years, an average of perhaps four feet per year. The swift rapids of the rocky gorge prevented steamboat traffic up to Minneapolis until locks and dams provided passage to commercial watercraft, including modern towboats and barges.

just above the crossing of Interstate Highway 35W. During the next 200 years, St. Anthony Falls was to move upstream the final mile to its present location, where it is now stabilized.

The history of industrial development at the falls, lumbering and flour milling, was long and turbulent. The military reservation that Zebulon Pike had secured from the Indians in 1805, and upon which Fort Snelling was built, extended upstream along both sides of the Mississippi to St. Anthony Falls. The abundant water power was first utilized in 1823 by soldiers of the fort to run primitive mills, supplying the garrison with lumber and flour. After the 1837 treaty with the Sioux passed the St. Croix Delta to the whites, the east side of the falls was open to settlers and claimants. Franklin Steele was the prime developer of the east side; he recognized the falls' unique position, with pinelands to the north on the Mississippi and the Rum and lumber markets to the south. Steele's efforts resulted in the first completed commercial sawmills using St. Anthony Falls waterpower in 1848, and the town of St. Anthony was established in 1849.

The St. Anthony industry, with Steele as its leader, was plagued by financial difficulties and legal and legislative maneuvers that extended to Washington. But the lumber-milling industry grew rapidly; from its modest beginning the mill complex cut 12 million board feet in 1855; later, in the 1890s, Minneapolis mills cut about a half billion board feet per year.

The first commercial flour milling began in 1851 and also grew rapidly. Franklin Steele became involved with flour milling, too, and in 1852 his mill ground flour, corn meal, and feeds. By 1860 St. Anthony Falls flour mills were producing up to 30,000 barrels per year; and then during the 1870s, over 2 million were produced. By this time flour milling had replaced lumbering as the leading industry.

While the town of St. Anthony developed on the east side of the falls, the west side, in military reservation, remained closed to private development. But the thus far unused water-power resources were not to be left untouched.

As early as the late 1830s, squatters from the Red River settlements were using the military lands; evicted by the soldiers in 1840, they moved across to the east side—downriver—and established a rough community known as Pig's Eye, named after a whisky dispenser, Pierre Parrant, who had a marked squint in one eye. In 1841 Father Lucien Gaultier built in this community a rough chapel which he named St. Paul—and thus the sister city to that developing around the falls began.

Squatters continued to appear in later years on the military reservation—illegally, to be sure. In 1852 the occupants began thinking of a name for themselves. "Minnehapolis" was the name selected, and in 1855 a new law permitted the sale of reservation lands, and a plat of "Minneapolis," without the "h," was submitted. Municipal government was established in the next year, and in the next the town was incorporated. The two cities grew up together, St. Anthony on the east side, and Minneapolis on the west. They shared the power source, St. Anthony Falls, for their most important industries of lumbering and flour milling. They were united as Minneapolis in 1872, and thereafter competed, not with each other, but with growing St. Paul downstream.

The territorial capital lay at the head of steamboat navigation, for the gorge left by the retreat of St. Anthony Falls up from the Mississippi-Minnesota confluence was too swift and rocky for even the most adventurous river pilots. Besides, Father Gaultier had selected an excellent site for a steamboat landing in locating his Chapel of St. Paul. Minneapolis prospered with industrial development, but St. Paul was favored because passengers and freight coming upriver had to stop at that end of the gorge. To satisfy both cities it was proposed in the 1870s that a lock and dam be built at Meeker Island in the gorge, on the border between the two towns. The dam would provide water power to St. Paul; the lock would allow boat passage to Minneapolis.

However, Minneapolis, though desiring navigation, did not want St. Paul to have water power competing with St. Anthony Falls; and St. Paul, however much the water power of the proposed dam was needed, would not agree to extending navigation to Minneapolis. Jealousies intensified, and the conflict and incriminations were bitter —in the end, the lock and dam were not built! (Locks and dams were built later, of course, but not until after the turn of the century.)

After the water-power resources of the falls had permitted development of valuable lumber and flour mills on both sides of the river, a series of near-catastrophes almost brought the cataract to an untimely end. In its upstream retreat, it could not go much farther anyway, for the limestone caprock did not extend beyond Nicollet Island, just upstream from the falls. And had the falls retreated that far, only a stretch of swift rapids would have been left. In 1866 a timbered water slide, or apron, was constructed over the natural falls to prevent further undercutting. But a devastating flood the next year destroyed the apron.

Far more damaging was the Nicollet Island tunnel, begun under Hennepin Island in 1868 and extending upstream. The tunnel was dug through the soft sandstone under the limestone caprock. Its purpose was to allow industrial development on Nicollet Island, providing a tailrace for discharged waters.

Then while digging continued, some cracks developed in the tunnel, and soon after, the limestone caved in near the upper end, creating a crumbling hole that threatened to break up the last remaining limestone covering and destroy the falls. With round-the-clock efforts, citizens of both Minneapolis and St. Anthony reapeatedly plugged the hole until it was repaired sufficiently to save the falls, albeit temporarily. Floods continued to batter the lip of the natural falls, and additional holes through the limestone upstream from the falls threatened to undermine the caprock by eroding the sandstone beneath.

In 1876 the Army Corps of Engineers completed the installation of a concrete dike 200 feet upstream from the falls, penetrating the riverbed forty feet and extending from bank to bank, to prevent water from percolating into the sandstone and endangering the protective cover. By 1884 a new timber apron to protect the limestone lip of the falls and two low dams upstream to maintain sufficient water over the limestone to prevent its freezing in low water were complete. The falls was stabilized at last.

Meanwhile, other calamities plagued the St. Anthony Falls lumber and flour mills. In 1870 a great fire destroyed the entire lumber-mill district on the east side, and the St. Anthony lumber company went out of business for good; financial problems plagued remaining industries; and in 1878 a gigantic explosion and ensuing fires in the Minneapolis flour mills killed eighteen men and destroyed one-third of the flour-milling district on the west side.

Reconstruction and further development continued, but it was in this troubled decade of the 1870s that the significance of St. Anthony Falls water power declined for other reasons. Steam was replacing water power, and by 1880 Minneapolis industry depended equally on water power and steam.

In 1882 the Minnesota Brush Electric Company operated its hydroelectric power plant on the flats of Upton Island just below the falls on the west side. It was the first hydroelectric station in the United States, ushering in an era when water power did not have to be used at streamside but could be transmitted by wire to industries far removed.

By 1890 Minneapolis was no longer dependent on the falls as a source of power. Shortly thereafter, Minneapolis lumber mills led the world in lumber production, up to a record half billion board feet annually, but production was not dependent on St. Anthony Falls water power. In 1960 the very last water wheel was turned by the falls. Today the once mighty cataract produces only a modest amount of hydroelectricity.

Lucy Wilder Morris Park, a small tract on the east side of the river below St. Anthony Falls, has now been expanded into the much larger Father Hennepin Bluffs, a park of rocky bluffs and wooded trails along historic Main Street. The park commemorates the spot from which Father Hennepin supposedly first viewed the falls three centuries ago.

For the better part of 200 years the bark canoe —portable and readily made—was the travel mode of the northern wooded wilderness. But eventually there was greater interest in the region than just exploration, salvation of Indian souls, and beaver trapping. There came the need to transport greater loads, especially on the main river—not only to float the harvests of trapping and hunting downstream, but also to move supplies, staples, and merchandise upstream. The capacity of the canoe, even the large transport sizes, was limited.

The immediate answer was the keelboat, used first on the Ohio and Mississippi above the Ohio's mouth. The first use of the keelboat on the Mississippi's upper waters was by the French in 1751, but not until the Americans increased their exploration and commerce on the upper river in the early 1800s did the keelboat become the mainstay of river transport. Pike, on his trip acquiring lands for military purposes and searching for the source in 1805, employed a keelboat for a portion of his trip from downriver.

The keelboat was so called because it was built on a keel, with plank ribs and sides. It was generally forty to eighty feet long, eight to ten feet wide, and usually carried a crew of ten men. Its load capacity was much greater than the canoe's—about 3,000 pounds of freight per man of crew. It was easy going downstream, of course, but the big advantage of the keelboat over, say, a raft, was that it was capable of upstream travel as well. Not that this was easy; it was propelled by poling, sometimes assisted by sail if an upstream wind was available, sometimes by pulling with ropes from tree stump to stump along the riverbank; but upstream it went. It could do eight to twelve miles per day upstream, still a long trip up from St. Louis. Nevertheless, in the 1820s and 1830s keelboats made many regular trips to Fort Snelling, carrying supplies of food, clothing, and rum upstream, and taking furs and produce down. Flat-bottomed, sharp-prowed at both ends, drawing only twenty inches draft or so, the keelboat in its best days was the "clipper ship of inland navigation."

By this time, also, steamboats were coming into general use on the lower river and on the Ohio and Missouri. In 1811, the *New Or-*

leans, the first of steam-powered craft on the Mississippi, had gone down the Ohio and through the river-wrenching New Madrid earthquake to the city of New Orleans. Then in 1823 the *Virginia* pulled into the landing at Fort Snelling, the first steamboat to the Minnesota region.

But shortly after this time, lumbering started in the upper river country, and throughout most of the mid-1800s lumber and log rafts were by far the most common floating vessels on the Upper Mississippi River. An important adjunct to the downstream traffic of lumber rafts and the early steamboat traffic was the flatboat. Evolved from a simple raft, by adding some sort of cabin or shelter and perhaps outer bulkheads, the flatboats were also known as "broadhorns." About sixty feet long and twenty feet wide, steered by oars fore and aft, they were meant for downriver traffic only, for they were assembled upriver of marketable lumber and logs and floated down with lumber, peltries, produce, and some manufactured goods. At the downriver port the goods were sold as well as the materials from which the flatboat was made. The flatboats frequently constituted floating markets —with blacksmiths, tinshops, grocery stores, dramshops—serving riverside farmers and settlers and occupants of other river vessels on the way down. At the end of the trip for the flatboats and lumber rafts, the rough crews rode back upstream on the steamboats—often to the consternation of more genteel passengers.

Keelboats, lumber rafts, flatboats—the transport of freight on the Upper Mississippi by these means was grueling work. It conditioned a company of hard, tough men. They fought perverse currents, rapids, and changing shoals, bitter weather, river pirates, each other, and whatever riverside law-enforcement elements tried to contain their shore-leave extravagances. They worked hard, drank hard, fought hard—through a colorful era that produced heroes like the legendary Mike Fink, two-fisted king of the river crews.

But these primitive types of river transport all led to an even more colorful era on the Mississippi. Primitive at first, no more than a tiny shack and woodpile on a raft that carried an inefficient boiler and engine, the steamboat eventually evolved into a giant floating palace. No effort was spared in design and construction to produce sweeping graceful lines, intricate, candy-colored gingerbread scrollwork on the outside, and the luxuries of silk, polished hardwood, and glass chandeliers inside—a setting more luxurious than anything on shore. But these elaborations came later, for at the beginning the steamboats were hard-working vessels.

After the *Virginia* in 1823, others followed, and traffic between St. Louis and St. Paul increased rapidly. The steamers were common in the 1840s (the keelboat was gone by 1845), and hundreds of steamboats annually made regular landings at the head of navigation at St. Paul, hauling lumber and grain, the principal produce of Minnesota, downriver. At the same time, they moved up the St. Croix, and, in the 1850s, up the winding Minnesota. Packets (steamboats that made prescribed runs carrying passengers and freight) followed regular schedules. In the 1850s, too, the steamboats brought thousands of European immigrants with their worldly goods to settle the forest lands along the St. Croix and the prairies along the Minnesota. The 1840-1860 period was the "Golden Age" of steamboating on the Upper Mississippi.

The Mississippi River steamboat was basically an engine-driven raft. It was built to glide over the surface of shallow river waters, rather than to cleave surging waves like an ocean-going ship. The engine was installed, therefore, not down in a hold, but on the top of the raft, or main deck, to preserve as shallow a draft as possible. Stern-wheelers came first, but the side-wheelers replaced them because the use of two engines, each independently driving a side-mounted paddlewheel, made maneuvering on twisting river bends easier. On the main deck, in addition to the engines, boiler, and furnace, freight, fuel, and the kitchen were carried. Above this the boiler deck held the staterooms for passengers. The term "stateroom" originated here, for each of these passenger rooms was originally named after one of the United States. This arrangement, with passenger quarters above the boilers, accounted for many river tragedies when boilers exploded.

The roof of the staterooms constituted the hurricane deck, and on this was the texas, a smaller group of staterooms or quarters for the boat's officers—added as the state of Texas was added to the United States in 1845. And above the texas, the pilot house overlooked the entire vessel and provided the best view of the river ahead. Two smokestacks, one on each side of the texas, completed the typical steamboat of the western rivers.

Most steamboats that plied the Upper Mississippi were constructed on the Ohio River, the center of steamboat manufacture, but later some were made at St. Louis, Dubuque, and Wabasha, and even at Kasota on the Minnesota River. They were all wooden-hulled, steel hulls coming into use only after 1900, and consequently fire was an ever-present danger and frequent occurrence. In fact, tragic events marked the demise of virtually all steamboats. They commonly struck snags and sank, boilers exploded, hulls were staved in by ice, floating trees, or collisions with log rafts or other vessels, and fires resulted from a variety of causes. Racing caused serious, if not frequent accidents accompanied by much loss of life; the early boilers had no gauges or safety valves, and the captain and crew's judgment of how much pressure could be attained without an explosion was at times faulty because of their enthusiasm for the race. The average life of a Mississippi steamboat was only five years, and wrecked hulks littered shoals and river bottoms during this period. Steamboating was interrupted by the Civil War, and although it increased to record-high traffic density afterward, the steamboats' days were numbered.

Railroads were numerous and hauled freight out of the Twin Cities by the 1870s. Numbers of steamboats increased (reaching a record 5,468 boats passing Winona in 1892), but the decline followed rapidly. The hauling of grain, in towed (pushed) barges, was the boats' big commercial business, but the railroads could carry it faster, and more directly to Chicago and eastern markets. Some steamboat-excursion traffic remained (as it does today), but by 1915 the packet lines were essentially gone. Furthermore, the logging of the white pine was over by this time in the St. Croix Delta. Screw-propeller, steel-hulled boats and barges were common in the early 1900s, and the gingerbread palaces—those that were not sunk or burned—were tied up somewhere as museums or showboats. The Golden Age of Steamboats was over, and many old pilots mourned its passing.

Steamboating on the Upper Mississippi, however, was not confined to the stretch between St. Paul and St. Louis. That is the reach usually conjured up, of course, when the subject is discussed, for Mark Twain never piloted an upper river steamboat (and probably would not have wanted to). For St. Paul was not the only head of navigation on the Mississippi. There were, in fact, two more. Both were important to the upper river in Minnesota, especially to the logging and lumbering industry, on the Mississippi side of the St. Croix Delta as well as in the headwaters region.

The first of these upriver stretches was from above St. Anthony

Falls to the rocky barrier at Sauk Rapids. Because there was no way to move a complete steamboat beyond St. Anthony Falls, the craft was assembled on the upper waters and then ran up to the rapids at Sauk Rapids. These boats ran from 1850 to 1879, when they were replaced by a railroad along the river. Usually the boats carried supplies upriver for the logging camps and also for settlers who were establishing farms in the wake of logging. Generally the rapids at the upstream end of this reach at Sauk Rapids was considered an absolute barrier, but a single instance in 1858 proved the exception. Anson Northup, St. Paul builder, took his *North Star* into the rapids in high water, scraped through, and steamed on up to Grand Rapids. Later he renamed the boat the *Anson Northup*, dismantled it, and carted it overland to the Red River of the North, the first steamboat to ply that northwestern stream.

The sound of steamboat paddles was also heard in the stretch above Sauk Rapids, particularly from Aitkin to Grand Rapids. Later, as logging and settlement followed upstream, steamboats on this 125-mile stretch prospered for the half-century from 1870 to 1920. Here the steamboat served primarily as an adjunct to the lumbering industry; it came into use in 1870 when the railroads reached Aitkin with logging supplies and left when the pine ran out. The river in this reach flows across the bed of Glacial Lake Aitkin and winds slowly in a deep, meandering channel. These factors made regular travel by steamboat possible up to Pokegama Falls at Grand Rapids, the uppermost head of navigation. Viewing the narrow, winding, tree-lined river today, it is difficult to imagine steamboats churning upstream. But the river had some help. The Army Corps of Engineers maintained a three- to five-foot channel by dredging, snagging, and constructing wing dams and cutoffs. It still is a deeper reach of stream, of course, but there were—and are—some shallow spots. So shallow that the river bed was, said the pilots, "dusty in places."

Nevertheless, the industry flourished, essentially serving as a northward extension of the end of the railroad. It supplied lumber camps with groceries, livestock feed, coal, and hardware; rafts with shacks built on them, or wanigans, were towed up to the mouth of tributaries and then were poled up to more remote camps to serve as cookshacks and bunkhouses; the steamers accommodated farmers with freight and passenger service along the way, stopping when summoned by a signal tied in the riverbank bushes; they helped with log drives, pulled snags, and broke up jams. The boats carried from 30 to

100 tons of freight and even towed barges of 40 to 50 tons. The largest, the *Andy Gibson*, was 140 feet long.

When the Army Corps dam was built on Big Sandy Lake, an operating lock was installed. Through this lock, steamboats sailed into Big Sandy and even up the Prairie River to the West Savanna. The *Lee*, the last boat on the Aitkin to Grand Rapids run, worked principally on Big Sandy and Prairie River, helping with log drives. And the *Oriole*, one of the biggest (125 feet) and last, worked for the Army dredging and snagging in the period 1910-1918; then it was beached on Big Sandy Lake where it was remodeled to serve as a resort hotel, "The Ark," until 1941.

The Aitkin County Park commission has prepared an excellent recreational guide to this stretch of the river, including historic photographs and river maps showing old steamboat landings and sites of steamboat wrecks as well as campgrounds and access points.

Despite the decline of steamboat traffic and the ascendancy of the railroads, many people continued to view the Mississippi as part of a vast inland commercial waterway that could, if appropriately improved for navigation, provide cheap transportation of bulk goods. The problem on the Upper Mississippi between St. Louis and the Twin Cities was a combination of changing river channels, rapids, and shallow water. What was needed, the navigation interests declared, was a maintained channel that could be relied upon to have sufficiently deep water at all times to handle the boats and barges then in use.

Of course, aids to navigation were not new in the early 1900s on the river. In fact, considerable effort had already been expanded by the Army Engineers to improve the river for steamboats by pulling snags, removing wrecks, and dredging. "Uncle Sam's Tooth-Pullers," they were called—double-hulled, fork-stemmed steamboats that winched sunken logs and trees from the shifting and settling silt beds of the river bottom.

But just the removal of snags was not enough. In 1878 a four-and-one-half foot navigation channel was authorized, and some rapids were bypassed by lateral canals and locks. Boulders were removed, and the channel in the gorge below St. Anthony Falls was dredged.

About this time, too, suggestions were made for water projects in the headwaters region where precipitation stored in big lakes and marshes served as water sources for the Mississippi. The mill companies near St. Anthony Falls were concerned about a reliable supply of water power at the falls and considered converting the large lakes in the headwaters into reservoirs for greater control of stable flows. And the Army Engineers were also interested in the reservoirs project, mainly as a means of improving navigation by releasing water from the reservoirs during periods of low flow. Upon authorization, five dams were built by the engineers between 1884 and 1895: at the outlet of Leech Lake on Leech Lake River, twenty-five miles from its mouth in the Mississippi; on the Mississippi at the outlet of Lake Winnibigoshish; the Pokegama dam on the Mississippi at Grand Rapids; at the outlet of Big Sandy Lake on Sandy River; and at the outlet of Cross Lake and the Whitefish chain on the Pine River. In 1912 a sixth dam was built at the outlet of Gull Lake on Gull River, which empties into the Crow Wing and then into the Mississippi.

At all sites the Corps maintains recreational facilities such as picnic and campgrounds, boat or canoe access, playgrounds, and swimming beaches, accommodating large numbers of users.

Although the reservoirs were constructed to dependably supply water power for the St. Anthony Falls mills, Minneapolis no longer relies on the falls because other power sources have been developed. And although a more stable river flow for navigation was the Corps' objective, the canalization by locks and dams in the lower reaches has largely met that need. The reservoirs now primarily serve recreational interests that require stable water levels—in the reservoirs themselves, not in the river.

In 1907 construction of a six-foot channel between St. Louis and the Twin Cities began. It was never completed (rather, it was superseded by an even more ambitious project), but the work partially completed left some conspicuous features in the river down from St. Paul: rock revetments, closure dams which shut off currents from backwater areas, and hundreds of wing dams. The last were long, narrow piles of broken limestone angling out from the riverbanks and intended to confine river flow to the main channel. They acted as deflectors, and they worked, partially. Many were constructed: in the thirty-mile stretch from St. Paul to Prescott, Wisconsin, 300 were built; from Wabasha to Winona (forty miles), 400. Most still exist today, submerged below the higher waters of later projects, and many are dangerous to unwary boaters because they are just under the water surface.

The history of development of the present nine-foot channel is sporadic. A lock and dam was installed in the gorge in 1906, later abandoned when Ford Dam (currently No. 1) was built and then enlarged in 1917, below the Ford Parkway bridge. A new No. 2 was built near Hastings and began operation in 1930.

From there downriver to Granite City, Illinois, twenty-five more locks and dams were built, numbered to 27. (One lock has no dam. No. 23 is missing, but No. 5A, near Winona, was added.) Most lock and dam construction was undertaken during the 1930s depression years, stimulated by President Franklin Roosevelt's public works program.

Each dam impounds a portion of the river as a navigation pool, and these waters cover the former floodplains, forming many backwater lakes, marshes, and wooded sloughs that did not exist previously. It is primarily the navigation pool that now creates the nine-foot channel, although continual dredging is necessary to maintain the required depth. The nine-foot channel, after completion, permitted navigation and barge traffic almost to the foot of St. Anthony Falls. Nine of the twenty-seven locks and dams are in or along Minnesota (including 5A), and No. 8 is nearest the Iowa border.

Much later, two new locks were added to enable navigation above St. Anthony Falls—the Minneapolis Upper Harbor Project. The Lower Lock and Dam, located just above the I-35W bridge, has a lift of twenty-five feet. The Upper Lock, at the falls, lifts fifty feet, the highest in the entire system. The project was completed in 1963 and now permits barge traffic upriver another four and one-half miles into Minneapolis. The total number of locks on the Mississippi is now twenty-nine.

As early as 1938 the Corps was authorized to conduct a study of the feasibility of a twelve-foot channel. But potential environmental damage to this unique river system is staggering; the plan has been strongly opposed by Minnesota's environmental scientists and citizens. According to Corps of Engineers' spokesmen, plans for a twelve-foot channel in the Upper Mississippi have been abandoned. But the Corps, supported by the barge and river shipping companies, plans new and enlarged locks and dam at Alton, Illinois, providing a twelve-foot channel capacity and quadrupling barge capacity. They argue that the present structure is unsound and too limited in capacity, and that the proposed new one, two miles downstream, should be classed "routine maintenance." Environmentalists, however, claim that lock and dam enlargement is an opening wedge and that the Corps will eventually extend the twelve-foot channel all the way up the river and greatly enlarge its navigational capacity. The twelve-foot channel, with its consequent additional dredge-spoil problem and its greatly expanded flooding of river bottomlands, would have a major detrimental effect on the Upper Mississippi River Wildlife and Fish Refuge. There would remain, in the words of the Izaak Walton League, a "Mississippi Canal, with all the scenic charm, recreation potential, and biological interest of a storm drain." The problem has not been permanently resolved.

Along the east side of the river beside St. Anthony Falls is the University of Minnesota's St. Anthony Falls Hydraulic Laboratory. Part of the flow is diverted through the laboratory, where hydraulic problems are solved by modeling, to scale, many proposed river projects. The Upper Harbor Project, including the Lower Lock and Dam and the Upper Lock, were modeled and planned in this way prior to construction of the actual project. The laboratory has modeled other projects in Minnesota's rivers, as well as in streams elsewhere in the United States and in other countries.

The channel catfish, basically a river fish, is a native to most streams in the midwestern United States. Often scorned in northern waters where it must compete with walleyes, northern pike, and smallmouth bass, the channel cat, despite its odd appearance, is highly regarded as a food fish throughout much of the Mississippi River basin. It is the most sought-after sport species in the middle river reaches and is increasingly popular in Minnesota.

Until modern fisheries management developed in Minnesota, the channel catfish was unknown in the Mississippi above St. Anthony Falls. This was also true of such other essentially river species as the lake sturgeon and white bass. The brook trout, also, was native to cold-water tributaries below the falls but not above. All told, of 123 species of fish known to have occurred originally in the Mississippi and contiguous waters below St. Anthony Falls, at least 59 were not found above the falls.

This peculiar distribution was not, as might be supposed, entirely or even mostly due to climatic reasons—that is, the exclusion of warm-water species from the northern, colder areas of the river—because many of the species absent from the upper reaches were found at similar latitudes in the St. Croix and the Red River of the

The channel catfish, long a favorite of anglers on the lower Mississippi, is increasingly popular in Minnesota as a food fish. The catfish has been introduced by man into the upper river above St. Anthony Falls.

North. It was, indeed, the precipitous St. Anthony Falls that prevented colonization of the headwater reaches of the Mississippi, whereas the upper St. Croix, which did not have a comparable barrier, and the Red River, which once connected with the lower Mississippi via the Glacial River Warren, were easily entered.

One may wonder, of course, how the sixty-four native species originally found above the falls got there. It is conjectured that many of these, more accurately described as lake species, apparently were able to cross drainage divides at times of floods or even when old glacial lakes connected the upper Mississippi with the St. Croix or the Red. These include well-known species such as the northern pike, walleye, largemouth bass, bluegill, black crappie, yellow perch, and bullheads. The interconnections among streams were essentially lake habitats, and these species dispersed, grew, and reproduced successfully while the typical river species could not.

When civilization arrived, the dispersal of fish species into previously unoccupied habitats increased—for some species intentionally, like channel catfish and brook trout. In other instances, such as dispersal of the European carp and freshwater drum, or sheepshead, introductions were probably accidental, an indirect result of increased human activity. At present the channel cat is abundant above the falls only to the Coon Rapids dam, but because it has been introduced upriver it may continue to extend its range.

The completion of the locks and dams at St. Anthony Falls in 1963 probably provides access for all species previously excluded from the upper river. Fishery scientists continue to observe fish distribution patterns to determine the effect of the St. Anthony project in particular and to study the effect of locks on fish dispersal generally.

Of course another effect of civilization on fish distribution is the severe pollution of the Mississippi below the Twin Cities. Some species of fish originally known from the river stretch immediately below St. Anthony Falls are no longer present because pollution has been an effective chemical barrier to fish from lower reaches of the river. Today, however, pollution abatement has alleviated this problem somewhat, and some species are returning.

Several species of catfish occur in the Mississippi's lower portions, but the channel cat is by far the principal one in Minnesota. The earliest explorers reported seeing, catching, and eating catfish, as well as such large and strange-looking species as sturgeon and paddlefish. The Indians, too, all along the river, appear to have used several species of catfish.

The catfish is by no means the only important sport species in the Mississippi. Others include huge muskellunge in some of the large headwater lakes and upper river, hard-fighting smallmouths in the rapids of the metropolitan reaches, walleyes in the island-studded lower river, and panfish such as yellow perch and crappies.

Our attempts to influence fishery resources have probably never been so striking as the introduction of the European carp into the United States in the late 1800s. At first it was so highly regarded as a valuable and desirable fish that it was jealously protected from potential poachers lest the supply be diminished before it could be established. But so adaptable and prolific is the species, and so successful is it in competing with other species in most kinds of water, that its spread and increase were devastating. In population density it has dominated the fish fauna of almost all waters in which it was introduced; in the Mississippi River, the catch by commercial fishermen of carp has exceeded that of any other species since 1900. The carp is being utilized as smoked fish, which is well accepted in Minnesota. Despite later attempts to control it with barriers, netting and seining, and even poisons, it is today so widespread, successful, and abundant that elimination or even significant reduction appears to be impossible.

Fortunately for the Mississippi in its uppermost reaches, the carp has not extended its range into the headwaters yet, for it apparently has not managed to become established in abundance beyond Blanchard Dam near Royalton. A few individuals have been observed above the dam, thus the carp may be further invading the Mississippi headwater streams.

The Atlantic salmon was introduced into Mississippi waters at about the same time as the carp. It is impossible to imagine two fish species less likely to successfully coexist; the salmon, it need hardly be reported, did not flourish in the Mississippi River.

Today, although the carp dominates river populations in approximately the lower half of the Mississippi's course in Minnesota and undoubtedly has reduced the production of more desirable species, the Mississippi remains a major producer of many game fishes throughout its course, providing recreational fishing opportunities of many kinds. Though the river has some angling devotees there are few compared with those on Minnesota's many lakes.

Virtually the entire river in Minnesota produces walleyes, and the fishing for this Minnesota favorite is frequently first-rate, even in the dog days of late summer when walleye fishing has declined in the more popular lakes. Smallmouth bass are high on the lists of those who know the river's fishing; even in the metropolitan reaches, hidden from the roar of traffic and industry only by a row of boulevard elms, the smallmouth provides choice sport.

In the reach on the bed of old Glacial Lake Aitkin, in Aitkin County, the river is deep and slow, with clay bottom and eroding clay banks. Here the principal game fishes are those typical of slow waters and lakes—northern pike, yellow perch, the sunfishes—and the walleye and smallmouth, although present, are less numerous. Both above and below the glacial lake section, the walleye and smallmouth predominate among river game fishes.

Of the species considered rough fish, the carp predominates in river populations, at least to St. Cloud and possibly to Blanchard

Dam. In reaches farther upriver, the redhorses strongly predominate among river fish populations. The shorthead, or northern redhorse, and the silver redhorse are most abundant, particularly the former. Both were native above St. Anthony Falls; they are essentially river species and occur in abundance in the swifter waters of many of Minnesota's rivers, frequently constituting as much as three-fourths of a river population. In swift streams like the St. Croix and Snake, the redhorses seem to be so much better adapted to fast currents than the carp that they continue in greater abundance than the European intruder. Although classed as rough fish, the redhorses are to a large extent unjustly maligned. They are fishes of swift, relatively clean waters. Redhorses are big, strong, and active on the end of a line, making heavy long runs when first hooked in fast water. Although bony like all members of the sucker family, their flesh is white and firm; in an iron skillet it can be fried with butter to a crisp golden brown that should tempt even the most critical epicure! The common white sucker, too, is held in high esteem by many, especially when taken in the spring spawning runs in small streams. When smoked, they are delicious.

The sheepshead, or freshwater drum, a rough fish which is abundant below St. Anthony Falls and in slower streams like the Minnesota and Red, was not originally found above the falls. Having somehow dispersed into the upper river, it now appears to be confined to the Mississippi below Coon Rapids dam. The sheepshead is another species that deserves greater respect as a sport and food fish.

The brook trout is the only stream member of the salmon family native to Minnesota's waters. Apparently it was left behind in cold-water tributaries of the Mississippi below the falls, mainly in streams of the southeastern driftless area, as the glaciers melted back and the climate warmed. However, the brook trout, as well as the brown (from Europe), was successfully introduced into many upper Mississippi tributaries. In addition to very small creeks where the brook trout now reproduces successfully, two larger streams have developed into perhaps the best-known trout streams in Minnesota—the Kabekona River, tributary to Kabekona Lake, for brooks, and the Straight River, in the Crow Wing watershed, for trophy browns (Chapter 11).

In addition to these recreational fisheries important in the Mississippi, a small commercial fishery provides seasonal and part-time work to fishermen who know and work the river in all its moods. Licensed commercial fishermen from either state may take rough fish for sale from the Wisconsin-Minnesota boundary waters, including the St. Croix from highway U.S. 8 south and the Mississippi down to the southern Minnesota border. Such fishing is permitted with seines and, in the Mississippi only, with set-lines and gill nets. The rough fish include gar, carp, and sheepshead, as well as buffalo, quillback, and other suckers; catfish of a prescribed size may be taken. However, carp dominates the fishery, constituting about two-thirds of the catch in pounds. Game fish such as walleyes, smallmouth and largemouth bass, northern pike, and others, must be returned if caught. Seining is often done in the winter through the ice.

In these interstate waters total production—that is, total catch of rough fish—has been declining in the last few years; from a high in Minnesota of a little more than 1 million pounds in the mid-1960s, the total for the last few years has declined to about one-third million pounds. Wisconsin catches, from the same waters, are higher. The number of licensed Minnesota fishermen is about 200, and the approximate value of the total catch is $25,000.

Fishery managers are worrying these days about the possibility of another carp problem. The grass carp, or white amur, is a native of Asian rivers. It feeds on submerged aquatic vegetation, and the benefit claimed for the fish by those who imported and promoted it is that it can control excessive weed growth in lakes and farm ponds. This claim has been challenged, however. Furthermore, it is feared that the grass carp will proliferate at a great rate and spread widely, competing with game fish. The real problem for Minnesota is that it is more a river fish than the European carp; its native habitats are similar to our warm-water, swift streams like the upper Mississippi, the Snake, and the St. Croix. Another concern in Minnesota is its effect on wild rice and other aquatic plants that serve as food for waterfowl. It has been stocked in some southern states and has been observed in the Mississippi, but so far, at least, it has not appeared in Minnesota.

Citizen interest in Minnesota's Mississippi is increasing at a rapid rate. A number of groups, spontaneously formed by persons interested in the river's problems, have sprung up and are active in working on specific solutions. On the state level, the 1974 legislature established an Esthetic Environmental Program; the first undertaking—a conference entitled *Mississippi I*—was a study of citizen interest in preserving the great river's values of all kinds; attendance and work at meetings and workshops was overwhelming, and in following years other conferences, *Mississippi II* and then *III*, were sponsored by the newly formed citizens' group, "Voice of the Mississippi." The federal- and state-sponsored Upper Mississippi River Basin Commission formed GREAT (GREAT River Environmental Action Team) as a forum for public discussion and involvement in planning the Mississippi's future with respect to floodplain management, fish, wildlife, recreation, and commercial transportation issues. Recently, the state of Minnesota designated the fifty-five-mile reach from St. Cloud to Anoka a component of the state's Wild, Scenic, and Recreational Rivers System. An amendment of the National Wild and Scenic Rivers Act designated the entire Mississippi from Lake Itasca to Anoka, a distance of 467 river miles, a study stream in the national system. The Mississippi was assigned top priority, and studies began in the same year to determine the river's qualifications to meet the criteria of the nationwide system.

GREAT river, indeed!

Chapter 14

The Southeast

Rivers of the Driftless Area

igh on a windy, wooded ridge overlooking the old townsite
of Beaver in the Whitewater Valley is a small graveyard.
Rows of white cedars, planted many years ago, mark the
cemetery borders and outline some grave sites. Many graves are more
than a hundred years old; the inscriptions carved on headstones are
difficult to read, if distinguishable at all, worn by a century of rain
and frost.

Here lie the settlers who first came to Minnesota—men and
women who lived to be very old, even by today's standards, tough-
ened by the rigors of the frontier. Here also lie row upon row of children, here and there a row from a single family, struck down by dis-
eases that have since been controlled. As in many other small ceme-
teries in the southeast, these stones and mounds are mute testimonies
to a half-century venture in self-sufficiency that failed. It failed because of agricultural practices destructive to the soils of the southeast
where running waters stripped the upper valleys and hillsides, deep-
ened the gorges, and carried the earth, disturbed by the plow, away
from the fragile slopes. Old Beaver now lies buried beneath twelve
feet of eroded and redeposited soil.

The land in the southeast corner of Minnesota is surprising in a state named after the North Star. It is a rugged land of wild timber and rushing streams, but it is also reminiscent of southern foothills—of parts of the Appalachians, of the Ozarks—a land of hills and hollows. It greens early in spring and wild flowers bloom first in the deep gorges. Its climate is more southern than the climate of the rest of Minnesota; its timbered valleys are lush with black walnut on the bottoms and hickory in the hills—neither found to the north; here are wild turkey, bobwhite quail, possums, and huge timber rattlers. It is a region with hundreds of small stream valleys and high, wild, bosky ravines. The southeast contains many superb trout and smallmouth bass streams; deep, misty gorges with placid canoe waters; caves and caverns of unsurpassed beauty; and clear, cold springs and cave-openings where sparkling trout streams erupt into rushing rapids.

The southeast has other surprises, too, for these hills are significantly unlike the southern mountains: more than one adventurer clambering up a wild streamcourse has emerged at the top to view not dark green valleys and shadowed rock ramparts, but the edge of a cornfield—and beyond, a vast rolling plain, dotted with farmhouse, barn, and silo. This is the "driftless area"—a land the glaciers missed —a rugged land carved by a sequence of geological events unique on the North American continent.

Long ago this region of central North America lay beneath a warm ocean, and later the deposited sediments, cemented and compressed, emerged to form a great, limestone-capped plateau. Much of that limestone, as well as deeper strata of other sedimentary rock, lies beneath the plains of southern Minnesota and the adjoining states to the east and south. Down the middle of it runs the mighty Mississippi River through a channel several miles wide, carved by the tremendous Glacial River Warren at the end of the last glaciation. Here the Mississippi's tributaries—our rivers of the driftless area—fed by melting glaciers and faced with steeper and steeper gradients on their way to the big river, also cut deep into the sedimentary rock.

The driftless area was an island of rocky uplands of 10,000 square miles in Minnesota, Wisconsin, Iowa, and Illinois, slightly

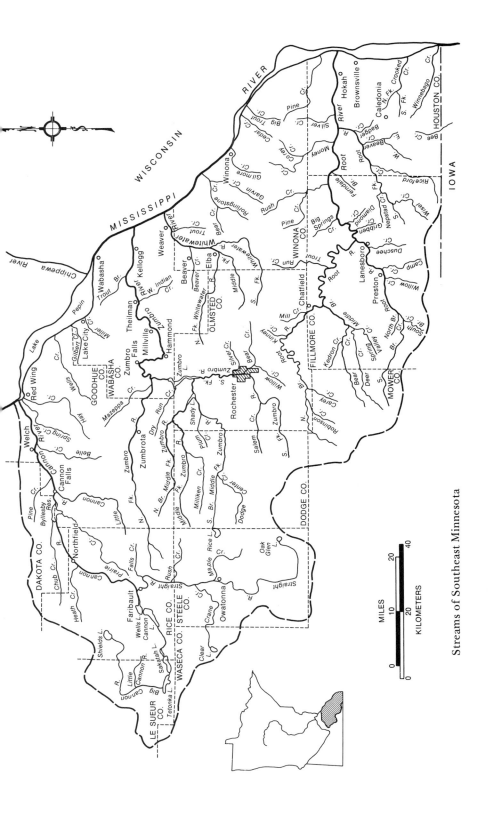

Streams of Southeast Minnesota

higher than the surrounding plains and therefore bypassed by the ice sheets of the last glacial period. Earlier glaciers may have covered the area, or at least intruded, but if they did, their deposits of clay, silt, and rock—glacial drift—have long since been eroded away. The last glaciers surrounded but did not penetrate this "driftless" island. Glacial drift, recognizable elsewhere in Minnesota today as moraines, till plains, rounded boulders, and sandy outwash plains, is absent from the region. The driftless area is a geologic relic—affected by surrounding glaciers, but not covered with their remains.

A significant characteristic of limestone that has had an impact on the physical environment of the southeast is its great solubility. Groundwater, resulting from precipitation that percolates through cracks and fissures in the limestone, dissolves the calcium carbonate of the rock and carries away the solution. The results are caverns, underground rivers, caves that discharge streams directly from valley walls, and, on top of the plain, sinkholes that drain underground and sometimes are plugged to form "sink" lakes. This karst topography is characteristic of southeast Minnesota and other parts of the driftless area, both before and after glaciation.

As glaciation was ending, much silt, sand, and gravel was carried by meltwaters in the rivers, including the Mississippi, and its channel filled with sediment to a level much higher than that of today's floodplains. The Mississippi's tributaries also formed wide, flat floodplains at this higher level. Later the clear waters of highly erosive Glacial River Warren eroded the valley floor several hundred feet. The tributaries also eroded to successively lower levels of the River Warren, leaving terraces of alluvial deposits perched along the sides of the valleys, in some places up to sixty-five feet above present floodplains. Such terraces now can be traced far upstream.

After Lake Agassiz ceased to drain south and the River Warren no longer flowed, the postglacial Mississippi River deposited its load of silt and sand on the valley floor to a thickness of 200 feet. The Mississippi today lies several hundred feet below the limestone plain, reflecting the tremendous erosive power of the glacial rivers.

The upper stream valleys of the driftless area are characterized by steep-walled bluffs of limestone and other sedimentary rock; thus runoff from snowmelt and torrential summer rainstorms produces flash floods, short-lived but severe. Combined with the great quantities of alluvial sediments in the old terraces, this "flashy" character of the streams resulted in much erosion in the past and accelerated erosion since immigration and settlement. In the lower reaches the streams meander back and forth across valley floodplains, eating into the terraces, changing course frequently, and carrying away or moving immense quantities of gravel, silt, and sand. Erosion occurred, though slowly, for many thousands of years after glaciation, creating rugged valleys, high bluffs, and rocky, swift streams.

But it was accelerated erosion that plagued the early settlers as they attempted to farm the fertile but vulnerable alluvial terraces and the headwater slopes. It was this activity of man that brought about in only a few decades, the ruin of farmers' hopes and the desolation on the land.

The southeastern corner was the first area of Minnesota to be reached by steamers bound upriver and carrying farmer-immigrants; therefore it was the first to be settled. The land was attractive with a moderate climate and the promise of agricultural productivity. The valleys contained rich soil, abundant timber for building and fuel, and water for power and domestic use.

It is difficult to pinpoint the time of initial settlement, for first cabins and gardens are usually impermanent and often leave no trace. But it appears that by the late 1840s there were some settlements in Houston County that survived. In 1851 the Mendota treaty of land cession from the Lower Sioux opened much of southern Minnesota to legal occupancy by whites; soon thereafter the railroads came overland from the east to the Mississippi, and then steamers reached Minnesota in an increasing tide of river traffic. Many towns and villages of Houston County were platted then, and soon the valleys of the Root, Whitewater, Zumbro, and Cannon were claimed by thousands. The density of settlement varied inversely with the distance from these streams.

At first, wheat production on the river terraces and surrounding prairies stimulated the prosperity of the farmers, and many small "flouring mills" were set up on the streams. Flour was a "money" crop that made some affluent. Ox teams carried wheat through the river valleys to market and brought lumber on the return trip. There was a sawmill at Brownsville by 1855, the year the Root River Steamboat Company formed; and the Southern Minnesota Railroad began to serve the entire area in the latter 1850s.

But as portents of the disaster to follow, storms and floods plagued the southeastern valley farmers. The Root flooded severely in 1865, though without much permanent damage; but the flood in 1876, far worse, resulted in several deaths. Not only floods, but also weather, insects, and soil exhaustion caused repeated wheat failures, and the need to diversify was recognized—to turn from dependence on wheat to a variety of crops and livestock. More and more marginal lands on the upland slopes were plowed, and pasturing on the hillsides increased.

The steep valley slopes were stripped of trees for lumber, and surfaces were even burned over in an attempt to establish grass for grazing. The result was severe erosion of the thin soil, formation of new gullies, and deep scouring of cool spring-water brooks to form steep, unstable, rocky dry washes. Continued grazing prevented reestablishment of vegetative cover. Soon the valley floors were buried with the alluvium of flash floods, and the once clear streams were choked with the debris of logging and deposited mud.

Finally, prosperity was gone. In its wake the valleys were left damaged almost beyond repair—the timber exhausted, fields inundated with barren deposits of rubble and sand, the waters fouled. Whole villages, like Beaver and Whitewater Falls, were entombed by erosional debris. Farms failed and were abandoned, and the former beauty of the valleys was replaced by the ugliness of eroded gullies and muddy waters.

Onto this scene of desolation in the mid-1930s strode a man to match the times. Richard J. Dorer was a giant of a man physically, and he was fired with intellectual energy and apostolic zeal. He was tough, like the junipers that clung to the sere south-facing slopes, but perceptive. He was responsive to the prairie wild flowers and would write insightful poetry about Minnesota's natural resources. He walked the wild valleys of the Whitewater and climbed the steep hills, and he looked at the eroded wasteland that was left. But he also looked into the future toward the beauty and productivity that others could achieve in these valleys if they would but work with fundamental ecological principles rather than against them—though he never expressed those principles in the language of the academic ecologist.

Dorer joined the Minnesota Department of Conservation in 1938, worked in several capacities and, ultimately, in the mid-1950s,

The Root River winds among steep, wooded hills in southeastern Minnesota. Now mostly incorporated in the Richard J. Dorer Memorial Hardwood State Forest, the deeply incised valleys and hills of the southeast constitute a rugged, picturesque land, called Minnesota's "little Switzerland." The Root and its branches are superb canoe streams, especially when the hardwoods are in flaming autumn color. Many of the Root's small tributaries are excellent trout streams.

he served as the Supervisor of the Bureau of Game. But his powers of observation, foresight, and evangelism were needed most in the years of depression and uncertainty—the 1930s and 1940s. He saw the Whitewater Valley not only as the magnificent public hunting ground that it could—and would—become. His interest was broader—he respected all wildlife, the native plants, the soil and rivers, and all the natural elements of what we now call an ecosystem working in harmony. And he saw man as a part of the ecosystem—hunting, fishing, learning, planting, and modifying his own impact on the system.

Concentrating on the Whitewater Valley, Dorer led the fight for restoration of the eroding slopes. Trees, shrubs, and grasses were replanted, gullies were blocked and filled, grazing stopped, improved cultivation practices were encouraged, and much abandoned land was placed in state ownership and brought under the protection of public management.

Dorer saw much land as inappropriate for agriculture but suited for other uses, and he wrote about them in his poetry and children's books. Dorer also was responsible for initiating the "Save the Wetlands" movement, a Minnesota program emulated around the world.

He did not appeal just to sportsmen for support to return game populations to the Whitewater; he sought out people whom he felt would appreciate all forms of life and land in harmony—he spoke to schools, churches, garden and bird clubs, the Izaak Walton League, the League of Women Voters, college classes, and many others. He fought untiringly for his plan to establish the Minnesota Memorial Hardwood State Forest.

Although flooding of the driftless area streams is still a major environmental problem to be dealt with, we have learned something about proper land use since the first settlers put plow to the soil—not only how to reduce flooding but also how to live with it. Even so, some rivers and streams are threatened anew as world food markets clamor and marginal headwater lands, once healed, are scarred again. It will take wisdom—and willpower—to reject unwise utilization and the consequent profits for the sake of a lovely river.

Dorer was an environmentalist before the word was coined; Minnesota is fortunate to have had him. The restored river valleys of the southeast are today living monuments to his stewardship.

The southeastern rivers include four major streams—Cannon, Zumbro, Whitewater, and Root rivers—and several smaller streams, all directly tributary to the Mississippi. Together, their watersheds comprise 5,708 square miles, primarily in Dakota, Goodhue, Rice, Wabasha, Dodge, Olmsted, Winona, Fillmore, and Houston counties. All streams originate on the cultivated glacial plains of southern Minnesota, wind slowly east, and drop abruptly into wooded gullies, ravines, and, eventually, the deep gorges of the driftless area.

The Cannon, the northernmost of the four, has its sources in an area of many lakes, some large, in eastern Le Sueur County and western Rice County; the main stem originates in Shields Lake. From Shields Lake, it winds first west as the Big Cannon River, then south, and eventually northeast. From the lake region of glacial drift and moraines, the Cannon begins its major drop into deeper valleys near Northfield, whose citizens in an earlier era frustrated Jesse James's raid and brought about the ignoble end of the Younger brothers. Near Cannon Falls is a hydroelectric station where the major dam on the river impounds Byllesby Reservoir; there are other large dams at Faribault and Northfield. From Cannon Falls down to the Mississippi, the Cannon flows through the most scenic and deepest part of its valley, at the foot of rock cliffs and bluffs towering as high as 360 feet above the river. A low dam and old mill remain at the village of Welch in this lower reach. The major tributaries of the Cannon are the Straight River, flowing north through Owatonna to Faribault, and the Little Cannon River, entering at Cannon Falls; lesser tributaries are Prairie Creek from Nerstrand Woods, Belle Creek entering in the lower gorge, and a few small trout streams.

Two state parks are located in the Cannon watershed. Nerstrand Woods State Park embraces Prairie Creek in eastern Rice County; the park includes an excellent area of relic big hardwoods in the steep creek valley and picturesque Hidden Falls on the creek, accessible after a pleasant walk down into the timbered ravine. In Sakatah Lake State Park, a spacious, heavily timbered park, the Cannon flows through the Sakatah Lakes; canoe access is available between the two, and there is boat-ramp access in the park. The Cannon River Scout Reservation located on the south shore of Byllesby Reservoir is used by many Scout troops. Several Rice County parks are also associated with the Cannon River or its tributaries — Falls Creek Park on a tributary of the Straight River, McCullough Park on Shields Lake, the source of the Cannon, and Shager Park on Cannon Lake, through which the river flows.

The Cannon is one of the major canoeing resources of the southeast included in the state's *A Gathering of Waters*. The upper sections include many lakes, several dams, and difficult portages, and in the lower water of late summer it may be too shallow for canoeing. The state guide suggests beginning at Sakatah Lakes; from there, in addition to Sakatah, Cannon, and Wells lakes, Byllesby Reservoir must be navigated; dams at Lower Lake Sakatah, Faribault, Northfield, and Byllesby must be portaged. From Sakatah Lake to Byllesby dam is about forty-five miles. Within this section the reach from Faribault and the mouth of the Straight to the upper end of Byllesby is twenty-five miles long, and the flow is generally sufficient for canoeing; there are no lakes and only one portage at Northfield. Probably most canoeists, however, prefer the reach from Cannon Falls (a municipal park provides excellent access) to a landing at the U.S. 61 highway crossing; this is the deepest reach of the Cannon's lower gorge and the most scenic, a section of seventeen miles; one portage is necessary around the old mill dam at Welch. Canoeists may have some problems immediately below Byllesby Reservoir unless there is sufficient discharge from the dam. The Straight River is also a pleasant canoe stream, small and flowing between wooded banks in a predominantly agricultural area. It is best in the higher water of springtime; the water is too low in late summer. The Straight is also described in the state guide, *A Gathering of Waters*.

The river's name is an English mistranslation of the French Rivière aux Canots, or Canoe River; the French and Indians cached their canoes at the river's mouth while hunting buffalo on nearby prairies.

The Cannon is the longest of the four major streams in the southeast, about 110 miles long from Shields Lake to the Mississippi. The upper stream, which includes several lakes, is known as the Big Cannon River in the forty-mile stretch above Sakatah Lake. (There is another Little Cannon River, a small stream tributary to this reach.) From Lower Sakatah Lake to Faribault is about fifteen miles, to Cannon Falls another thirty miles, and from there to the mouth in the Mississippi near Red Wing another twenty-five. The Cannon drains a watershed of 1,462 square miles, mostly in Dakota, Rice, and Goodhue counties. For most of its length, the Cannon is gentle water, with moderate currents but few rapids. Its total drop is about 400 feet, an average gradient of slightly less than four feet per mile; between Northfield and Cannon Falls is the greatest drop, but much of this is in the fall over the Byllesby dam. The gradient is again lower from Cannon Falls to the mouth. Average annual discharge is about 560 cubic feet per second, with a maximum of about 40,000; alkalinity is high, about 225 p.p.m., the result of the limestone bedrock.

The Zumbro River is not quite as long as the Cannon, its watershed is more compact, and its tributary system is more extensive. The Zumbro consists essentially of three major forks —North, Middle, and South—all originating in cultivated till plains in the western part of the watershed and all flowing roughly east and joining to form the main stem near Mazeppa. The river then flows through a deep gorge to its mouth in the Mississippi near Kellogg.

The headwater tributaries are slow-flowing and generally turbid, draining the plains of southern Minnesota. The water is clearer, at least in late summer, where the deep gorge is lined with hardwood timber in the lower section. The river meanders through a wide, flat floodplain, much of which is cultivated for corn and soybeans. In the lower reaches the river is as much as 500 feet below the uplands. Unlike the Cannon's, the Zumbro's watershed contains few natural lakes, although there are several impoundments of the stream. One of the most notable is Shady Lake at Oronoco, formed by damming the junction of the Middle Fork and its South Branch; Oronoco County Park on the reservoir provides camp and picnic grounds but no boat access. In 1858 gold was discovered in the riverbed of the lower Middle Fork, precipitating the short-lived Oronoco Gold Rush. Subsequent floods, after which the diggings were no longer profitable, ended the rush. Several impoundments were formed by dams constructed near Rochester on the South Fork—Lake Mayowood, a recreational lake created a few miles west of Rochester in the 1930s and now nearly filled with silt; Silver Lake, a millpond constructed in Rochester in the mid-1800s; and large Zumbro Lake, also on the South Fork north of Rochester, a reservoir impounded by a hydroelectric dam serving Rochester. Silver Lake harbors many thousands of Canada geese, during both winter and seasonal migrations; it is the site of the discovery in 1960 of the giant Canada goose, a subspecies previously thought to be extinct. Flood damage has occurred in Rochester, the result of rapid expansion of residential and commercial development in floodplains where floods are common, and the Corps of Engineers proposes channelizing natural streams in the area as a means of flood control. Several miles of channelization and levee construction along lower reaches of the main stem below Kellogg have been completed to control flooding of agricultural lands near the mouth of the river.

The major tributaries of the Zumbro are its three forks and their branches; most tributary names are variants of the name Zumbro: the North Fork originates in southeast Rice County and flows east to join the main stem near Mazeppa; the Middle Fork, with both North and South branches, joins the main stem in Zumbro Lake; and the South Fork flows through Rochester and north to Zumbro Lake and the other forks.

There is one state park in the Zumbro River watershed, Rice Lake State Park in Steele County; Rice Lake is a headwater source of the South Branch of the Middle Fork. Olmsted County parks include Oxbow Park on the South Branch of the Middle Fork and Oronoco Park on the Shady Lake impoundment of the Middle Fork. There is also an unimproved park below Zumbro Lake dam, with good canoe access. Five miles up the valley from Kellogg, in the lower gorge, is the new Kruger Campground and Recreation Area, administered in the Memorial Hardwood State Forest. It includes trails, river access, picnic area, and a campground perched high on a wooded plateau overlooking the valley; it is named after Willis Kruger, former game warden in the southeast district who contributed significantly to the rehabilitation of the southeast and the establishment of the state forest.

Canoeing on the Zumbro presents another view of the deep, wooded gorges of the driftless area. Most upper tributaries are too small, thus canoeists generally prefer the reach downstream from the junction of the forks. First access is at Zumbro Falls, at a riverside picnic ground maintained by the Zumbro Valley Sportsmen's Club. Other landings exist at Hammond, Millville, Theilman, and Kruger campground. The lower reach, Zumbro Falls to the mouth, is a wild section of clear water, gentle rapids, steep bluffs, and heavily wooded riverbanks. The Zumbro is mapped and described briefly in the state guide, *A Gathering of Waters*; it deserves a place in the itinerary of Minnesota canoeists.

The name Zumbro is an English approximation of the French Rivière des Embarras—*embarras*: an obstruction by log jams and driftwood, which is characteristic of the lower river.

The Zumbro and its many tributaries comprise a watershed of 1,428 square miles, primarily in Goodhue, Wabasha, Dodge, and Olmsted counties. The North, Middle, and South forks all flow about fifty miles each; the main stem, beginning at the junction of the South and North forks a few miles up from Zumbro Falls, flows another fifty miles to its mouth in the Mississippi near Kellogg. From the highest headwaters to its mouth the Zumbro's waters fall about 600 feet, but the main stem, from the junction of the North Fork and the other branches, drops only 180 feet to its mouth, a gradient of about three and one-half feet per mile. The mean discharge is about 650 cubic feet per second, with a maximum over 30,000; alkalinity, like that of the Cannon, is about 225 p.p.m.

Much of the spacious Whitewater watershed of streams, valleys, and wooded hills is in the Whitewater Wildlife Management Area and two state parks, although the planned land acquisition for the wildlife area is not complete. The watershed of 296 square miles is much smaller than the other three major ones in the southeast. It does not extend very far west and thus includes none of the glaciated plains. Instead relatively more of the area is wooded ravine and rocky bluff. Present state ownership of land in the wildlife management area includes 25,000 acres (about forty square miles), and acquisition of an additional 14,000 is planned for completion of management objectives.

The Whitewater Wildlife Management Area began in the early 1930s as a game refuge, and hunting became common in the area in the 1940s. A small interior portion of the management area is retained now as a refuge, where pools and marshes are diked to hold water and serve the needs of migrating waterfowl. However, most hunting is probably for deer, much of it with the bow, an increasingly popular sport. Cottontail rabbits and squirrels, abundant in the wooded ravines, are popular quarry, and hunting for ruffed grouse and woodcock is increasing. The Whitewater is also the scene of a successful reintroduction in 1964 of the wild turkey. Although they are extremely wary birds, they are now plentiful enough that large flocks are occasionally seen, and surplus birds are live-trapped and introduced to other areas in the southeast. A limited hunting season will soon be instituted.

There are about 30,000 days of hunting in the wildlife area per year, but this is by no means the greatest use of the area. It also serves as an outdoor classroom for many thousands of students, teachers, and scientists. Also, more than twice as many fishermen use the area as hunters, taking advantage of the superb stream-trout fishing. A few years ago, indiscriminate use of four-wheel drive and off-road vehicles created serious problems of vegetation destruction and erosion on stream banks and steep slopes; all such motorized vehicles, including snowmobiles, are today prohibited off regular roads in the wildlife management area. However, snowshoe travel and, more recently, cross-country skiing are increasingly popular winter sport activities and are much more compatible with wildlife objectives. Camping is not permitted in the management area, although

In the Whitewater Valley, hunter and dog enjoy the splendor of towering lime-stone outcrops. Upland bird hunting can be enjoyed in the Whitewater Wildlife Management Area, along the same riverbanks that provide superb trout fishing in season.

The wild turkey, once native to the rugged hill country of Minnesota's southeastern watersheds, has been successfully reintroduced in the Whitewater and Root River valleys, and self-sustaining populations are flourishing. Extremely shy, they are seldom seen. Although not legal game now, their growing numbers will provide some excess birds for a limited open season in the near future. Because of their wariness, they will provide an unusual sporting challenge, in which only the most skilled hunter will be successful.

some private campgrounds and the state parks provide accommodations in the watershed.

The Whitewater system consists principally of the three forks—North, Middle, and South—and two smaller tributaries, Beaver Creek from the north and Trout Creek from the south. Beaver Creek flows through the old village site of Beaver; both were named for the earlier fur-trapping enterprise. The route from the fur country passed through Beaver to the Mississippi where flatboats were waiting to be loaded with peltries and produce.

Floods have always been the scourge of the Whitewater Valley. They followed man's unwise scarring of the steep slopes and contributed to the desolation of the 1930s. Probably the worst series of floods occurred in 1938, when twenty-eight storms ravaged the valley and tore away topsoil. But it was very recently—1974 and 1975 —that the most intense storms, torrential summer thunderstorms, occurred. And the floods that followed taught a striking lesson in land use: the South Fork, where the watershed is almost entirely covered by vegetation and is protected by state ownership in the wildlife management area, subsequently ran clear and full of trout; but the North Fork, recently returned to intense cultivation on marginally productive land, flowed with thick mud and silt almost all year long. It has become an augury of spring when the Whitewater overflows its banks, and Minnesota Highway 74 is closed between Weaver and Elba. But when floodwaters recede, the Whitewater floodplain again provides wildlife habitat, rippling streams, and scenic beauty—a wise use of this kind of land.

The two state parks in the Whitewater watershed are Whitewater State Park on the Middle Fork and Carley State Park on the North Fork. Whitewater, with close to 1,000 acres, is one of the most popular state parks in Minnesota—it provides trails below splendid bluffs and atop scenic lookouts, camping, picnicking, and trout fishing. Carley, smaller, is more primitive and isolated; hiking and camping can be enjoyed along the rocky bluffs rimmed with giant white pines. The deeply eroded limestone ravines and wooded slopes of the driftless area contribute to scenic values in both parks.

The Whitewater is not a canoeing stream, but the main stem from Elba downstream is minimally passable. The upper three forks are too small—just as well, for they are outstanding as trout streams.

The name "Whitewater" conveys a picture of sparkling rapids and shining pools, and so it did to the Sioux, whose name for the stream was translated and adopted—the word for "white," *ska*, appended to "water," *mini*. The name of the nearby town of Minneiska has the same origin.

The main stem of the Whitewater is about fifteen miles long, from the confluence of the three forks to its mouth in the Mississippi, and the mean gradient is five feet per mile. Gradients on the three forks, as expected in these tumbling trout waters, are considerably higher, usually about twenty-five feet per mile on each. Mean discharge near the mouth is probably about 200 cubic feet per second; the maximum in the 1974-1975 summer storms was perhaps a hundred times greater.

The Root River watershed, 1,670 square miles, is slightly larger than either the Cannon or the Zumbro, but it seems much larger because the watershed includes more streams, valleys, and hills. More of the Root's watershed is put to recreational use than to agriculture. Some of the tributary headwaters do originate in the glacial drift of agricultural areas such as eastern Mower and Olmsted counties, but virtually the entire network of rivers and streams in Winona, Fillmore, and Houston counties lies in a system of steep coulees, timbered slopes, rushing streams, and deep, winding valleys. The main-stem Root has three main branches—North, Middle, and South—which rise in thin glacial drift in northeast Mower County. The North and Middle branches join near Chatfield, and the South Branch confluence with the main stem is near Lanesboro. The section between Chatfield and Lanesboro (North plus Middle) is also officially termed the Middle Branch, but it is known locally as the North. From Lanesboro downstream, the Root flows in a valley that becomes deeper and deeper in its course to the Mississippi; the gorges are 400 to 550 feet below rugged ranges of wooded hills and the steep buttresses of tributary valleys. The floodplain of this lower reach is in some places a mile wide; here corn and soybeans are cultivated. Even tobacco—a few acres—is produced. There are no natural lakes in the Root watershed.

The Root's tributaries might have been named more imaginatively. In addition to the North, Middle, and South branches, the main stem in its lower reach receives the South Fork from the south near Houston. Upstream from Preston on the South Branch, are North Branch Creek and South Branch Creek. Smaller named tributaries enter the longer branches and forks in a highly dendritic pattern.

There are two state parks in the Root watershed — Beaver Creek Valley State Park near Caledonia and the new Forestville State Park near Preston. The former includes one of the most beautiful spring brooks in the southeast, East Beaver Creek, a tributary of the South Fork. Beaver Creek begins in large springs and flows through extensive watercress beds below high bluffs. Camping, picnicking, hiking, and trout fishing are available. Forestville State Park is located on the upper South Branch where it is a clear-water trout stream of deep green pools and sparkling riffles. Campsites are located on the South Branch, and picnic grounds at the mouth of North Branch Creek. The latter is one of the most productive of the southeast's trout streams, and its headwater source is in a large cave. The focal point of Forestville State Park is the old Forestville store, a stage stop and post office which opened in the mid-1800s; the last proprietor, Thomas Meighen, closed the shop in 1910, leaving in place an inventory of hardware, bottled medicines, dry goods, and other items (including a straw hat for a horse). The store may now be viewed by park visitors in much the same condition as Meighen left it.

The Root must be regarded as one of Minnesota's outstanding canoeing resources. Several routes exist on the upper three branches, for example, beginning at Forestville State Park on the South Branch (at moderately high water levels) or near Chatfield below the junction of the North and Middle branches. The lower gorge from Lanesboro down — a distance of fifty miles to the Mississippi — is the outstanding reach for rugged hills, bluffs, and slowly meandering river. In the fall the floodplains are yellow with ripening corn and soybeans, but the wooded hillsides are bright with autumn leaves. The upper branches have series of pools and small rapids, and are too shallow for canoeing in low water; a few modest rapids occur in the lower gorge reach. Guides to the river have been prepared by the Root River Canoe Trails Association in Rushford, and the Commercial Club of Chatfield; the Root canoe trail is also included in the state's *A Gathering of Waters*.

The name Root, like Whitewater, is derived from a Sioux name for the stream, and possibly refers to tree roots exposed along the stream after floods. Their word for "root" was *hokah* or *hutkan*, and the town of Hokah on the river reflects this origin.

In all, the Root drops about 550 feet from its upper headwater tributaries to the Mississippi. The highest gradients are in the three branches in fast-water sections; the lower reach of fifty miles from Lanesboro to the Mississippi drops 170 feet, a mean gradient of only about three and one-half feet per mile. Mean discharge of the main stem at the mouth is close to 1,000 cubic feet per second, the highest of all the southeast rivers; maximum flow reached perhaps 50,000 in the 1974 summer storm. Alkalinities in the headwaters and small tributaries that flow from limestone are high, over 200 p.p.m., like the alkalinities of other streams in the southeast, but they are a bit lower in the downstream reaches.

Between and south of the four major watersheds are smaller drainages from which several streams flow directly to the Mississippi. Like the small tributaries of the four major streams, these Mississippi tributaries are deeply incised in bedrock of limestone and other sedimentary rocks and have steep gradients. Between the Cannon and the Zumbro, an area bordered by Lake Pepin on the Mississippi, the watershed is drained by several small streams, Spring, Hay, Wells, Gilbert, and Miller creeks, all emptying into Lake Pepin or the head of Lake Pepin through Red Wing; the cities of Red Wing, Lake City, and Wabasha are included in this small watershed, as is Frontenac State Park, high on a point overlooking Lake Pepin. Between the Zumbro and the Whitewater is a small area drained by Gorman Creek and East Indian Creek (just over the hill from West Indian Creek, a tributary of the Zumbro). And between the Whitewater and the Root is a larger area including the city of Winona and a number of streams — Rollingstone Creek (or Rupprecht Creek in upper reaches), Garvin Brook, and Gilmore Creek. These are all trout streams, as are Cedar, Big Trout (or Pickwick), and Pine creeks, farther south. This area includes John A. Latsch State Wayside on the Mississippi, its three prominent bluffs Points Faith, Hope, and Charity overlooking Lock and Dam No. 5. Also in this area along the Mississippi just north of La Crescent is the proposed O. L. Kipp State Park, including many scenic bluffs along the big river. Finally, below the Root River watershed, in the southeasternmost corner of Minnesota is an area that drains partly to the Mississippi directly and partly into Iowa and the Upper Iowa River. The streams here include Crooked and Winnebago creeks to the Mississippi, and Bee (or Waterloo) Creek into Iowa; Waterloo Creek in Iowa is a highly valued trout stream, as is the short headwater section in Minnesota. These small additional watersheds cover a total of 852 square miles, draining either directly or indirectly to the Mississippi River.

The fishery resources of the southeast are varied and delightful. Except for the headwater areas of the Cannon, there are no natural lakes in the region. But the southeast's streams and rivers offer superb angling, particularly for trout and smallmouth bass. Fisheries can be classed in three principal categories: trout in the cold-water headwaters and small tributaries, smallmouth in middle reaches where fast-water riffles and rapids are present, and rough species which predominate in the lower reaches of the main-stem rivers. The last category includes several species of the sucker and redhorse family, catfish, and carp. An occasional walleye, northern pike, or smallmouth bass is also taken. Catfish are perhaps more common in the middle reaches than in the lower main stems.

There are about seventy-five named and identified trout streams in the southeast, constituting one of the two major trout areas in Minnesota (the other is the North Shore), and totaling about 275 miles of trout water. More than half the streams are classified by the Minnesota Department of Natural Resources as offering "good" or "prime" trout fishing; these comprise over 100 miles of stream. Most are small creeks, with fast-water riffles flowing over broken limestone bedrock, and many rise in caves and springs in the sedimentary rock. Generally they are cold and rich with invertebrate food organisms. Some are so small that they are best approached through bankside vegetation with great care; others, though small, flow through pasture and have ample room for a back cast. A few are big enough for the classic approach of the fly fisherman wading slowly upstream with dry fly and a long cast. Among the larger streams are the upper South Branch of the Root in Forestville State Park, Trout Run Creek tributary to the North Branch of the Root east of Chatfield, and the three upper forks of the Whitewater. Other popular trout streams are Duschee Creek near Lanesboro State Fish Hatchery, East Beaver Creek in Beaver Creek Valley State Park, South Branch Creek and North Branch Creek, both tributary to the South Branch of the Root in Forestville State Park, Mazeppa Creek (or Trout Brook) in the Zumbro watershed, and Garvin Brook tributary directly to the Mississippi near Winona. Other favorites are Hay Creek near Red Wing;

Beaver Creek in the Whitewater Wildlife Management Area; Gribben (or Whalen) and Diamond creeks near Lanesboro; upper South Fork of the Root, including its tributaries Nepstad and Wisel creeks; Crooked Creek with both North and South forks flowing directly to the Mississippi near Caledonia; and Bee Creek which flows south into Iowa. The adventurous can find many more with the help of a guide map distributed by the Department of Natural Resources, "Trout Streams in Southeastern Minnesota."

But a half-century ago, the streams of the southeast were not the cherished resources they are today. Severe erosion was starting to affect the fishery resource, and it did not pass unnoticed. Some of the earliest ecological research on fish and fish habitat was stimulated by the deteriorating conditions in this part of the state. Thaddeus Surber, an early biologist with the Minnesota Game and Fish Department, made the first extensive studies of the Root River watershed streams, beginning in 1920. He walked a thousand miles along the streams, listing and describing them in detail and observing the fishes present. He investigated stream conditions in relation to requirements of fish and recommended fish management procedures. As the result of his observations of the effects of erosion on trout stream conditions, he urged improved management of the stream valleys. He also found the large springs near Duschee Creek. Surber selected this site for what later became the Lanesboro State Fish Hatchery and promoted restocking of trout where conditions appeared suitable. However, it was long thought that the streams in the southeast were so prone to flooding that natural reproduction could not be successful. Today, however, with the return of vegetative cover in some watersheds and improved fish habitat in some streams owing to intensive management, reproduction of wild trout now appears to be common in many streams. And as a consequence, stocking of hatchery trout has been eliminated in some streams, and management goals now include establishment of the better-quality fishery provided by wild trout.

In most streams of the southeast the brown trout is the principal, or only, trout species. An import from Europe, the brown was

An angler wades Trout Run Creek, one of the southeast's better known and most productive trout streams. In late summer most of these streams are characterized by sparkling clear water, shaded by the lush vegetation in the deep valleys.

first stocked in the Root River watershed in 1888. It has now adapted to the southeast's streams, as it has to many throughout North America, because of two important traits. The first is that the brown is an unusually wary species and a permanent population can be maintained in the face of heavy angling; second, large individuals can grow and will remain in a relatively small stream, competing successfully with other species. Our other two common stream trout, the brook and the rainbow, do not share these characteristics. The brook trout is indigenous to streams in the southeast, relic populations apparently having been left in streams suitable for trout as the glaciers retreated, and the early settlers found the native trout in these streams. But the brook is not a wary fish and does not normally grow to be as large as the brown; native populations of brook trout probably were overexploited when civilization arrived. They have been widely stocked by the state, and naturally reproducing populations are now found in a few streams. The rainbow, a native of western North America, grows to a large size but prefers larger streams. It was first introduced in the Root's tributaries in 1887; it is now stocked widely by the state essentially for early-season fishing, but the rainbow rarely develops self-sustaining populations in small inland streams.

The brown trout, however, is ideal for the streams of the southeast. The brown rises well to an artificial fly or nymph (placed by the expert angler, of course) and is therefore highly prized by the fly fisherman. The individuals usually caught are about ten to twelve inches long, although specimens between fifteen and twenty inches (one to three pounds) are not uncommon. The very few unusually large—thirteen- or fourteen-pound—browns that are taken receive front-page coverage.

The popularity of some streams and extensive stocking of hatchery fish just before the trout season opening led to large crowds and a carnivallike atmosphere at some of the better streams on the opening weekend. The result was erosion of streambanks, litter, and a diminution of the very values that attract stream trout anglers. Now, with improved watershed cover and stream water quality, and a greater emphasis on wild trout than on hatchery stock, it seems appropriate to spread out fishing pressure and decrease the undesirable aspects of the opening day. Seasons have been lengthened, with an earlier opening (late winter) to provide more opportunity for recreation.

The southeast also offers some fine smallmouth bass fishing in its rivers. The smallmouth requires water only slightly warmer than do trout and also somewhat larger streams, preferring relatively fast water. The middle reaches of several of the southeast rivers provide ideal habitat.

Although all the main rivers provide some smallmouth fishing, the favorite reaches are the Middle Fork Zumbro, South Fork Zumbro upstream from Rochester, Salem Creek, the three upper branches of the Root, and the lower reaches of the South Fork of the Root. The stretch of the North Branch of the Root between Chatfield and Lanesboro is one of the most productive reaches of smallmouth water; also good are the lower South Branch, the Middle Branch, and lower reaches of the Middle Branch tributaries Bear and Kedron creeks. Angling may be done by wading in most reaches, and these streams are large enough so that often fishing can be combined with a canoe trip. In these stretches the channel catfish is also a common resident, usually taken from pools or quiet-water reaches between the smallmouth's rapids.

The dream of Dorer, Kruger, Surber, and many others for protection and wise management of the natural treasures of the driftless area became a possibility with the establishment by the Minnesota legislature in 1961 of the Memorial Hardwood State Forest, embracing essentially the Minnesota portion of the driftless area. In terms of administrative area, it is the largest of Minnesota's state forests, about two million acres (3,100 square miles); of this area, an estimated 460,000 acres are in forest, primarily the wooded stream valleys; it is intended that, of this, roughly half will be acquired in public ownership. The objectives of the enabling legislation are to "preserve the scenic beauty of the marvelous bluffs . . . provide camping sites, canoe routes, hiking and bridle trails and facilities for every type of winter sports and . . . furnish excellent hunting and fishing in exceptional surroundings." Within the administrative borders, the land will remain largely in private ownership, with public ownership concentrated along the streams and river valleys. Its management objectives are many, including high-quality timber production through restoration of damaged woodlands, protection of water quality, preservation of outstanding scenic resources, enhancement of fish and wildlife through habitat protection, and encouragement of outdoor recreation with proper use of unique natural areas. It is fitting that in 1976 this forest was renamed the Richard J. Dorer Memorial Hardwood State Forest.

The outstanding recreational values of the southeast were recognized early, and some of Minnesota's first state parks were established along the streams. Today the state forest's borders include seven state parks, many wildlife management areas including the large Whitewater, the Kruger Campground and Recreation Area, and many local parks and waysides; eventually it will probably include some units of the state Wild, Scenic, and Recreational Rivers System. The state forest also borders the Minnesota portion of the Upper Mississippi River Wildlife and Fish Refuge with its vast recreational resources along the big river. The dream proceeds toward reality.

Richard J. Dorer died October 11, 1973, and according to his wishes, he was buried the following day in the cemetery on the wooded ridge above old Beaver. His evangelism will be missed, but he left a colossal legacy of better understanding and clearer waters.

Minnesota owes much to the poet of the Whitewater Valley.

Chapter 15

The Upper Iowa and Cedar

Outlets to Iowa

Rising in the sunny pastures of southern Minnesota, the turbid Upper Iowa River flows slowly south over the plains of Minnesota into Iowa. After its initial entry into Iowa it loops north across the border four times before the river finally leaves Minnesota, heading east to its mouth in the Mississippi. Coursing through the clear pools and beneath the towering limestone bluffs of the rugged northeast corner of Iowa, this stream is one of the midwest's outstanding scenic resources, Iowa's proffered contribution to the National Wild and Scenic Rivers System.

The wild rivers legislation enacted in 1968 provided for eight "instant" wild rivers and twenty-seven "study" streams designated for possible addition. The latter were rivers identified as potential units of the national system, streams with recognized recreational and cultural value, but requiring additional investigation before being officially included. One of these was the Upper Iowa. In 1972 the Department of Interior recommended that the Upper Iowa be included with a scenic or recreational designation, and be administered by the state of Iowa. Thus far, Congress has not acted on this recommendation. Meanwhile, the river has been placed in a Natural River category by the Iowa State Scenic Rivers Law.

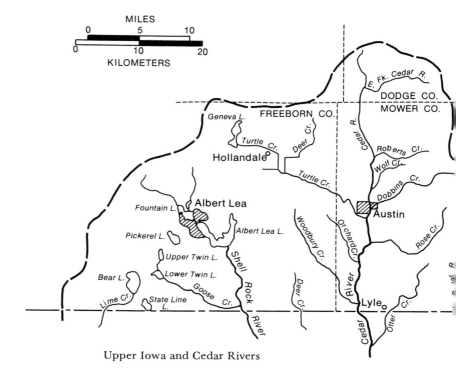

Upper Iowa and Cedar Rivers

The Upper Iowa begins as a small pasture creek in the rolling plains of southeastern Mower County. In its course south it accumulates several Minnesota tributaries, including the North Branch and the Little Iowa River. The stream near the town of Le Roy was dammed for water power to run a gristmill in the late 1800s. The old impoundment now is the central feature of Lake Louise State Park, an oasis of woodland flowers and hardwood timber in otherwise almost unbroken plains. Camping, swimming in the old mill pond, and numerous hiking trails are available at the park. From Le Roy the river flows southeast and crosses the Iowa-Minnesota border for the first time. At Lime Springs, Iowa, the river is dammed again, and the old mill still stands, in a county park. Good access to the river is available below the mill, the recommended beginning of the canoe route.

Downstream the river meanders north. Four times it recrosses the border until near Granger it finally leaves Minnesota. To the east, the Upper Iowa enters the driftless area of northeast Iowa—rugged, deeply eroded, superbly scenic country with the same geologic his-

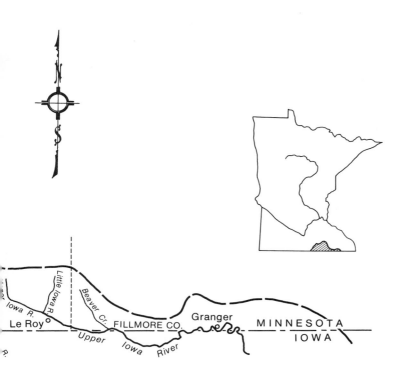

tory as southeastern Minnesota and southwestern Wisconsin. The Upper Iowa in this reach is the state's outstanding canoeing stream and also provides some fine smallmouth bass fishing in a pastoral setting of clear running water and gentle beauty. The river is spectacular in its lower reaches; limestone cliffs and palisades rise more than 100 feet from the river's entrenched meanders, and near the mouth bluff tops tower 450 feet above the valley floor. In addition to the popular smallmouth, a few trout are caught in the river. Trout are more common in many smaller tributary streams that emanate from the base of high limestone bluffs as springs, cool throughout the summer.

Even in Minnesota, considerable smallmouth and catfish angling is done, especially along the larger river loops in the state. Canoe access is also available in Minnesota, especially near Granger.

The Upper Iowa drains about seventy square miles of Minnesota, including that drained by its Minnesota tributaries. Minnesota can claim only a small part of the Upper Iowa River as its own. But we use the river and are responsible for the quality of its headwaters. With our Iowa neighbors and other Americans, Minnesotans are for-

The Upper Iowa River originates in southern Minnesota, where it was dammed to provide water power for grinding flour and feed. The old mill pond, now the central feature of Lake Louise State Park, remains to provide a spot for contemplating wild flowers, skipping rocks, or chewing a grass stem. Downstream in northeastern Iowa, the Upper Iowa River becomes a spectacular stream flowing at the foot of limestone bluffs that tower hundreds of feet above the water surface.

tunate to have the Upper Iowa included in the nation's river resources.

Although the 1851 Treaty of Mendota, by which the Sioux ceded most of southern Minnesota to the land-hungry whites, had not yet been officially ratified, settlers began their advances into the Cedar River watershed in 1852. Following these trailblazers, the greatest influx came between 1855 and 1860. They found this watershed in Mower County rich with agricultural potential. The dark prairie soils were well drained by the river and its tributaries in the upper watershed. The high central prairie—a flat plateau that divides the Cedar from the watersheds of the Root River to the east—was thought to have a more comfortable climate than lower elevations. Timber for building and fuel was ample, especially along the streams, and the first settlements in the county were located along the Cedar where Austin, the present county seat and largest city in the watershed, eventually was founded.

The watershed of the Cedar was soon peopled with industrious immigrants from central Europe, who created prosperous communities in this region where the prairie was fertile and the water supply reliable. They built cabins along the river, watered their stock from the creeks, and built numerous water-powered flouring mills as early as the 1860s. In 1908 the Cedar, after one of the greatest storms in its history, went over its banks and flooded Austin. Even so the development of the region was little slowed by such problems. Today it is bustling with industry as well as agriculture.

The Cedar rises in a group of small creeks, including the East Fork, in the pastures of southwestern Dodge County and flows south. Entering northwestern Mower County below the confluence of creeks, it is in many reaches wide and slow with little gradient. But in stretches north of Austin the gradient is steeper; here the Cedar is a scenic stream of riffles and pools, tumbling small rapids and fishing holes. At Ramsey an old mill dam still exists and impounds Ramsey Mill Pond, providing fishing for bluegills, crappies, northern pike, and largemouth bass. Driesner Park, an extensive municipal recreational development virtually in the downtown district, provides camping, picnicking, and other activities as well as fishing in the Cedar, which forms a natural border for this river park. Above Austin the major tributaries, besides the several headwater creeks, are Roberts and Dobbins creeks, both small streams flowing from the east; Dobbins Creek is also dammed in the city.

The Cedar's largest tributary, Turtle Creek, joins the river just below Austin from the west. Turtle Creek drains a large area in the western part of the Cedar watershed; many vegetables, particularly onions and potatoes, are raised in the vicinity of Hollandale, where low-lying peat lands occupy an old, drained lake bed. Here Turtle Creek, and its tributaries as well, are ditched deeply and straightened for many miles. A number of shallow lakes previously existed in the Turtle Creek watershed but have been drained; the only one left is Geneva Lake in northern Freeborn County, the headwater source of Turtle Creek and essentially the only lake in the entire Cedar River watershed. It is shallow and productive of waterfowl but not of fish.

Below Austin, the Cedar receives the tributaries Rose Creek

from the east and Orchard and Woodbury creeks from the west. Orchard Creek has some attractive characteristics in its lowest few miles; with its clear water and stony riffles, it resembles the trout streams of the Root River region to the east, but it is just a bit too warm. Some smallmouth bass habitat exists in this reach.

About three miles west of the village of Lyle the Cedar enters Iowa, having flowed in Minnesota about 40 miles; its total length is more than 300 miles. In Minnesota the Cedar drains 584 square miles, its mean discharge is about 225 cubic feet per second, and the maximum in flood stage was over 10,000.

The Cedar is one of Iowa's major rivers. South of the Minnesota border, but still in its upper reaches, the Cedar is one of the state's outstanding scenic river resources, its valley lined with limestone bluffs and hardwood and red cedar timber. The Cedar offers excellent canoeing and good smallmouth fishing, both in the main stream and the tributaries. In the lower reaches, channel catfish and flathead catfish provide the major fishery resources. Eventually the Cedar empties into the Iowa River in central Iowa. The Cedar is sometimes known as the Red Cedar River—for example, on Nicollet's maps of the region, no doubt named for the prominent stands of red cedar trees on its valley slopes.

Other streams enter Iowa from southern Minnesota. Some of these, such as Otter Creek and the Little Cedar River, are small tributaries of the Cedar, emptying into the main stream below the Iowa border. A larger one is the Shell Rock River, which heads in Albert Lea Lake in the city of Albert Lea and is the principal stream in Freeborn County. A wooded island is the outstanding feature of Helmer Myre State Park in and along Albert Lea Lake. In contrast to the Cedar watershed, many lakes occur in the Shell Rock drainage, the result of more recent glaciation in this region; in addition to Albert Lea Lake, the larger ones are Pickerel, Upper and Lower Twin, Bear, and State Line lakes. Albert Lea and the smaller lakes near it were formed behind glacial drift deposits that dammed depressions in an older Shell Rock Valley. The Shell Rock River and other smaller streams drain 570 square miles of Minnesota; the main stream flows twelve miles from Albert Lea Lake to the Iowa border and enters the Cedar in central Iowa. Goose Creek originates in the Twin Lakes and flows southeast to empty into the Shell Rock. Lime

Creek flows from Bear Lake, enters Iowa, and then empties into the Shell Rock. The Shell Rock is considered a smallmouth river in Iowa, but has many catfish and walleyes as well. Alkalinities in the Upper Iowa, Cedar, and Shell Rock systems, all originating in Minnesota and flowing into Iowa, are relatively high, ranging from about 150 to over 200 p.p.m.

In southwestern Minnesota, the Rock and Des Moines rivers also leave Minnesota for Iowa, but these streams, originating on the Coteau des Prairies (and discussed in Chapter 17), are separated from the Cedar-Upper Iowa by the Blue Earth River, which flows north from Iowa and into Minnesota.

Most streams rising in Minnesota and flowing into Iowa provide important recreational resources, partly in Minnesota but more significantly in the Iowa reaches of the rivers. Several are outstanding canoe streams, especially the Upper Iowa, and the smallmouth bass is the major sport fish. The streams that leave southern Minnesota are ideal for smallmouth as well as the canoe. Although these rivers are often muddy in the pastures and cultivated plains of Minnesota, they are clearer and cooler in the rugged limestone valleys of northeast Iowa.

It is little wonder that these streams are prized among northern Iowa's natural resources.

Chapter 16

The Blue Earth

Fool's Copper

Among the earliest French adventurers in Minnesota was Pierre Charles le Sueur, fur trader and explorer along the upper Mississippi River in the late 1600s. From a smaller, more western river Le Sueur had obtained a sample of strange, bluish-green clay, and he took the clay to France, so the story goes, where a king's officer, one Le Huillier, assayed it and concluded that it contained copper. Consequently in 1700 Le Sueur came back to the wilderness with an expedition fully prepared to ascend the Rivière St. Pierre and a southern tributary they named the Rivière Verte (Green River) to establish a copper mine.

Arriving in the fall, they quickly built Fort l'Huillier, named for the legendary assayer, and wintered on the stream we now call the Blue Earth River, about five miles from its mouth.

In the spring Le Sueur and his fellow copper miners set to work. Another mile upriver, on the bluffs overlooking the river valley from the north side, they dug 30,000 pounds of the blue-green clay from a layer four to ten inches thick. Selecting 4,000 pounds of what appeared to be the best of the ore, Le Sueur left Fort l'Huillier to sail for France — carrying the ore and a supply of furs obtained from the Sioux. Le Sueur left a company in charge of the fort. While he was gone, a war party of Foxes, angered at Le Sueur's trade with the

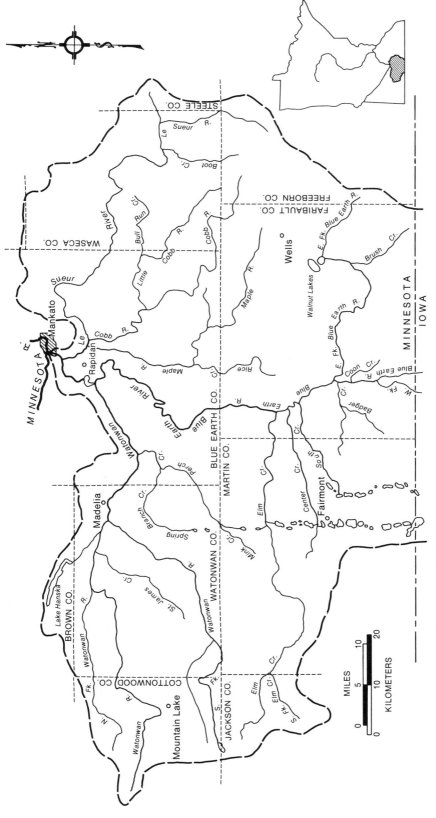

The Blue Earth Watershed

Sioux, attacked the fort. Three Frenchmen were killed, and the rest fled down the Mississippi.

Nothing more was left to history concerning the fate of the copper ore. It contained no copper, of course. Probably it was thought to be valuable ore because its color resembled that of copper salts, which are blue-green. Historian Theodore Blegen raises the possibility that Le Sueur, knowing all along that the clay was worthless, nevertheless held out the prospect of copper to his official patrons as a means of financing his fur-trading ventures.

French scholar Joseph N. Nicollet, more than a century later, found only cavities were the Indians had extracted the clay for decorating their faces and bodies; he found no mining ruins. He believed that Le Sueur's mine was on the Le Sueur River (which Nicollet named after the earlier explorer) rather than on the Blue Earth.

At any rate, the clay is no longer visible nor are traces of Fort l'Huillier nor the mines. We have instead a beautiful name for a beautiful river and a lovely Sioux name for the thriving city at its mouth: Mankato, which means blue or green earth.

Nicollet was so impressed with the area's rivers, high wooded banks, and the network of deeply incised small streams that he termed it the "Undine Region," after a beautiful water sprite in German folklore. The Blue Earth and its two major tributaries—the Watonwan from the west and the Le Sueur from the east—make up a wide, fan-shaped watershed that is unique in Minnesota because it is broader than it is long. Each major tributary is almost as large as the Blue Earth itself, so that the watershed is composed of three major streams, with many tributaries, coming together near the mouth of the main stem in the Minnesota River at Mankato.

The Big Woods, the large tract of virgin hardwoods that covered much of east-central Minnesota, extended into the northern part of the Blue Earth drainage. But to the south were flat plains with natural grassland where the buffalo roamed in Le Sueur's day. Into these plains the streams cut deep ravines, and along the steep riverbank hillsides extended fingers of the Big Woods from the north. This streamside supply of timber furnished fuel and material for buildings and furniture to the early settlers of these otherwise treeless prairies. The three rivers were also important for their abundant water power to run the sawmills and gristmills.

In contrast to watersheds on either side, the Blue Earth's flow is to the north and the Minnesota River; on the west, the Des Moines River flows south into Iowa, and to the east, the Cedar and its tributaries do likewise. In the downstream reaches of the Blue Earth watershed, all streams have cut through glacial drift to expose sedimentary bedrock. In some places the resultant deep channels are 200 feet deep.

The headwaters of the Blue Earth rise in Iowa and flow north across the state boundary as the West Fork and the main stem; both are small and ditched. The East Fork, a larger stream, originates entirely in Minnesota.

The upper watershed of the East Fork has the only trout stream in the Blue Earth basin: Brush Creek, a small, cold stream emanating from the Kiester Hills. The elevation of these morainic uplands in the southeast part of the watershed is as high as 1,475 feet, whereas most of the surrounding till plains lie at 1,000 to 1,150 feet.

Two notable chains of lakes oriented north-south form part of the upper reaches of two creeks directly tributary to the Blue Earth, Center and South creeks, near Fairmont in Martin County. These lake chains with headwaters in Iowa are partly filled glacial river valleys, bordered and confined by parallel moraines. Some of these lakes contain largemouth bass and bluegills, although many are too shallow to sustain game fish populations through the winter in all years, and consequently rough fish are abundant.

Walnut Lake Wildlife Management Area, including South Walnut Lake, is located on the East Branch south of the village of Wells. This 2,000-acre public hunting area is one of the major wildlife management areas in south-central Minnesota. It is managed primarily for waterfowl, but also for pheasants and other small game. Even a moose, normally an inhabitant of the far north, spent a winter here recently.

Near the village of Rapidan, about twelve miles from the mouth and at the head of the present lower gorge, Northern States Power Company previously operated a hydroelectric power generating dam above the confluence with the Le Sueur but slightly below the Watonwan. After the completion of the present dam in 1910, the reservoir, impounded Rapidan Lake, filled very rapidly with silt and mud and today is virtually a marsh. The hydroelectric facility is no longer operative.

Two views on stream management. *Above:* Main stem of the Blue Earth River at the Minnesota-Iowa border, ditched and drained to increase agricultural production. *Below:* East Branch of the Blue Earth as it comes out of the Walnut Lake Wildlife Management Area.

The Blue Earth has a total drainage area of about 3,550 square miles, 3,106 of which are in Minnesota and 450 in Iowa. The mean discharge of the Blue Earth at its mouth is nearly 1,300 cubic feet per second, including flow from both major tributaries; maximum flood discharge was about 60,000 and occasionally constitutes over half the flood flow in the Minnesota River. The length of the Blue Earth, from its junction with the East Branch, is about 100 miles. It drops 285 feet, an average gradient of less than three feet per mile; the gradient through the lower gorge, however, is about five feet per mile.

The Le Sueur River heads up in a series of many small streams in Waseca and Freeborn counties. These form the two major tributaries of the Le Sueur, Cobb, and Maple rivers. They, like the main stem, have deeply incised ravines in the surrounding plains of the lower reaches; all had southward extensions of hardwood forests in their upper valleys. The Le Sueur watershed includes about 1,100 square miles. The stream is about 100 miles long and has a gradient of about four feet per mile; its average discharge is about 400 cubic feet per second, with a peak flow of about 25,000.

The Watonwan consists of three main branches: the main stem and the North and South forks, all originating near Mountain Lake in east Cottonwood County. Because the plains are flat and channels are shallow here, agricultural lands of the western part of the watershed are subject to periodic flooding. Considerable ditching and channelization have been completed on all three branches and more is proposed. In contrast with the purported advantages to cultivation, such ditching has the disadvantage of intensifying downstream floods on the Blue Earth and the Minnesota. The area is an important part of Minnesota's pheasant range, and it also includes many small potholes and marshes for waterfowl production. A number of wildlife management areas with public hunting would be lost if the proposed drainage in the upper North Fork watershed is carried out.

The Watonwan's watershed is slightly greater than 800 square miles. The main stem, after all three branches have joined, is about forty miles long. Gradients in the three branches are very low, and even in the lowest section of the main river the gradient is only about three feet per mile. Mean discharge at the mouth is about 350 cubic feet per second (slightly less than in the Le Sueur), and the maximum flow has been nearly 20,000.

Most waters of the Blue Earth network are now at least somewhat muddy, draining agricultural lands subject to accelerated erosion. All waters are quite hard; the alkalinity of most exceeds 200 p.p.m.

The gorge area of the lower Blue Earth includes perhaps the principal river fishery—for smallmouth bass—among the streams of the watershed. Even so, fishing for this prized species has declined, and carp are more abundant, apparently as a result of increased silting from headwater regions. Compliance with new federal water quality standards, including improved soil conservation and water retention practices in upstream cultivated areas, may restore the smallmouth fishery to its former importance. Rough fish, especially the ubiquitous carp, predominate in river fish populations, although walleyes, northern pike, and channel catfish are taken by anglers in places. Many lakes of the watershed, including the two lake chains in Martin County, have only marginal game fish populations and winter-kill frequently, but many are valuable as waterfowl-production areas.

Where the Watonwan River enters the Blue Earth, there is an angular piece of land that once was the center of a beautiful valley, shaded by great oaks on the river's bluffs and containing a sparkling, clear-water lake and outlet stream. Wild game, fish, berries, and other wild fruit were abundant. But the Sioux, so the legend goes, believed the valley was haunted by evil spirits that roamed the beautiful land, seeking blood. The Indians avoided the area despite the tempting pleasures—except War Eagle, a brave young chief who discovered the valley's loveliness and, not being superstitious, indulged in the pleasures of the beautiful rivers and the cool woodlands. The evil spirits, however, were not to be denied, and tragedy struck the young chief. After a skirmish with the Chippewa, in which War Eagle's band successfully defended their village, War Eagle took for his bride a beautiful Chippewa maiden, the daughter of the enemy chief. This displeased the Sioux who could not reconcile this relationship with their ancient enmity for the Chippewa. They harassed the young couple until War Eagle and his bride retired to the beautiful valley and lived many happy moons along the rivers where the rest of his band dared not trespass.

One day while hunting, War Eagle ventured too far beyond the valley; he was discovered by his own people, attacked, and killed. In her grief, the young bride rushed to him, drew the knife from his hunting sheath, and plunged it into her own breast. The Haunted Valley had exacted its tragic tribute.

However fanciful the Indian legend, other violent events along the Blue Earth's streams actually happened, among them the ending of the criminal careers of some of the most infamous outlaws of the west. On September 7, 1876 Jesse and Frank James, the three Younger brothers, and three other gang members rode boldly into Northfield to raid its single bank. It was the James gang's only criminal act in Minnesota, and it ended with inglorious defeat—Jesse's only real mistake as an outlaw.

In Northfield two of the gang members were killed in a gunfight by the town's citizens; the rest—Jesse and Frank James, the three Youngers, and Charlie Pitts—fled west. Posses were formed, and virtually all of southern Minnesota was alarmed; eventually, a thousand volunteers joined in a great chase. Jesse and Frank slipped from their pursuers and eventually escaped to the Dakota border and south. But the Youngers—Bob, Jim, and Cole—and Charlie Pitts headed up the Watonwan River and into the wild swamp country around Lake Hanska, where they were spotted and recognized. They ran for the shelter of the Watonwan bottoms, but an armed posse followed, and in a tangled thicket of brush and grape vines along the river all four outlaws were brought down by a hail of deputies' bullets that shredded their covert. Pitts was dead, all three Youngers badly wounded, and later imprisoned.

Today, a concrete and granite marker on a country road not far from Madelia marks the spot along the Watonwan River where the battle took place.

The Blue Earth River between Rapidan Dam and its mouth in the Minnesota is unique in southern Minnesota and exceptional in the watershed. Swift rapids alternate with quiet pools throughout the twelve-mile section. It is the outstanding stretch of wild-water canoeing in southern Minnesota, and it is utilized by many, especially in the high flows of spring that occur at the same

The Blue Earth River in its lower twelve miles flows in a deep channel lined by rocky bluffs and wooded hills, a fast reach with a significant smallmouth bass fishery. Its swift rapids and scenic quality make it popular with canoeists.

time springtime vegetation flowers on the riverbanks. The river flows between high, wooded bluffs and rocky escarpments, eroded through glacial drift to sedimentary bedrock. No other stream section in south-central Minnesota contains similar resources of fish, wildlife, and scenic views of valley and wooded hills.

A few years ago the Army Corps of Engineers proposed a large reservoir on the Blue Earth as part of an extensive flood control program in the Minnesota Valley. The dam, to be constructed about two miles above the mouth of the river, would have impounded many miles of the Blue Earth and Le Sueur rivers, including all of the lower gorge between Rapidan and the new dam. At flood stage, it would have inundated all the major rivers and tributaries for hundreds of stream miles.

The loss of natural beauty and recreational resources would have been enormous. A wild-water canoeing river would have been destroyed; migration from the Minnesota River of fish such as walleyes and catfish would have been stopped; the smallmouth bass, a stream resident, would have had its spawning and feeding habitat destroyed; thousands of acres of wildlife habitat, marshes, wetlands, and woods, including that of the major deer population in this part of the state, would have been eliminated. The result, instead of the fish and wildlife enhancement claimed by the dam's sponsors, would have been a heavily silted reservoir suitable only for rough fish species. The water level would have fluctuated so much (up to thirty feet) that the shallow-water edges would have been worthless for game fish spawning and for waterfowl production. The Minnesota Department of Natural Resources concluded that the reservoir's value in recreational, fish, and wildlife resources would have been virtually nil and that the measures offered to compensate for these losses would have been inadequate.

Flood-control benefits in the Blue Earth watershed, as well as downstream on the Minnesota and Mississippi rivers, were claimed for the big dam and reservoir. But the acreage proposed to be permanently flooded in the Blue Earth basin behind the dam was nearly as great as the acreage covered by record floods in 1965.

Vigorous opposition to the Minnesota Valley dams developed, led by citizens groups as well as the Minnesota Department of Natural Resources. The big-dam program in the Minnesota Valley, including the Blue Earth proposal, has now been dropped.

Vigilance, however, will be required to retain our heritage of beauty in Nicollet's Undine Region.

Chapter 17

The Southwest

Rivers of the Coteau des Prairies

The broad, flat-iron-shaped Coteau des Prairies is an elevation of the plains of northeastern South Dakota, its northern tip just touching the North Dakota border and its eastern edge cutting the southwestern corner of Minnesota. This plateau, "the highland of the prairies" 500 to 800 feet higher than the central plains, is the most conspicuous surface feature in southwestern Minnesota and sets the topographic stage for the streams of the region.

The Coteau exists because it rests in part on a base of hard quartzitic rock, the remains of an ancient mountain range. Ridges of this very old rock resisted erosion for hundreds of millions of years, and glaciers deposited high moraines on top of the hard rock. Sioux quartzite, sometimes called red rock or jasper, crops out in several places in southwestern Minnesota, such as in the extreme southwest corner of the state, the "Blue Mound" along the Rock River, and in the quarry near the town of Pipestone. (Pipestone rock, or catlinite, from which Indians made their ceremonial pipes, is a softer layer of siltstone inter-bedded in the quartzite.)

The glacial moraines making up the plateau could even be termed rugged along the edge—early explorers looking back at the lowlands below must have had a feeling of being in high country.

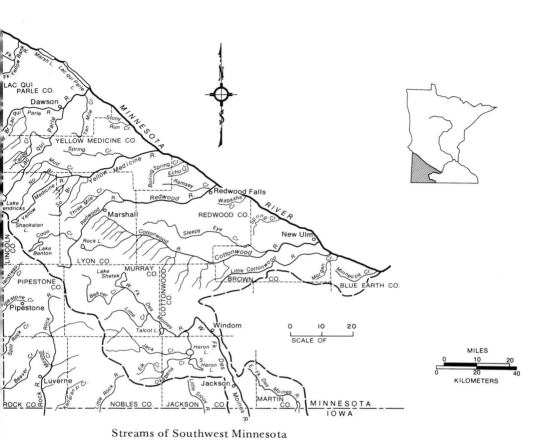

Streams of Southwest Minnesota

And although the top is generally smooth, the rolling topography is poorly drained and includes many lakes, ponds, and marshes, particularly within the northern tip in South Dakota where elevations are greater than in Minnesota.

All along the edge of the Coteau, small streams and creeks, some that flow only temporarily in normally dry ravines, run down the rugged slopes perpendicular to the plateau's edge. From the western edge in South Dakota, their waters eventually find their way to the Missouri; from Minnesota's eastern edge they flow into the Minnesota River Valley. Especially on the eastern side, small streams cut steep gorges and rugged valleys, where wooded, cool oases contrast sharply with surrounding wind-swept prairies. These gorges protected the woodlands from prairie fires and originally provided almost the only hardwood timber in this part of the plains.

Among the hills of the eastern edges of the Coteau in Minnesota are the headwaters of four of the state's major streams: the Lac qui Parle, Yellow Medicine, Redwood, and Cottonwood rivers, all flowing to the Minnesota Valley. Along the top of the plateau, but near the eastern edge, is the divide between the Minnesota-Mississippi drainage to the east and the Missouri drainage to the southwest. Here two other major rivers rise on top of the Coteau and flow south into Iowa, one from either side of the divide. The Des Moines River on the east eventually becomes Iowa's largest stream, emptying into the Mississippi after flowing southeast across the entire state of Iowa. And the Rock River, west of the divide, flows out of the most southwestern corner of Minnesota, soon into Iowa's Big Sioux River, and then into the Missouri.

The waters of the Coteau streams are generally hard, with alkalinities from about 150 to 200 p.p.m.; streams originating in the underground waters of the calcareous glacial drift are very hard. The highest alkalinities in this range occur in the waters of the deeply eroded Coteau slopes and of spring tributaries flowing on the Coteau and in the Minnesota Valley.

The four rivers emptying into the Minnesota—Lac qui Parle, Yellow Medicine, Redwood, and Cottonwood—share many characteristics. Each has three distinct reaches: a swift, rocky stretch as the headwaters come down the slope of the Coteau; a long, slow, meandering course across the lowland plains; and a deep rocky gorge section where waters plunge into the 200-foot-deep Minnesota River Valley. The headwaters are relatively clear, flowing through rapids and over gravel bars, the lowland stretches in the plains, where the channels are in glacial drift high in clay and extensively ditched, are turbid with suspended clay and flow over soft, silty bottoms; and in the lower gorge, although stream bottoms are generally of large rocks and boulders, the waters retain much silt from upstream reaches, and silt coats the rocks. In the low water of autumn and winter, however, the four rivers may become clear throughout their courses.

All four rivers begin on the Coteau at elevations of about 1,600 to 1,900 feet, drop sharply for the first 500 feet, level off at about 1,000 to 1,100 feet on the low plains, and empty into the Minnesota at about 800 to 900 feet. Gradients in the headwater reaches range to 50 feet per mile, 1 to 2 feet per mile on the lowlands and up to 100 feet per mile in the Minnesota Valley gorge of the lower Redwood where many falls and cascades occur.

The lowland reaches of these four rivers may seem slow and uninteresting, especially because they have been extensively ditched and straightened, but some reaches resemble unmodified prairie streams, with winding bottomlands shaded by willows and cottonwoods. In these low plains sections some streams, such as the Cottonwood, follow courses set by glacial meltwaters that flowed southeast along the edge of the retreating ice.

In swift-water reaches, some stream sections have been set aside as state or local parks. In the upper reach of the Redwood, for example, is Camden State Park, a spacious section of densely wooded river valley, surprising but welcome amid the flat plains. Camden is much used for camping, picnicking, and hiking, and for skiing in winter; it is unique among the southwestern streams in having sufficient springwater tributaries to provide some trout habitat, and trophy browns are occasionally taken by trout fishermen. Lyon County's Garvin Park on the upper Cottonwood encloses a spreading, wooded valley of steep slopes and rushing stream, offering camping, picnicking, and trails.

The lower gorge reaches of all four rivers are outstanding areas of recreational use or historical significance. On the Lac qui Parle, northeast of the village of Dawson, is Lac qui Parle County Park, a large area with woods and open space for camping and other outdoor activities along the stream banks. The river here is rushing and noisy in high water, full of boulders and white water, flowing between high wooded banks. At the mouth of the Lac qui Parle in the Minnesota River is Lac qui Parle State Park, and along the lake is the large Lac qui Parle Wildlife Management Area. Originally, the Lac qui Parle River formed a delta in the Minnesota Valley and impounded Lac qui Parle Lake, but the lake level is now controlled by a man-made dam (Chapter 18). Near the lower end of the Yellow Medicine is the Upper Sioux Agency State Park, site of bloody Indian war in the summer of 1862; this was also known as the Yellow Medicine Agency. Although the emphasis in this park is on the historical importance of the Indian agency, the Yellow Medicine River contributes its wild-water scenic beauty to the site. The gorge section of the Redwood River includes Alexander Ramsey City Park in Redwood Falls. The park contains some of the most unusual river environment in Minnesota. The swift rapids and cascades rushing over ancient granite are reminiscent of northern Minnesota, and the falls of Ramsey Creek, a straight, muddy ditch in its plains headwaters, plunges into the Minnesota Valley with beauty equal to the most remote

Spring-fed in its steep reach down the slope of the Coteau des Prairies, the Redwood River remains open in winter. This rocky stretch in Camden State Park resounds with the roar of rapids in springtime. It also yields some trophy-sized brown trout to the skilled angler.

waterfalls of the north. Many miles of trails, campgrounds, soaring bluffs of weathered granite, and rocky river rapids can be enjoyed in this island of wild river on the prairie. The lower Cottonwood flows through a wooded gorge and thence through Flandrau State Park at New Ulm. The park memorializes territorial supreme court jurist Charles Flandrau, hero of the defense of New Ulm in the Sioux Uprising. It includes a swimming pool, camp and picnic grounds, primitive canoe access, and many trails.

The Lac qui Parle has its ultimate origin in Lake Hendricks, a lake with good walleye fishing on the South Dakota border in northwestern Lincoln County. Winding northward on the Coteau, it is a temporary stream at best and here flows only in the wettest periods. Entering Yellow Medicine County to the north, the stream plunges down the slope of the Coteau for about eight stream miles and drops 250 feet. Near Canby it reaches the lowland

Dropping down into the Minnesota Valley, the Redwood plunges over granite ledges in cascades and rapids, cutting a deep, scenic gorge into some of the oldest rock formations on earth. The Redwood gorge is in Alexander Ramsey City Park, Redwood Falls.

plains, and then it begins a long, slow course generally northeast across the western panhandle of Yellow Medicine County and diagonally across Lac qui Parle County to the Minnesota. It falls 210 feet in its final eighteen-mile descent into the Minnesota Valley. In both the headwaters and lower gorge sections it flows through wooded valleys, and on the low plains an occasional willow or cottonwood grows along the banks. Paralleling the river's course down the Coteau is Canby Creek, a small trout stream joining the Lac qui Parle farther downstream. As it flows toward the Minnesota, the Lac qui Parle receives near Dawson its largest tributary, the West Branch, which drains much of western Lac qui Parle County and originates in South Dakota. In the lower Minnesota Valley reach, the Lac qui Parle collects from the south Ten Mile Creek (the lower section is also known as Three Mile Creek), the only designated and stocked trout stream in Lac qui Parle County. Many other small tributaries enter the Lac qui Parle on the lowlands, all having been largely channelized or ditched.

The Lac qui Parle drains a watershed of 767 square miles in Minnesota as well as another 343 in South Dakota. It flows for sixty-six miles from Lake Hendricks and empties into the Minnesota River just below Lac qui Parle Lake. It drops over 800 feet, an average gradient of more than twelve feet per mile. Its mean discharge at the mouth is slightly more than 100 cubic feet per second, but it has been over 10,000 in its maximum flood.

The river's name is a French translation of the Indian name for the lake it impounded — "The Lake Which Talks."

The Yellow Medicine River also rises on the Coteau in Lincoln County, not far from the sources of the Lac qui Parle, but it originates in three branches: the North Branch, main stem, and South Branch. The main stem heads in Lake Shaokatan, western Lincoln County, and winds northeast along the highland as a temporary stream; roughly between Ivanhoe and Taunton it descends the slope of the Coteau and drops 250 feet in about five miles. The North Branch comes off the slope near Porter, and the South Branch, just south of Minneota in Lyon County. The three join north of Minneota, and the Yellow Medicine proper begins its lowland plains course, essentially east toward its mouth in the Minnesota. It falls eighty-five feet in its final ten-mile drop into the Minnesota Valley. Like the Lac qui Parle, the Yellow Medicine courses through wooded valleys in both the upper and lower reaches, but its channel across the low plains is treeless except for an occasional stream-bank willow or cottonwood. Besides the headwater North and South branches, its major tributaries are Mud Creek and Spring Creek, both draining from the west; many other small tributaries enter the Yellow Medicine and its main branches, and most are ditched. In all, the Yellow Medicine and its branches drain 665 square miles. The main stem flows about eighty miles from Lake Shaokatan to the Minnesota River, dropping more than 850 feet, an average gradient of slightly more than ten feet per mile. The Yellow Medicine's flow averages about 100 cubic feet per second near its mouth, similar to the Lac qui Parle, and has reached nearly 12,000 in flood.

The Sioux named it Yellow Medicine for the bitter, yellow roots of the moonseed plant, growing as lush vines in thickets along the stream banks.

The Redwood River, too, begins on top of the Coteau des Prairies. It wanders around the corners of Lincoln, Pipestone, Murray, and Lyon counties as a temporary stream, then flows northeast toward the slope of the highland. Between Russell and Marshall, the Redwood drops off the Coteau, and in about fifteen miles it falls nearly 300 feet. In this reach, where it tumbles along the bottom of a wooded valley 100 feet deep, is Camden State Park. At Marshall the river reaches the lowland plain and then flows east toward the Minnesota Valley with a gradient of only two to three feet per mile. At the city of Redwood Falls, the Redwood River plunges into the wooded Minnesota River bottomlands, dropping 100 feet in one mile, tumbling and cascading over granite ledges in Alexander Ramsey City Park. A forty-foot dam at Redwood Falls was previously operated as a hydroelectric generating facility. The impoundment is now utilized for recreational purposes. The Redwood's main tributaries include Coon Creek, originating in Lake Benton up on the Coteau, Three Mile Creek, which joins the Redwood on the plains below Marshall, and Ramsey Creek, which empties into the Redwood in the Minnesota Valley after a spectacular waterfall in Ramsey Park. A large portion of the Redwood is ditched on the low-plains reach as are hundreds of miles of small tributaries. The watershed of the Redwood is 739 square miles. The stream flows about ninety miles from its highest sources in tiny tributaries to its mouth in the Minnesota and drops about 1,000 feet, an average gradient of twelve feet per mile. The Redwood's mean discharge at Redwood Falls is, like that of the Lac qui Parle and the Yellow Medicine, about 100 cubic feet per second, but its maximum flood discharge was nearly 20,000 after an intense thunderstorm in the late spring of 1957.

The river's name is not derived from big redwoods like those of the Pacific coast; rather, the name is from the reddish bark of the willowlike dogwood called by the Indians "Kinniqkinnic," growing along the streams. They used the white inner bark as smoking "tobacco."

The Cottonwood River is somewhat different from the other three. It is longer, larger, and has a greater drainage area and different drainage pattern. Like the other three, however, it rises on top of the Coteau. Its main source is in the marshes of Rock Lake, in southwestern Lyon County, from which the river wanders on the Coteau for about twenty miles as an intermittent stream. Above Amiret, the Cottonwood, still a very small stream, plunges through a deep, wooded valley and drops 200 feet off the highlands in about five miles. Turning southeast, the river flows along the base of the Coteau's moraines and receives many small tributaries and intermittent streams that also come down the highland's slope. Leaving the base of the Coteau, the Cottonwood crosses the lowland plain flowing east to its mouth in the Minnesota at New Ulm. The lower reach of the river, including that in Flandrau State Park, is in a heavily wooded valley. Very few tributaries enter the Cottonwood from the north side; the major one is Sleepy Eye Creek, entering near the upper end of the lower reach on the lowland plain. The Little Cottonwood River, flowing roughly parallel to the Cottonwood on the lowlands, enters the Minnesota directly below New Ulm. Garvin Park is located on the Cottonwood's descent on the Coteau slope; there is a city park on the Cottonwood at Springfield and a wayside park near Sleepy Eye where canoe access is available. The lower section, from the Sleepy Eye wayside down to Flandrau State Park, usually can be canoed. It is a scenic trip along a mostly wooded course, especially in the lower gorge reach; however, water levels are not always sufficient for canoeing, especially in late summer. A dam in Flandrau State Park once impounded Cottonwood Lake, a recreational lake in the park, but since high waters washed out the dam in both 1965 and 1969, it has not been rebuilt. A Redwood County park is located near Walnut Grove on Plum Creek, a small tributary of the Cottonwood made famous by the books of Laura Ingalls Wilder. Plans for a large dam on the Cottonwood, part of an extensive seven-dam proposal of the Army Corps of Engineers for the Minnesota Valley, have been dropped. In all, the Cottonwood flows about 100 miles, draining a watershed of 1,295 square miles; it drops a total of 750 feet from Rock Lake to the Minnesota River, an average gradient of seven and one-half feet per mile. The mean flow is about 280 cubic feet per second at New Ulm and the maximum was about 28,700.

The Sioux called the river "Waraju" for the cottonwood tree, which was common along this and other prairie streams.

In addition to the four major rivers, a number of smaller streams flow across the southwestern plains and empty directly into the Minnesota. These include the Yellow Bank River, originating in South Dakota and flowing into the Minnesota above Marsh Lake, Stony Run Creek, between the mouths of the Lac qui Parle and the Yellow Medicine rivers; Boiling Spring and Echo creeks, between the Yellow Medicine and the Redwood; between the Redwood and the Cottonwood, Wabasha Creek and Spring (Hindeman) Creek, the latter a small trout stream, enter the valley; and below the mouth of the Cottonwood at New Ulm enter the Little Cottonwood, Morgan Creek, and Minneopa Creek with its splendid double-waterfalls in Minneopa State Park near Mankato. Together, these streams drain 1,187 square miles of watershed in Minnesota; the total southwest drainage into the Minnesota River is 4,653 square miles in Minnesota and about 350 square miles in South Dakota.

The Des Moines River originates in lakes on top of the Coteau in northern Murray and southern Lyon counties, principally in Lake Shetek, one of the few large lakes of the southwest. On the southeast shore is Lake Shetek State Park, through which the Des Moines flows as it leaves the lake; the state park memorializes an Indian massacre during the 1862 Sioux Uprising. From Lake Shetek, the river (actually the West Fork of the Des Moines) flows southeast toward the Iowa border and Jackson County. In this reach the river makes the Big Bend, a northeastern loop over the Cottonwood-Jackson county line.

The upper reach is in a heavily cultivated area, and the valley is shallow. But in the highland reach below Windom the river cuts a deeper valley, much of it densely wooded. About ten miles north of Jackson is Kilen Woods State Park, where the valley becomes a gorge 150 feet deep in places; this scenic stretch is heavily timbered with oak and other hardwoods. Except for moderate rapids in the park area, the river is mainly slow, flat water. The park is the site of early Indian attacks on white settlers, five years before the 1862 conflict. Ten miles below Jackson, the Des Moines leaves Minnesota eventually to become Iowa's largest river.

In contrast to the lowland plains of the four Minnesota River tributaries, the watershed of the Des Moines River is dotted with lakes and ponds. Many of these have been acquired as state wildlife management areas and federal waterfowl production areas. One of the largest is Talcot Lake Wildlife Management Area, an extensive waterfowl marsh in southwestern Cottonwood County; the Des Moines flows through Talcot Lake, its level maintained by a state-operated dam at the river's lake outlet. The Des Moines is included in the state's *A Gathering of Waters*, which describes a fifty-mile canoe trip from the Talcot Lake dam to the Iowa border, including the steep scenic valley in Kilen Woods State Park.

The Des Moines in its upper reaches has many small tributaries including Beaver and Lime creeks in Murray County and Jack, Elk, and Okabena creeks in the Heron Lake watershed in Jackson and Nobles counties; the outlet of Heron Lake flows into the Big Bend reach of the Des Moines in Cottonwood County. Almost all tributaries of the Des Moines flow east from the divide to the river, with virtually none entering the river from the east side. The East Fork of the Des Moines, rising in southeast Jackson County and flowing into Martin County, leaves Minnesota and flows into Iowa and then into the main stem, or West Fork.

The main Des Moines, or West Fork, flows ninety-four miles in Minnesota and descends about 235 feet from its upper headwater lakes at about 1,510 feet to the Iowa border at 1,275, an average gradient of two and one-half feet per mile; it is a relatively flat stream. The average discharge near the Iowa border is about 350 cubic feet per second; in a previous flood stage it reached nearly 20,000. In Minnesota the West Fork drains 1,350 square miles and the East Fork, along with several other small creeks, 200 square miles.

Rivière des Moines is French for "River of the Monks." Early explorers simply assigned it a French name that sounded like its Indian name. The river had been named for an Indian village in Iowa.

T he Rock River is unique in Minnesota because it is the only one of Minnesota's major streams in the Missouri River drainage. The rest flow north to Hudson Bay, east through the Great Lakes and the St. Lawrence River to the Atlantic, or directly to the Mississippi as it courses through or along Minnesota.

Nevertheless, the Rock is not very different from other Minnesota streams originating on the Coteau des Prairies. The river's origins

The Rock River, Minnesota's only major stream in the Missouri River watershed, flows across the rolling plains of southwest Minnesota at the foot of the sheer bluffs of Blue Mounds State Park. Plains Indians lured herds of bison over the bluffs to their deaths, a primitive means of harvest. Joseph Nicollet named the outcrop "The Rock," the name later transferred to the river and Minnesota's southwesternmost county.

are in Pipestone County at an elevation of about 1,800 feet. From here it flows south, with much meandering, to the Iowa border. On farther, it empties into Iowa's Big Sioux River, which flows south through a central cleft on the Coteau to the Missouri.

The Rock River flows through a region that was undulating prairie, well drained by many small tributaries. There are no natural lakes in the watershed and little timber, although the main stream flows in a well-defined valley with occasional trees typical of river-banks, such as cottonwood, willow, and soft maple. In the town of Luverne, a welcome shady city park is located by a bend of the river.

In addition to the Rock itself, several tributaries rise in Minnesota and join the Rock in Iowa—for example, Kanaranzi Creek and the Little Rock River (Nobles County). To the west, Flandreau, Pipestone, Beaver and Split Rock creeks originate in Pipestone and Rock counties and flow west into South Dakota, eventually emptying into the Big Sioux in Iowa. Split Rock Creek State Park offers camping, picnicking, a swimming beach on an artificial lake, and trails; the name is derived from some exposed red Sioux quartzite that was fractured and split by weathering. To the east, the headwaters of the Little Sioux rise in Jackson County, flow south into Iowa and toward the Missouri.

The main stem of the Rock flows over fifty miles in Minnesota, dropping about 450 feet from its headwaters in Pipestone County, an average gradient of about nine feet per mile; there are no precipitous rapids along its course. The Rock drains 558 square miles in Minnesota. Other tributaries of the Big Sioux River drain 921 square miles in Minnesota, then flow through either South Dakota or Iowa; to the east, the headwaters of the Little Sioux and tributaries drain 314 square miles of Minnesota land. The total Missouri River watershed in Minnesota is 1,793 square miles. The Rock River has a mean discharge near the Iowa border of about 100 cubic feet per second, although precise data are not available.

About two miles north of Luverne, overlooking the Rock River from the west, is a sharp escarpment of old, hard rock—Morton Gneiss, estimated to be 3.5 billion years old. Over this escarpment, the Sioux drove bison to their deaths—their way of harvesting part of the vast herds for meat, hide, and fur. This area is now set aside as Blue Mounds State Park, including camp and picnic grounds, an artificial lake (on Mound Creek, a small western tributary of the Rock), and trails. A herd of bison grazes this original prairie. The name of the park is derived from the appearance of the high mounds as viewed against the western sky by migrating settlers, but also perhaps from the bluish lichens that cover almost all exposed rock. This was the "The Rock," on Joseph N. Nicollet's map. It overlooks the meandering stream to which its name was given—Rock River.

Fish and game made up a large part of the often scanty food resources of the earliest settlers. The lakes on the Coteau, the major plains streams, and the Minnesota River itself all provided abundant food fish supplementing a limited agriculture. Northern pike, walleyes, catfish, and bass were taken then as now, but probably many more of those species we now disdainfully consider rough fish were a part of the settler's diet, too—suckers and redhorse, buffalo, sheepshead. They were taken with hook and line and, without the legal constraints of today, more efficiently with spear and trap.

Fishing in these waters is considerably different than it was in the early years of settlement and, with few exceptions, is now very light. The section of the Cottonwood downstream from Sleepy Eye, with clear waters and clean stony bottoms, once supported a moderately large smallmouth fishery, but it has declined because of an increased silt load in the stream. A modern addition is the European carp, which often is predominant in river populations.

Because the streams flowing south to Iowa from the top of the Coteau—the Des Moines and Rock—differ hydrographically from the other four, the fisheries are also different. The Des Moines and Rock lack both the swift headwaters and lower gorge of the other four; their waters are slower, more turbid. Both can be characterized as primarily catfish streams, as far as sport fish are concerned. In Iowa both are considered important fishing streams, the upper Des Moines primarily for channel and flathead catfish, but also for walleyes, smallmouth bass, and northern pike, and the Rock, with similar species sought, is considered the best fish habitat in the Missouri River tributaries of Iowa. The carp and many members of the sucker family frequently are the most abundant species. Because the Rock is the only major Minnesota stream tributary to the Missouri River, some small and less-known minnows and darters occur here, but are not found elsewhere in Minnesota.

There are only a few streams in southwest Minnesota that can support trout; all are in the Minnesota River drainage and are stocked with hatchery trout. As may be expected, those few trout streams are located either in the swift waters that tumble down the slope of the Coteau or in lower reaches entering the Minnesota Valley. These include Canby Creek, a tributary of the Lac qui Parle in Yellow Medicine County on the Coteau slope; Ten Mile (Three Mile) Creek, emptying into the Lac qui Parle in its lower section; the lower reach of Ramsey Creek, in Ramsey City Park in Redwood Falls; the Redwood River in its upper reaches in Camden State Park; and Spring Creek tributary directly to the Minnesota. All are marginal trout waters, although some stocked brown trout grow to a large size in a short stretch of the Redwood in the state park.

When the white settler arrived in Minnesota, the southwestern prairie was not a marshy land like much of the Red River Valley. It had not been blanketed by broad glacial meltwaters and was not a flat glacial lake bed. Rather, it was a region of gently undulating plains, the result of glaciers having scraped over it and melted back, leaving rolling glacial till and low moraines. Everywhere was rich, fertile prairie, on the Coteau and the low plains as well. Here were dry prairies, moist swales, wetlands, and shallow lakes.

The topography was more rugged on the Coteau, and there were more wetlands and deeper lakes. But even on the low plains, in the many slight depressions and between the low moraines, were myriad small lakes and sloughs, tiny streams wandering through the moist bottomlands and poorly drained surrounding marshes. Between these wetlands were the fertile grasslands where bison, elk, and antelope had fed, the deep, black soils that attracted the farmer-settler. The marshes and creek bottoms supported huge populations of wildlife — ducks and geese "that darkened the sky," and abundant fur-bearers such as mink, muskrat, beaver, and otter; the surrounding grasslands supported diverse smaller mammals, shorebirds, and songbirds that added variety and beauty to the land. The prairie chicken had either followed the settlers, or become quite abundant in the habitat produced by the limited agriculture of the day. Introduced after settlement, the Hungarian partridge and pheasant depended on the wetlands and associated grass and brush cover.

Now except for a few isolated wetlands set aside by state and federal agencies as wildlife habitat, the marshes are drained and converted to cultivated fields. Thousands of miles of small creeks and stream bottomlands have been converted to barren, straight ditches.

Ironically, the massive drainage was not necessary for the general cultivation of crops. The channelization of streams and drainage of wetlands simply placed more acres in cultivation or permitted earlier planting.

It is difficult, impossible in most cases, to estimate the loss of wildlife habitat attributable to the ditching and draining of these once rich prairie wildlife habitats, for we have little early survey information for comparison. But the early settlers' accounts of the area's wildlife are impressive. And earlier drainage and ditching projects surely had effects similar to those of recent channelization projects where losses have been measured. It must be concluded that truly immense losses in wildlife and beauty have been sustained.

One example will suffice. The watershed of Ten Mile Creek, a tributary of the Lac qui Parle River in Lac qui Parle and Yellow Medicine counties, was subject to an extensive ditching project, authorized as Judicial Ditch No. 8 and completed between 1967 and 1969. Watershed area of Ten Mile Creek is a little less than 100 square miles, the drainage system comprised nearly 300 miles of open ditch and tile. A thorough evaluation of wildlife habitat had been conducted by the U.S. Fish and Wildlife Service before the project; the Minnesota Department of Natural Resources inventoried wildlife lands remaining after the project with both field observations and aerial photographs. The project was devastating to wildlife, for more than 80 percent of the wetland habitat was lost. More than 350 separate wetlands comprising nearly 5,000 acres were gone. Except for nine publicly owned acres, almost all marshes of the watershed were drained. Estimated losses of wildlife production were 12,000 ducks, 8,000 pheasants, 9,000 muskrats, and innumerable other smaller mammals and birds, annually.

Small streams throughout the southwest corner of Minnesota have been similarly treated. Considering that additional drainage and channelization had also been done in the past, it is likely that only a small fraction of the original wildlife habitat now remains. Additional proposed channelization, ditching, and drainage would reduce it even further.

The realization of loss and consequent change in our priorities have been slow to come about. Some new trends are emerging, however. At a public forum held at Southwest Minnesota State University, Marshall, in 1973, the need for research on preservation of wetlands and erosion control by storage of upland waters was emphasized; no importance was attached to the need for further drainage.

It was a hopeful sign.

Chapter 18

The Minnesota

Corridor West

During the mid-1800s many significant changes occurred in the land that was to become Minnesota. It was a dynamic period of rapid settlement, improvements in transportation, and increasing trade, and the Minnesota River played a large role in this development. But two events took place along the river's banks that were to have a profound and disastrous effect upon the settlement of the valley and the new state. The first occasioned great hopes and aspirations for the future; the second, with its bloody violence, shocked civilized North America.

At the village of Traverse des Sioux (named for the traditional crossing of the river by the Sioux), near present St. Peter, negotiators from the United States government met on July 23, 1851 with representatives of the Upper Sioux bands and concluded a treaty of land cession. Territorial Governor Alexander Ramsey was the principal negotiator for the United States; thirty-five Indian leaders represented the Upper Sioux.

The Indians were to receive small land reservations along the upper river and cash payments. The payments actually were withheld to satisfy claimed traders' debts and for investments. The annual interest from the investments, in the form of annuities, was to pay for supplies, food, medical care, and education, and the principal was to

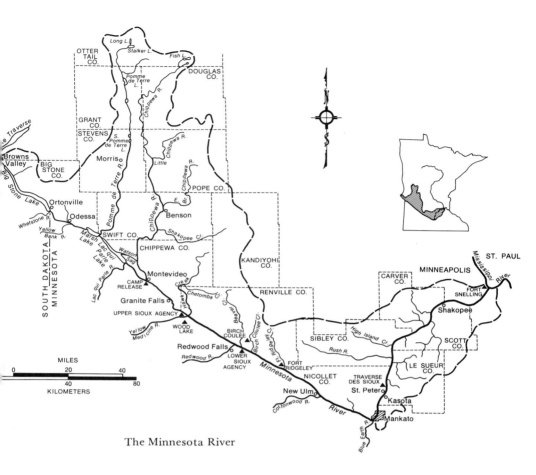

The Minnesota River

be retained by the United States government. It was a sharp business deal on the part of Governor Ramsey; the Indian leaders, in their naïveté, signed away their ancestral heritage.

This cession and a similar treaty with the Lower Sioux bands at Mendota the same year gave the United States what was later estimated to be twenty-four million acres. The region comprised essentially the southern one-third of the present state of Minnesota and parts of Iowa and South Dakota. The Minnesota Valley led northwest through the center of this great prize; the transportation potential of the river and rich bottomlands of its valley assured settlement. The Minnesota Valley was advertised in expansive terms to prospective immigrants recently arrived on the east coast from Europe, and the wave of settlers surging west moved up the river.

The times were good—for the white invaders. So good, in fact, that the disastrous panic of 1857, and even the outbreak of the Civil War in 1861, failed to dampen westward expansion in the Minnesota Valley. Squatters, quick to move onto new lands, were given preemptive rights to purchase, and land sales soared. Statehood was attained in 1858. Steamboats soon arrived on the river, and frequent river service was initiated. The times were so good, in fact, that few noticed the growing unrest on the upper river reservations.

During 1861 and 1862, the Indians' situation at both the Upper and Lower agencies deteriorated seriously. The government failed to provide annuities and promised supplies and food on schedule, creating conditions that were further aggravated by unscrupulous traders at the agencies, crop failures on the Indians' farms, and internecine fighting among the bands crowded together; their plight became desperate. Chief Little Crow, respected by both Indian and white, and a responsible leader desiring peace and willing to accommodate to the new ways, acted as negotiator in the growing tension of late summer 1862. But, pleading for provisions for his people, Little Crow was humiliated: Andrew Myrick, a trader at the Lower Agency near present Redwood Falls, contemptuously counseled the agent in charge, in front of Little Crow and his people: "If they are hungry, let them eat grass!" That was the end of peaceful negotiation.

On August 17, without provocation, four Indians murdered five whites at a settler's homestead in Acton Township, Meeker County. Certain of retribution, the four met in council with Little Crow and other chiefs at the Lower Agency, and the decision for war was made.

The Sioux Uprising of 1862 began at the Lower Agency at dawn the next day, August 18. After the Indians' initial rage was vented upon the traders, Andrew Myrick lay dead, his body pinned to the ground with a scythe and his mouth stuffed with grass. The war raged for five weeks along the Minnesota River. The Lower Agency was virtually destroyed; the Upper Agency at the mouth of the Yellow Medicine River was attacked and burned. Throughout the upper valley, settlers panicked and fled downriver as the Indians massacred and burned every vestige of white occupancy they could find —homesteads, farms, missions, trading posts.

Fort Ridgely, from the Indians' viewpoint the most important military objective in the whole of southwestern Minnesota, was besieged. The fort's garrison was tenacious in its defense. When a rescue force of troopers sent from St. Paul under command of Colonel

From its position on the rim of the broad Minnesota Valley, Fort Ridgely "kept the door shut" and firmly withstood Indian attack in the Sioux Uprising of 1862. It was conceded by Indian leaders afterward that the defense of Fort Ridgely prevented a general Indian attack on the lower valley and the St. Paul-Minneapolis settlements. The fort has been excavated, partially restored, and incorporated into Fort Ridgely State Park, on the river between Redwood Falls and New Ulm.

Henry H. Sibley arrived, the Indians' purpose was thwarted. But a burial party led by Major Joseph R. Brown, reconnoitering upriver from Fort Ridgely, was ambushed at Birch Coulee Creek and suffered the heaviest military losses of the conflict. Downriver, then, attacks on the village of New Ulm were successfully repelled by its citizens under the command of Indian agent and territorial supreme court justice Charles E. Flandrau.

Despite the Indians' victory at Birch Coulee, their defeats at Fort Ridgely and New Ulm broke the offensive. And three weeks later, on September 23, the war ended as Sibley crushed Indian resistance in a battle near Wood Lake in eastern Yellow Medicine County. Three days later 269 white and half-breed prisoners were taken under protection by Sibley at a place quickly named Camp Release, near present Montevideo, and there the last of the Indians surrendered.

The uprising left many white settlers and soldiers dead—estimates were as high as 800—as well as an unknown number of Indians. The aspirations and possessions of thousands of immigrant families were destroyed, the upper Minnesota River Valley depopulated. The great hopes of westward settlement, rich opportunities on the frontier, and fertile valley farms were gone. The clamor for revenge was loud, and it resulted in summary trials and the sentencing to death of more than 300 Indian leaders, although all but 38 were reprieved by President Lincoln. The 38 were hanged in Mankato the day after Christmas, and the Sioux were forever banned from Minnesota.

Indian war swirled across the Dakota plains for several more decades. But the Sioux's hopes of retaining their old ways of life were extinguished in a senseless massacre in 1890 along the banks of a more distant stream—Wounded Knee Creek, South Dakota.

The events along the Minnesota left a legacy of regret and guilt to Minnesota citizens. Although it can be argued that the exploration, exploitation, and settlement of western Minnesota by white Europeans were inevitable, there remains the feeling that perhaps it could have been done differently.

Today the scars of tragedy are still visible on the banks of the river. Locations of buildings, forts, and battles have been identified, excavated, restored, and preserved in state parks, waysides, and monuments. An excellent visitor's interpretive center has been constructed on a wooded valley bluff at the site of the Lower Sioux Agency. Traverse des Sioux, Fort Ridgely, Birch Coulee, and the Upper Sioux Agency are included in our state park system; monuments and markers identify the significance of events at New Ulm, the Lower Agency, Wood Lake, Camp Release, and others.

The trail west up the Minnesota Valley is a road marked harshly by history.

Long before the events at Traverse des Sioux and the Lower Agency shaped the cultural history of the Minnesota Valley, geologic forces shaped its physical characteristics. More than one visitor to these relatively tiny, twisting waters have wondered how such a small stream could be responsible for the broad, deep, straight valley of the Minnesota. As a matter of geological fact, the present Minnesota River is not responsible. Another river, a swollen torrent of icy currents, filled the developing Minnesota Valley and carved it millennia ago. This was the Glacial River Warren, named for

Swinging back and forth from bluff to bluff, the Minnesota River seems too small for its broad valley. Actually the valley was formed by the ancient Glacial River Warren, a much larger stream that once drained the glacier meltwaters of giant Lake Agassiz.

General G. K. Warren, Union officer in the Civil War and army engineer, who first described the origin of the wide valley. It flowed from the south end of Glacial Lake Agassiz some 9,000 to 12,000 years ago, south because the northern outlets to the Arctic and Atlantic oceans were blocked with ice. Today's Minnesota is termed by geologists an underfit river, a small stream flowing in the great valley cut by the Glacial River Warren.

The last glaciers in the southern Minnesota area retreated northwest, and when the southeastern margin was near the area of the present Twin Cities, the meltwaters flowed only a short distance to the lower Mississippi; its course was shaped by older moraines and the edge of the ice itself. As the ice continued to melt, the incipient Minnesota River worked its way upstream—first to the southwest and then (turning at present Mankato) to the northwest. Evidence of the river found far above the present valley floor, such as sandy terraces and potholes, attest to the presence of the river at a much higher elevation than that of today's stream. After the ice edge and the river headwaters reached the continental divide at Browns Valley and vast Lake Agassiz was formed to the north, the River Warren began cutting the Minnesota Valley. Today, in some areas the valley is five miles wide, and it lies as much as 250 feet below surrounding plains, a reminder of the great volume of water that once raged down its course.

The high, steep bluffs along the sides have had a profound effect on the character of tributary streams. Rivers and creeks winding slowly across the southern plains, or flowing down from the northern lake and hill regions through marshes and swamps, suddenly plunge into the Minnesota Valley. The results are varied but always interesting from both aesthetic and hydrological viewpoints. Indeed, some of the most delightful river environments in Minnesota are along the bluffs, rims, and bottoms of the Minnesota River Valley. Plunging waters of the tributaries have formed rapids, waterfalls, and deep gorges. Examples are the rapids in the lower gorge of the Redwood River, the lovely waterfalls of Minneopa Creek in Minneopa State Park (Minneopa, from the Sioux, means Two Waterfalls), the trout stream Eagle Creek near Savage, and the beautiful wooded gorge of the Blue Earth River in and immediately south of Mankato.

We usually think of a continental divide as a mountain or plateau, or at least a small ridge. The continental divide at Browns Valley, however, is a long depression rather than a ridge. It is, in fact, a glacial river valley that contains a slightly higher, hardly distinguishable area from which precipitation now flows away in two directions. South of Browns Valley (the village is located on the divide itself), the headwaters of Big Stone Lake begin, receiving the Little Minnesota River from South Dakota. Down-valley the Whetstone River also flows in from South Dakota. Here the fan deposited at its mouth formed a natural dam near Ortonville, impounding Big Stone Lake, which is the border between South Dakota and Minnesota for its entire length of twenty-five miles. The Whetstone now flows directly into lower Big Stone Lake through a diversion completed in 1973. Below Ortonville the Minnesota is a small but distinct river, flowing entirely in the state of Minnesota. It flows for fifteen miles, receiving the waters of the Yellow Bank River, whose headwaters are also in South Dakota; then it meets Marsh Lake, a natural impoundment dammed by the fan of another tributary, the Pomme de Terre, coming down from the hills of the lake country to the north. And yet another reservoir, Lac qui Parle Lake (meaning The Lake Which Talks), is formed because a fan is deposited by the Lac qui Parle River coming from the southwestern prairies.

The plunging waterfalls of Minneopa Creek are typical of streams suddenly entering the deep Minnesota Valley from the higher woodlands and prairies. Minneopa, from the Sioux language, means "Two Waterfalls"; the upper falls may be seen below the bridge in this view from a Minneopa State Park foot trail.

Eroding steep terrain, swift waters can carry great loads of sand and silt. But when a receiving stream is met by a tributary, current velocity diminishes abruptly, and sand and silt loads can be carried no farther. This material, or alluvium, is dropped in the bed of the receiving stream, forming alluvial deposits that are often fan-shaped. Such a "delta" or "fan" may become so large that it dams the receiving stream, and in the Minnesota Valley, Big Stone, Marsh, and Lac qui Parle lakes have been formed in this way. Although they are natural reservoirs, the lakes were subject to some natural fluctuation; thus dams have been built at the outlets for greater water control.

From Lac qui Parle the Minnesota begins a tortuous, 270-mile journey to its mouth, swinging across the valley floor from bluff to bluff. In the upper course to New Ulm, the valley has been cut through glacial drift and sedimentary rock to older igneous and metamorphic rock. Near Granite Falls were two natural waterfalls; although not high enough to be classified among waterfalls of great significance, they nevertheless were the river's only waterfalls. There are igneous rock exposures in this area, and granite quarrying is a major industry. Both waterfalls were developed—that is, modified by manmade dams—for the production of hydroelectric power, but only the upper one in Granite Falls still operates. The river's only major rapids are just above Granite Falls. Downstream, no further man-made obstructions mar the natural meandering of the Minnesota.

Below the present valley floor, the granite bedrock dips sharply to the east; consequently downstream from above Mankato the River Warren exposed only sedimentary rock—sandstones, siltstones, limestones, and dolomite. These layers are much younger than granite and were formed by the deposition of fine materials on the bottom of ancient oceans. Because the layers vary in hardness and ease of erosion and solution, some striking features developed along the sides of the valley: tributary waterfalls, sheer bluffs such as those at Fort Snelling, caves and caverns, and river terraces called "prairies." One of these prairies is formed by the beautiful Kasota stone, salmon-pink sedimentary rock quarried near the town of Kasota and used as building material. The Kasota Prairie Natural Area of thirty acres is preserved by The Nature Conservancy as an example of the original landform and is used by ecology classes from nearby colleges.

Besides the large headwater lakes, the valley floor contains many oxbow lakes—old river bends that have been cut off by natural erosion of the river and left isolated, often in a horseshoe or oxbow shape. All are shallow, and the fish in them are subject to frequent winterkills. In the lower reaches of the river are several shallow saucer lakes, where natural river levees of flood-deposited materials trap floodwater. Rice, Fisher, and Blue lakes, near Shakopee, are good examples. The lower fifteen miles from above Savage to the mouth have been dredged to provide a nine-foot-deep channel, like that in the Mississippi, for commercial barge navigation.

Alkalinities are generally high, about 200 p.p.m., at most points in the river and tributaries draining lands that are covered by calcareous glacial sediments. Except in low-water winter conditions, the Minnesota is a muddy stream. Of the major rivers in the state, often it carries the most sulfates and carbonates and is the most turbid, with great quantities of clay and silt.

Waters from many sources make up the Minnesota. From the trickles of marshy depressions and pastures near Browns Valley, Big Stone Lake collects some small tributaries as well as the Little Minnesota and Whetstone rivers (some of the few streams originating outside the state and flowing into Minnesota).

Major tributaries fall into well-defined groups. From the south and the Coteau des Prairies enter the Lac qui Parle, Yellow Medicine, Redwood, and Cottonwood—plains streams that originate as swift creeks on the highland of the Coteau, meander across the southwest's low plains, then plunge through gorges and ravines into the Minnesota (Chapter 17). From the north come the Pomme de Terre, Chippewa, and Hawk. And from the south the Blue Earth River—carrying the waters of its own major tributaries, the Watonwan and Le Sueur rivers—enters through its lower gorge (Chapter 16). Other small tributaries enter the Minnesota throughout its long course; some, tumbling over waterfalls or originating as springs at the base of bluffs, flow only as short, though highly productive trout streams.

From Browns Valley to its mouth at Fort Snelling, the Minnesota is 355 miles long, including the headwater lakes; the river flows 270 miles from the outlet of Lac qui Parle Lake to the mouth, and downstream from the lower dam below Granite Falls the Minnesota River flows unobstructed for 240 miles. From Big Stone Lake, at an elevation of 964 feet, the river falls to 690 feet at its mouth, a total drop of only 274 feet. The average gradient is less than 0.8 feet per mile, so low a gradient that the present Minnesota would have been only a meandering prairie stream without the great glacial river valley.

The total watershed comprises nearly 17,000 square miles—14,751 in Minnesota and about 2,000 in South Dakota and Iowa. The Minnesota portion constitutes nearly one-fifth of the state's area. In Minnesota the southwestern watersheds—Lac qui Parle, Yellow Medicine, Redwood, Cottonwood, and some contiguous areas—contribute 4,653 square miles of watershed; the major northern streams—Pomme de Terre, Chippewa, and Hawk Creek—contribute 3,560; and the Blue Earth from the south, 3,106. The remaining about 3,400 square miles of watershed drain through smaller tributaries directly to the headwater lakes and the main stem of the Minnesota River.

The discharge of the Minnesota is highly variable; the watershed in all three states has a continental climate characterized by extremes. The annual mean discharge near the mouth is nearly 5,000 cubic feet per second; the maximum has been more than 100,000. The southwestern rivers contribute an average of about 600 cubic feet per second, the northern streams about 450, and the Blue Earth about 1,300; the rest flow from smaller streams emptying directly into the Minnesota.

Floods occasionally cover parts of the valley floor; economic losses from floods, however, are proportional to man's encroachment on the floodplains. Seven dams were proposed for the Minnesota Valley in the name of flood control, five on the main stem and one each on the Cottonwood and Blue Earth (Chapter 16). Ironically, the reservoirs would have inundated far more of the Minnesota floodplain than would have been protected.

One project has been completed: the Big Stone-Whetstone dam and reservoir built by the Army Corps of Engineers. The dam, near Odessa, impounds the Minnesota River seven miles upstream toward Big Stone Lake and should benefit wildlife in the area. The project will be managed by the U.S. Fish and Wildlife Service, primarily for waterfowl production. For the present, at least, plans for the other six dams and reservoirs in the Minnesota Valley have been dropped. When river bottoms remain unmodified and floodplains unoccupied, the beauty of springtime woods and riverbanks returns quickly after floodwaters recede.

Three important tributaries of the Minnesota flowing from the north are the Pomme de Terre and Chippewa rivers and Hawk Creek. Together, their watersheds constitute nearly one-fourth of the total Minnesota River watershed in the state and their flow about one-tenth of the total discharge at the Minnesota's mouth. These, also, are hard-water, productive streams.

The Pomme de Terre begins in the high country of Minnesota's famed lake region. Its origins are in lakes and ponds of the rugged glacial moraines; it begins as a distinct stream tumbling cool and clear from Stalker and Long lakes in southern Otter Tail County. Bordered by wooded hills and grassy meadows, the Pomme de Terre flows south through many lakes in Otter Tail, Grant, and Stevens counties. Most of these lakes have small water-control dams in the outlets, maintaining lake levels. The Pomme de Terre has no major tributaries.

In many stretches between lakes, it meanders quietly through cattail and reed canary grass marshes. Many state wildlife management areas and federal waterfowl production areas are located in the watershed—along small tributaries, saucerlike marshes, and the river itself. Below the town of Morris, however, the character of the river changes; from here down, the river is bordered by eroding, muddy banks. The river becomes increasingly turbid toward its mouth.

For 100 miles the Pomme de Terre River runs from Long and Stalker lakes to its delta creating Marsh Lake. It drains 977 square miles of watershed, and the annual mean runoff is about 100 cubic feet per second, although the maximum has been more than 5,000. Its overall gradient is about three and one-half feet per mile, more than four times that of the Minnesota. Pomme de Terre is French for "potato," and the river was named for the prairie turnip, a potatolike food of the Sioux.

The Chippewa River is a larger stream, and its watershed lies just to the east of the Pomme de Terre and is twice as great—2,080 square miles. It, too, originates in high headwater lakes of central Minnesota, and it flows 130 miles to its mouth in the Minnesota River at Montevideo, where it contributes an annual mean flow of 200 cubic feet per second; the maximum flood was nearly 10,000. The Chippewa's gradient is slightly higher than that of the Pomme de Terre—four and one-half feet per mile—and the high country character of the headwater region is similar to that of its western neighbor, although the river does not flow through scenic lakes as does the Pomme de Terre. Also in contrast to the Pomme de Terre, the Chippewa has several major tributaries—Little Chippewa River, East

Branch Chippewa, and Shakopee Creek; together these contribute nearly half the flow of the main stem, and their drainage comprises half the Chippewa's total watershed. Much of Shakopee Creek has been channelized, and wildfowl marshes have been greatly reduced in this area through drainage.

An interesting topographic feature in the lower watershed is a glacial river channel known as Watson Sag, now modified by the engineers. This channel connects the lower Chippewa to Lac qui Parle Lake above the outlet dam. During periods of floods on the Chippewa, high waters are diverted into Watson Sag—upstream, really—to Lac qui Parle Lake, reducing floodwaters in the lower Chippewa and thus in the Minnesota itself. Part of the mean annual discharge, then, flows through the channel to Lac qui Parle Lake. The east end of the channel, near the village of Watson, is relatively dry and is used as pasture; the west end is usually under water and constitutes an imposing swamp of floating vegetation and bare trees, known as the "Big Slough."

The lakes and wetlands of the Pomme de Terre and Chippewa river watersheds provide rich fish and wildlife resources. Especially in the higher headwater regions, many lakes are clear yet fertile, and these contain the larger sport fishes characteristic of central Minnesota lakes—walleye, largemouth bass, and northern pike, as well as panfish such as bluegills, crappies, and yellow perch. Rough fish—bullheads, sheepshead, buffalo, suckers, and carp—are usually abundant in the marginal lakes (those subject to occasional winterkill). There is some fishing in the pools formed in the rivers below lake-outlet dams. In the lower area of the watersheds many marshes, wetlands, and small tributaries provide rich resources for production of waterfowl and pheasants. Many of these areas are protected in state wildlife management areas and federal waterfowl production areas, both open to public hunting.

The Hawk Creek watershed, 503 square miles, lies directly to the east of the lower Chippewa. The stream flows sixty-five miles and contributes 150 cubic feet per second annual mean flow directly to the Minnesota. In contrast to the two other northern streams, Hawk Creek does not rise in the high moraines, but on a marshy glacial till plain not much above the level of the Minnesota Valley bluffs. Much of the watershed contains, or contained, marshes and wetlands well suited to waterfowl production, with habitat for pheasants and other small game on the edges. One of the outstanding—and best documented—losses of Minnesota's stream resources was sustained here; over sixty miles of Hawk Creek and its major tributary, Chetomba Creek, were channelized by excavating a wider, deeper, and straighter stream course. Although the purpose of channelizing is to alleviate local floods by allowing water to run off faster, it produces greater flow and raises flood crests, thereby intensifying downstream floods. Furthermore, this channelization made it possible to drain many private wetlands, and in the channeled portion of the Hawk Creek watershed over half the marshes and wetlands were drained. Wetland loss in the channeled portion of the watershed was nine times that in the unchanneled portion. The loss of habitat and wildlife production was devastating.

The French called the Minnesota the Rivière St. Pierre. But aside from the record of Pierre Charles le Sueur's fort and abortive attempt at "copper" mining on the Blue Earth, the French left little to history along the Minnesota. Instead it was the British who were most interested in searching the big valley for a route to the Pacific and the Orient, part of the long and unsuccessful quest for the Northwest Passage. Jonathan Carver, an English-colonial and most noted of the earlier chroniclers of America, spent the winter of 1766-1767 in Sioux tepees 200 miles upstream from the mouth of the Minnesota. He explored farther upstream the following summer and provided the earliest written descriptions of the upper river, recording for the first time the beauties of the Minnesota Valley. "A most delightful country," he wrote, "abounding with all the necessaries of life that grow spontaneously . . . Wild Rice grows here in great abundance; and every part is filled with trees bending under their loads of fruit, such as plums, grapes and apples." The river's name was soon anglicized to St. Peter's.

With the Louisiana Purchase in 1803, the Minnesota River and its watershed became part of the United States. In 1805 Lieutenant Zebulon M. Pike was ordered to ascend the Mississippi to establish military posts and search for the source of the river. At the mouth of the Minnesota, on the island that now bears Pike's name, he concluded a treaty with the Sioux for lands bordering the Mississippi upstream for nine miles, the first treaty of land cession in Minnesota. Here Fort Snelling, the great armed outpost of the northern wilderness, was later constructed.

The fort was built between 1820 and 1824 by Colonel Josiah Snelling, soldier-hero of the War of 1812, engineer, architect, and public administrator. The fort was named for its builder in 1825. It was a masterpiece of design and construction; never laid to siege, its imposing architecture and great height above the rivers apparently discouraged Indian attack. Its commandant was a hard master, thorough, precise, and fair in his administration but harsh in discipline. The fort stood the tests of Indian internecine war, traders' intrigues, and speculators' maneuverings; it furnished troops for the Civil War and the Sioux Uprising of 1862 and training grounds for later wars; it provided sanctuary for refugees from remoter wildernesses, arbitration of frontier quarrels — Indian and white alike — and education and social amenities to the men, women, and children who lived within this northern bastion. Today, there are many reminders of the frontier fort — military stations, federal offices, a veterans' hospital, a national cemetery, and Fort Snelling State Historical Park. The park encompasses the restored and preserved original buildings, Pike Island, and the wooded confluence of the two great rivers; it is also designated as a National Historic Landmark.

Although Fort Snelling guarded the mouth of the Minnesota and overlooked activities on the small military reservation, the valley stretching west remained the domain of the Sioux. Squatters and traders trespassed, but settlers did not enter. The principal exploration of the area was led by Major Stephen H. Long of the U.S. Army, who, with Josiah Snelling's son William, geologist William H. Keating, and the Italian adventurer Count Beltrami, traveled the length of the valley in 1823 with a military expedition. Keating produced the first American account of the valley, including botanical and hydrological observations and descriptions of its economic prospects. Beltrami, however, was more expansive: "Nature seems to have lavished all her treasures on this beautiful valley," he wrote.

Henry H. Sibley arrived a decade later, representing the American Fur Company's interest in the fur resources of the valley. His limestone house, the first private home in Minnesota and still standing, was in Mendota, and there Sibley entertained in elegant style the more civilized travelers of the time as well as Indians. From his trading business he acquired a wealth unprecedented in the region. Sibley later left the banks of the Minnesota for St. Paul and a part in the making of the Treaty of Traverse des Sioux, the state of Minnesota's first governorship, and a battlefield role in the Sioux Uprising.

When the *Virginia*, the first steamboat up the Mississippi, turned into the St. Peter's River and Fort Snelling's landing on a spring day in 1823, there was no thought of steamboat travel up the valley. Navigation developed on the sweeping St. Croix and on the Mississippi to St. Paul; but the Minnesota was too winding, too shallow, too unreliable, and the suggestion of steam navigation on the Minnesota River provoked only ridicule. But a quarter of a century after the *Virginia*, the *Anthony Wayne* pushed upstream a few miles and signaled a new day for the long river. In the same year four more exploratory trips were made, including one by the *Yankee*, which went up the river more than 150 miles. There were many enthusiastic accounts of the wonderful stream and the beautiful valley in the decade ahead, especially when the treaty at Traverse des Sioux opened the valley to settlement. Henry D. Thoreau, in Minnesota in 1861 for his health, eloquently described the turns and twists of a steamboat on the Minnesota River. A new kind of hydrologic principle emerged in his reaction to the tortuous stream: "Ditch it straight," he wrote, "& it would not only be very swift, but soon run out."

Through the 1850s and until the outbreak of Indian war, hundreds of steamboats plied the river, although a regular schedule was out of the question. The sharp bends and uncertain water levels were the main problems, but short, shallow-draft boats, built especially for the Minnesota, continued to twist and turn their way upstream even in low-water seasons.

Inevitably someone proposed taking a steamboat up the Minnesota on a spring flood and across the divide at Browns Valley to the Red River of the North. The *Freighter* tried it in 1859 but was wrecked below Big Stone Lake; no steamboat ever sailed through Browns Valley. A proposal for a canal, linking the upper Minnesota and the headwaters of the Red, was never implemented.

In this period just before statehood was attained, the capital of Minnesota was nearly located on the river. The territorial capital had been St. Paul, and it was carelessly assumed by most citizens that it would remain so in statehood, soon to come in 1858. But in early 1857 the territorial legislature quickly passed a bill to move the capital to St. Peter on the Minnesota River. The scheme was the idea of the river-town promoters, including territorial Governor Willis A. Gorman. But the promoters had not reckoned with colorful Joe Rolette, fur trader, famed pioneer in the oxcart transportation system on the Red River Trails. Rolette, no-nonsense legislator, absconded with the capital transfer bill and hid in a hotel room, drinking and playing poker with cronies for a week, until he returned to the legislative chambers at the moment of adjournment. The capital of the new state was to remain in St. Paul, and was not moved to the banks of the Minnesota River.

Prosperity slowly came back to the valley after 1862. Only gradually did the settlers return; some did not go back to their desolated homesteads at all. But the Indian threat was gone, and the railroads first started up the valley in 1865, a portent of the steamboats' demise. The surge west started again, and the fertile valley yielded new and greater agricultural produce. Civilization, with its problems as well as its advantages, moved up the river, and the valley flourished. Railroads were extended, and when the last steamboat went downstream in 1874, the river, artery of westward expansion, slipped into relative obscurity.

Events and people made brief appearances in the history of the river: the James gang, whose first planned raid in the Minnesota Valley in 1876 was frustrated when they were recognized by Mankato citizens; the construction at Port Cargill near Savage of U.S. Navy tankers that were floated downriver to sail on distant seas in World War II; and the indomitable Charlie Poliquin, who in 1958 dreamed along the riverbanks, built a seventy-foot-long, aluminum-covered boat, and, after an initial 400-yard voyage that left him firmly aground, finally made it after many months to New Orleans—where the boat promptly sank.

Today the valley's history is being painstakingly retold as the result of successful efforts of the Scott County Historical Society to restore Murphy's Landing, a Minnesota Valley Restoration Project, just east of Shakopee along the old steamboat landing. To these grounds old homesteads, shops, inns, mills, cabins, churches, and a depot, as well as Indian villages, are being carefully transported and restored. Murphy's Landing makes an old valley come alive again.

Fish and wildlife of the river valley constitute a valuable resource in Minnesota. The river and floodplain today retain much wildlife habitat similar to that encountered by the early explorers and settlers because there are no high dams, no large reservoirs, no extensive industrial developments. Floodplain vegetation includes many species of wild flowers, marsh plants, shrubs, and such typical floodplain hardwoods as cottonwood, willow, and soft maple. Oak and elm woods and many grassy meadows are found on south-facing hillsides; maple-basswood forests are characteristic of the moister north-facing slopes.

In the Minnesota River channel catfish predominate in the sport fishery, although walleyes, smallmouth bass, northern pike, and panfish are also taken. Channel catfish, northern pike, crappies, and smallmouth bass have been stocked by the state since 1962. Fish populations, however, are predominated by species considered rough fish—sheepshead, buffalo, quillback, several other kinds of suckers and redhorse, and the introduced carp. Commercial fishing is pursued for certain rough fish species—mostly carp, buffalo, and sheepshead —generally in the upper reaches below Lac qui Parle. The Minnesota is famous for some large rough fish, including a legendary catfish— perhaps a mud cat—weighing 157 pounds, taken in 1930.

The valley bottoms provide a rich, diverse habitat for many species of wildlife—hunted game, song birds, waterfowl, and fur-bearers. The many marshes and wetlands, ponds and oxbow lakes provide excellent habitat for waterfowl, primarily the wood duck along the riverbank woodlands, as well as for aquatic fur-bearers like the mink and muskrat. The headwater lakes, Marsh and Lac qui Parle, are incorporated into some of the largest and most important wildlife management areas and public hunting grounds in the state, and are stop-overs for great concentrations of migrating waterfowl in spring and fall. Other, smaller, state wildlife management areas have been acquired in the valley for public hunting; similarly many federal waterfowl production areas managed by the U.S. Fish and Wildlife Service are scattered throughout the Minnesota watershed. The principal upland game bird is the introduced pheasant. Deer are plentiful —and fat—in the valley; brushy, wooded hills bordering the river bottoms with agricultural fields, swamps, and wetlands, provide both food and cover. The river valley is probably best known, however, for small game such as cottontail rabbits in the brushy bottoms and fat fox squirrels on the hillsides wooded with butternut and oak; the quality of habitat is excellent for these two favorites.

Recreational facilities of many kinds have been developed in the valley of the Minnesota and its northern tributaries. There is public access to most of the fishing lakes in the headwater regions of the Pomme de Terre and Chippewa rivers and to numerous points on the streams and river-bottom lakes and the Minnesota River itself. The watershed has many public hunting grounds for waterfowl and pheasants. There are no state or national forests in the Minnesota watershed, but many state parks have been developed, principally in locations of historic interest; campsites are available at some of these. In addition to the parks associated with military and Sioux Indian history are Big Stone Lake State Park, with three separate units along the headwater lake; Lac qui Parle State Park, at the lower end of Lac qui Parle Lake, site of an early fur trading post, church, school, and mission serving the Sioux; Glacial Lakes State Park in the upper Chippewa watershed, including outstanding examples of glacial moraines and outwash plains; Monson Lake State Park in the eastern part of the Chippewa River watershed, the site of an Indian massacre of settlers during the 1862 uprising; Appleton Lake County Park, Swift County, providing boat access to the Pomme de Terre; Swift Falls County Park, on a wooded rocky section of the Chippewa which includes waterfalls; Sibley State Park on Lake Andrew, a headwater lake of Shakopee Creek; Flandrau State Park at the mouth of the Cottonwood; Minneopa State Park with its double waterfalls; Sibley Park in Mankato, at the mouth of the Blue Earth; and many other county and municipal parks on the smaller streams of the watershed. Four large Renville County parks are located near or along the Minnesota River—Beaver Falls, Camp Town, Skalbekken, and Town and Country parks—including natural bottomland and river environments.

In September 1963 a river traveler put in his canoe at Ortonville and floated some 330 miles downriver to the mouth in the Mississippi. Clyde Ryberg, of Burnsville, long a champion of Minnesota rivers, undertook this trip with his friend Senator Henry McKnight, to obtain information upon which a sound plan for managing the river's recreational resources could be based.

Ryberg's efforts were important in later plans to preserve the unique historical, recreational, and cultural values of the Minnesota River Valley.

Today, ambitious proposals have been drawn for further protection of the valley's resources, including a major recreational trail along the lower river. The state legislature authorized the study for a second segment, from Le Sueur upstream to the South Dakota border below Big Stone Lake. More than a hundred important historic sites have been identified along the river, though many have not been acquired or restored. The Minnesota is included in *A Gathering of Waters*, which describes a designated canoe route of 263 miles from Ortonville to Shakopee.

The Lower Minnesota River Valley Citizens' Committee, concerned with the preservation of the environmental quality of the lower Minnesota Valley, proposed a federally sponsored program of protection and development of the river. And in 1976 the Minnesota Valley National Wildlife Refuge was established along the lower stretch of floodplain between Carver and Fort Snelling. The refuge extends along a twenty-five-mile stretch; its four separate units will be administered by the U.S. Fish and Wildlife Service. And, more recently, the Minnesota Department of Natural Resources have proposed a ninety-five-mile stretch from the outlet of Lac qui Parle to Franklin in Renville County as a component of the Minnesota Wild, Scenic and Recreational Rivers System.

Those who would use and protect the valley's beauty share Count Beltrami's enchantment with the river's natural treasures.

Many states, including Minnesota, are named for major rivers because the significance of a river usually emerges long before statehood is attained. "Minnesota," from the Sioux, is popularly translated as "sky-tinted"; thus Minnesota is known as the land of sky-blue waters. But did the Sioux really see the muddy Minnesota River as a stream of sky-blue water? Probably not. In fact, a more accurate translation is "whitish" or "sky-clouded."

Minnesota will probably stick with sky-blue, anyway.

Minnesota's Streams

A Call for Stewardship

*A river belongs to no man. And it belongs to every
man. And no man has any right to contribute to the
desecration of a river by irresponsible and abusive
acts, at the expense of his neighbors and fellow American citizens, near or far removed from the stream
itself.*

Richard J. Dorer

The Conservation Volunteer, Nov.-Dec. 1968, p. 37.

Sky-blue or not, the Minnesota River is a stream that has been
put to trial and has emerged almost unscathed. The soil, trees,
wildlife, and muddy waters of the Minnesota Valley sustained
the men and women of central Minnesota for more than a century,
and when representatives of a government cadre of engineers de-
manded that hills and homesteads be buried beneath dammed waters,
they were met with the resistance of a people whose values are rooted in their land.

No stream in Minnesota—perhaps in the nation—has had its future so threatened, its natural character so marked for destruction,
its existence made so uncertain by serious development proposals,
and yet has emerged to symbolize an awakened ethic of land stewardship, as has the Minnesota River.

Surely among the ancestors of the human species is that industrious and sometimes notorious dam-builder, *Castor canadensis*. Imitating the beaver, the ancients constructed obstacles to the flow of water. Ingenious water works were built, only to fall into decay. Through prehistory, civilizations rose and fell among some of the world's great rivers. Only modern cultures—actually within the most recent decades—have raised an alarm over the effects of large dams on man's relationship to the earth's life-supporting natural resources.

Almost all large dams are built with flood prevention as one objective. Yet a dam, large or small, can no more prevent a flood than it can prevent rainfall. A flood is the release of high waters from the stream channel out over the floodplain, and a dam merely transfers the floodplain inundation from one section of stream to another; the impounded reservoir is frequently larger than the downstream floodplain that is protected. Even this protection is temporary.

There are only two effective means of ameliorating the effects of a flood: (1) by retaining excess precipitation in the watershed's uplands in lakes and marshes, and (2) by keeping valuable property that may be prone to flood damage off the floodplain. Man has violated both these principles. We have ditched and drained headwater wetlands in our pursuit of high agricultural productivity, rushing floodwaters downstream. And downstream we have built our homes and factories on the floodplain, where damage will result when the flood inevitably occurs.

The problems with flood-control dams related to their alleged function alone are many-fold. First, the dams are impermanent; concrete dams are highly vulnerable to damage by water, weather, and earthquake. The great loss of property and life in dam disasters is evident—the 2,200 lives lost in the 1889 Johnstown flood, the Rapid City tragedy in 1972 which killed 236, the more recent Teton Dam disaster in Idaho. Second, a dam built on a river that carries even a modest sediment load will soon "silt in"—the impoundment will fill with the soils eroded from headwater regions—and therefore become useless for flood control. Third, in order for a reservoir to operate for flood control, it must have a large enough capacity to accommodate the anticipated flood. Then it must release enough water so that it can hold the next flood; the result is a wildly fluctuating water level, even more than a hundred feet. The reservoir has a "conservation pool"—a permanent lake—and also a "flood pool"—a larger, temporary lake that holds the flood. Between is a no-man's-land, alternately dry and inundated and of no more commercial use than the original floodplain. And the fluctuating level of such a reservoir virtually precludes production of the fish and wildlife that depend on shore and littoral habitats.

The floodplain of a river valley usually develops in the lower part of a major watershed and is composed of alluvial materials—silt, sand, and gravel—spread by a thousand floods. The river erodes this plain laterally with meanders that move from one side of the valley to the other. Additional floodwaters spill over the plain when deep snow melts or heavy rains fall on hillsides and headwater creeks, adding alluvium and enriching the floodplain.

The first settlers saw the rivers' floodplains as areas of utility and potential productivity. They usually arrived by river; the floodplain was handy and flat. It was rich in black soil, wildlife, and green plants and woodlands that, in a treeless prairie, promised well-watered fields, wood for building and fuel, and wild game. The river water was available for domestic and industrial uses and for transportation. There on the floodplain the settlers built farms, homes, industry, transportation systems, and, eventually, complete cities. And the settlers prospered in the beauty and productivity of these riverside lands.

That is, until one stormy spring night when the flood came raging down the valley to bring destruction and tragedy. Of course when floods occurred, the river was considered to have gone wild. And man began to devise ways to tame it. Eventually governmental agencies of public works engineers were established and encouraged, agencies which today have attained such power and influence that they are virtually independent of citizen control. The result, since big-dam building began just after the turn of the century, has been the construction of high dams on almost every major river in the United States—a national program that has failed to provide either effective, permanent flood control or more than a small fraction of today's electrical power production. These dams have caused staggering destruction of our environment in loss of fish and wildlife production, river-based recreation, floodplain productivity, cultural, historical, and archaeological sites, and magnificent scenery. Man today views the disasters of human industriousness—and because powerful bureaucratic forces have been unleashed, the awakening has come almost too late.

We can use the floodplain for many purposes other than the construction of homes and businesses that are subject to damage by flood waters. These include parks and playgrounds, recreational trails, scenic drives, wildlife production for nature study areas and public hunting, canoe, boat, and fishing access, winter sports, picnic and campgrounds, historic monuments, and pristine examples of wild America for scientific study. These activities can fully utilize the floodplain—yet withstand occasional flooding with practically no damage. And the stream remains intact—dynamic, changing with the seasons—rather than covered by the conservation pool of a high-dam reservoir, or channelized and polluted in the center of floodplain industrial development.

Let us review two mistakes made in Minnesota—there were high aspirations for these dams when they were built, but today they are burdens.

The Rapidan dam was first constructed on the Blue Earth River near the present village of Rapidan in 1867; a later structure, still standing, was built in 1910. With a head of sixty-two feet it impounded a reservoir of about 500 acres, filling the wooded gorge that now ends abruptly at the plunging falls which thunder through damaged spillways. Its generation capacity was 1,500 kilowatts, today a small fraction of Minnesota's power needs. Soon mud and silt from the prairie soils of southern Minnesota were carried into the reservoir and settled to the bottom of the inundated gorge, and the reservoir began to fill.

The big flood in 1965 delivered the coup de grace to the Rapidan dam, and today it neither generates power nor controls any flood. It was planned that Blue Earth County would acquire the dam (a county highway crosses it) and continue to operate it; it was proposed that the reservoir be maintained as a "scenic setting for housing development." But mud continues to pour into it.

Beneath the mud lies the real "scenic setting," the river gorge. But short of disastrous accident, it will not be uncovered. For the sediment is too deep, and it is too costly to move. The threat of dam failure is too serious to ignore, the result too devastating for areas downstream, including the city of Mankato. What can be done?

The Coon Rapids dam on the Mississippi River was completed in 1914, designed as a hydroelectric generating plant with a 6,500-kilowatt capacity. It had a head of twenty feet and included twenty-eight spillways and gates. The reservoir extended upstream five miles to Anoka. At the time of its construction it was one of the biggest hydroelectric plants in Minnesota, exceeded only by the plants at St. Anthony Falls, St. Croix Falls, and the huge Thomson plant on the St. Louis. Only three hydroelectric plants with greater generating capacity were built afterward in Minnesota — at Royalton and St. Paul (both Mississippi River) and Fond du Lac (St. Louis River).

In December 1966, fifty years later, Northern States Power Company ceased all generating operations at the Coon Rapids dam and closed it down. It was damaged from weather, inefficient, and competed unsuccessfully with other means of electric production that were more efficient and had greater capacity.

The list of structural damage was long: leaks through the dam and the gates; earth sunken near the dam; spillway walls tilted; piers eroded and broken; ice damage; faulty sills, beams, and struts; and supporting walls bowed, twisted, bent, washed out. In 1967 all power production equipment was removed. In 1968 the Minnesota Department of Conservation recommended removal of the dam.

However desirable it was from the standpoint of economics to simply remove the dam and return the river to its natural level above Coon Rapids, from the viewpoint of residents upstream and other users of the reservoir, it was simply unthinkable that the pool be drained. What could be done?

Understandably Northern States Power Company, with no further interest in power production at the site, wished to divest itself of responsibility for the dam. Northern States Power had a piece of land near the dam that, they felt, would be suitable for a park. Would someone be interested in the gift of 170 acres (with the dam, of course) to be used for public recreation and enjoyment?

Someone was. In 1969 the dam and property were transferred to the Hennepin County Park Reserve District to be developed as a park. The company agreed to provide some funds to assist in dam repair and maintenance — $800,000. But even the initial repair would cost far more than that, to say nothing of the permanent obligation to maintain, protect, and operate the dam. And in 1975 the Park Reserve board approved, by a close vote, a contract for repairs that would cost $2.4 million, including $1 million to be diverted from projects in other programs of the Park Reserve. Later in the same year the Park Reserve complained that the county could not afford the repairs and appealed to the federal government for assistance. Hennepin County wished it had looked at that particular gift a little more closely.

The experience with the Rapidan and Coon Rapids dams is being repeated again and again throughout the state and the nation, for many of our early dams are now silted in or dangerously damaged. Of the approximately 2,500 dams built in Minnesota, about 1,000 are still in existence. And currently more than fifty Minnesota municipalities and counties own dams for which state assistance has been requested—dams taken as gifts for public parks and recreation and no longer wanted by their former private owners. It is discouraging that new and bigger dams continue to be proposed.

For comparison let us consider again the dynamic valley of the Minnesota River. Here there are wide, flat floodplains, contained on each side by the steep bluffs of Glacial River Warren; it is a valley of great beauty, of rich wildlife habitat, of tradition and history.

The seven dams and reservoirs that threatened the Minnesota would have irreversibly changed the watershed, particularly the floodplain, of the Minnesota Valley. Five dams on the main stem of the river and one each on the tributary Blue Earth and Cottonwood rivers, were proposed. All would have flooded huge areas of floodplain. The largest of these would have been near New Ulm and would, at flood stage, have impounded water in the Minnesota Valley for forty miles, covering sixty miles of actual river channel. Far more area of the valley would have been permanently inundated than would have been protected. The reservoir would have flooded many thousands of acres of choice wildlife habitat in lakes, marshes, and woodlands—an enormous loss of river bottom environment.

Except for the Big Stone-Whetstone dam and reservoir recently completed, the plan was dropped. The proposed benefits did not equal the enormous costs of dam construction and environmental loss.

In 1976 Congress passed an act creating the Minnesota Valley National Wildlife Refuge along the lower river. It is remarkable that most of the floodplain in this largely urbanized section of the valley is in a natural state, rich in wildlife cover, woodlands, marshes, saucer lakes, and river bluff scenery. It is planned that the river bottoms be administered in several separate units from near Carver downstream to Fort Snelling. The project in its entirety will encompass a total of 17,500 acres, slightly more than half to be administered by the U.S. Fish and Wildlife Service and the rest by the state of Minnesota and local units of government. Among the proposed programs are management for wildlife production, particularly waterfowl; visitor centers for the observation and study of wildlife by the metropolitan public; environmental interpretive centers that are near innercity schools; limited public hunting in designated wildlife management areas; fishing and boating access and canoe trails on the river; and the preservation of approximately forty sites and monuments significant to Minnesota history. It is a new concept within the function of the national wildlife refuge system. The refuge is the result of the efforts of many concerned individuals and citizens' groups who worked over many years to protect this part of the valley and its rich floodplain resources.

The contrast between present reality and the earlier proposed network of big dams and reservoirs is striking; the refuge itself is an outstanding example of our growing understanding of the value of our river resources.

Nationwide, our federal flood-control program has built 260 major flood-control reservoirs, 8,000 miles of artificial stream channels, and 6,000 miles of levees and floodwalls, at a cost to American taxpayers of 25 billion dollars. Despite this, flood damage continues to mount annually—and we must conclude that our dam-building, as a national program, has been a costly failure. It is apparent that the most effective solution to flood problems is floodplain management—keep people away from the floods, rather than trying to keep floods away from people.

Water power for cheap generation of electricity has always been a temptation. But the potential production of electric power by hydroelectric dams is tiny compared to total electricity needs; the development of all likely dam sites in the United States would provide only 5 percent of national electricity demands projected for the year 2000. Even within the enormous Tennessee Valley Authority—once the answer to southern electric power needs—hydropower now provides only 12 percent of total electric power produced by TVA. If future electric power needs are to be met, it obviously must be done by means other than dam-building. Why destroy our rivers now?

Dams are not the only threat to Minnesota's streams and rivers. The catalogue of problems caused by man is great. Perhaps the worst of these affecting smaller streams is channelization. The agencies' term for it is "channel improvement." In practice it means dredging and widening to change a meandering, winding stream with pools, riffles, sand and gravel bars, and bank vegetation into a straight ditch—with no diversity in substrate or gradient, with no streamside cover. The purpose is to enlarge the flow capacity of the stream to hurry downstream the high waters of spring melt or rainstorms. Channelization works. It does, indeed, speed excess waters downstream, preventing overflow onto the floodplain locally— and incidentally intensifying flood conditions downstream, where additional water control projects are then often proposed as the next "structural solution."

Stream channelization has three basic objectives:

(1) Improvement of navigation. This is the purpose of work on larger rivers, usually undertaken by the Army Corps of Engineers.

(2) Flood control. "Excess" waters run off more rapidly because the channel is enlarged and straightened. Containing walls and levees are often constructed using spoil from the stream dredging. This procedure prevents overflow onto the floodplain, but the effect is only local; it increases the severity of downstream flood damages because it essentially removes the floodplain (in the area of the channelization) from the storage capacity of the watershed. This is the objective of work on urban floodplains, usually by the Army Corps of Engineers, and in cultivated floodplains, usually by the Soil Conservation Service.

(3) Increased acreage of arable land. Ditching of natural streams to facilitate drainage and accelerate runoff, making wetlands, marshes, and swamps suitable for cultivation, was done by some early settlers and farmers, sometimes by huge "bull plows" drawn by several ox teams. Most of the more easily accomplished work of this type

has been done. Additional ditching and draining of wetlands continues on a more costly basis, with the aid of federal funds primarily
administered by the Soil Conservation Service. Strangely enough,
federal subsidization continues at the same time – to farmers to keep
arable land out of production as a price stabilization measure. A
particularly insidious element in such stream channelization is the
construction of many small ditches on private land after major public
ditches are created with federal funds. These drain additional wetlands into main arteries, causing incalculable losses of wildlife and
water storage regionally. And the straight stream, even with attempts
to renew wildlife and fisheries habitat along it, may be substantially
shorter than the original stream – as much as one-half or even one-
third the original length.

In 1971 members of the North Central Division of the American Fisheries Society, the oldest scientific society concerned with
natural resources in the United States, held a symposium on stream
channelization in Omaha, Nebraska. Representatives from the Soil
Conservation Service and the Army Corps of Engineers also had been
invited to participate. Under discussion was an attempt to tally the
number of stream miles that had actually been channelized in fourteen states and provinces of midwest North America. Thus symposium
participants wanted, first, to assess the magnitude of the problem ad-
dressed. Of course such a tally is difficult, for much ditching had
been done long ago. Furthermore, as already noted, a channelized
stream is shorter than the original, and it may be impossible to determine the length of the original stream lost to the straightening
process.

Only half the states and provinces were able to provide numbers,
and the final figure reported was therefore a marked underestimate –
though still impressive – more than 29,000 miles. Significant to Minnesotans was the tally reported for their state, by far the largest
proportion of the total – 21,700 miles of streams channelized in Minnesota alone!

What happens to the biota – fish and other aquatic life, wildfowl
and other streamside wildlife, and vegetative cover – when a natural
stream is turned into a straight ditch? The general answer is, of
course, that they are virtually eradicated. Many researchers have reported the same general findings: fish populations almost eliminated,
or shifted from game fish species to rough fish such as the carp; aquat-

ic invertebrates, the food base for fish and other water-supported wildlife, reduced to tiny fractions of original abundance; higher stream gradients and consequent increased erosion; large areas (frequently the major proportion of wetlands originally present in a watershed) supporting waterfowl and aquatic fur-bearers drained.

Symposium authors concluded: "When a stream is channelized, it is permanently disabled . . . it lives on a pitiful remnant of its former self, unable to function productively . . . a continuing burden on . . . society."

A major channelization threat now confronts a unique Minnesota river resource—major in the sense that it will destroy a fishery resource unmatched elsewhere in the state—the channelization of the Roseau River, currently proposed by the Army Corps of Engineers.

The Roseau is unique in Minnesota with respect to its northern pike population which has a reproductive capacity far above the average for the state and greater than any other riverine northern pike population in Minnesota. Conditions in the swamp and marshland adjacent to the river are particularly conducive to successful pike reproduction, especially because the river is connected by old oxbows, wetlands, and sloughs to the pools of the Roseau River Wildlife Management Area. Many thousands of northern pike fingerlings are recovered from the wildlife management area pools and transferred each year to other lakes in Minnesota. Nowhere else in the state do the particular spawning conditions exist in such high quality and great quantity.

The channelization proposal calls for widening and straightening the river channel for approximately forty-five miles, for the purpose of lowering flood levels in the village of Roseau and reducing flooding over some agricultural lands, mostly pasture.

The cost of this benefit will be the destruction of the major source of northern pike fingerling production in the state and the only major river sport fishery in northwestern Minnesota and adjacent Canada. The Roseau will be widened to the extent of removing pool areas for northern pike cover, removing all streambank cover, destroying riffle areas that produce fish food organisms, causing excess heating of stream waters, losing the diversity of stream bottom and thus biological productivity, and, most important, preventing access of adult pike to the spawning areas of the sloughs and pools of the wildlife management area.

If approved, the Roseau channelization project will result in the loss of one of the major fishery resources in Minnesota. It is a resource that can never be replaced.

There are, however, some signs that we may have turned the corner and are at last facing the fact that human populations are interdependent in the earth's community, and not the rulers of it. There is a new organization of citizen effort, a new system of environmental laws and programs, new interpretations of old customs, new cracks in the old order. Among professional and scientific organizations, there is a new activism that rejects the old ivory-tower isolation and enters the public arena to apply basic ecological principles to critical environmental problems. These developments are a result of the growth of environmental concern that mushroomed little more than a decade ago, and some bear specifically upon the management of our streams and rivers.

Certainly one of the major implements of the environmental movement is the National Environmental Policy Act (NEPA), passed by Congress in 1969. The outstanding element of this landmark legislation is that it requires environmental impact statements (EIS). Any project by a federal agency that might have significant environmental effects must include in its plans a statement outlining the effect, or impact, of the project upon the environment, opening the potential effects to public view. The act has been termed "the touchstone of modern environmental litigation."

Minnesota has enacted its own version of NEPA, in some respects stricter than the federal act. State legislation controlling floodplain and shoreland use and other acts bolster natural resource management programs. Of major significance to Minnesota's rivers and streams are both the national and the Minnesota river protection systems. To date, the Upper and Lower segments of the St. Croix are in the National Wild and Scenic Rivers System, and a large segment of the Mississippi, and the Kettle and Big Fork rivers are under study for inclusion. The Kettle is the first river of the Minnesota Wild, Scenic and Recreational Rivers System; the Mississippi from Anoka to St. Cloud and a scenic reach of the North Fork of the Crow were added, and others are under consideration. These two acts, within current natural resource legislation, provide the greatest protection specifically of our rivers, although progress, especially in the national system, has been agonizingly slow.

At its annual meeting in March 1977 the Minnesota Chapter of the American Fisheries Society recognized the outstanding value of Minnesota's free-flowing rivers and unanimously passed a resolution, calling upon the governor of Minnesota to declare a moratorium on dam construction and channelization on all rivers of the state capable of supporting substantial sport fisheries and other recreation.

Many citizens' groups are increasingly active in advancing protection programs and legislation concerned with the environmental values of streams and rivers. Established organizations, such as the Izaak Walton League, the National Wildlife Federation, National Audubon Society, The Wilderness Society, and the Sierra Club, have long been active and concerned about river resources, and newer groups like the Environmental Defense Fund, Environmental Action, and the Natural Resources Defense Council are militantly active in litigation, lobbying, and public information. The American Rivers Conservation Council is specifically active in considering current river environment problems, and groups like the Minnesota Canoe Association and Trout Unlimited are concerned not only with their specific interests but also with the natural qualities of streams and rivers. The Voice of the Mississippi, recently organized in Minnesota, speaks for the values and protection of the Mississippi in Minnesota.

Many environmental problems are resolved in the courts including the supreme courts of the state and nation; an important segment of the legal profession now specializes in environmental law. Many specific river problems are solved legally and, increasingly, to the benefit of our streams and the people who love them.

Significant, too, are the cracks appearing in the previously solid front presented by the developers. The Army Corps of Engineers now has responsibilities to protect streams as well as to develop them; individual officers have made decisions in favor of environmental considerations; and the Director of Civil Works for the Corps recently stated that in his opinion a law like NEPA was ten or fifteen years overdue. The Corps is now teamed with the U.S. Fish and Wildlife Service in a cooperative effort (GREAT) to chart a course of proper management of the Upper Mississippi River. The Corps recently made several decisions to leave sections of the floodplain

alone and undeveloped rather than to build dams, and the Corps provides services to communities such as floodplain studies to serve as a
basis for wise use of floodplains. In Minnesota the Corps has itself
rejected the plan to connect navigation between Lake Superior and
the Mississippi. New policies of the Soil Conservation Service de-
emphasize channelization and drainage and have returned to water
conservation, a founding principle of the SCS.

But the greatest influence in protection of our flowing waters
is a citizenry newly aware of the value of this resource. This will also
mean greater utilization of our streams for recreation and some problems caused by local overuse, but the general effect of a concerned
population is a positive influence, and that influence has been clearly
demonstrated in recent years.

To preserve river values, our streams must be deliberately managed for diversity—not just for the canoeist, not just for the species
of fish that provide sport to the angler, but rather for the myriad life
forms that, living interdependently, are unique to flowing waters.
Management must set aside some wild areas for enjoyment and
study, protecting them from human manipulation and allowing natural succession.

Awakened public concern for our river resources must be sustained if we are to preserve them for future generations. In Minnesota we have not yet made irreversible decisions concerning the use of
many of our streams—not the case in some other regions of the nation. We in Minnesota still have some time. And we have some goals
at last clearly identified.

We are beginning to place short-term economic benefits in per-
spective with the enduring value of a protected free-running stream;
we are beginning to realize that, under man's assault, our streams and
rivers will not survive. We are beginning to look ahead, a century,
perhaps, to some future Minnesota—to wonder what the winding, remote pools of the Little Fork will be like then, to ask whether the
western prairie rivers will still rush in springtime flood through their
glacial beach gorges, to hope that the North Shore waterfalls will still
be awesome and clear.

If we use our time and our remaining options wisely, we might
yet make secure the magic of flowing waters in our green valleys.

Bibliography

Bibliography

Ackermann, W. C., G. F. White, E. B. Worthington, and J. L. Ivens, eds. 1973. *Man-made lakes: Their problems and environmental effects*. Am. Geophys. Union, Geophys. Monogr. No. 17.

Allison, I. S. 1932. *The geology and water resources of northwestern Minnesota*. Univ. Minn., Minn. Geol. Surv., Bull. No. 22.

American Heritage. 1962. *Steamboats on the Mississippi*. New York: American Heritage.

Bachman, E. 1969. *A history of forestry in Minnesota*. Association of Minnesota Division of Lands and Forestry Employees, St. Paul.

Baker, J. H. 1887. The sources of the Mississippi, their discoverers, real and pretended. *Minnesota Historical Society, Collections* 6:3-28.

Bardach, J. 1964. *Downstream: A natural history of the river*. New York: Harper & Row.

Blegen, T. C. 1963. *Minnesota, a history of the state*. Minneapolis: Univ. Minn. Press. (Revised edition, 1975.)

———. 1968. *The Kensington rune stone: New light on an old riddle*. Minn. Hist. Soc., St. Paul.

Bolz, J. A. 1960. *Portage into the past*. Minneapolis: Univ. Minn. Press.

Bonnema, K. W., 1972. *Wildlife habitat losses in Ten Mile Creek watershed (Judicial Ditch 8), Lac qui Parle and Yellow Medicine counties, Minnesota*. Minn. Dept. Nat. Res., Sec. Tech. Serv., Spec. Publ. No. 99.

Breining, G., and L. Watson. 1977. *A gathering of waters, a guide to Minnesota's rivers*. Minn. Dept. Nat. Res., St. Paul.

Brown, M. H., and I. J. Nygard. 1941. *Erosion and related land use conditions in Winona County, Minnesota*. U.S. Dept. Agriculture, Soil Conserv. Serv., Erosion Survey No. 17.

Carlander, H. B. 1954. *A history of fish and fishing in the Upper Mississippi River*. Upper Mississippi River Conserv. Committee.

Carlander, K. D. 1942. *An investigation of Lake of the Woods, Minnesota, with particular reference to the commercial fisheries*. Minn. Dept. Conserv., Div. Game and Fish, Bur. Fish. Res., Invest. Rep. No. 42.

Carley, K. 1961. *The Sioux Uprising of 1862*. Minn. Hist. Soc., St. Paul.

Carter, H. 1942. *Lower Mississippi*. New York: Farrar and Rinehart.

———. 1970. *Man and the river: The Mississippi*. (Photography by D. Guravich) Chicago: Rand McNally.

Choate, J. S. 1971. *Wetland drainage in the Hawk Creek pilot watershed, Minnesota*. Minn. Dept. Nat. Res., Div. Game and Fish, Spec. Publ. No. 91.

Christianson, R. W. 1974. *Commercial navigation on the Upper Mississippi River: An economic review of its development and public policy issues affecting Minnesota*. Water Resources Res. Ctr., Univ. Minn., Bull. No. 75.

Colby, P. J., and L. L. Smith, Jr. 1967. Survival of walleye eggs and fry on paper fiber sludge deposits in Rainy River, Minnesota. *Trans. Amer. Fish. Soc.* 96:278-296.

Coleman, Sister Bernard, Sister Verona LaBud, and J. Humphrey. 1967. *Old Crow Wing*. Duluth.

Colingsworth, R. F., B. J. R. Gudmundson, W. L. K. Schwarz, and C. W. Rudelius. 1973. *Environmental impact assessment study, St. Croix River Pool*. North Star Research Inst., Minneapolis.

Dobie, J. 1959. *The Itasca story*. Minneapolis: Ross & Haines.

Dunn, J. T. 1965. *The St. Croix, midwest border river*. New York: Holt, Rinehart, and Winston.

Eddy, S., J. B. Moyle, and J. C. Underhill. 1963. The fish fauna of the Mississippi River above St. Anthony Falls as related to the effectiveness of this falls as a migration barrier. *Proc. Minn. Acad. Sci.* 30:111-115.

Eddy, S., and J. C. Underhill. 1974. *Northern fishes*. 3rd ed. Minneapolis: Univ. Minn. Press.

Eifert, V. S. 1957. *Mississippi calling*. New York: Dodd, Mead.

———. 1959. *River world, wildlife of the Mississippi*. New York: Dodd, Mead.

———. 1966. *Of men and rivers*. New York: Dodd, Mead.

Elliott, R. R. 1968. Our headwaters canoe trail. *Conservation Volunteer* 31(177):14-16.

Fisher, W., N. Gruchow, and C. Wechsler. 1972. *Minnesota environmental education areas*. Minn. Dept. Nat. Res., St. Paul.

Fridley, R. W. 1976. Debate continues over Kensington rune stone. *Minnesota History* 45: 149-151.

Fugina, F. J. 1945. *Lore and lure of the Upper Mississippi River*. Winona, Minn.: published by author.

Gluek, A. C., Jr. 1965. *Minnesota and the manifest destiny of the Canadian Northwest*. Toronto: Univ. Toronto Press.

Goldman, C. R., J. McEvoy III, and P. J. Richerson, eds. 1973. *Environmental quality and water development*. San Francisco: W. H. Freeman.

Grant, U. S. 1895. The international boundary between Lake Superior and the Lake of the Woods. *Minnesota Historical Society, Collections* 8:1-10.

Hale, J. G. 1969. An evaluation of trout stream habitat improvement in a North Shore tributary of Lake Superior. *Minn. Fish. Invest.* 5:37-50.

Harlan, J. R., and E. B. Speaker. 1969. *Iowa Fish and Fishing*. 4th ed. Iowa Conserv. Commission, Des Moines.

Hart, I. H. 1952. Steamboating on Mississippi headwaters. *Minnesota History* 33:7-19.

Hartsough, M. L. 1934. *From canoe to steel barge on the Upper Mississippi*. Minneapolis: Univ. Minn. Press.

Harza Engineering Company. 1971. *Report on abandonment and transfer of ownership of dams*. Prepared for Minn. Dept. Nat. Res., St. Paul.

Hassinger, R. L. 1967. *The Cloquet River, its ecology and recreation*. Minn. Dept. Conserv., Div. Game and Fish, Tech. Serv. Sec., Spec. Publ. No. 41.

Hassinger, R. L., J. G. Hale, and D. E. Woods. 1974. *Steelhead of the Minnesota North Shore*. Minn. Dept. Nat. Res., Div. Fish and Wildlife, Sec. Fish., Tech. Bull. No. 11.

Haugstad, M. C. 1969. *Guidelines for trout fishing in eastern-central Minnesota.* Minn. Dept. Conserv., St. Paul.

Havighurst, W. 1937. *Upper Mississippi, a wilderness saga.* New York: Farrar and Rinehart.

————. 1964. *Voices on the river.* New York: Macmillan.

Hella, U. W. 1972. The Minnesota River Valley Trail. *Hut!* Sept. 1972:17-18.

Heuvelmans, M. 1974. *The river killers.* Harrisburg, Pa.: Stackpole Books.

Heyerdahl, E. G., and L. L. Smith, Jr. 1972. *Fishery resources of Lake of the Woods, Minnesota.* Univ. Minn. Agr. Exper. Sta., Tech. Bull. No. 288.

Hollenstein, G. H. 1962. *Power development in Minnesota.* Minn. Dept. Conserv., Div. Waters, Bull. No. 20.

Holmquist, J. D., and J. A. Brookins. 1972. *Minnesota's major historic sites, a guide.* Minn. Hist. Soc., St. Paul.

Hopeman, A. R., Jr. 1973. *An economic analysis of flood damage reduction alternatives in the Minnesota River basin.* Water Resources Res. Ctr., Univ. Minn., Bull. No. 58.

Hynes, H. B. N. 1970. *The ecology of running waters.* Toronto: Univ. Toronto Press.

Jenkinson, M. 1973. *Wild rivers of North America.* New York: E. P. Dutton.

Johnson, M. W. 1967. *A fisheries and recreational survey of the Crow Wing River, 1964-65.* Minn. Dept. Conserv., Div. Game and Fish, Tech. Serv. Sec., Spec. Publ. No. 40.

Johnson, R. E., J. B. Moyle, and W. A. Kenyon. 1949. *A biological survey and fishery management plan for the streams of the Root River basin.* Minn. Dept. Conserv., Div. Game and Fish, Fish. Res. Unit, Invest. Rep. No. 87.

Jones, E. 1962. *The Minnesota, forgotten river.* New York: Holt, Rinehart and Winston.

Jung, L. J. 1965. *The Great River Road in Minnesota.* Minn. Outdoor Rec. Res. Commission, St. Paul.

Kane, L. M. 1966. *The waterfall that built a city.* Minn. Hist. Soc., St. Paul.

Keating, B. 1971. *The mighty Mississippi.* (Photography by J. L. Stanfield) National Geographic Soc., Washington.

Kelsey, V. 1951. *Red River runs north!* New York: Harper & Bros.

Knudson, G. 1971. *A guide to the Upper Iowa River.* Decorah, Iowa: Luther College Press.

Kuehn, J. H. 1948. *A reconnaissance of the Blue Earth River to determine present status of smallmouth bass and to evaluate present environmental conditions.* Minn. Dept. Conserv., Div. Game and Fish, Fish. Res. Unit, Invest. Rep. No. 81.

————. 1951. *1950 Nemadji River Survey.* Minn. Dept. Conserv., Div. Game and Fish, Fish. Res. Unit, Invest. Rep. No. 110.

Lane, F. C. 1949. *Earth's grandest rivers.* Garden City, N.Y.: Doubleday.

Larson, A. M. 1949. *History of the white pine industry in Minnesota.* Minneapolis: Univ. Minn. Press.

Lawrie, A. H., and J. F. Fahrer. 1973. *Lake Superior, a case history of the lake and its fisheries.* Great Lakes Fish. Commission, Tech. Rep. No. 19.

Leopold, L. B. 1962. Rivers. *Amer. Scientist* 50:511-537.

Littlejohn, B. M. 1965. *Quetico-Superior country.* Quetico Foundation, Toronto.

Longley, W. H., and J. B. Moyle. 1963. *The beaver in Minnesota.* Minn. Dept. Conserv., Div. Game and Fish, Tech. Bull. No. 6.

Lund, D. R. 1975. *Lake of the Woods, yesterday and today.* Staples, Minn.: Nordell Graphic Communications.

MacCrimmon, H. R., and B. L. Gots. 1972. *Rainbow trout in the Great Lakes.* Ontario Ministry Nat. Res., Toronto.

Martin L. 1911. Physical geography of the Lake Superior region. In *The geology of the Lake Superior region,* eds. C. R. Van Hise and C. K. Leith. U.S. Geol. Surv. Monographs 52:85-117.

Meyer, R. W. 1974 Forestville, the making of a state park. *Minnesota History* 44:82-95.

Meyer-Oakes, W. J., ed. 1967. *Life, land and water: Proceedings of the 1966 Conference on*

Environmental Studies on the Glacial Lake Agassiz Region. Winnipeg: Univ. Manitoba Press.

Midwest Planning and Research, Inc., and U.S. Geol. Surv. 1966. *Selected rivers of Minnesota, recreational analysis.* Minneapolis and St. Paul.

Minneapolis City Council. 1972. *Mississippi/Minneapolis.* Minneapolis.

Minnesota Conservation Department (now the Minnesota Department of Natural Resources). 1959. *Hydrologic atlas of Minnesota.* Div. Waters, Bull. No. 10.

Minnesota Department of Natural Resources. n.d. *Trout streams in southeastern Minnesota.* St. Paul.

Minnesota Outdoor Recreation Resources Commission. 1965. *Minnesota's Memorial Hardwood Forest.* Rep. Subject No. 4.

Minnesota Outdoor Recreation Resources Commission. 1965. *Recreational use of rivers and streams in Minnesota.* Staff Rep. No. 9.

Morgan, A. E. 1971. *Dams and other disasters.* Boston: Porter Sargent.

Morse, E. W. 1962. *Canoe routes of the voyageurs.* Quetico Foundation of Ontario and Minn. Hist. Soc., Toronto and St. Paul.

Moyle, J. B. 1940. *A biological survey of the upper Mississippi River system.* Minn. Dept. Conserv., Div. Game and Fish, Fish. Res. Invest. Rep. No. 10.

———. 1950. How big can a fish get? *Conservation Volunteer* 13(77):36-37.

Moyle, J. B., and Walter A. Kenyon. 1947. *A biological survey and fishery management plan for the streams of the Saint Louis River basin.* Minn. Dept. Conserv., Div. Game and Fish, Bur. Fish., Invest. Rep. No. 69.

National Park Service. 1971. *Master plan, St. Croix National Scenic Riverway.* Washington.

Needham, P. R. 1940. *Trout streams.* Ithaca, N.Y.: Comstock.

Nute, G. L. 1925. The Red River trails. *Minnesota History* 6:278-282.

———. 1941. *The Voyageur's Highway.* Minn. Hist. Soc., St. Paul.

———. 1944. *Lake Superior.* Indianapolis: Bobbs-Merrill.

———. 1950. *Rainy River country.* Minn. Hist. Soc., St. Paul.

———. 1955. *The voyageur.* Minn. Hist. Soc., St. Paul.

Oglesby, R. T., C. A. Carlson, and J. A. McCann, eds. 1972. *River ecology and man.* New York: Academic Press.

Outdoor World. 1973. *Rivers of North America.* Waukesha, Wisc.

Palzer, B., and J. Palzer. 1973. *Whitewater; quietwater.* Univ. Wis., Hoofers Outing Club, Madison.

Petersen, W. J. 1937. *Steamboating on the Upper Mississippi.* State Hist. Soc. of Iowa, Iowa City.

Peterson, A. R. 1962. *A biological reconnaissance of the upper Mississippi River.* Minn. Dept. Conserv., Div. Game and Fish, Sec. Res. and Planning, Invest. Rep. No. 255.

———. 1975. *Analysis of the composition of fish populations in Minnesota's rivers and streams.* Minn. Dept. Nat. Res., Div. Fish and Wildlife, Environ. Sec., Invest. Rep. No. 335.

Pringle, L. 1973. *Wild river.* Philadelphia: J. B. Lippincott.

Rector, W. G. 1953. *Log transportation in the Lake States lumber industry 1840-1918.* Glendale, Cal.: Arthur H. Clark.

Reedstrom, D. C. 1964. *A biological reconnaissance of the Snake River.* Minn. Dept. Conserv., Div. Game and Fish, Sec. Res. and Planning, Invest. Rep. No. 275.

Replinger, J. S. 1974. *Minnesotans and their Mississippi River: A citizens' review of Minnesota's Mississippi River environments.* Prepared for the Esthetic Environment Task Force, State of Minnesota, St. Paul.

Rommel, S. 1973. Canoeing the Vermilion River. *Hut!* Jan. 1973:4-7.

Ryan, J. C. 1973. *Early loggers in Minnesota.* Minn. Timber Producers Assoc., Duluth.

Ryberg, C. N. 1963. *1963 rivers survey, St. Croix River.* Rep. No. 1. North Central Marine Assoc., Minneapolis.

———. 1963. *1963 rivers survey, Little Fork River.* Rep. No. 2. North Central Marine Assoc., Minneapolis.

———. 1963. *1963 rivers survey, Big Fork River.* Rep. No. 3. North Central Marine Assoc., Minneapolis.

———. 1963. *1963 rivers survey, Minnesota River.* Rep. No. 4. North Central Marine Assoc., Minneapolis.

Ryder, F. J. 1972. *A century of service.* Water Resources Fact Sheet, U.S. Army Corps of Engineers, St. Paul.

Schneberger, E., and J. L. Funk, eds. 1971. *Stream channelization, a symposium.* North Central Div., Amer. Fish. Soc., Spec. Publ. No. 2.

Schwartz, G. M., and G. A. Thiel. 1963. *Minnesota's rocks and waters.* Minneapolis: Univ. Minn. Press.

Severin, T. 1968. *Explorers of the Mississippi.* New York: Alfred A. Knopf.

Sheldon, W. G. 1967. *The book of the American woodcock.* Amherst: Univ. Mass. Press.

Sierra Club. 1970. *A wilderness in crisis—the Boundary Waters Canoe Area.* North Star Chapter, Minneapolis.

Sims, P. K., and G. B. Morey, eds. 1972. *Geology of Minnesota: A centennial volume.* Univ. Minn., Minn. Geol. Surv., St. Paul.

Smith, B. R., J. J. Tibbles, and B. G. H. Johnson. 1974. *Control of the sea lamprey* (Petromyzon marinus) *in Lake Superior, 1953-70.* Great Lakes Fish. Commission, Tech. Rep. No. 26.

Smith, L. L., Jr., and J. B. Moyle. 1944. *A biological survey and fishery management plan for the streams of the Lake Superior North Shore watershed.* Minn. Dept. Conserv., Div. Game and Fish, Tech. Bull. No. 1.

Stenlund, M. 1965. The beaver, split personality in a pelt! *Conservation Volunteer* 28(163): 23-26.

Surber, T. 1924. *A biological reconnaissance of the Root River drainage basin, southeastern Minnesota.* Sci. Invest. Lakes and Streams, Appndx. to Biennial Rep., State Game & Fish Commissioner, Minn., for period ending June 30, 1924.

———. 1941. Some early biological surveys on Minnesota waters, 1918-1934. *Conservation Volunteer* 1(4):46-50.

Thiel, G. A. 1944. *The geology and underground waters of southern Minnesota.* Univ. Minn., Minn. Geol. Surv., Bull. 31.

———. 1947. *The geology and underground waters of northeastern Minnesota.* Univ. Minn., Minn. Geol. Surv., Bull. 32.

Underhill, J. C., and J. B. Moyle. 1968. The fishes of Minnesota's Lake Superior region. *Conservation Volunteer* 31(177):29-53.

Upham, W. 1920. *Minnesota geographic names, their origin and historic significance.* Reprint. Minn. Hist. Soc., St. Paul, 1969.

U.S. Army Corps of Engineers. 1973. *Water resources development in Minnesota.* Chicago.

Usinger, R. L. 1967. *The life of rivers and streams.* New York: World Book Encyclop. and McGraw Hill.

Utter, J. G., and J. D. Schultz. 1976. *A Handbook of the Wild and Scenic Rivers Act.* Univ. Mont., School of Forestry, Missoula.

Water Resources Research Center. 1973. *Proceedings of public forum on water resources problems and research needs in southwestern Minnesota.* Univ. Minn., Minneapolis.

Wheeler, R. C., W. A. Kenyon, A. R. Woolworth, and D. A. Birk. 1975. *Voices from the rapids, an underwater search for fur trade artifacts, 1960-73.* Minn. Hist. Soc., St. Paul.

Whitmarsh, S. R., and W. C. Brabham. 1970. Upper Iowa River—a case study. In *Proceed-*

ings: National Symposium on Wild, Scenic, and Recreational Waterways, St. Paul, Minn., Sept. 10-12, 1970. U.S. Dept. Interior, Bur. Outdoor Rec., Washington.

Wilkinson, J. M. 1973. *Report on channel modifications, volume I*. U.S. Council on Environ. Quality, Washington.

Wright, H. E., Jr. 1972. Quaternary history of Minnesota. In *Geology of Minnesota: a centennial volume*, eds. P. K. Sims and G. B. Morey. Univ. Minn., Minn. Geol. Surv., St. Paul, pp. 515-547.

Wright, H. E., Jr., L. A. Mattson, and J. A. Thomas. 1970. *Geology of the Cloquet Quadrangle, Carlton County, Minnesota*. Univ. Minn., Minn. Geol. Surv., Geol. Map Series GM-3.

Wright, H. E., Jr., and W. A. Watts. 1969. *Glacial and vegetational history of northeastern Minnesota*. Univ. Minn., Minn. Geol. Surv., Spec. Publ. No. 11.

Ziebarth, M., and A. Ominsky. 1970. *Fort Snelling, anchor post of the Northwest*. Minn. Hist. Soc., St. Paul.

Indexes

Index to Minnesota Streams

General Index

Lake Traverse, 110; dam on Mud Lake, 110; proposed Roseau River channelization, 112, 122; dam on Red Lakes, 117; proposed Huot Dam on Red Lake River, 118; proposed Wild Rice River dam, 120; navigation channel in St. Croix River, 138, 147-48; navigation connection between Lake Superior and Mississippi River studied, 147; Mississippi River Headwaters dams and reservoirs, 190-91, 209, 210, 211, 237-38; locks and dams on Mississippi River, 220, 237; navigation charts, Mississippi River, 223; repair of St. Anthony Falls, 230; channel maintenance from Aitkin to Grand Rapids, Mississippi River, 236, 237; Zumbro River channelization, 257; proposed Blue Earth River dam, 286-87; proposed Cottonwood River dam, 296; built Big Stone-Whetstone Dam, 314; and channelization, 331, 332; teamed with U.S. Fish and Wildlife Service in GREAT, 335; floodplain management, 335-36

U.S. Bureau of Reclamation, and Garrison Diversion project, 128-29

U.S. Fish and Wildlife Service: in sea lamprey control, 65; and waterfowl production areas, 128; surveyed wetlands in Ten Mile Creek watershed, 303; to administer Big Stone-Whetstone reservoir, 314; to administer part of Minnesota Valley National Wildlife Refuge, 323, 330; teamed with U.S. Army Corps of Engineers in GREAT, 335

U.S. Navy, tankers built on Minnesota River, 320

University of Minnesota: Cloquet Forest Experiment Station, 39, 164; fisheries research on pollution, 88; research on ruffed grouse, 164; research on American woodcock, 172; Cedar Creek Natural History Area, 183; Lake Itasca Forestry and Biological Station, 208; St. Anthony Falls Hydraulic Laboratory, 240

Upper St. Croix Lake (Wis.), 137

Verendrye, Sieur de la. *See* La Verendrye, Sieur de

Vermilion Lake, 77, 81, 84, 102

Vineland, Minn., 176

Virginia, Minn., 77, 86

Voice of the Mississippi, citizens action group, 246, 335

Voyageurs, French-Canadian, 68-71, 72-76, 79: route from Lake Superior to Mississippi River, 28-29, 32; route from Montreal to Grand Portage, 73-74; route from Grand Portage to Fort Chipewyan, 75; used alternate routes, 80, 83; route on St. Louis and Vermilion rivers, 80-81; route from Lake Superior to Lake of the Woods, 82; assisted in setting U.S.-Canada boundary, 84

Voyageur's Highway, 72-76, 88, 94

Voyageurs National Park, 75, 81, 93, 94

Wabasha, Minn., 219, 221, 234, 238, 249, 264

Walleye, 31-40 *passim*, 51, 63, 88, 90, 100, 104, 115-27 *passim*, 148, 149, 157, 158, 159, 161, 162, 174, 176, 181, 188-92 *passim*, 222-45 *passim*, 265, 277, 284, 286, 292, 300, 301, 316, 321

Warman, Minn., 157

Warren, Gen. G. K., army engineer, 309

Warroad, Minn., 83, 85

Watap Lake, 70

Waterfalls: in St. Louis River, Thomson, 37; barriers to fish distribution, 39-40, 65; along North Shore, 44-46, 48, 53, 70; barriers to steelhead migration, 64; between border lakes, 79, 80; in Minnesota River Valley tributaries, 310, 311
—individual falls: Baptism River, 54; Beaver River, 54; Big Falls, Big Fork River, 100, 101; Big Falls, Pigeon River, 63, 70; Brule River, 62; Caribou River, 57; Cascade River, 48, 59; Cross River, 57; Curtain Falls, 80; Devil Track River, 60; Hananen's Falls, Little Fork River, 102, 103, 104; Hidden Falls, Prairie Creek, 255; Horn Rapids, Pigeon River, 63, 70; Kadunce Creek, 61; Kakebeka Falls, Kaministikwia River (Canada), 68; Kettle Falls, 81; Kimball Creek, 61; Koochiching Falls, 78, 81, 81, 82, 87; Lake of the Woods outlet, 78; Little American Falls, Big Fork River, 100, 101, 101; Little Fork River, 102, 104; Loon River, 80; Lower Basswood Falls, 80; Manitou River, 57; Middle Falls, Pigeon River, 63, 70; Minnehaha Falls, 217, 227; Minne-